D1263189

IN THE EYE OF THE STORM

OTHER BOOKS ABOUT AFRICA BY BASIL DAVIDSON

History

The Lost Cities of Africa
Black Mother: The African Slave Trade
The African Past: Chronicles from Antiquity
    to Modern Times
The African Genius: An Introduction to African Social
    and Cultural History
Africa in History: Themes and Outlines
A History of West Africa AD 1000–1800; with
    J. A. Ade Ajayi and F. K. Buah
A History of East and Central Africa to the Late 19th
    Century; with J. E. F. Mhina
African Kingdoms; with the editors of Time-Life Books
Guide to African History
Discovering Our African Heritage

Contemporary Affairs

Report on Southern Africa
The New West Africa; symposium edited with A. Ademola
The African Awakening
Which Way Africa? The Search for a New Society
The Liberation of Guiné: Aspects of an African Revolution

Fiction

The Rapids

IN THE EYE
OF THE STORM

ANGOLA'S PEOPLE

BASIL DAVIDSON

DOUBLEDAY & COMPANY, INC., GARDEN CITY, NEW YORK
1972

ISBN: 0-385-03179-3
LIBRARY OF CONGRESS CATALOG CARD NUMBER 72–76710
PRINTED IN THE UNITED STATES OF AMERICA
FIRST EDITION IN THE UNITED STATES OF AMERICA

226628

To Marion
   in love and gratitude

       and

To the memory of Américo Boavida
   surgeon patriot revolutionary
   killed by the Portuguese air force
   while tending the sick
   in the Cambule Forest of Angola
   September 25, 1968

CONTENTS

INTRODUCTION   xi

THE SEED OF MIDWINTER
       Guerrilla Days, Guerrilla Nights   3

PART ONE   ANGOLA IN HISTORY   31

   1 Themes and Outlines   33
   2 Early Development   47
   3 The "Take-off" into Kingship   52
   4 Marauders from the Sea   68
   5 The Hundred Years' War   77
   6 Primitive Extraction, 1600–1850   85

PART TWO   THE YEARS OF SILENCE, 1850–1960   95

   1 Carving Out a Colony   97
   2 Extending the System: From Slavery
      to Forced Labor   105
   3 The Years of Salazar   119
   4 On the African Side   131
   5 From Reformism to Revolt   143
   Documentary One   155
   6 "The Time of the Leaflet"   160
   7 On the Eve   170

PART THREE   GUERRILLA WAR   181

   1 Luanda, February 1961   183
   2 The Rising in the North   187

Documentary Two   194
3   Congo Diversions   207
4   Riding the Storm   229
Documentary Three   244
5   The Eastern Front: Toward the At-
    lantic   251
Documentary Four   275
6   Midwinter's Harvest: From Revolt to
    Revolution   282

PART FOUR   THE REVOLUTION OF THE POOR   299

1   The End of a Road   301
2   The Colonial Answer   305
3   The Neo-Colonial Variant   322
4   The Road Ahead   339

MAPS

1   Portuguese Angola: Districts, district capitals,
    railways   32
2   Angola: Some principal ethnic groups (approxi-
    mate locations)   35
3   Middle Africa (West and Central): Main pre-
    colonial centers of power and kingship (approxi-
    mate locations)   54
4   Eastern Angola   255
5   Central Angola: Location of some guerrilla ac-
    tions in Bié   269
6   Areas of guerrilla presence and penetration,
    1971–72, and of national liberation organization.   283

ACKNOWLEDGEMENTS   349

BIBLIOGRAPHICAL NOTE   351

INDEX   353

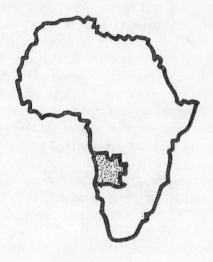

INTRODUCTION

1961. A few hundred men and women take to arms in a land of silence and obscurity. They mean to free their people from foreign rule, yet have everything to learn except determination. All but crushed by the power they have rebelled against, some of them survive to rethink their problems, reapply themselves, gradually expand their ranks. By 1972, eleven years later, they lead a national movement deeply rooted in the soil of native hope and loyalty, participation and support.

As the roots deepen, so do their aims and thoughts widen. Their principal aim is still to free their country from foreign rule, but now they believe they must build a new society as well;

freedom and revolution have opened a partnership here. How
has this come about, and why? With what actual and potential
consequences for Angola? With what implications for the rest
of Africa, for the rest of the world?

Their country is a vast region, more than five times as large
as Britain, more than twice as large as France, nearly one sixth
the size of all the U.S.A. While its people number fewer than
six millions, it is also a most deprived country, even in African
terms. Viewed from the outside, its hopes of creative change can
only seem small. Yet pessimism is rich man's property. The deprived have at least this advantage: they must act to save themselves. The interesting question is whether they act wisely.

The question of whether the deprived act wisely is the question of whether they act successfully. For the success of the deprived in acting creatively against conditions of barbarism that
the endowed may deplore, but, being endowed, will continue to
accept for others, has now become the survival test of any civilization worth the name.

Angola's people are among the most deprived of any people
anywhere. Do they act successfully? "When power has been as-
sembled by those who have grievances," Gunnar Myrdal has replied, "then is the time when ideals and the social conscience
can become effective." There is of course nothing automatic in
the process: ideals and the social conscience may become effective, or they may not. Is this a case, a test case, where they have?
To change fear into confidence, despair into hope, anger into
understanding, even hatred into love; these are essentials of
success in such a case as this one is, even though, or perhaps
above all because, the path to creative change must go through
the wretchedness of war. Are these essentials to be found here?

Angola's case is certainly extreme in its deprivation. Not because nine tenths of Angolans still live in thatched villages or
woodland homesteads scattered across remote plains, lost in
long, slow hills, niched in solitude along the banks of languid
streams or broad, forgotten rivers; at least in principle, there
may be much to be said for living thus. But in 1972 these people
were living there, and have long lived there, in acute material

distress and hunger, while other Angolans, somehow surviving in urban slums, suffered conditions not much better and sometimes worse. During the 1960s about 98 per cent of all Angolans were completely illiterate, were denied any effective control over their own lives, and were unable to participate in any legal action to improve their lot.

This extremity of Angola's situation gives more than drama to the scene. In wider terms—in terms of an inquiry into the possibilities of constructive change—it can and does shed light on less extreme cases, since the issues here are desperately plain and clear, and yet, at the same time, inherently characteristic of all other parts of the colonial or formally colonial world. More than that: in one degree or other, these issues may even be those, substantially, that matter today for almost every people, whether living in the "backward" countries or in those that are called "developed." What must Angola's people now do to build a good society, a society worth living in? What can they do? The questions are particular to Angola; the problems they pose are general to mankind. The study of these problems is the study of ourselves.

This book is an attempt to ask such questions, and to portray their actual or possible answers, against the background of Angolan history and the living reality of the past few years as well as today. It derives from a personal experience of "Portuguese Africa" that began in 1954 and has since continued, latterly with visits to guerrilla-held areas of Guinea-Bissau in 1967, of Mozambique in 1968, and of Angola in 1970. This last involved a walk of some three hundred miles in eastern Angola, partly in company with the leader of Angola's national movement, Dr. Agostinho Neto: to him and his comrades, especially to Lara and Iko, to Paganini and Petrov and Rui (the *noms de guerre* are as various as those who bear them), to Pupa and Luta and February-Four and many others, I record my thanks for companionship and information. So far as possible, I have left them to speak for themselves, though responsibility for what I have written is mine alone.

Some direct impressions of the people and the country are followed by a first part concerned with the formative background of Angolan history, a second part concerned with the colonial period, a third part concerned with the 1960s and the early 1970s, and finally a fourth part devoted to a discussion of aims and objectives—of what development may really mean for Angola's people, and, at least by implication, for every other people caught in the tangle of our times.

IN THE EYE OF THE STORM

THE SEED OF MIDWINTER

"As with seed that has long lain waiting for conditions propitious to the germination that will preserve the species and assure its evolution, the culture of Africa's peoples now springs forth again, across the continent, in struggles for national liberation."

Amilcar Cabral

"Like the seed of midwinter, unheeded, unperished,
  Like the autumn-sown wheat 'neath the snow lying green"

William Morris

GUERRILLA DAYS, GUERRILLA NIGHTS

Out here in the wide expanses of the east it is a country that
might well be like the surface of the Moon, if only the Moon
grew gray-green trees or long yellow grass, and were always deep
in dust. Or this is how it seems in the time after dawn, tramping
from some chance woodland bivouac across soil as friable as
sand, mile upon mile, hallucinating miles, or after sundown
while making camp beneath a cloud of stars. Then these hidden
plains of eastern Angola gain a majesty and graven beauty of
their own, and the soil that is really sand, long-mingled and composed by millennia of pluvial attrition, turns to a carpet of silvered snow. Then the small quick rivers of the east, Luati and

Mussuma, Shekului and Cambule, flowing even in the months of drought, become mirrors for the Moon and the Milky Way, and promise destinies of calm and peace. Petrified in silence, these nightlit landscapes reflect MacDiarmid's lines:

> The moonbeams kelter i' the lift,
> An' Earth, the bare auld stane,
> Glitters beneath the seas o' space,
> White as a mammoth's bane.

The mammoths have given way to the elephants; and that was long ago. Yet the day's hard brilliance shows a land that seems caught in an immemorial past which cannot change. The country's dense and tangled woodlands reach out as though they outrun time, climbing to the west in low skylines backed one upon another. Through them, flowing east, the rivers move in corridors of sodden grass that widen into lakes in the season of the rains. Now in the drought, along these grassland channels, there are paths of dust imprinted by the track of buck and lion. A primeval country.

The impression is mistaken. There are other footprints in the dust. Some of them are ours. Others are theirs. Mozambiki and February-Four, excellent trackers, slow down and cast about and give judgment as to age and origin of prints they find upon our path. They inspect them with expert eye, and sometimes, when the prints are not ours, they follow them into the bush and return with telltale signs, a sardine tin or a can that once held chocolate milk. The enemy eats well.

Much has changed; more has changed in the past five years than in any other period of history. Along the grassland channels where the people used to live, close to their fishing and their fields of millet or maize on the margin of the woods, the huts lie empty under tumbled thatch. Now there is nobody living along these open grassland channels; the war has seen to that, first the reprisal columns, then the commandos, now the helicopters with their swiveled automatics.

Today we find no people. We have come across the road to Gago, south of the Mussuma River: a long hard trek, for the Gago road is important to the enemy. Gago itself is a helicopter base for the far east; beyond it, southward again, the convoy road goes on to Ninda and other garrisons. Here there is no population either side of the road for four hours' marching; they've pulled back to escape ground raids and bombing.

Yesterday Paganini's saboteurs blew a road bridge not far from Gago, one of the innumerable wooden plankways that cross the rivers flowing east to the Zambezi, and today there's a helicopter buzzing up and down the road, minding the lives of a bridge-mending team. We hear its arrival soon after dawn, when we are still ten miles from the road. "Detour round it," Paganini decides. No risks with a visitor present. Another two hours on top of the eight.

The road is a red slash through the woods, its surface furrowed by wheel tracks a foot deep into the sand. Two hours beyond it we hear the distant thump of bombing somewhere at our backs. There is nobody there to be bombed, neither civilians nor guerrillas, but the enemy's calling in of bombers is said to be good for the enemy's morale. Weeks later, we learn what Paganini's saboteurs did in those days: five bridges destroyed and as many trucks. They are five young men who know their business, shrewd and cool, having all the confident secrecy of men who follow mysteries of their own: they don't blow bridges unless they can blow trucks with the same charge. Going east over the road some weeks later, heading back for Zambia, we shall slip across within a mile of a bridge-mending team.

Now, westward bound, we stop soon after sunset and get to sleep while fires give heat that will not last. By the small hours of the morning it will be too cold for anyone to sleep, even those who have blankets. Not many have blankets, not many have clothes that are more than rags, though the dry-season nights on this three-thousand-foot plateau are viciously chill. Only in the wet season, when the rivers fall and the grassland channels vanish into mirrors of water, and the dusk grows dense with mosquitoes, will any of these fighters take cover in a hut.

Birds were calling till near sundown, piping to a cricket's drone somewhere out beyond the woodland verge that borders the river, a deep cold stream. These orioles have only one song. They rehearse it with a careful discouragement, ever-repeatedly dropping half a dozen notes into the background silence as though filling a pot of woe, and then not knowing what to do but fill another. If they have a message, it is one suggesting that men should give up this fight and go quietly away.

The advice will not be followed, but now the orioles have taken it themselves, and the night has other, foreground noises, comforting and comfortable, concerned with us. Small fires crackle while men feed them with twigs, load them with branches. Paganini calls for the can of forest honey that we have and hands it around. He is a tall thin man of twenty-eight or so, a man of Bié, in central Angola, who commands a guerrilla zone as big as half of Wales. He has not yet quite forgiven me for coming to disturb his war. But grievances, however small, are not susceptible of long nursing under guerrilla conditions. Tonight he draws a little plan for me, to explain his grievance, and forthwith forgives me. He had had it all arranged: the blowing of a bridge under the first truck of a convoy, with fire from this point and that point.

"I would have got them all, but at one go. And their troops."

He looks across at me with large eyes glinting in the firelight, and offers a rueful smile.

"That's it, you see. We called it off. There's President Neto directly here, and now there's you as well. Of course we called it off." Now the plan is changed; he launches into logistic details, talking away his grievance. His vivid eyes are wistful, full of memories. Why "Paganini"? Because "I had a sorrowing childhood, and so did he." A childhood in Bié, Angola's colonial heartland where the settlers rule, a youth in emigration at Léopoldville, in the Congo, a youth of elementary schooling and clerking and careering in a small way, the only possible way, a youth of trying to understand. . . .

Now Paganini is a skilled commander of a movement in full expansion; judged by my own experience of other guerrilla wars, he is an excellent commander. Paganini takes nothing for granted, never allows anyone to see him upset, humps his own pack, marches with the rest, thinks and acts with nerves honed by experience. Between January and June this year he has had only seven men killed and ten lightly wounded, but estimates about forty enemy dead. And it's not only that: for as well as forming an internal base area, his zone is also a principal channel of communication with the west, with Bié and eventually the Atlantic lands beyond.

He sits on the other side of the fire, and talks about his life. He talks well, throwing off ideas and incidents. It's clear that he sees his life make sense at last. So many lives have found their meaning here. I think of my friend Américo Boavida, killed by bomb splinters two years ago in the Cambule Forest not far from here: an intellectual and successful surgeon who could have passed by comfortably on the other side, as some other Angolan intellectuals have preferred to do. Our last meeting had occurred in Dar es Salaam, a chance meeting caused by Boavida's arrival from Angola on some question of medical supply and my own from a journey in Mozambique. The blue-green pool of the Kilimanjaro Hotel was offering its comfort when Boavida's shout stopped my plunge; I dressed again and we went for coffee. We sat in luxury for half an hour while Boavida explained the manner of guerrilla life in Angola. He was a man who had raised himself in Lisbon and Barcelona to a summit of gynecological specialism: he could have had any one of a dozen senior jobs in European hospitals. "But I am doing what I have to do, and I can tell you that I have realized myself in a way that I can never regret. I have thrown away my career, my personal career, and I am glad. I am working for my people. I am where I belong." Two months later he was dead. He must have hated dying, but not the road that led to his death.

We who are alive lie on our backs and are content, resting our weariness. Pillared on slender trunks, a dome of faint green leaves encloses the world of our night, the closed world of our companionship. There is nothing to be done but eat whatever Pupa may still be able to produce, whether of millet or of rice, and sleep till the early cold makes sleep impossible. Tomorrow we shall find people.

Meanwhile we can listen to the world, which sounds a strange place when heard from here.

Petrov's transistor—"they gave me that name in Bulgaria because they couldn't pronounce my real name"—whistles in a search for Brazzaville while his stubborn fingers twist the knob. He lingers for a while with a *fado* from Radio Luanda that wails with sentimental sorrow to sad Portuguese soldiers in this land so far from their own, moves to and loses a smooth English speaker from South Africa, pauses for the Zambian news, arrives at Brazzaville and stays. In Brazzaville, as in Dar es Salaam, the national movement has broadcasting facilities.

This listening to a range of stations relaying London, Paris, Luanda, and a dozen other contesting or protesting voices, thrusts us back into a world that is both ours and not ours in a dialectic that is very much a part of this war: a confrontation between worlds that are altogether different and yet the same. Only Petrov listens with any care. It's his job, after all. One job among others. Collecting information, sorting intelligence. Petrov is about the same age as Paganini and comes from Cabinda, in the far northwest, a veteran whose father was a docker and whose mother was a peasant of Cabinda—a slim-built man bent to a severe self-discipline, speaking with an inner strength that does not fail him. From Cabinda he came out here to the east in 1967.

"We had to learn about these eastern peoples, we had to learn their languages, we had to find out how they think about each other, even what we should call them." A long and tangled business. "Most of these eastern people are called Ganguella by the

Portuguese. It's a name we can't use. Why not? Because the Portuguese took it from the Ovimbundu long ago"—the Ovimbundu, Paganini's people, live westward in the central districts—"and the Ovimbundu used it in the old slaving times. Just the same, the other way around, the Chokwe of the east call the Ovimbundu *Bunitali*. That means 'the people who came with the Portuguese,' the profiteers of the slave trade if you like. That's another name we can't use. Because it's another name that goes against our unity."

Petrov thinks as an Angolan and reproves me gently for inquiring into ethnic identities. "It's tribal talk; it's greatly harmed our people." All the same, facts are facts. He wrinkles his brow under its Portuguese military cap and continues to explain. "Then there's the Luvale, northeast of us here, they're a big people too. The Portuguese call them Luena. But the Luvale say Luena is the name of their big river, not of themselves. Besides, in their language, it's like *kaluena,* a word they have for venereal disease. We can't call them Luena. We had to learn that too."

Unity: it's the word that states the central problem. Without unity nothing can be done. But how do you make it? Petrov hammers on the point. "We are building this unity. We have become a national movement. There's nothing now to compare with the difficulties of 1961, when we began. If the Portuguese had given us independence in 1961, it'd have been worse in Angola than in the Congo." I think of some words of Amilcar Cabral's: "We do not like war. But this armed struggle has its advantages. Through it we are building a nation that is solid, conscious of itself." The war presses hard upon every kind of weakness; but the weakness can be overcome. "That is what struggle means: turning weakness into strength."

Petrov's transistor hits upon an urgent voice in French, interrupting firelit comfort to explain the disasters of a world that is not here: conflicts in the Middle East, miseries in Southeast Asia, worries in the countries that are called Developed. But here in the countries that are not called that, truly in the very eye of the storm, there are twenty men at rest beneath a dome of leaves and stars and silence, and, so far as worries are concerned, a wonderful simplicity of choice and outcome.

Our solitude is another mistaken impression. In other woodland bivouacs, ten miles away, twenty, two hundred, and farther still, other groups are also resting by their fires. They rest while the road of their lives forks ahead of them with death on one side and survival on the other. They have lived this life for years; they will go on living it. The war is nowhere near its end, but the fork in the road is always there, moving with them, waiting with each pale dawn.

There are also the garrisons of the enemy, stood down for the night save for sentries and searchlights. In Paganini's fighting zone there are eight such garrisons. We shall go as far as the outskirts of Muié and perhaps beyond. It depends on the situation. Tomorrow we shall find people again, and news.

Men stir and doze and await the dawn. Paganini leans across the fire between us and thrusts another branch upon the ashen heap; blowing, he brings it to life, small flames leaping from the ashes. So it is with this war, this whole uprising, the colonized history of these people. Their grievances might seem forgotten, their hopes abandoned, their cause defeated, they themselves silenced. But it was not like that. It was really that the ashes were alive, waiting only for fuel and draft. Now they have burst into strong life again, glowing as these flames do with an inner heat that resists and stays even beside the ice-cold waters of Cambule in the chill hours before dawn.

Paganini sits up and claps his hands. He looks across the fire and says that it is just past five. In half an hour it will be light, though a gray light with yet another hour to the sun. Luta comes for my little pack and my privileged pair of blankets. A frail-seeming man of eighteen, Luta is like February-Four and Chapayev and almost all our group, born here and broken to the country's ways. He takes my pack and his own belongings, which go into a miniature canvas bag, and he carries them all without any bother. He also has a hand grenade, so far his only weapon; and he carries this in his right hand, a yellow-green hand grenade. At night he shares a blanket with Mozambiki, who, despite his name, is a Kasakelle Bushman from the far southwest.

If there is anything to eat, this is the time to eat it; if not, we drink water from bottles, provided there is any left. With an advance guard of three, Chapayev breaks ahead, a thin young man of Ninda—but everyone here is thin, and most are young —who walks with the spring of an antelope and whose ethnic group (with apologies to Petrov) is Luchazi. Chapayev is another who, like Luta, has lately learned to read and write: in ciMbunda, with Portuguese the next target. "They taught me in a *kimbo* school," he has explained, "while we were waiting in the wet season last year." Every guerrilla detachment has its protected circle of *kimbos,* woodland villages where people have found refuge from the enemy, and which govern themselves through local committees formed by the national movement.

We stumble after the advance guard, snapping branches on the tree-lined path. The magic of the night is altogether gone: the dome of trees is nothing now but a meager shield of branches, the trunks upholding them mere six-inch tubes of lichened wood. Until another sundown we are back to reality, back to the war.

Around eleven we find the first *kimbo* west of the road. Now we shall find others. West of the road there are plenty of people, though you have to know where to look for them.

These kimbos, one or two a day on an eight-hour march, vary in appearance and stability. Here to the west of the road, southward from the Mussuma River, they are little more than flimsy camps where people may not stay for more than a few days at a time. For the Portuguese specialize in harrying the regions near their roads with reinforced ground patrols and commandos helicoptered from Luanda, on the far Atlantic coast, by way of Gago or Canavale or some other eastern air base. The first we

find is a group of about fifty people, most of them women and
men beyond fighting age, who are debating whether to return
westward or continue eastward into Zambia. It is a frequent
debate among those who live within a few days' walking of the
frontier: they skip back and forth according to the tide of war.

All kimbos are under the protection of at least one of Paganini's detachments, which are placed at four to six hours' march
from each other and entrusted with a number of specific tasks.
Farther westward we shall find much bigger kimbos established
on a more or less permanent basis in the deep forest, complete
with good huts of thatch and clay, shrines for their ancestral
spirits, frames for their textile work, kitchen clearings for their
fires and cooking pots.

Each of them has its committee, and each committee presents itself by way of its chairman or its secretary or some other
official person, elderly men for the most part who smoke metal-
stemmed pipes of local wood made by their own craftsmen.
Among these people, mostly Mbunda here, the ironsmiths have
long been famous. They make good knives, hatchets, pipestems,
fishhooks, a range of useful things.

There are usually a couple of rickety chairs and perhaps a
wooden table. There the visitor sits, a little ceremoniously, and
receives a chicken or a pot of *masangwe* (pounded millet)
from the proper person, usually a committee leader, while Paganini and Petrov listen to the news and give their own. Sometimes men find parents or relations. Once, we passed through
February-Four's father's village; it was deserted, but the kimbo
was nearby. One is reminded of the fiction of the Portuguese
who say, and never tire of saying (but what else, after all,
could they say?), that their aim is to liberate these kimbo people from the "terrorists' grip." From their own brothers and fa-
thers, cousins and sons?

Sometimes the kimbo is big enough to yield a meeting. People gather, the elders in front, the women standing in a row
singing. Two days ago there was just such a meeting for

Agostinho Neto, a big meeting of a couple of hundred people. They listened carefully to Neto, a man of unswerving moral purpose whose character achieves its full dignity and value here, among people whose judgment is without mercy for those who would lead them; and they asked for rifles. "Give us rifles," they said, "and we shall not fear the *tugas*," a common pejorative word deriving from the Brazilian slang for Portuguese-from-Portugal, *Portugas*. The national movement has brought it here, and everyone seems to use it now. *Os tugas terroristas*, say the guerrillas in their communiqués: *os turras terroristas*, throw back the Portuguese, having also invented a word.

This is chiefly a war for people, not territory. The Portuguese concentrate on seizing any people they can find; when they find any, they drive them behind the barbed wire of "strategic hamlets"—a technique learned from the Americans in South Vietnam, who learned it from the British in Malaya—which they call, with a peculiarly Portuguese preference for the inappropriate, *senzalas do paz* (peace villages). The guerrillas concentrate on preventing the Portuguese from filling these "peace villages," and on liberating people from these villages when they can; otherwise on prosecuting their war. In the end, the side wins that remains "on the ground" when the day is over. By 1970 this is undoubtedly the national movement's fighting units. In 1971, when small detachments begin to be formed into large mobile units supplied with light artillery, the superiority of the guerrillas will become clearer still.

The war is nearly ten years old. It's become a familiar pattern. In these parts the people call the "strategic hamlets" *ndandandas*, "a Chokwe word," Petrov explains, his eyes winking with the interest of the fact, "that goes back a long time, before the Second World War, to a time when the Portuguese began concentrating the Chokwe in villages so as to control them better. When the Portuguese began making these concentration camps here again, a few years back, the Chokwe said: 'It's the *ndandandas* come again.'" I think this relates to the

policy of concentration introduced at the beginning of the
1920s by Norton de Matos, a governor who laid the foundations for Portuguese administrative control of the interior.

At every kimbo where we halt or bivouac, Dr. Eduardo dos
Santos, who heads the national movement's medical service and
is making a tour of inspection, spreads out his drugs and holds
a clinic. His movable store of drugs goes into one large suitcase
and sits through the day's marching on the head of Boavida, a
student nurse (whose name is not, it seems, related to
Américo's). This Boavida is a man of the Mbunda, who will
act as medical assistant, if he is good enough, when the doctor
has moved elsewhere. The means are slender, for little help
comes from outside, but they are better than nothing. Files of
people await their turn: elders, a man with a bullet in his but-
tock, ailing women, mothers with tearful babies. Pills and in-
jections are apparently in great demand.

People ask what they should do, where they should go? Paganini listens. Saying little, he tells them what he can. Just
now, he cannot tell them much, for a Portuguese raiding offensive has begun west of Muié and is moving this way. We're
marching toward it and will find it shortly. Meanwhile, people
should shift more deeply into the forests, keep good watch,
move every few days. . . . The committee responsibles listen
and nod their heads. They know it already, but there is comfort
in being told, there is comfort in being listened to by one's own
men, one's own fighters.

The Portuguese commanders and politicians in Lisbon claim
that "the terrorists" have no intimacy with the people. Their
troops in the field know better. A guerrilla movement deprived
of intimate and enduring links with its own people would be a
movement doomed to rapid destruction. Such fighters could not
even eat, much less fill their ranks.

This movement has an everyday intimacy with its people that
reaches into every aspect of their lives. But the unity thus forged

is not a simple thing: it has had to be struggled for. There is the tricky problem of magic.

Like other traditional societies, those of the Mbunda and their neighbors are cemented by religious beliefs which suppose that all evil, even death, has an ultimate cause as well as an immediate cause. A man may die of a hunting wound or a fever or some other obvious ill. But it is the power of evil that really will have killed him. So the question is: Who has unleashed this power against him? Who is responsible for calling in witchcraft against his neighbor? Contrariwise, what can be done by counterwitchcraft to save him and preserve him from further perils? When the Mbunda first went to war again, after many years of accepted defeat, they looked for help to bullet-liquefying charms. That was before the coming of the national movement. The charms failed and the defeats were crushing. Yet the national movement has still to deal with the distractions of witchcraft.

One day around seven in the morning, north of the headwaters of the Cambule toward the forests of the Shekului, we come into a large kimbo. There are chicken and *masangwe* for our hungry stomachs, a good welcome. Yet something seems amiss. The committee of the kimbo has gathered in their stamped-earth space beneath the trees—half a dozen men of middle age and one elder. Two of them have even contrived clean shirts and ties. None of us has anything like that, though Petrov, true to an exemplary discipline, had polished his boots before breaking camp and some of the polish has survived. They gather around and give us food. Yet something is clearly wrong.

There ensues a lengthy palaver between the committee on one side and Paganini and Petrov on the other; in the middle, as it were, is a lanky young man with a rifle, the sector chief in charge of protection for this and neighboring kimbos. This sector chief is the center of the trouble. Tall and rather handsome, he appears badly disturbed. His hands are trembling and his face is drawn with anxiety.

The meeting unwinds its drama.

Petrov explains afterward. This sector chief is a local man in good standing with the movement and the kimbos under his charge. But magic has struck at him. A long story. Briefly, he had married a woman of this kimbo and paid full bride gift for her. But he was not her first husband. Some years earlier she had married another guerrilla of the national movement; this other man had been transferred elsewhere, for training, before having paid his full bride gift to the woman's parents; then he had stayed away and not returned. So in due course this woman married the sector chief, and her own parents were well pleased with this second marriage. But the first husband's parents were not. They were strongly discontented, holding that the woman was still their son's wife and that he would surely return; besides, hadn't they started paying bride gift for her, and was the part that they had paid to go for nothing?

Now, says the sector chief, they have bewitched him and mean him to die. Petrov has to sort it out, and it's difficult. It's very difficult, because the first husband's father, the author of the witchcraft according to the sector chief's conviction, happens also to be the chairman of the kimbo committee. The "civil power" and the "military power" must act closely together if they are to act at all; here they are bitterly at odds. "No doubt," says Petrov afterwards, "our sector chief has a bad conscience for having married his comrade's wife. Anyway, he's completely demoralized." And so he is. The man's whole frame trembles with omens of disaster. "He's got these shaking fits," Petrov continues, "and he says that the chairman will in any case kill him, now that he's accused the chairman of witchcraft and the chairman knows he has."

"The chairman says it's all nonsense about his having laid a spell, but he also says we'll have to move this sector chief. And we shall have to. We shall have to move him right away. He'll never recover if we don't, and there'll be more trouble." Petrov sighs. "Yes, there's got to be built an entirely new kind of Angola. . . ."

Petrov handles all this with a careful patience. "It's not the first time. No, we've learned not to act in this kind of case till we've really got at the facts on the spot." He recalls another case, a more serious one, as an illustration of why getting at the facts on the spot is more than desirable. "Up in northern Moxico, the secretary of a committee accused the chairman of a committee of passing information to the Portuguese. But the comrades decided to look thoroughly into the matter before shooting the chairman for treachery. And what did they find? An old story, going back long before the war, as many of these conflicts do.

"Long before, two men had gone to work in the west together. There one of them had died. But the other one said nothing about that when he came home again, though meanwhile he'd taken over his dead friend's possessions. Then it got around that the man had died. Years passed. But they didn't forget. The dead man's family, our comrades found, had been trying ever since to avenge themselves on the other man's family. When the national movement was formed up there, the son of the dead man became secretary of a kimbo committee, and the son of the man who had come back became its chairman. So then the dead man's family thought that false accusations of treachery would be a good way to bring about the death of the other man's son. By way of compensation, if you like. . . ."

At one of our bivouacs along the Shekului River, Paganini talked again of this kind of problem. We'd passed the grave of a fisherman shot by the Portuguese; at the head of it, a stick thrust in the ground was surmounted by a tin plate. What was that for? "Part of the task we have is to explain how things really are. In the past it was always believed that you shouldn't use the cooking pot or plate of a man who'd died. These should be placed on his grave. Very well, but we're at war, and we're short of cooking pots and plates. So now and then we've said: Go and take them from this or that grave. Some of our comrades would say it should not be done. All the same, it was done, and no evil came of it, so gradually the old custom dies away. . . .

"Or they'd say we shouldn't pass through a burial ground,

especially at night, because the spirits of the dead would harm us. But all the same we do pass through burial grounds, and no evil comes of that either. We explain: It's what you imagine that makes you believe you see ghosts, you don't really see them, they aren't really there."

"Yes, much has changed with this war. Before, if you went on a long walk from, say, Ninda to Muié, people would receive you in a friendly way but they wouldn't give you anything to eat. They do now, though; you've seen that for yourself—people come and give us food if they have any, they're offended if we don't take it. Or crossing a river: You'd have to pay fifty escudos to a man with a canoe. And then he'd stop in the middle and demand another fifty, and he'd threaten to drown you if you didn't pay. There was no love, you see, among people then."

Unity is a vital thing, no doubt, but it has to be a unity of men and women thinking in the same way, going in the same direction.

We come down southward to the Shekului, toward the big forests that reach out to Bié, in the center of Angola. The offensive has begun to the west, but what is happening with it? There will soon be news of that. Meanwhile there is the marching and the talk and the meetings on the way, and the feeling of this country in one's bones.

The young men have gone into the fighting units; not all of them, but more than enough for the arms available. "We have about five thousand men in the east," Agostinho Neto said the other day, "but only about half of them have modern weapons, and many have none at all." The best of them, maybe a few hundreds, have had training in the Soviet Union or some other part of Eastern Europe or in a friendly African country, perhaps Tanzania, perhaps Algeria. February-Four is one of these, Chapayev is another, the road-and-bridge miners too; they come back with skills and a badge or two for their caps, a few words of Russian and often a *nom de guerre* like Chapayev. Sometimes they come back with claims to privilege and comfort. But the movement takes them in again and reshapes them to a common purpose, if only because the movement can do nothing else and survive. "We should prefer to do all our training in Africa," Neto said, "for that reason: for the reason that people who train in Europe grow accustomed to conditions of life that we cannot offer here."

The young men stay in the fighting units for months and years. That is the destiny of partisans, however harsh. There is no alternative except defeat. On the other side, the Portuguese army rewards its special troops, commandos and others, with privileged pay if they stay out on bush operations even two or three weeks at a time. Then they can return to base for praise and comfort. Here there is no chance of comfort, and precious little in the way of praise; what counts for praise in partisan armies is the absence of blame.

Do all of them stay? This is a volunteer army which people can leave as they can join—by their own decision. "It's the case," Paganini said on this point during one of our nights along the Shekului, "that some of our early fighters gave up and went to Zambia. Not many, but some. They didn't go because they'd changed their minds about the struggle. They went because they were worn down by the conditions here, year after year since 1966 or 1967—no blankets, not enough food, no rest." He himself had been a year farther north, and down here already nearly half a year; others had been longer. "We don't regard it very badly that they leave. They'll come back. Besides, they do it openly, they don't run away in secret. A man will come and say, Look, I've no blanket, I've nothing, I'm going to Zambia. And if you say, No, don't go, he'll go anyway. So what do you do?"

Paganini throws back the question with a quiet self-confidence: here there is nothing to hide. And if lack of a blanket sounds anything but fatal, try sleeping without one on these plains, night after night, month after month. They have given me two blankets, but my own nights, even so, are carved and cut by the cold. And I am here only for a few weeks.

The peasants reflect all this; after all, they are the same people as the fighters. The question is not about resistance; the peasants in their majority were for resistance from the start. They have that in their history. This is what their old men, their "senior warriors" or middle-aged men as we should call them, remember and respect: the old tradition of resistance. "When the Portuguese came here we fought them and we defeated them," an old man said one day as we bivouacked above the headwaters of the Cambule. "That was long ago. But I was a chief then, even then, before the Portuguese came. My power was from the ancestors, not from the Portuguese after they'd defeated us." And he talks about the last great chief of the Mbunda people, *Mwene* Bando, who ruled beside the waters of Luati.

When did *Mwene* Bando rule? "It was long ago, it was in my youth." There are no dates to hand. But the old man's memory is not at fault. Writing in 1918, the administrative annalist of the years of Norton de Matos' first long term here, José de Oliveira Ferreira Diniz, has told the tale. "The chief of the [Mbunda] tribe is the *soba* Bando, who has exercised his authority nigh on twenty years, and is one of the few tribal authorities to have conserved power and prestige among his subordinates. This chief has his *lombe,* his residence, on the banks of the Luati. . . ."

Diniz was referring to the period of the First World War, when the whole country of the Mbunda and Luchazi, for a long way west of the Zambian frontier, still was unsubdued. Coming back after the war was over, Norton de Matos began trying to subdue it, and with some success. This was the time, early in the 1920s, when *Mwene* Bando's men began to be defeated.

But the defeat was partial for a long time, "considering that today, in 1931," as another historian of Portuguese colonial rule has noted in a book of 1934, "our influence, Portuguese occupation and territorial organization, are incomparably less intense and perfected [here in the east] than after the expeditions of João de Almeida," just before the First World War.

So the old chief of 1970, in refuge in the woodlands, would have been a "young warrior" of *Mwene* Bando's back in the 1920s; his life has spanned the whole colonial experience of these people, and memories of precolonial independence overleap the gap of fewer than fifty years. "There," they say to me one day, checking in our march along the Luati. "That is where *Mwene* Bando had his *lombe;* that is the very place, do you see it?"

They point to a few stakes in the ground, silvered like old bones along the grassland verge, the skeleton of a vanished age. But, close by, there is another structure of today or yesterday, a burned-out house of wood. A Portuguese tax-collecting post, they explain. There is pleasure in regarding it; laughter spreads. And the history of the Mbunda comes full circle, here beside the antique frame of *Mwene* Bando's *lombe.* Forty years of colonial tax collecting—and *Mwene* Bando's warriors have become men with modern rifles and with thoughts that belong to today and possibly even more to tomorrow.

The question for these peasants is not about resistance, but about ways and means. Unlike others, farther to the west or north, they are near enough to Zambia for refuge there. But should they go there, and add more hundreds to the camps? Or should they stay? Stay, says the national movement, stay and help us fight. "Yes, we have the courage to stay," the chairman of a kimbo committee along the Shekului one day tells me, while the rumble of occasional bombing can be heard in the west, where the Portuguese offensive is getting under way. "But we need rifles." He is a powerfully built man of about forty-five, wearing a pair of ragged shorts and some kind of ancient army jacket, a committee leader since 1966. "If we have rifles we shall not fear the Portuguese or the militia"—African conscripts in Portuguese service—"but we need rifles. Now they can take us like women, because we have no rifles."

"You have a few rifles," Paganini tells a meeting the next day, "and now we are going to bring you more." He speaks to them in ciMbunda, a language he has learned since coming here. "We shall give you enough rifles to defend yourselves against the militia and the GE"—"special groups" consisting of African mercenaries armed and trained by the Portuguese for bush warfare, and intended as "better" than the militia.

"We are giving each kimbo group two of our fighters to train you in using these rifles. And because there are few young men among you now, the women must bear arms as well." Neto said the same thing in several meetings held here before he left, the other day, on a journey to Europe. "The women must bear arms; the women can fight as well as the men. And we on our side will then be able to send away our detachments so as to attack the Portuguese where they are." They listen, a ring of watchful faces. Paganini enlarges upon other points. The prices charged by the national movement's warehouses—retail stores that sell goods brought in from Zambia in exchange for locally grown food—are said to have been too dear. "Yes, so now we have changed these prices, we have lowered them. . . ."

These things are known, but hearing them spoken of has its comfort, above all now when the *mujimbo* is not good, when the *mujimbo*, the "bush telegraph," speaks of bitter fighting on the way. Another kimbo leader rises to reply, a man of cramped muscles, a man of skin and bone, a man without illusions. Yes, there are people who are at the Portuguese post, at nearby Muié, where the Portuguese have a garrison of maybe a hundred and fifty men: they have been taken but they will come back, they will come back whenever they can escape. "Those without courage to stay have gone to Zambia. But we who are here will stay. We know that our guerrillas have courage. We know that Guimarães has courage."

There is a pause while this severe old man nods toward Guimarães, their young commander, the commander of the fighting detachments that encircle Muié. Guimarães grins an acknowledgment: if he is popular here, it has not been an easy popularity to win. Every pair of peasant eyes judges by what it sees and by what its owner, with village skepticism, infers from what it sees. No commander here will escape judgment by any

reference to superior orders or tactical mysteries. Courage is
what a man does, what he is seen to do. The *mujimbo* says that
Guimarães has courage; it is not everyone's reputation.

The old man continues, turning now to the visitor. "We protest against their killing of our people. We protest against their
arrest of our people." He turns to Paganini. "We demand that
our movement send a big force to support us. We demand that
all our people be armed. You, the responsible ones, have the
task. It is the task to give arms to those who have the courage
to stay. Our people will stay. Yes, but we need rifles."

Nobody supposes that any such big force can be sent, or even
should be sent: it is rather a question of everyone's speaking his
mind, airing his thoughts, expounding his solutions.

Paganini answers with his own stubborn patience. Arms are
coming, and will be given out. Then he speaks about the coming offensive, its timing, its probable objectives, what people
must do to escape its consequences. The watchful faces do not
change. These are also things that everyone knows, for everyone
has done it all before and expects to do it many times again
before this war can be won. Paganini discusses the *mujimbo*
and says where it is right and where it is wrong, and generally
how things will be. There is a comfort in hearing all this. Nobody is being clever. Nobody is telling lies.

The meeting ends, and there is food to eat.

Muié lies about seven miles distant, "a town of the fourth class"
according to an official description of 1952: "Like so many
others in these distant and sparsely occupied regions, it has
nothing but the stores of a few traders." A town of the fourth
class in Angola is not much of a town: Muié is really nothing
more than a village at the end of a road to nowhere.

Muié can be inspected from woodland cover at a distance
of about four hundred yards, though at the cost of a harsh bout
of forced marching there and back. Today it has more than
the stores of a few traders. Its rectangle of barbed wire, enclosing the whole camp save for its helicopter landing strip just

outside, is furnished with eleven timbered guard posts and three searchlights. A road bisects this wired-in rectangle from east to west. On the northern side, inside the wire, there are the main garrison buildings: barracks for the white troops, a canteen, a small hospital, a resthouse for the officers. South of the road, still inside the wire, are barracks for the black troops, space for "liberated" villagers "recaptured from the terrorists," and what looks like a warehouse.

Petrov's intelligence says that Muié has a company of white troops from Portugal; these are normally relieved every three months and otherwise supplied by twice-monthly truck convoys from battalion HQ at Cangamba, up the road to Silva Porto in the "colonial heartlands." The trucks, Petrov says, are all Unimogs or Mercedes from West Germany: the Portuguese, he thinks, have few others. Muié also has about sixty GE and maybe thirty militia. For the most part, these troops sit within their wire and do nothing but guard, or try to guard, their "liberated" prisoners. But now and then they are reinforced for offensive sweeps through the neighboring countryside. That is what is happening now. "Operation Zaga" is about to get into its stride.

In the summer of 1970, the United Nations will duly report, "Portuguese forces launched a series of special military operations against MPLA (national movement) bases in Moxico District. Operation Zumbo s/H was carried out in an area bound by the Alto Cuito, Cuito, and Cuvelai rivers, close to the central district of Bié."

That is to the west of us, where Paganini's further detachments lie, and by way of which the transport convoys march their supplies westward from the Zambian frontier. Paganini's zone is a decisive one for transport and supply, as well as for its own importance in itself; through Paganini's zone, the fighting units reinforce their push toward the west, toward the High Plateau which eventually will take them still farther westward down the watershed to the Atlantic seaboard.

Meanwhile, continues the same UN report, "another operation, code-named 'Zaga,' was aimed at eliminating MPLA (national movement) forces from an area in the southeastern part of Moxico District, bounded by Muié, Cangombe, Chiume, and Ninda." This is the central zone of Paganini's area, where we were during part of "Operation Zaga." "Elimination"? It will be giving away no secrets to report that Paganini's forces are several hundred strong; among their other duties, they protect thousands of village people in woodland kimbos. According to Petrov's intelligence while we are outside Muié, "Zaga" begins on June 10; it undoubtedly continues for several weeks. But with what true result?

The Portuguese command will claim for Operation "Zaga" the killing of twenty-one guerrillas, the wounding of seven, and the "freeing" of 145 village people. These figures will be a large exaggeration of the truth; even if they were not, they would betoken nothing remotely like "elimination" of the national movement in this area.

The operation will have failed.

The "freeing" of village people "seized by the terrorists" and "kept" in woodland kimbos is a frequent theme in communiqués of the Portuguese command. What is the truth about that?

Today and tomorrow, outside Muié, the people of the national movement will demonstrate their answer to Operation "Zaga"; and the words of the Portuguese communiqués will once again appear too absurd even to be cynical. There may be readers far away in Lisbon who can believe these communiqués. If so, this can be only because there is no straight reporting of the war in the Portuguese press, and very little reporting of any sort. Whenever there is any such straight reporting from the Portuguese side, the truth comes singularly clear.

It is not necessary to rely on witnesses with the guerrillas.

In March 1971, six months after Operation "Zaga" had "eliminated" the national movement from the Muié region, an Ameri-

can reporter, Jim Hoagland, of the Washington *Post,* was taken
to that region, and to Muié itself, now acquiring for the first
and doubtless for the last time a certain fame upon the world's
stage. Mr. Hoagland is one of the best reporters of the African
scene and took his assignment on the chin, or rather on the
feet. He marched with a Portuguese raiding party and watched
them at work.

"Three large French-manufactured helicopters, just arrived
for duty in Angola," he wrote for his newspaper of March 14,
"lifted off from Muié" a little before dawn. "Forty miles south,
they hovered over a clear space, the wind from their blades
flattening the yellow-green swamp grass as Monteiro's men
jumped. . . ." They set off on the familiar mission described
in the Portuguese communiqués as "freeing" village people
"seized by the terrorists." Hoagland went with them.

"The rain began a few minutes after the Portuguese soldiers
had captured the first African woman," Hoagland reported.
"She watched in wonderment and fear as the young infantrymen
smashed down a field of ripe corn. The second woman was
caught on the other side of the deserted village. . . . The
white troops let the woman collect her possessions, which barely
filled the porcelain basin she balanced on her head, before they
pulled down her stick-and-thatch hut. Then the 44 soldiers
marched the two women prisoners into the Angolan forest. Behind them in the deepening mud lay the ruins of a small village
the Portuguese suspected of having provided food to African
guerrilla fighters. . . .

"This was the first hour of a 'hunt and persecute' patrol, the
more elegantly phrased Portuguese equivalent of Vietnam's
'search and destroy.' Hunting and persecuting have become Portugal's main tactical tools in trying to repress Africa's longest
black nationalist war. . . .

"The emaciated, aged African women—'captured population'
in the terminology of this strange war—stumbled under the
weight of the 40-pound field packs the soldiers had given them
to carry. . . .

"'These patrols are the key to getting the population to our side and winning the war,' 2nd Lt. Filipe Monteiro, the patrol leader, said. . . . 'Besides, if we let these women go free, they would go and tell the terrorists where we are. Then we all would be ambushed and perhaps someone would be killed.'"

Returning, they had seven "liberated prisoners." They reached "the last danger point, a wooden footbridge across a small river. . . . The seven African civilians were lined up to cross the bridge one at a time before the soldiers. The first four made it. The fifth, a woman, deviated slightly from the path. She stepped on a mine. . . ."

The visitor on the guerrilla side sees the same scene as Mr. Hoagland, only in reverse.

On the day after the meeting by the Shekului we sleep later than usual: there is nothing to do until tonight, when "Operation Zaga" will cause us to move again. There is time to write one's notes, to embark on the collecting of a little oral tradition from a kimbo elder, to question the handful of fighting men who have remained as a kimbo guard, the rest of their detachment being away on the same duty elsewhere. With any luck, it will be a day of rest.

It begins like that. The five fighting men, and a sixth who is concerned with food supply, gather in a circle. Four are Mbunda; two others are Kankangala, members of an Mbunda subgroup who speak a variant of ciMbunda. Three are from villages in this immediate area, one is from the Canavale region, to the southwest of Muié, another from Cangombe, not far west of Muié, while the sixth is from the boundaries of Lunda, in the north. Two have seen action eight times each, and one seven times, having all joined the national movement in 1967; two have seen action only once, having joined in 1968; the sixth has so far seen none. Two have learned to read and write ciMbunda in the kimbos of the areas; only one of them can speak a little Portuguese. They are a random sample, but probably a fairly representative one.

There is a meeting of leaders. Paganini and Petrov set forth the position. They estimate the direction of the coming offensive; they discuss the evasive movement of local kimbos; they consider detachment positions, both now and those to follow in the next days and weeks. Pupa triumphs with his cooking pots; there is even some rice to eat, and honey to rescue the sour boredom of *masangwe*. Mozambiki plays his marimba, his finger xylophone; so does February-Four, sitting on a tree trunk, listening to his fingered notes and the songs they mean to him. Chapayev wears a towel about his neck, fresh from bathing in the river. It is a day of rest; with any luck it will continue so. Tomorrow may even be another. Perhaps we shall not march tonight? Perhaps we had better wait until such-and-such a courier returns tomorrow? We have marched hard for many days; everyone would like a rest until tomorrow.

Nothing of the kind. Movement stirs behind the veil of nearby trees. Newcomers.

They are three women with three children from the Muié concentration camp. They have slipped away into the forest while cultivating a field under Portuguese guard. They are village women of twenty-five to thirty years old, it is hard to be sure of their ages; two of the children might be ten or eleven, the third can be scarcely more than four. Two of these women are wives and wear blue-striped cotton dresses, but the third has only a skirt and so is presumably unwed; there is no time to go into the sociology. Others, they say, have also just escaped, and are coming the same way. "But we were the first among them."

It has been the usual story. Unable to supply their captives with food, having to get their own by threatened convoys from Cangamba, the Portuguese have to allow their captives out of the wire so as to cultivate nearby. But in allowing them out they can't prevent them from trying to escape. "There is nothing to eat in that place," the women say, "there is nothing for us there."

They are badly frightened. "If they come here after us," says the third, who speaks for them, "they will find us and they will kill us." She repeats this in a refrain, a matter-of-fact refrain lined with fear, as Paganini softly questions her and listens. There is the smell of fear now, and little to be done about it. The escapees' direction of flight will have been marked; the trail will be followed. Paganini speaks to reassure them and others who gather; and they are glad to be reassured. That's about all: guerrillas cannot hold a front, and people committed to guerrilla war, as these people are, pay a price that can be mortal. Everyone knows this. But there are rules for these situations. People should understand and sympathize with each other's fears and problems, and should take care to say so.

The women listen to Paganini's words, and fall silent. Paganini turns to me with a slow gesture, deprecating his helplessness. "They are bombing again, do you hear?" The women wait for more reassurance, but Paganini does not give it to them. There is no more to give. Faintly in the distance, the bombing continues. Somewhere over there, trees crash to the ground, tear themselves from their roots, spout fire and smoke from shattered branches.

We shall march at first light. The kimbo will disperse.

Before dawn we are heading for the southeast through the woodland slopes of the Shekului Forest, raising one low horizon after another beneath a sky that lifts and pales. As we go, we pass kimbo groups that are also getting ready to move, packing up their cooking pots and putting out their fires, stamping on wisps of smoke that may otherwise mount and linger on the forest cover, betraying human presence to any helicopter that may come this way in daytime, when the Portuguese make their raids. They will tramp away to another location in the forests, more distant from Muié, and there they will again build flimsy shelters that will serve until the offensive peters out and people can return to the riverside locations they prefer. They may be safe where they are going, or they may not; nobody has anything to say about that, if only because there is nothing useful to be said. It is not the first time, or even the twentieth. It will not be the last.

We march till past sundown, circling Muié to the southward, and stop at last where people are at rest. Or rather where their fires are burning, for they themselves have vanished in the night. We stand beneath green domes of firelit foliage and wait. They begin coming back within minutes, having seen us from their hiding places. They show where we may bivouac and light our own fires. We gather around leaping flames that lift new domes of leafy magnitude. We lie beside the fires and sleep, waiting for the cold that will drive away sleep.

Deeper into the forest, on the next day and the next, there are kimbos of long standing, where people do not think of moving, confident in their guerrilla protection here.

Some days later we reach the marshy waters of Cambule within a gray-green wilderness beneath a milky sky, and Rui shoots an eland. Soon there is good grilled meat beneath a fire-charred crust, and all of us are pricked with hunger. But then, as though by magic, there are people too. They come out of the woods; they materialize from the thickets; they gather around in knots of eagerness, a little shy at first in case their hope of sharing in the eland is ill placed. But it is not ill placed —Rui's eland is a large one, young and yet full grown. Fifty people can eat their fill from it, and still leave meat for smoking that will not rot upon the march. Paganini supervises the grilling and the butchering and the sharing of the meat, cutting it himself, handing it around, taking the occasion to hold a meeting and discuss the news and the movement and the right thing for them to do. There is laughter and companionship; and people find acquaintances and time for gossip. Petrov says with a carefully emphatic pride: "They will sleep well tonight, they've their own fighters to protect them." And what might appear as mawkish propaganda, if delivered in some communiqué or bulletin, strikes here a note of obvious and moving truth. They do sleep well, and so do we.

We cross the Cambule and leave them behind us, waving their farewells before they leave themselves. We march into the marshy wilderness, our boots sucking at our feet. The war is ten years old. The war goes on.

PART ONE

ANGOLA IN HISTORY

"I was a chief before the Portuguese came.
My power was from the ancestors. . . ."

Elder of the Mbunda,
Moxico District, 1970

"The government of Bailundo is democratic. These heathen mix
with the infamous humiliations of the orientals, the unbridled coarse-
ness of the English people at election times in England. The kings
defer to and flatter their counsellors; these are they who elevate a
king to the throne and also cast him down."

De Almeida Sandoval, 1837
(trans. G. M. Childs)

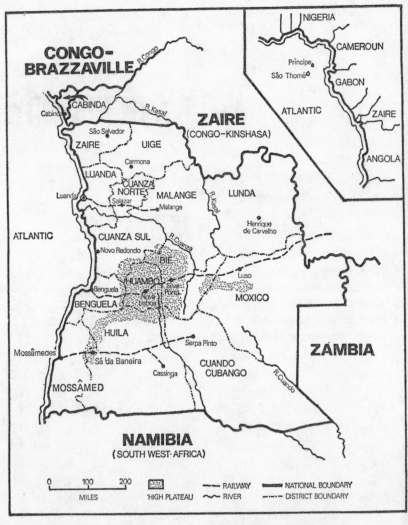

Portuguese Angola: Districts, district capitals, railways

1   THEMES AND OUTLINES

"Out there to the east," wrote in the tenth year of the war a somewhat excited South African journalist, reporting to Johannesburg from the inland Portuguese garrison town of Serpa Pinto, "is one of the great becalmed areas of Southern Africa— 100,000 square miles of bushveld, home for scattered groups of primitive tribesmen and herds of game which make it a dream for hunters and lovers of the Africa of old." Now, he added, "it is changing," and "is a strategic area which is becoming the focus of attention in the Angolan rebel war. . . ."[1]

This traveler's picture of the Angolan east depicts a favored theme of traditional "outside thought" about that "great becalmed area" and neighboring regions of the same reputation. It is the theme to which the Portuguese have always returned when talking of these inland regions as "the lands at the end of the Earth," where no one lives save the "most primitive tribes"—the same theme, with a wider frame of reference, that inspired a prominent English historian of Africa, some forty years ago, to believe that "the heart of Africa," till Europeans came upon the scene in the middle of the nineteenth century, "was scarcely beating."

And so in fact it did appear to the early travelers from "outside"; at first glance, it sometimes looks like that even today. There stays with you a sense of having penetrated to the heart

[1] Robin Drew, *The Star*, Johannesburg, July 25, 1970.

of a mystery and attained an ultimate truth, an "inner truth" about Africa, only to find that the mystery continues to elude you and the truth lies hidden within timbered solitudes. This, you want to say upon returning, is "Africa's Africa," untouched, peculiar to itself, preserving its strangeness intact and unalloyed.

Here, for example, there lives one of the strangest of all creatures, unknown outside these central African plains: *Kasolo*, "the Discoverer," as the Mbunda call the little bird that sits high on a tree and pipes a signal to passing humans, early in the morning, that it knows the whereabouts of a bees' nest. If you follow this bird through the woods it will lead you to where the honey lies, and then, when you have opened the nest and taken your share, *Kasolo* will take his.

"*Kasolo* calls at 05.55. Everyone delighted . . ." begins my note for June 18, 1970. A century earlier old Silva Pôrto the *Sertanejo*, the Backlands-Traveler, most sympathetic of the nineteenth-century explorers, modest, persevering, gently inquisitive, had known exactly that sensation. "We, obscure pilgrim of Destiny, pay our tribute to this marvelous messenger of sweetness. . . ."[2]

Yes, a strange country, and the echoes of its strangeness continue with the people themselves. Marching in 1853 along the Ninda River toward the Zambezi, east of the Shekului,[3] Silva Pôrto came upon a group of "Cassaqueres [Kasakelle] . . . a nomad tribe you will find all over the interior of this enormous land"; in fact a Khoi people, related to the Bushmen

[2] Several singularly unpleasant Portuguese will pass through these pages; here I am glad to pay tribute to one who was quite the reverse. The quotation from Silva Pôrto is in his diaries: *Viagems e Apontamentos de Uma Portuense em África*, referring to his African decades (1847–90) though published in 1942, Lisbon, Ministry of the Colonies, page 209.

As to *Kasolo*, Mr. D. W. Snow of the British Museum (Natural History) has been kind enough to furnish me with an authoritative note: "The 'honey messenger' is the bird usually known as 'honey guide,' and the species in eastern Angola is probably the Black-throated Honeyguide (*Indicator indicator*). . . . The bird leads people (and also some wild mammals) to bees' nests, with the object of eating the grubs and wax, and a little honey as well, after the nest has been opened up. It is one of the most remarkable cases of specialised feeding behaviour known in birds."

[3] See Map 4, page 255.

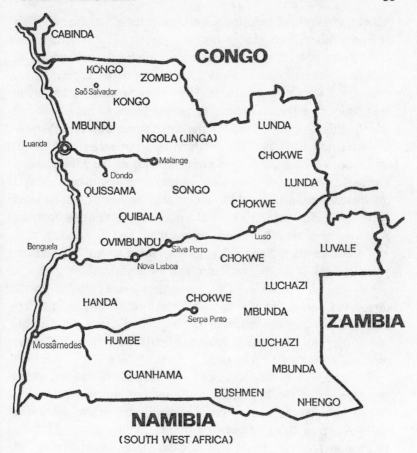

CABINDA

CONGO

KONGO   ZOMBO

Saõ Salvador

KONGO

MBUNDU

LUNDA

NGOLA (JINGA)

Luanda

CHOKWE

Malange

Dondo

LUNDA

QUISSAMA   SONGO

CHOKWE

QUIBALA

OVIMBUNDU

Luso

Silva Porto

Benguela

CHOKWE

LUVALE

Nova Lisboa

LUCHAZI

HANDA   CHOKWE

MBUNDA

Serpa Pinto

ZAMBIA

Mossâmedes   HUMBE

LUCHAZI

MBUNDA

CUANHAMA

BUSHMEN

NHENGO

NAMIBIA
(SOUTH WEST AFRICA)

Angola: Some principal ethnic groups
(approximate locations)

of the south, whose ideas and loyalties have been largely those
of the Stone Age. Of such, in the visitor's small party of 1970,
was Mozambiki the Kasakelle, who wears a monkey-skin hat
with a tail flicking around his pale brown face, and whose eyes
for spoor in the sand, whether animal or human, are those that
urban man has long since lost. Mozambiki is not in the Stone
Age. He carries a rifle and begins to think as an Angolan of
today. Yet the truths of the Stone Age, of all that long unwritten

history of mankind before the gates of Eden shut, are probably still somewhere with him.

A great lack of information about these peoples, a lack of written information, helps to deepen the strangeness. Urban man looks for words on paper. Here you can find next to none that bear upon the problem. "There are zones of Angola about which little is known," writes the Portuguese ethnographer De Lima as late as 1964, "about which one can really write nothing."[4] So it is, for the best modern account of the Mbunda and Luchazi has no more than stray notes covering a page or two.[5] So far as I have been able to discover, nothing of eyewitness value has been written about them since the time of João de Almeida and Ferreira Diniz more than half a century ago, while before that there are only the scant notes of travelers such as Silva Pôrto, Serpa Pinto, and F. S. Arnot.[6]

Of these, the only ones of value are those of Silva Pôrto, direct and curious though tantalizingly brief: "Reached the territory of *Mwene* Gambo, where we pitched camp. Paid right-of-passage money to the lady of the land (*dona de terra*), who gave us a goat and some bowls of millet flour. . . . Went on and pitched camp in the country of *Mwene* Canunga, paramount chief of the Mbunda. . . . Sent right-of-passage money to the lady of the land, whom I saw in our camp when she brought us a goat, bowls of millet flour, cups of mead (*minzundo*). . . ." What rights, what status, what manner of appointment concerned these "ladies of the land"? What ties held fast his chiefs to *Mwene* Canunga, king of the Mbunda? Silva Pôrto does not say; nor do any of the others.

There is much more information about some other parts of

4 Mesquelita de Lima, *A Etnográfia Angolana*, Luanda, 1964, p. 17.

5 Merran McCulloch, *The Southern Lunda and Related Peoples*, International African Institute, London, 1951.

6 J. de Almeida, *Sul de Angola: Relatório de un govêrno de distrito (1908–10)*, Lisbon, 1911, repr. 1936; José de Oliveira Ferreira Diniz, *Populações Indígenas de Angola*, Coimbra, 1918 (much the fullest historical description of eastern Angola's populations); Silva Pôrto, op. cit.; Serpa Pinto, *How I Crossed Africa*, London, 1881, vol. 1, e.g. p. 254; F. S. Arnot, *Missionary Travels in Central Africa*, London, 1914 (but relating, so far as these peoples are concerned, to two decades earlier).

Angola, especially in the west and the center. These contain peoples—some of them large peoples such as the Kongo, Kimbundu, Ovimbundu—who first had contact with intrusive whites in a distant past, and whom a few of these whites studied with some care. Yet these whites, even those of missionary intention, knew the Africans they encountered here as opponents, rivals, or objects of coercion; and the histories they wrote were invariably the histories of themselves.[7] Thus the history of the Africans of Angola can be understood only with distortion and foreshortening when seen from the European records.

These distorting effects have been repeatedly enlarged by characteristic European attitudes of evaluation. One such attitude has been to suppose a great distinction of kind between the western peoples, of whose strong kingdoms much was known even by 1550, and the eastern or southern peoples, about whom nothing or very little was known—in Portuguese parlance, between the western peoples of "the colonial heartlands" and the eastern or southern peoples of "the lands at the end of the Earth."

Another familiar distortion has derived from a European preoccupation with ethnic distinctions seen as some sort of "primitive nationalism," as what is nowadays called "tribalism." Thus, many of the traditional intergroup relationships of tolerance and common culture between neighboring language groups have become obscured, by European misunderstanding, to the benefit of an often false picture of violent rivalry in the past.

So it has come about, for example, that the Chokwe, a numerous people who expanded their settlements southward from Lunda in the eighteenth century and after, have been generally presented as "invaders" or "dispossessors" of the already indigenous ciMbunda-speaking peoples. No doubt there were many minor clashes and disputes. But the truth seems rather to have been that the Chokwe were accepted as like-thinking and useful neighbors for whom easy room could be found in a

[7] An outstanding exception is G. M. Childs, *Umbundu Kinship and Character,* Oxford, 1949.

little-filled land. The experience of the national movement during the 1960s—an intense experience now yielding the first real surveys of how these eastern peoples have thought and think about themselves—suggests that most of their conflicts in the past were based not on ethnic rivalry or on "tribalism," but on much more narrowly political struggles for power among appointed chiefs; and that even these conflicts were often the exception and not the rule. If nationalism is a new idea in Angola, so also is "tribalism," its natural child.

The historiography of Angola's people is in any case notably deficient. The country's archaeology is practically unknown, prolonging an ignorance especially bad for any grasp of the formative periods of early Iron Age development during the first millennium A.D. Almost no work has gone into the systematic assembly of oral history, save for the western peoples and the Lunda in the northeast, whose king lists and other dynastic data have provided a chronological outline covering several centuries.

Even so, the science of history has made some progress here during the past two decades, though seldom by Portuguese effort, and a general view of its meaning and development is now possible. Several basic points emerge.

One of these is that nearly all Angola's people—like nearly all their neighbors of middle Africa—share ultimately common origins and cultures, and speak related languages that are often little more than variants of a few of the western Bantu tongues. The chief exceptions to this rule are the Khoi groups of southern Angola; these derive from a different line of phenotypes and corresponding languages.

Another basic point is that certain attitudes of conflict and distinctiveness have developed at various times: for example, between the Kimbundu and the Kongo of the west, or between the Ovimbundu of the center and the peoples of the east.[8]

[8] Generally lumped together in the Portuguese literature as "Ganguella." They sometimes lump themselves together, at least in Zambia, as the Wiko, "the people of the west." Kafungulwa Mubitana, "Wiko Masquerades," *African Arts*, Los Angeles, Spring 1971, p. 58, notes that this term is used by Angolans living in western Zambia, applying to the "Luvale, Luchazi, Chokwe and Mbunda, all

But these attitudes have been largely the consequence of direct or indirect pressures arising out of European intrusion from the Atlantic seaboard after 1500. The Portuguese imperialist claim to "five centuries of presence in Angola" is completely mythical beyond the coastal country. Yet the indirect consequences of that presence penetrated after 1600 far beyond the seaboard, and helped toward political and economic changes that entered Angolan history long before anything even faintly resembling the Portuguese colonial system. Some of these consequences were absorbed constructively into the fabric of African society; of consequences of this kind, probably by far the most important was the inland spread after about 1600 of American food crops, such as cassava and maize. Other consequences went toward social disintegration; of these, the worst, beyond any doubt, was the steady inward spread of the slave trade and its search for captives who could be marched westward to the coast and sold there.

Much of Angola's history, after Portuguese arrival just before 1500 and continuing with Portuguese effort along the seaboard, thus reflects a sequence of African initiatives and responses to direct or indirect outside challenge. In various ways and under various leaders—some of whose names are still remembered with pride and admiration—this or that Angolan people sought to contain the challenge from outside, or absorb it, or turn it to their advantage. Angolan history, in other words, offers a "typology" of initiative and response just as much as Portuguese history does.

This way of looking at the past can offer some advantages. In the first place, the Angolan typology of initiative and response to white intrusion can be shown to link up closely with the actions and reactions of other Africans, and so build toward a meaningful historical synthesis for many peoples of the continent. Secondly, it can serve as a useful corrective to the fa-

---

characterized by a tradition of common origin and sharing a homogeneous culture. . . ." One finds this same sense of identity among members of all these and other, neighboring peoples in the woodland kimbos and fighting units of the national movement.

miliar "no-heart-beating" school of thought—to the notion that "Africans stood still" before they felt the "guiding hand" of Europe, but afterward became the more or less helpless objects of European policy and precept.[9]

The Angolan typology, as it happens, is unusually rich. As elsewhere, it begins with "primary initiatives" of resistance. The western kingdoms, those of the Kongo and Kimbundu and others, stand firm on their own state power. When pushed to it, they gather their armies and fight the Portuguese. Otherwise, their rulers find ways of accommodating the demands of the maritime whites to their own dynastic or state interests. All these ways tend to modify existing forms of society. Some of them, such as the acceptance of Christian ideas at the courts of kings, have little modifying effect: the Christian missionaries are few, often feeble in their faith, seldom of more than fleeting influence on events and loyalties. Other influences, and, most of all, the development of the sale of African captives for the benefit of oversea plantation owners, become terribly destructive of existing law and order: their consequences will slowly undermine the whole fabric of society in these lands.[10]

Exceptionally rich in its display of "primary initiatives and responses," Angola's history continues to foreshadow and encapsulate the whole long and complex experience of African-European interplay and adaptation. It was here, for example, that there appeared upon the scene the earliest systematic effort to Africanize the meaning and the teachings of Christianity as a means of African self-defense, and of the enhancement of African power over destiny. In 1706 there was burned at the stake, under Capuchin priestly authority backed by a sufficient secular force, a young Kongo woman, Dona Beatrice, *Chimpa*

[9] The "typological" method of analyzing African history, and of thereby moving toward a coherent understanding of the African historical situation, notably since 1800, owes much to the pioneering work of T. O. Ranger and some others. I would like to acknowledge my debt to them here; and I have tried to suggest some of the fruits of this approach in *The Africans*, Longmans, London, 1969 (*The African Genius*, Atlantic-Little, Brown, Boston, 1970).

[10] Cf. David Birmingham, *Trade and Conflict in Angola (1483–1790)*, Clarendon, Oxford, 1966; James Duffy, *Portuguese Africa*, Harvard and Cambridge (Eng.), 1959.

Vita, who had proclaimed herself the reincarnation of Saint Anthony, and, as such, called on the Kongo to reassert the dignity and independence of their ancient kingdom after invading Portuguese had trampled both beneath their soldiers' heels.

Like others later, Dona Beatrice taught her multitude of devotees that Jesus and His Mother Mary and Saint Francis were all black people; that the birthplace of this black Jesus was the old Kongo capital of São Salvador, not far south of the Congo River; and that nearby Sundi had played Nazareth to São Salvador's Bethlehem. Every Friday she died for a while "and went up to Heaven to sup with God and plead the cause of the blacks, her partisans, and especially for the restoration of the Kongo kingdom, returning to life on Earth each Saturday."[11]

For all this, by Catholic orthodoxy mingled with local political intrigue, Dona Beatrice was burned as Joan of Arc had been burned by the English in France three centuries earlier; and very striking, as it happens, are the parallels between these two martyred women, whether in their simplicity of faith or in their practicalities of aim and action. The memory of Dona Beatrice died no more than did that of Joan of Arc: for years afterward the echoes of her prophecy stayed vividly alive, producing, as one of its side effects, a remarkable religious art devoted to the iconography of Saint Anthony and the crucifixion of a black Christ. Other effects, however indirect, were more important. Two and a half centuries after Dona Beatrice had perished in the flames, with Fr. Lorenzo da Lucca holding aloft his crucifix, new African Christian prophets were to take up her mission in circumstances very different, but essentially, as to the regaining of independence, just the same. One of these was to be Simão Toco, among the direct forerunners of the great rebellion of 1961. A persistent thematic continuity runs through the history of these lands.

Many other types of "intermediate or secondary" initiative and response mark this history: the desperate reassertion of old

[11] Louis Jadin, "Le Congo et le secte des Antoniens. . . ." *Bull. de l'Inst. hist. belge de Rome,* 1961, pp. 519–20. Quoted from the account (there *in extenso,* with other contemporary documents) of Fr. Bernardo de Gallo.

sovereignties, sometimes successful, at other times plunged in defeat; minor revolts against administrative abuse; mass emigrations to other lands; shrewd efforts at carving out a share in the white man's trade or the white man's power; a whole range of individual ploys and enterprises; finally, the modern movements of the twentieth century.

These last form the central matter of this book; and they, too, seem often to foreshadow and encapsulate the general African response to "modern times." They do this in their early forms of political thought and protest, beginning before 1900; in those many columns of invective journalism that an earlier Portuguese regime was ready to tolerate seventy and eighty years ago; in the living drama of the men who wrote them. They do it in their shift from "cultural" forms of self-identification to outright politics and political organization. They do it in their demands for reform, in their reliance on the possibilities of reform, in their expectation that reason can evoke an answering reason. But it may well prove that they prefigure the general African response in quite another way as well—in the framing of a new type of indigenous and fundamental change: the modern shift from ideas of reform to ideas of revolution.

Much else can be argued for the sheer and vital interest of Angola's case. Perhaps nowhere else in "settler Africa," in the Africa where whites have put down roots and made their homes, may one better see in all its ambivalence the curious relationship of blacks to whites, coupling an acceptance of white humanity with a rejection of white oppression. What a western Sudanese diplomat said about the invading French in 1880 might be said by the Angolans about the Portuguese. "We like the French," he observed, "but do not trust them; they, on the other hand, trust us but do not like us."[12]

In this respect, Angola is rich in social history with a wide context. That is not because the Portuguese have been long in this land. So far as most of Angola is concerned, they have not been long, or no longer than other whites in other African

[12] Seydou to Galliéni, quoted in J. D. Hargreaves, *Prelude to the Partition of West Africa*, Macmillan, London, 1963, p. 260.

lands. It is because most of the Portuguese who have come to live here have been poor people of small pretensions and even smaller education, whose ideas about wealth, comfort, or their own careers have not been greatly different from many of the Africans they have lived among. If in the old British saying about settler emigration to colonial Africa it used to be "officers to Kenya, and sergeants to Rhodesia," it was enlisted men or privates to Angola (or to Mozambique); and the footsloggers of Portugal were mostly peasants. Their economy at home was near "subsistence," their literacy was nil.

This tended to a certain easygoing tolerance "at the base," if seldom to anything approaching friendship. Does this argue for the Portuguese regime's ever-repeated claim to operate a non-racist system, a non-discriminatory system? Unhappily, not in the least. The Portuguese claim to "non-racism" is empty of truth in any systematic sense, just as is the myth of "five centuries of presence." As late as 1950, even on the frequently quoted sexual side of the question, the figures could not support it: they showed, even as late as that, a total of only about 30,000 *mestiços* in Angola—of people, that is, recognized as being of "mixed blood." Apart from that, of course, "the sexual side of the question" proves nothing about non-racism by a ruling group. The Republic of South Africa has more than a million "Coloureds," people recognized as being of "mixed blood," but nobody will care to say that they have derived from white attitudes of social or political enlightenment.

Yet in everyday relations, wherever aspects of the system and its built-in coercion did not arise, there could be tolerance and even a mild affection on either side of the Angolan color line, and probably to a degree more widely felt as meaningful than in any of the non-Portuguese colonies of white settlement. It may not be sentimental to say that on the African side, at least before 1900, it was something of the case of *Kasolo* the Discoverer calling to the better-equipped traveler to help in sharing out the riches of the land. The famous King Affonso of Kongo (1506–40) had set the tune for that almost at the start of Afro-Portuguese contact, praying that his "friend and brother" in Lisbon would send him "two physicians and two apothecaries and one surgeon," and for skilled woodworkers who could build him a ship capable of sailing to Europe; while he, on his part, would do his best to satisfy Portuguese wants.[13]

But the traveler had another idea; and sharing played no part in it. The traveler was not a friend, much less a brother. This is no kind of anti-Portuguese statement. It may be permissible here (if otherwise pretentious) to affirm that the Portuguese are a singularly laborious and peaceful people, full of wit and savor, hard to dislike. But they are also a much abused people. More than most others, they have suffered from the greed and irresponsibility of rulers, especially over the past fifty years or so. Their conduct in Angola has often reflected these miseries at home. Yet the Africans are well aware of this: they, too, have suffered from bad rulers, whether their own or the Portuguese, and this too has made for a certain tolerance and sympathy in mutual woes.

There has even been a certain numerical equality in this suffering. If more than half a million Angolans have fled from Portuguese rule since 1961, not counting other thousands who fled in earlier times, about as many Portuguese have smuggled their way out of Portugal, illegally for the most part, escaping from hunger and unemployment to the factories of Paris and Toulouse.

Surprisingly, perhaps, the ferocious years of the 1960s seem not to have destroyed this consciousness of belonging to a common humanity, at least on the African side.

Throughout 1968–69 the responsible leader of the national movement in the crucial Luso area of Moxico District was a tall, thin lathe of a man, courageous and intelligent, whose *nom de guerre* is Iko. Interviewed elsewhere in 1970, he discussed the national movement's treatment of the grouped Portuguese farming settlements in that area, dotted here and there

[13] Rather more than a score of Affonso's letters to Lisbon have survived; twenty-two of them were reproduced by the Visconde de Paiva Manso in 1877: *História do Congo* (*Documentos*). They are yet to be translated in full, but a small selection will be found in my *Black Mother,* London and Boston, 1961, and idem, *The African Past,* London and Boston, 1964.

about Angola though chiefly in the central districts, and known as *colonatos*.

"From many *colonatos* we have seized large numbers of cattle to feed our own population in the forests, and we have driven their farmers into the refuge of fortified towns. But not in every case. Around Luso, for instance, we have spared two of its *colonatos,* 'Luchea' to the north and 'Sacassange' to the south. We've let them be, we haven't touched their cattle. They don't bother us. Even our population doesn't really have anything against them. After all, they're poor folk. They go barefoot, they've no wealth to spare, and actually their lands belong to no one else. Besides, they grow useful things." Here and there, if rarely, individual Portuguese have quietly made their peace with the national movement; you will hear them spoken of as friends. And Portuguese remains and will remain the national movement's lingua franca, its language gateway to the outside world.

There have been exceptions to this kind of attitude; no doubt there will be others in the future. But the general sentiment among responsible men and women in the national movement —as in its companion movements of Guinea-Bissau and Mozambique—is rather that the bulk of Portuguese have become the victims of a disaster from which they are able to extricate themselves far less than the Africans, who suffer from it worse. And the basis for this sentiment is not hard to trace, whether in African action or conversation. Large numbers of Africans have taken their destiny in their own hands, and feel that they are opening a new and altogether better chapter in their lives. Yet it is difficult, in these lands, to think that Portuguese people can take their destiny in their own hands, much less open a new and better chapter in their lives. Or that they can do this until the Africans have prevailed, and have thus helped to lighten Portugal of a regime that may benefit a privileged oligarchy but can only ruin and degrade the mass of ordinary folk.

An underlying continuity in the interaction of diverse communities, often sharp in contrast, is a basic factor of Angola's history of development. It is very much a history of African development, for the Portuguese were scarcely on the scene till late in the nineteenth century; even in the far west their presence barely dominated the coastal country, save in spasms of military effort, before 1850.

Even so, this is a history of particular value and interest for anyone concerned with charting the chancy enterprise of contact between blacks and whites, at least over the past hundred years. Here, during those years, the blacks have tried to keep what they had, little enough though it might be, and to add what might possibly be added, even less though that might be; while the whites, prefiguring their onslaught of the 1960s, have sought to reward their lives of adventure or weary isolation in the bush, their homesickness and boredom, their sadness and their sense of failure, with some golden scoop or strike of luck, no matter what the laws might say.[14] Here, in an often crystalline clarity of detail, even in a detail that a later age may think malicious, lies the core of the white man's history in Africa, and of the black man's answer to it.

[14] What it was like to live in a Portuguese administrative town of the third or fourth class during the colonial period is told in Castro Soromenho's memorable novel *Terra Morta,* available in French translation as *Camaxilo, Présence Africaine,* Paris, 1960.

2   EARLY DEVELOPMENT

The formative periods of early Angolan history lie far back, beyond any contact with the world outside Africa. Stone Age archaeology being still in its infancy here, little is known of the country's aboriginal inhabitants. But they appear to have belonged to that fairly wide range of hunting-and-gathering cultures that sparsely populated the southern continent in middle and late Stone Age times, and whose remote descendants are the Khoi peoples of our own era.

This situation began greatly to change some two thousand years ago, or perhaps a little less. New populations were taking shape here by A.D. 500. These new populations were adapted by previous development to the wooded grassland country that forms the major part of Angola; their ancestors had probably come from closely similar country in the southern Congo Basin. They were prepared for the problems of finding a livelihood, whether by fishing or hunting, cattle-raising or cultivating millet, in vast plains whose over-all ecology seems to have changed little since Stone Age times.

Their adaptation continued. Spreading and settling, they produced new variants of their "initial" cultures. The process had to be slow, because conditions were often adverse. It was hard to increase the food supply to support an expanding population. But it was possible: most of Angola was relatively free of the tsetse fly that is fatal to cattle, and the soil, though regularly leached by tempestuous rainfall, could yield sparse crops. If the timber of these woodlands was seldom of much value in making useful things, being largely of little-workable genera such as *Brachystegia,* it was certainly good for fires, and fires were even more important to settled peoples then than now. The rivers were many, and were rich in fish as they are today.

The "incoming ancestors" of these new populations seem to have been offshoots of the Bantu group, who are taller and darker than the Khoi peoples. Their early expansion, before A.D. 500, is thought to have taken place from the Katanga region of the southern Congolese grasslands. These "incoming ancestors" were few in number; and the cultures they fathered were made possible by the absorption of existing peoples, presumably of "proto-Khoi" or Khoi stock. Yet these new cultures were markedly different from the Stone Age hunting-and-gathering systems already in existence here. Like other Bantu cultures, to the north and east, they had made the long revolutionary leap into food growing, cattle domestication, and the working of metals. They were, in other words, capable of making fixed village settlements in a single place, or in a series of closely neighboring places inhabited by rotation every few years.

With these capacities in early technology and organization, they were able to multiply in numbers. As they multiplied in numbers, so also did they spread across the land; and as they spread across the land, they produced new variants of their "original" cultures, new ideas about self-identity, new religious customs and loyalties, new languages. They developed an ever-greater diversity; but this diversity rested always on the basic unities of Bantu culture in general. In religious matters, for example, wisdom and truth continued to be expressed by a divine source transmitted through lines of accredited ancestors, themselves "speaking" to living people through oracles and priestly interpreters.

Little can be known of their early development into more complex social structures. But the evidence for a regular division of labor—as, for example, between cultivators and metalsmiths—is fairly conclusive. Social divisions arising from this evolving practice of labor division appear to have crystallized into loose forms of hierarchical structure, into "protochiefdoms" or "protokingdoms," soon after A.D. 500.

This process of "take-off" into new forms of social organization must in any case have been slow, for in these circumstances the accumulation of productive power and the advance of technology could be nothing else. But the process continued, enclosing more and more of these developing peoples within social structures that were basically alike, not only in Angola but throughout the greater part of the southern continent as far south as the inland country of the Cape of Good Hope, and as far east as the lands along the Indian Ocean seaboard.

Factors contributing to this process would necessarily have included the "feedback" consequences of labor division as technology improved: the growth in size of individual settlements, or groups of settlements, able to stay longer in a single place as better technology increased their food supply; the need for more complex patterns of self-rule as settlements grew larger and more stable; and, increasingly after A.D. 1000, the organizational demands of long-distance trade.

This last was especially important for those inland cultures that could feed the eastern demand for African ivory and gold, a demand that became regular and large after the Swahili seaports of the East African seaboard became closely linked to the Indian Ocean trading community around A.D. 900. Though long-distance trade at this relatively early period seems to have had little importance for Angola's people, its value to their neighbors was undoubtedly great. It almost certainly helped to promote the growth of the remarkable Zimbabwe culture in the country that would long afterward become Rhodesia. Thus "there is scarcely a modern gold mine in Southern Rhodesia which is not on the site of an 'ancient working.' . . . It has been deduced that originally the zone from the surface down to about twenty feet was exceptionally rich in gold, and it seems very probable that immense quantities were exported" to the

Swahili seaboard towns and thence to Arabia, India, and China.[1]

With limited though growing capacities, development was therefore unequal among these populations. It varied with the local possibilities. Sometimes, as with the Zimbabwe culture, it was relatively rapid and far-reaching; elsewhere, especially in zones of unusual ecological hostility such as eastern Angola, it was slow and small. But this was an inequality that emerged from socioeconomic foundations basically similar; and so it came about that relatively advanced peoples remained within the same general cultural orbit as their less advanced neighbors. This may be seen very well in what is known, or reasonably presumed, about the growth of political authority.

All these peoples possessed a ready means of developing secular authority once they felt the need for it. If wisdom came from a divine source interpreted or transmitted by priests, then secular authority could operate with priestly sanction: in this respect, the growth of secular authority followed the same course as in other continents. It would be a simplification to say that the priests became kings, but not that the kings were all, in some sense, priests. Secular and spiritual power went hand in hand, but the second was the foundation for the first: power was mediated through a hierarchy, but the hierarchies were subject to their duties, and their duties were controlled by religious rules framed for the advancement of the common good.

If the obscure "dona de terra" to whom Silva Pôrto paid his passage fee among the Mbunda was a "person of importance," she was by no means a landowner in any material sense: on the contrary, her importance will have derived merely and solely from her religious office, and this office will have served a social purpose guaranteed by the rules of Mbunda religion. It was certainly no different with *Mwene* Bando and with all the other rulers of this wide panorama of peoples. What gave *Mwene* Bando his power was a political consensus sanctioned

[1] Roger Summers, "The Southern Rhodesian Iron Age," *J. of African History*, 1 of 1961, p. 5.

by religious belief. The same nexus of ideas and beliefs limited his power and regulated its use in relation to like-minded neighbors. This was the nexus that varied throughout Iron Age times according to local productive capacities and other influences, and has given this African history its scheme and pattern of developmental change.

3   THE "TAKE-OFF" INTO KINGSHIP

The variety of these evolving structures in most of middle Africa—in all the grassland countries west of the great Rift Valley —appears to have consisted of modifications of two main types or models. One of these developed in the far western areas of the region, the other in the east; each gave rise to a numerous progeny.

The model for the western type is said to have crystallized not long before A.D. 1300 in the neighborhood of the Congo river-lake known since the late-nineteenth century as Stanley Pool, after explorer Sir Henry Morton Stanley. It lies some 400 kilometers from the river's end in the Atlantic. Here, on Professor Vansina's reading of the evidence available in the 1960s, much of it the fruit of his own research, there emerged "a single original state" from which "all the [Atlantic] coastal states derived their political institutions."[1]

This does not in the least mean, of course, that a fully organized "working model" of kingship sprang overnight from the knees of fate. It will have been a gradual work of creation. It may have been a work more or less deeply influenced by some memory or inheritance from the far older kingships of the Niger-Benue region: recent archaeological evidence suggests that some of these were already in existence by the eighth or

[1] Jan Vansina, *Kingdoms of the Savanna,* University of Wisconsin Press, 1966, p. 40.

ninth century A.D.[2] There is no present means of guessing how much influence such precedents may have had farther south; but the possibility, strengthened as it is by the little that is known of southward migration routes from the Niger-Benue area, should be kept in mind.[3]

Here as elsewhere, early development into forms of kingship would have corresponded to local forms of mastery over environment. More permanent and larger settlements would have multiplied the complexities of community life. Purely local trade, village trade in food and tools, would have expanded into trade over longer distances. Markets at geographically favored points, such as the environs of Stanley Pool, would have attracted distant customers. Little by little, royal authority would have become, as Ibn Khaldun remarked in 1400 of kingships in northern Africa, "an institution natural to mankind."[4]

Large kingships grew out of small ones in the measure that developmental factors pressed that way. Finding the need for it, men found means of channeling peripheral or rival powers into a unified power to meet new needs and opportunities. There is much supporting evidence for this kind of process, whether in Africa or elsewhere. Thus the strong dynasties that emerged in southern Uganda around A.D. 1400 are known to have followed smaller and more localized experiments in the concen-

[2] By radiocarbon datings: See Thurstan Shaw, *Igbo-Ukwu*, Faber, London, 1970, 2 vols.; vol. 1, pp. 260–61. These indications of unexpectedly early dates for kingships east of the lower Niger River have been somewhat confirmed, during the past few years, by radiocarbon datings for the Ife kingship in Yorubaland, west of the river. See Thurstan Shaw, "On Radiocarbon Chronology of the Iron Age in Sub-Saharan Africa," *Current Anthropology*, vol. 10, 2–3, 1969.

[3] The little that is known, or presumed, derives mainly from linguistic evidence. Most linguistic authorities now agree that the initial homeland of "Proto-Bantu," the presumed mother language of all the later (often much later) languages of the Bantu group, was the Niger-Benue region. It is further supposed that migration of the people who carried this language southward, and evolved its derivatives, was southward as well as eastward around (though also possibly through) the Congo River rain forests. Recent summaries of the "state of the Bantu problem" are in David Dalby (ed.), *Language and History in Africa*, Cass, London, 1970, espec. papers by M. Guthrie and J. D. Clark; and in Joseph H. Greenberg, "Linguistic Evidence Regarding Bantu Origins", *Journal of African History*, XIII, 2 (1972).

[4] Ibn Khaldun, *Muqaddimah*, vol. 1, p. 380 (trans. F. Rosenthal), Routledge, London, 1967.

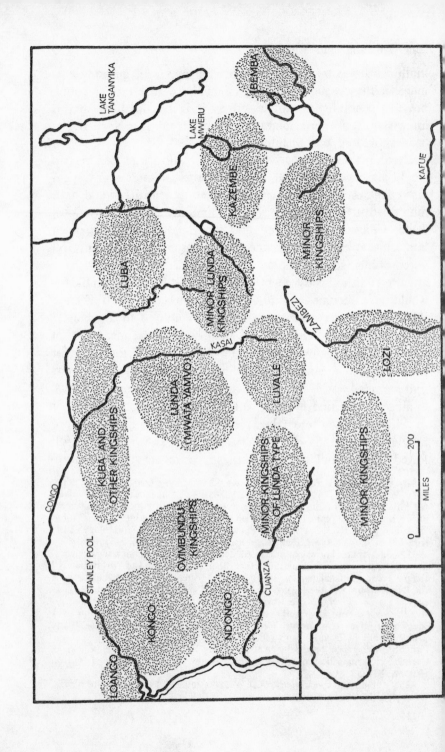

tration of secular power. The same thing happened in the
Niger-Benue region, and indeed in almost every region for
which there is evidence. The written records of medieval Europe depict the process in some detail. The oral records of
Africa, though less illuminating, are often adequate to a general reconstruction of what happened.

By about 1450, the strongest kingdom in the western area,
not far from the Atlantic seaboard, was that of the Kongo people; and the Kongo have conserved their history with some care.
Their traditions sketch a picture of migration, new settlement,
and adjustment to local conditions that is markedly similar in
its essence to the consequences of the Norman invasion of
Anglo-Saxon England three centuries earlier. Around 1350 a
leader and his warriors crossed southward over the Congo River
from the region west of Stanley Pool, their homeland, and obtained supremacy south of the river. With them they brought
ideas about kingship that derived from their own history; if
Professor Vansina is right, ultimately from that "single original
state" that had already taken shape near Stanley Pool. They
grafted their rule upon a people, the Ambundu, who had already developed an embryonic kingship of their own.

But what came out of this, the historical Kongo kingdom,
was clearly no more a mere transfer of "Stanley Pool structures" to the Ambundu country, or a mere elaboration of already existing Ambundu structures, than the Norman kingship
in England was a mere variant of the polities of northern France
or Saxon England. William the Norman, and the Kongo conqueror, Ntinu Wene (or *mwene*, meaning ruler), had the same
basic problem, and they set about solving it in the same basic
way.

Each had to legitimize his authority and thus the presence
of his followers in a land that was not theirs by ancestral and
thus divinely sanctioned right. Just as William the Norman inserted himself into the Saxon ancestral structure, and so "became" King Edward the Confessor's rightful heir upon the
Saxon throne, so also did the Kongo conqueror reconcile himself by appropriate rites and rituals with Ambundu beliefs

about legitimacy. As in England after 1066, there evolved a
kingship of a new type, differing from Ambundu custom by its
absorption of Kongo custom, but differing also from Kongo
custom by its reconciliation with Ambundu custom. It was a
process of synthesis that would have occurred wherever kingships now emerged.

Seven kings had ruled over the Kongo kingdom when the
Portuguese first dropped anchor in the estuary of the Congo in
1483 and found there a state that was "great and powerful,
full of people, having many vassals."[5] Later they found other
kingships which had developed by the same process. The most
important of these, north of the estuary of the Congo, was
Loango, along the seaboard of what is now the enclave of
Cabinda. To the southward, south of the Kongo kingdom, the
most important was Ndongo, the kingdom of the Kimbundu.
Its king's title being *ngola,* the Portuguese would call this country Angola, but meaning, for a long time, only the seaboard
country south of Kongo.

All these western kingdoms were organized in much the same
way. Most of them, by the 1480s, were in vassal relationship to
the Kongo kingship, although Ndongo also claimed an independent status of its own. Exactly what these relations were is
hard to know, since each kingship produced its own tradition,
and the traditions naturally conflict. By the 1480s they seem to
have settled into a mutually tolerant pattern. There is little
evidence of violent rivalry between them.[6]

In the Kongo kingdom, for example, each village had its
own headman, who was also the representative of the dominant
village lineage or "extended family," and subsumed in his person both the ritual power endowed on him by religious com-
pact with the spirits of the land and the political power derived
partly from this spiritual position and partly from the kingship
structure. The same order of ideas linked each headman, or
village ruler, to the district ruler above him; in their turn, the

[5] A variant tradition says four kings; this seems improbably few.
[6] There is a large bibliography relating to these western kingdoms; much of
it is usefully summarized in David Birmingham op. cit. and in Vansina op. cit.

many district rulers were similarly linked to the six rulers of provinces. These rulers were duly subordinate to the king: in European terms, they were the king's provincial governors. At the top of this pyramid of power was the senior *mani,* or king. His spiritual and thus political power rested on the supposition that his ancestors were the "national" ancestors, subsuming in their persons, as it were, the sum total of all the ancestral lines of Kongo authority, whether at a village, district, or provincial level.

Some of the ideas projected in this structure derived from a period when these Iron Age societies were first taking shape. Thus the kings of the Kongo were endowed traditionally with a special relationship to the art of smithing: initially, perhaps, their authority had arisen from their forefathers' capacity to penetrate and possess the mysteries of smelting and smithing, and to make metal tools and weapons, which for a long time were rare and marvelous objects. A mixture of religious belief and political manipulation completed the accumulation of power by these kings. This manipulation produced aspects of kingship markedly different from those of medieval Europe, notably in the matter of succession to the throne.

Africans have shown a great capacity for handling the problems of political power. It may even be that the peaceful regulation of "community relations" has been their supreme accomplishment. In the Kongo kingdom, as in others down to the upheavals of the nineteenth century, great care was taken to prevent the accumulation of hereditary power, whether at the center or at the periphery. All titles to office had to be filled anew at the accession of a new king: no narrow family, not even the king's, could count on any right to keep the power that any one generation might wield. This had the advantage of "handing around" the power of rule and its privileges among the country's clans and provinces: it discouraged the rise of permanent centers of rivalry, and so tended to hold the kingdom together.

But it had, of course, a corresponding though lesser disadvantage: there was no "presumptive heir," no appointed successor. When a king died his successor had to be elected from a more or less large number of candidates. In the Kongo kingdom the only indispensable qualification for candidature to the throne was descent by one line or another from Ntinu Wene, the "founding king." This meant that the death of a king signaled an immediate crisis in which rivalries between candidates were settled according to the push and pull that each could bring to bear, through alliances or allegiances, upon an electoral council of nine or twelve senior lords. Often enough it came to fighting between rival candidates' followers, sometimes to great moments of single combat between champions. But once the succession was settled, the system took over again. The new king called in all the lesser authorities and confirmed or replaced them in office; peace among the nobles was restored.

These accession wars and intrigues grew complex as time went by and the nobles became numerous. According to Vansina, there were so many of these nobles by 1700 as to form "a social class by themselves." Portuguese ideas also helped toward this development of a ruling group. They may probably be seen at work as early as 1540 with the death of King Affonso, when rules were changed and accession to the throne became hereditary, at least in principle. Possibly the royal interest and claimed monopoly in the new oversea trade—the trade in captives for Portuguese enslavement—had something to do with this, if only because the slave trade provided an entirely new means of material accumulation in individual hands. But the "royal descendants" conserved their status; and their personal ambitions repeatedly gave the Portuguese a channel for their own influence upon events. As history was to show, it became almost always possible for the Portuguese to find a royal candidate "of their own" who, once in power thanks to Portuguese influence, was willing to repay the Portuguese with subservience. Later on, in colonial times, this was to become a familiar pattern of "collaboration" by chiefs.

One other aspect of the system was to have a profound influence upon events. At the other end of the scale from the nobles, there was a group of men who had altogether lost their civic rights, either by sentence of the courts for serious offences, or because they were strangers captured in warfare with neighbors of the Kongo. These were the "disposable persons" who appeared in every such system. They were not slaves in the familiar Euro-American sense of the word, but they could be bought and sold. There were never very many of them. The economies of these kingdoms had no use for plantation labor and thus for large quantities of slaves. But they were enough to make a crucial difference once the Portuguese appeared on the scene.[7]

Soon after 1500, whether for their new sugar plantations on the offshore Angolan island of São Thomé, or later for transport to Brazil, the Portuguese became keenly interested in acquiring captive labor for enslavement. The sale or gift to them of the Kongo's "disposable persons" was the key that opened the gate to a slave trade that afterward engulfed the whole near-coastal country.

Once fastened into the trading relationships of these kingdoms by the initial exchange of "disposable persons" for imports from Europe, this trade rapidly undermined and corrupted all previous rules about the duties of powerful men toward ordinary folk. "Kings, rich men and prime merchants" who ran the trade on the African side—the words are those of John Barbot, writing in the 1680s[8]—turned their backs on social responsibility and eagerly "joined hands with the Europeans in exploiting the African masses."[9]

A second center of development into kingship lay in the grassland country of the upper Congo River, where there were

[7] Many Europeans afterward believed (and some still do) that very large numbers of Africans, from the earliest days of the slave trade, "were living in a state of servitude," and that black Africa was little more than a vast reservoir of persons who were slaves before being sold to oversea buyers. It is a view that will not stand serious inquiry. See, for instance, B. Davidson, "Slaves or Captives? Some notes on fantasy and fact," in N. I. Huggins, M. Kilson, and D. M. Fox (ed.), *Key Issues in the Afro-American Experience,* Harcourt Brace Jovanovich, New York, 1971.

[8] "A Description of the Coasts of North and South Guinea," in J. and A. Churchill's *Collection of Voyages, etc.,* London, 1732, p. 364.

[9] Walter Rodney, "African Slavery . . . on the Upper Guinea Coast . . . ," *J. of African History,* 3 of 1966, p. 434.

similarly favorable conditions for the expansion of small polities
into larger ones. The process seems to have begun considerably
earlier here, and may have been related to the early growth of
Bantu-speaking peoples, since this was the probable "mother
region" of Bantu expansion two thousand years ago. But the
"original pattern" or model kingship for this wide area crystallized only around A.D. 1500, when a Luba leader, Kongolo,
established his power in the neighborhood of Lake Kisale
(Katanga).

Kongolo's successors confirmed this power along lines not
far removed from those of the Kongo kingship. All candidates
to the throne or to lesser posts of authority in the political system had to belong to a dominant lineage or ruling group whose
members called themselves *balopwe*. By a conflation of their
own beliefs about legitimacy with the beliefs of those they ruled,
balopwe gathered power to themselves in this and in neighboring Luba-type states.

There set in the same process as had given rise to the Kongo
kingdom. Junior sons of rulers or frustrated royal candidates
mustered their followers and marched away on careers of their
own. The traditions speak vividly if vaguely of this process of
separation. Thus Kibinda Ilunga, brother of a Luba ruler about
1590, marched westward into the country of the Lunda along
the upper reaches of the Kasai River, a country later to be divided into two parts by the colonial frontier between Belgian
Congo and Portuguese Angola. Kibinda is said to have married a
Lunda queen; in any case, he inserted himself into the legitimate
line of Lunda kingship, and his successor, Luseeng, and Luseeng's successor, Naweej, elaborated a new structure of centralized rule.

This was new in form as well as time. Unlike the Luba kingships, it embodied two sociopolitical inventions which gave this
Lunda kingdom a long life, great flexibility of operation, and a
ready means of absorbing neighbors. These inventions are known
to anthropologists as "perpetual kingship" and "positional succession." Elements of both ideas have existed in all kingdoms,
whether in Africa or not, but the Lunda carried them to subtle

lengths. Without entering on details, one may note that they ensured both permanence at the center and tolerance at the periphery. They raised the structure, as it were, above the actual ties of kinship between persons and groups, and gave it a dynamism and legitimacy of its own. These were mechanisms for centralized rule which "divorced the political structure from the real descent structure, since they were not bound to any principal of descent in particular. . . . Therefore the mechanisms could be diffused without necessitating any changes in the existing social structures, which explains why so many Central African cultures could take over the system with little or no cultural resistance."[10]

Within the Lunda system, for example, an incorporated people who had been previously independent could and did retain its local kingship with traditional dignity and privilege, but was grafted into the empire by the grant to this kingship of a perpetual Lunda title to office; this title imposed certain obligations but also recognized certain privileges. It was, in other words, a form of "indirect rule" aimed at the accommodation of local sovereignties to the needs of an over-all sovereignty.

Lunda structures of this kind proliferated through the grasslands. New kingships were founded westward in Angola, southward in Angola and Zambia, eastward in the Katanga grasslands. By about 1750 this whole inland area was more or less divided among kingdoms of Lunda type.

Whether in this way, or in other forms of kingship such as that of the Kongo and Kimbundu, or in still other forms such as the kingship of the Kuba on the lower Kasai, nearly all these many peoples were embraced within systems that resembled each other more or less closely, though with many local variants. In the largest of these states, such as the far-ranging Lunda empire of the Muaant Yaav or Muata Yamvo, the "Lord of the Viper," elaborate court systems were supported by tax and tribute from vassals far and wide. At least in principle, each subordinate title paid tribute to its superior. So long as the tribute was paid, each

[10] Vansina, op. cit., p. 82.

was left largely to its own devices. Only when tribute was with-held, and not always then, was force applied.

This middle African network of kingships, some large and others small, reached practically from the Atlantic coastland to the plains of Tanzania. By 1800, if not earlier, men and goods were passing from one zone of royal authority to another all the way across the continent. These trans-African links were after-ward exploited by African and Afro-Portuguese traders in Portu-guese service, and the trails they followed were used, still later, by the European explorers of these latitudes. But they were forged and organized by indigenous peoples in their own interests or in those of the kingdoms to which they belonged or paid trib-ute. How effectively they worked became clear to Portuguese on the Atlantic seaboard in 1852, when three "Zanzibari" traders—not necessarily from Zanzibar Island, but certainly from the eastern seaboard—arrived at Benguella to see what trading op-portunities they could find there. They found none, but their arrival gave the signal for a greatly renewed Portuguese interest in establishing a trans-African trading route between Angola and Mozambique. Silva Pôrto was sent off to pioneer the trail. He got no farther than the Zambezi, although that was no mean feat.

Portuguese travelers had already provided some intriguing eyewitness accounts of the kings of the inland country. Of these, the most detailed concern the kingdom of the Kazembe, an east-ern offshoot of the Lunda network. Its first titleholder established his power in southeastern Katanga in about 1740. In 1796 a Goan trader, Gonsalvo Gaetano Pereira, who was in business at the little town of Tete on the middle Zambezi River (north-western Mozambique) and "who had long carried on the gold trade in this part of the interior of Africa," sent his son, presuma-bly by an African mother, on a voyage of discovery to the north-ward. This young man traveled with a company of traders, said to have numbered five hundred, through what is now western Malawi and eastern Zambia until he reached the country of the Bisa, "a good, peaceable, and industrious people, trading chiefly in cloth."[11] He found that they controlled the export trade in ivory, while importing cloth and other goods from the Yao, who in turn obtained these items from the eastern seaboard. The cloth in question would have come mainly from India.

Nineteen days after leaving Bisa country, young Pereira and his companions at last entered the kingdom of the Kazembe, a prestigious monarch who was the second of his line, and were well received. "The first thing the monarch did was to bestow upon them a title, which, by rendering their persons sacred, secured them from injury and insult." Following the Lunda pattern, in other words, the Kazembe absorbed these possibly useful visitors into the political structure of his kingdom, and gave them an appropriate status and identity. Having done that, he "next assigned them a plantation of ripe manioc [cassava], as a maintenance during their stay; besides which they were publicly exempted from the customary punishments of that country, such as cutting off the ears, hands, and other members, inflicted for particular offences."[12] Judicial barbarity was as much a characteristic of the Kazembe's rule as it was to most other kings of his period, whether African or not.

Pereira's account also reveals something of the relations of formal vassalage that linked the Kazembe to the Lunda emperor, far away to the westward. "Immediately on their arrival, a messenger was dispatched to the King of Moropooa, informing him, that if he had seen white men from Angola"—that is, from the Atlantic seaboard—"his son, the Cazembe, had now received a visit of the like kind from Mozambique." This "King of Moropooa" was clearly the Lunda ruler, the Muata Yamvo, who, like the Kazembe, needed little prompting to realize the possible trading benefits of linking the east coast with the west.

Like later visitors, Pereira was impressed by the power and ceremonial authority of the Kazembe. "This Prince, who lives in a style of great magnificence, has many wives; a silk robe with enormous folds invests his person, and on his head he wears

[11] From the ms. account reproduced in T. E. Bowdich, *Discoveries of the Portuguese in the interior of Angola and Mozambique,* London, 1824, p. 88.
[12] Ibid., pp. 90–91.

a cap or bonnet, ornamented with a red feather, beads and a fringe of gold and silver."

Of spiritual as well as secular power, "the sovereign keeps up so high a state that even during the ceremony of receiving his foreign visitors, he remained most part of the time behind a curtain, as if his august presence was a favour to be witnessed only at intervals by the chosen few," which, of course, it was. His troops were "remarkably well disciplined, and very orderly in their behaviour, the military manoeuvres being directed by signs," while the Kazembe's capital, "which is under the direction of a police, is some miles in circumference."[13]

This and later accounts of the Kazembe and his court are valuable not only for themselves. They also allow one to guess something of the majesty and state of the Lunda emperors to the westward. These remained beyond European reach till the 1840s, when a Portuguese trader called De Graça made a long visit to the court of Naweej II, and learned a little of his political arrangements.[14] Yet De Graça's description is singularly bare, and to grasp the range of the Muata Yamvo's power and prestige one needs to turn to African sources.

Most of the peoples of east and northeast Angola, as well as of north and northwestern Zambia looked to the Muata Yamvo and his court. It goes without saying that they did not always do so happily. In De Graça's time the Luvale were protesting bitterly against the quantity of tribute they had to send to the Lunda emperor. But they continued to recognize their ultimate subordination to him. As late as the 1950s British colonial officials in northwestern Zambia (Northern Rhodesia then) were noting with some surprise that the current paramount chief of the Luvale, Shinde, who had entered upon office in 1912 and was the twelfth of his line, claimed descent from the first son of the first Muata Yamvo. This son, Shinde affirmed, was the

[13] In 1952 the then Kazembe, a chief within the Northern Rhodesian colonial system, told Commander Thomas Fox-Pitt (to whom I am grateful for this information) that the Kazembe's capital at the time of Pereira's visit was "on the side of a ridge not very far north of Mbereshi Mission," near Johnston Falls.

[14] J. R. de Graça's account, "Expedição ao Muatayanvua," is in *Boletim da Sociedade de Geografia e de História de Lisboa,* IX (1890), pp. 265–68.

founder of the Luvale kingship, having come from the Kasai
in about 1750.[15]

Even in colonial times, all administrative frontiers notwith-
standing, the Luvale continued to send at least a nominal tribute
to the Muata Yamvo, powerless though he was within the Belgian system. This tribute was acknowledged in a directly political
manner. "During 1954 the Luvale chieftainess Ndungu sent an
embassy to Chief Mwatiamvwa in the Congo, bearing him presents. In return two men were sent from Mwatiamvwa to Mize
to make ceremonial hats for the Luvale Chief. These two men
were Mwatshumbu and Chitambula [and] described themselves as Mwatiamvwa's servants. They stated that they were the
'Royal hatmakers' but that they also had other duties for which
they received no regular wage. They informed me that Chief
Ndungu and Chief Chinyama Litape had received 'crowns' for
senior chiefs while Kucheka and Sakavungu had received junior
chief crowns."[16]

It is a remarkable picture of continuity: of the persistence of
cultures otherwise submerged by deprivation of power and the
means of self-respect. Some five decades after the whole great
network of Lunda loyalties has passed under colonial rule,
whether British, Belgian, or Portuguese, the "royal hatmakers"
quietly continue their work, and the chiefs of the Luvale can be
properly installed only when they receive crowns that have the
sanction of the Muata Yamvo, living symbol of their own legitimacy.

Much changed during the nineteenth century; the system frayed
along its edges. East of the kingdoms of the Ovimbundu, in
eastern Angola, many small kingships shared the land, and few
of them seem to have had any conscious links with the distant
lord of Lunda. These were the little states of the Ambwela,
Mbunda, Luchazi, and others. Each was ruled by its own
mwene, and they often joined in linked alliances for their com-

[15] Balovale District Book KTW 1/1, Nat. Archives, Lusaka.
[16] loc. cit.

mon good, so Silva Pôrto could pass among them without let or
hindrance save for paying passage money to "the ladies of the
land."

"Their language and customs are the same throughout," wrote
Serpa Pinto in the 1870s, not much oversimplifying the truth,
"but there is a difference in their political organisation." Outside
the Caquingue country, "they form confederations . . . each
large village or township being governed by an independent
chief."[17] These confederations appear to have lived in general
tolerance of one another. Some of them, like that of the Mbunda,
were capped by a "senior king" on a pattern that was no doubt a
distant echo of the Lunda system, from which all of them had
variously derived their political ideas and customs.

Westward on the high plateau of Angola, the seventeenth
century saw the growth of a large number of more or less closely
related Ovimbundu kingships. Southward, among the Cuanhama or Ovambo and their neighbors, the Lunda network seems
to have had no effect, and the kingships followed a southern
Bantu pattern. In nearly all parts of this middle African interior,
the picture by 1800 was one of settled communities held within
systems of centralized power. These varied in their efficacy and
organization. But between them they were capable of ensuring a
general maintenance of law and order.

This is not to say that peace was invariable or government
always enlightened, nor that progress into new forms of production and productive relationships was anything but very slow.
Triggered by dynastic rivalries or the search for more farming
land as populations grew in size, and as trans-Atlantic crops
such as maize and cassava became more readily available, new
migrations could have a disturbing effect. But pressures such as
these could be easily absorbed; and the records, such as we have
them, suggest that they were.

The "ifs" of history are tempting; but they offer no reward.
What would have happened here if the impact of the outside
world, the world of rampant nationalism and imperialist ambi-

[17] Serpa Pinto, op. cit., vol. 1, p. 127.

tion, had been an altogether different one: had been content, that is, to limit itself only to "trade and contact," eschewing invasion and enclosure? Very clearly, all these peoples would still have had to undergo their own process of transition from the world they knew, and build new systems of production and self-rule along modern lines. It can be argued that some of them were already moving in that direction—at least, that there were men among them who understood the need for substantial change, and tried, if briefly, to achieve an understanding of the way to meet this need. As it was, history dealt differently with them. History produced the Portuguese.

The early capacities and intentions of the Portuguese were by no means clear to the kings of western Angola, as the records amply indicate; nor, in the nature of things, could they have been. Early contacts were surrounded by a mutual ignorance—tentative, suspicious, mingled with grave misunderstandings.

These strangers from the sea had useful things to offer. But not many. Though the Portuguese in Lisbon assumed their own superiority, this was far from demonstrated at "the point of contact." They came in larger ships than West Africans had seen before, and these ships carried cannon and men with guns at a time when none of these had yet appeared in western or central Africa south of the Sudan, or even south of the Sahara. Otherwise the only material evidence of superiority rested in elaborate clothing. Much was made of this.

"We command you," says an order of John II in 1493, "to give Don Pedro who came [to Lisbon as ambassador] from Mani Kongo, a hood and cloak and trousers of *pre* [presumably a woolen stuff] and a doublet of *catim* [a kind of ticking?] and four shirts of Holland, and a leather belt and buskins and a lined beret and half a dozen silk laces and a dozen and a half of leather ones . . . ," adding, as became that cautious merchant prince, "and register it in your book to be later signed by me." It was not much, and one may think it roused no great enthusiasm in the recipient.[1]

The Portuguese, in any case, had fatter fish to fry elsewhere. At least until the 1560s their interest in the Angolan seaboard and its hinterland was a merely local one, always much subordinate to their effort in the Indian Ocean. There in the "Golden East" they despoiled and plundered for half a century, wrecking the trade and often the cities of the East African seaboard, India and Ceylon, Malaysia, and beyond, burning and stealing, piling their ships with loot. In the quarter century after Vasco da Gama's three small ships had led the way in 1497, the court in Lisbon presided over the dispatch to the East of no fewer than 243 voyages by galleons and caravels, while sailings to and from India recorded for 1497–1612 totaled as many as 1,231.[2]

Sailings to the Congo seaboard, where no such plunder could be found, were far fewer and less well equipped. They so remained until the rise of a Portuguese slave economy in Brazil after 1550. Then Angola became little more than a reservoir from which colonial Brazil drew enslaved captives, a system that continued until late in the nineteenth century.

Yet this system had been implanted, with all its essential aspects and assumptions, in the earliest years of Portuguese contact. Resting then, as afterward, upon a theory and practice of primitive extraction, its economic foundations lay in the growing of sugar cane on the island of São Thomé, while its sociopolitical assumptions were those of racial superiority.

In 1952–53 the present prime minister of Portugal, then a professor at the University of Coimbra, gave a course of lectures on Portuguese ideas about Africa. "The natives of Africa," he declared, "must be directed and organized by Europeans but are indispensable as auxiliaries. The blacks must be seen as produc-

---

[1] Paiva Manso, op. cit., p. 2. The story of Portugal's early contact with Kongo has been often told: see, e.g., Birmingham, op. cit.; Duffy, op. cit.; and my *Black Mother*, 1961.

[2] Luiz de Figueiredo Falcão, *Livro em que se contem Toda a Fazenda e real património dos reinos de Portugal, Índia e Ilhas Adjacentes,* a statistical report by a secretary of King Philip II's early in the 17th century, published in Lisbon, 1859.

tivetoorganizedineconomy

tive elements organized, or to be organized, in an economy directed by whites."[3] It was a doctrine already old by several centuries. In no other terms, and with no other meaning, did the governors and missionaries of Portugal in Angola speak about Africans during the sixteenth century and after.

Typical was Father Gouveia, a Jesuit at the court of the King of Ndongo in 1560–75, at a time when the Portuguese were preparing to invade that kingdom. Gouveia wrote to Lisbon that the only way to seriously convert this heathen people was to subject them to Portuguese rule. Had they not indulged in the insolence of taunting him with their own power, boasting that if it were not for the sea they would turn the tables on the Portuguese, and go to Portugal and take its riches? "Gouveia stressed that the Portuguese king must give exemplary punishment to those who expressed such ideas, and show once and for all that he was the real master of all Africa."[4] Professor Caetano would have found this only right and proper. "The past is a foreign country: they do things differently there."[5] But they also do things much the same.

Until about 1500 there were no sugar plantations outside the Mediterranean, where sugar cane was grown in Cyprus by slave labor brought from southern Russia.[6] Advances in maritime technology then opened the possibility of similar enterprises elsewhere. The first took shape on the previously uninhabited island of São Thomé, reached by Portuguese mariners sometime after 1470. In 1485 the king in Lisbon gave São Thomé to one of his vassals, João de Paiva, and sent out a company of conscripted Jewish men and women and common-law criminals.

They and their successors, working for the profit of the fief holder, turned to the growing of sugar soon after 1500, while the fief holder, always a law unto himself, saw to the import of captive labor from the mainland. This early slave trade was vastly expanded after the 1550s by similar demands from Portuguese

[3] Marcello Caetano, *Os Nativos na Economía Africana*, Coimbra, 1954, p. 16.
[4] Birmingham, op. cit., pp. 44–45.
[5] L. P. Hartley, *The Go-Between*, London, 1952, p. 1.
[6] Philip Curtin, *The Slave Trade and the Atlantic Basin*," in Huggins, Kilson, Fox, op. cit., p. 79.

fief holders who had opened sugar plantations in coastal Brazil. "By 1580, the Portuguese settlements in Brazil had already reached a population of about 57,000. Of this number, about 44 per cent were European, 32 per cent Indian, and 29 per cent African—and the African population was steadily increasing."[7]

Such was the framework on the Portuguese side. It governed the whole connection, being reinforced from time to time by flickers of ambition to find silver, gold, or the legendary Prester John, and driven always by the ambition of local governors and soldiers, in whose general term of three years' African service lay their recognized "right" to make their fortunes, or at least to pay their debts. Established in outline from the very first, this was the framework that enclosed the Luso-African connection then and later.

It could yield little good to Africans. For them, all its major effects were negative, whether in the undermining of constitutional authority, in the opening of a wide gateway to the rapacities of the slave trade, in the confusions of mind that derived from medieval Catholic attitudes toward missionary effort, or in the sowing of hostility between neighboring states.

The kings maneuvered or temporized. Affonso of Kongo accepted Christianity and regular alliance with Lisbon, hoping for technical aid in teachers and artisans. His long reign was marked by a deepening disillusionment and despair. "Your Highness," he writes to his royal "friend and brother" of Lisbon in 1526,

> should know that our kingdom is being destroyed in many ways. These are the fruit of excessive freedom given by your officials and representatives to men and merchants who come here and set up stores with goods and many things which we have forbidden. These they spread throughout our kingdom and domains in such abundance that many of our vassals, whom we had in our obedience, no longer obey. They have these things in greater abun-

[7] Curtin, op. cit., p. 81. The African population of Brazil increased so greatly that figures for 1810 show 843,000 whites and 1,887,500 blacks. During much of the 18th century there were probably as many as a million Africans working on Brazilian sugar plantations; most had come from Angola. R. P. Simonsen, *História Económica do Brasil*, São Paulo, 1937, 2 vols.; vol. 2, pp. 56 and 205.

dance than we ourselves, and yet it was with these goods
that we kept them contented and subject in our vassalage
and jurisdiction. All this does great harm not only to the
service of God, but also to the security and peace of our
kingdoms and state. . . .

We cannot even reckon how great is this damage, since
every day these merchants take hold of our people, the
sons of the land and the sons of our noblemen and vassals
and our relatives who are seized by thieves and men of
evil conscience . . . and so great, Sire, is the corruption
and licentiousness that our country is being completely
depopulated. . . .[8]

But the slave trade had become a system, and no power then
could overturn it. Too many reckless people, whether black or
white, had their hands upon its gains. Vainly, Affonso returns a
few months later to the same subject. Will not the king in Lisbon
make good his earlier promises of aid, and send out medical
personnel? And will he not discipline his own subjects so as to
help the Mani Kongo discipline his own? Once more he launches
out on explanation:

Many of our subjects so covet the rewards and goods of
your kingdom, such as they are brought here by your subjects, that in order to satisfy their greed they seize upon
free men—very often it happens that they even kidnap
noblemen and the sons of noblemen and of our own relatives, and sell these to white men in our kingdom. . . .
And as soon as these are bought by white men, they are
ironed and branded with fire and taken to be embarked. If
then they are caught by our guards the whites allege that
they have bought [these captives], though they cannot say
from whom. . . .[9]

Explanation did no good. Within another fifty years nearly a
third of the population of Brazil would be slaves from Angola, or
their children.

[8] Paiva Manso, op. cit., p. 58. I have slightly modernized the language.
[9] Ibid., p. 56.

A long misery followed. The details make a story that is nothing if not dramatic, but need not be told here. For a while after
Affonso's death, in about 1540, the Kongo retained their sovereignty. Late in the 1560s the ruling Mani Kongo was able to call
on Portuguese military aid to help expel an invasion from the
east—an early offshoot of the Lunda migrations—by a people
called Yaga. These entered the eastern fiefs of the Kongo kingdom and appear to have settled there, absorbing local men as
well as marrying local women. In the absence of a strong state
structure, they would doubtless have done the same as others of
their kind, and founded another state on the Lunda model. As it
was, they collided with a power that could defend itself with
Portuguese aid. In 1572 the Yaga were driven elsewhere.

Yet the kingdom's sovereignty was increasingly contested by
the disloyalty of coastal vassals who had gone into the slave trade
with the São Thomistas and others, as well as by the Portuguese
Crown. It lasted for most of another century partly because of
the failing effort of the Portuguese, now extended half across the
world but incapable of holding what they had, and partly because the Portuguese in Kongo, like the Africans, were divided
among themselves.

Just as the São Thomistas played their own hand at the expense of the Crown's authority and interests, so too did other
Portuguese on the mainland. By 1592, for example, Abreu de
Brito is explaining to the Crown that the king of Kongo is anything but friendly, and is even harboring "evil intentions of
rebelling against Your Majesty's authority": is contemplating, in
other words, the reassertion of his own. But, continues De Brito,
the fault is not entirely with this wicked Kongo monarch. For the
latter would never have entertained these ideas of rebellion were
it not for the white men who live in his kingdom—"white men
who are guilty of many infamies so shameful to our fatherland
that I cannot mention them."

Disobedience to the Crown's agents was no doubt the worst of
these "infamies," for De Brito calls on the Crown to insist that
these whites—with their "war slaves," their private armies—must

be made to join the Crown's agents in helping to conquer the Kongo's neighbor, Ndongo. Already there is struck a note of local Portuguese disloyalty to Portugal that will become familiar in later years, and a Portuguese party has arisen that sees its interests as conflicting with those of Lisbon.

Relations worsened as the Crown's pretensions grew. In 1642 the old alliance broke at last in pieces. A year earlier the Dutch maritime rivals of Portugal had seized the main Portuguese base along this seaboard, São Paulo de Loanda.[10] At once the Ndongo leader, the famous Queen Zhinga, hastened to ally herself with the Dutch against the Portuguese. King Garcia II of Kongo followed suit. For a brief while it looked as though the Portuguese must lose their last footholds on this coast. But the Dutch had no great interest here, and failed to reinforce their challenge. In 1648 the Portuguese replied with a squadron of fifteen ships and nine hundred men-at-arms, sent from Brazil under Salvador Correia de Sá Benevida, who retook Loanda and Benguella from the Dutch, and a year later imposed peace on Garcia and Zhinga.

Then the 1650s bring an uneasy lull in which neither side has any confidence. Finally, in 1665, the Portuguese invade Kongo with a force from Loanda consisting of 200 troops from Portugal, 150 local Portuguese, 100 African musketeers, and 3,000 African bowmen. They are met in battle by King António of Kongo with 190 African musketeers, a huge force of bowmen said to number 100,000, and—intriguing detail—190 Portuguese musketeers serving under an Afro-Portuguese captain, Dias de Cabra. These two armies fight it out at Mbwila on a day of driving rain, and the force from Loanda narrowly prevails. Many of King António's commanders are left on the field; he himself, wounded and taken prisoner, is decapitated by the Portuguese. They take his head and crown and scepter to Loanda as trophies of their victory, and, no doubt, as proof of it as well.

[10] Loanda begins to be spelt Luanda late in the 19th century, the unaccented "o" sound being more or less equivalent in Portuguese to "u."

Mbwila signaled the downfall of the structures set in place by Ntinu Wene and his successors. The Kongo kingdom survived in memory, and in some of its local loyalties and organization; it never again recovered. This in itself might have been no loss from the standpoint of African development, provided that an overturn of traditional structures led to the development of new ones more useful to self-defense and advancement.

But nothing better replaced it or could have done so, given the nature of the Portuguese connection and its system of primitive extraction operated by Crown and settlers alike. Developmental for the Portuguese—in so far, that is, as their own feeble economy could take advantage of the profits—the system was entirely retrogressive for the Africans. And it was intended to be that.

How far this was the case may be seen in microcosm by an incident of the years 1605-7. King Alvaro II of Kongo, still independent within his own domains although, according to the Luso-Spanish doctrine now evolved, "subject to royal patronage and placed within that obedience," sent two ambassadors to Lisbon. Like others before them, their mission was to obtain technical aid. They were to ask for masons and metalsmiths.

Just why King Alvaro needed metalsmiths is not explained in the documents: the Kongo, after all, had considerable skills in smelting and forging metals. However that may be, the two ambassadors were received with no joy. Landing at Lisbon in November 1605, they were told to wait while King Philip of Spain's viceroy in Portugal asked Madrid for instructions. Their wait was long; delay, after all, had always been a chief response to Kongolese requests. Not until March 1607, by which time Alvaro's ambassadors had managed to get to Madrid, did the Council for Portugal find it possible to present the ambassadors' requests, advising their rejection.

"It appears to the Council that these workers [masons and metalsmiths] should not be sent. It is undesirable that anyone who can work in stone and lime [cement], or in iron, should be in that kingdom, because it would only lead to disobedience. . . ." To which King Philip scribbled in the margin: "Very well."[11]

What could be clearer? To promote technological progress among the blacks would lead to "disobedience." As such, it was to be deplored and if possible stopped—although, as the Council advised Philip in the manner of other such councils concerned with Africa in our own times, this should be done with as little "scandal" as possible.

The whole doctrine of colonial exploitation, whether primitive or not, whether Portuguese or other, lies enshrined there like a gem winking its undeniable presence. Three and a half centuries later Professor Caetano would describe it in modern terms: "The blacks must be seen as productive elements organized, or to be organized, in an economy directed by whites." Outside that framework, outside the exploitation of Africa in service of the white man's world of empire, "aid for development" could only be at best a nuisance, at worst a prelude to revolt.

Was the Kongo kingdom exceptional in this experience? It fared less well than Loango, north of the estuary, but far better than its southern neighbor, Ndongo. These variants add their own commentaries to the story.

[11] Documents in J. Cuvelier and L. Jadin, *L'Ancien Congo d'après les archives romaines (1518–1640)*, Brussels, 1954, pp. 527–28, and passim.

5   THE HUNDRED YEARS' WAR

Portuguese policy toward Ndongo, the other strong kingdom of western Angola, was much the same as toward Kongo. But it induced a more painful outcome.

The rulers of the Kimbundu people proved wary of Portuguese blandishments. They had learned some useful lessons from experience in the north. It had been their northern clans who were raided for captives by their neighbors of Kongo when, early in the 1500s, São Thomista and other Portuguese demands for plantation slaves outran the Kongo kingdom's available pool of disposable persons. To the Kimbundu, accordingly, the Portuguese appeared not as allies but as enemies. This was to lead to a century of marauding warfare as the Portuguese tried to force the gates of Kimbundu country.

After 1500 the court in Lisbon ordered that all maritime trade should pass through royal agents established in Kongo ports such as Mpinda, in the estuary of the Congo River. The São Thomistas had little taste for this, and ran their own maritime trade as they wished, trafficking illegally with Ndongo as well as Kongo. The court took thought to overreach them.

In 1520 they sent the Kimbundu an ambassador, Balthazar de Castro, with companions. Their orders were to look for silver mines in Ndongo and provide for Christian conversion of the *ngola,* the Kimbundu king, and his court. The *ngola* had other ideas. He confined De Castro and his companions to the royal township and refused conversion. Meanwhile his agents continued their illegal trade with the São Thomistas, selling off their own disposable persons.

Yet direct links with Lisbon, such as the Kongo enjoyed, could still seem desirable. The São Thomistas naturally tried to prevent any from being forged, fearing for their illegal monopoly of trade with Ndongo. Kimbundu ambassadors dispatched to Lisbon in the middle of the sixteenth century are said to have been held on São Thomé for as long as nine years, finally reaching Lisbon in 1557. There they affirmed that the *ngola* would now accept Christianity, though perhaps they did not have authority for doing so: by this time, no doubt, they were fairly desperate men. Lisbon responded. Another embassy, under Paulo Dias de Novais, made its way to the *ngola*'s court in 1560, together with two Jesuits and two secular priests.

They were amiably received, but that was all. What had gone wrong? Discussing their failure afterward, the Portuguese blamed the king of Kongo for advising his neighbor of Ndongo against any official dealings with Portugal. By this time, the king of Kongo had solid reasons for giving such advice; apart from his opinion of the Portuguese, however, there was probably another factor in his mind. Any Portuguese alliance with Ndongo would infringe on Kongo's official monopoly of oversea trade. The Kongo king is said to have warned the *ngola* that the Jesuits had really come to discover how far the wealth of Ndongo would justify Portuguese invasion. No doubt the São Thomistas told stories of the same kind, and possibly there was more than malice in these stories: ideas of invading Ndongo were already in the air. In any case, the *ngola* withdrew into hostility and held Dias de Novais until 1565. This man then went home and urged military conquest.

He was listened to. Late in the 1560s a force of some six hundred Portuguese troops proved decisive in evicting the Yaga from Kongo. If that kind of force could tip the balance in one place, surely it could do so in another? In 1575 the same Dias de Novais disembarked at São Paulo de Loanda with seven hundred troops, of whom half were regular men-at-arms; three years later he was actively at war with Ndongo.

He was unsuccessful, but others followed. Not until the 1680s would these wars with Ndongo drag wretchedly to an end. By then Ndongo lay in ruins; Portuguese rule was established, if feebly and erratically, along the whole seaboard of what is central and northern Angola today; and the shape of the future colony was fixed, at least in the west.

This hundred years of warfare offers a rich if painful study in types of "primary initiative and response" to the coming of Europeans. Like other threatened African kings, the *ngolas* and their representatives fought when they had to fight, often victoriously, but tried repeatedly to confine the issue within the limits of diplomacy and negotiation. In 1580 they settled accounts with Portugal's ally of Kongo by shattering an invading Kongolese army said to have consisted of sixty thousand African and fifty European troops. In 1590 they routed a Portuguese expedition composed of 125 European musketeers and fifteen thousand African bowmen. But meanwhile they were running into other troubles. New states were taking shape in their own hinterland; new sources of division once more offered openings to the Portuguese; new constellations of power began to make an impact on the situation.

Early in the 1620s the reigning *ngola*'s sister, Queen Zhinga, went to Loanda to make peace with João Correia de Sousa, a governor who had just arrived. He refused her a chair, whereon she called up one of her servants and, seating herself on his back, began to negotiate. Formally, her negotiations were successful. Zhinga induced De Sousa to accept Ndongo as an ally instead of a vassal, and sealed the bargain by accepting baptism as Dona Ana de Sousa, the governor acting as her godfather.

This settled nothing, the peace being broken almost as soon as it was made. In 1627 the Portuguese inflicted a serious defeat on Zhinga's forces. She built a new kingdom in Matamba, to the east. There came the Dutch, offering for a while the hope of European alliance against the Portuguese. But seven years later

the Dutch were gone again, and the wars resumed with fresh
Portuguese incursions.

Already Ndongo had practically ceased to exist as an organized polity. "The kingdom of Angola [Ndongo] . . . is very extensive," the Portuguese bishop of Congo and Angola was
reporting to the Pope in 1640. "At one time it was rich. Now it is
completely ruined."[1] The way was open for the extractive system
of the Portuguese, as slapdash and wasteful as it was stubborn,
to thrust inland from the seaboard, here in Ndongo as already
in Kongo.

North of the Congo estuary the different experience of another seaboard kingdom, Loango, offered a contrast that proved
little more than a variant on the same theme.

Loango was one of a cluster of little kingdoms in the area of
what is now Cabinda and its confines. They kept their independence for a number of reasons, partly because the Portuguese
were busy elsewhere. After 1600 they became focal points of trading interest for Portugal's more powerful European rivals.

Slaving was their business, and it flourished. By 1776, according to a French missionary who had lived there, "the principal
trade of these peoples of Loango, Kakongo, [and other small
neighboring kingdoms north of the Congo estuary] is that of
slaves which they sell to the French, English, and Dutch, who
carry them to their American colonies."

The method of obtaining these captives was the same as elsewhere: "they are taken in warfare by those who sell them . . .
and those who take these captives sell them to merchants of the
country, and these merchants march them to the coast." Such
raids "scarcely trouble the peace of the kingdom, since they take
place far away beyond the kingdom's frontiers."[2]

Like Benin and other kingdoms of the Guinea coast, but unlike Kongo, the Loango ruler and his neighbors retained full

[1] Cuvelier & Jadin, op. cit., p. 511.
[2] Abbé Proyart, *Histoire de Loango, Kakongo, et Autres Royaumes d'Afrique*,
Paris, 1819, but completed in 1776; p. 115.

control of their own side of the trade. They allowed their own traders no direct contact with European buyers, but obliged them to work through royal agents controlled by the king's minister of commerce. Thus Loango's chief trading representative had the job both of supervising European behavior and safeguarding the royal monopoly. This minister of commerce "makes frequent voyages along the coast where the Europeans have their warehouses. He has to keep himself informed of the exchange rates between Europeans and Africans, and to ensure there is no cheating on either side. He also presides over the payment of the customs dues which the king exacts from strangers who trade here, and he is in charge of policing the markets."

A peaceful situation, then, with a proper respect for African rights and sovereignties? And therefore one in which the development of this African society could benefit and move ahead to new forms of production and organization? To think this would be to overlook the nature of the trade; it had in fact no "developmental content." As a first point, it was a highly restricted trade, if also a steady one. "Only a very small number of individuals, whom one may call the rich and powerful, are interested in it. As for the people at large, their interest in trade is as simple as their needs, which are few and primitive."[3]

Even so, a means of developing at least the embryo of a capitalist class? And so of shifting this society into line with European examples? Again, not in the least.

These "rich men, kings and prime merchants" were in no way concerned with accumulation even of a primitive capitalist character. They were uniquely interested in exchanging raw material in the form of human labor for goods of a non-productive type. As in other African countries involved in the trade, the goods imported had no aspect that could lead to new forms of local industry. Their arrival and distribution brought no transfer of technological know-how, no stimulus to local efforts at reproduction. On the contrary, the effect was rather to discourage local industry by disseminating foreign substitutes, even when, as of-

3 Ibid., p. 121.

ten, imports were not guns and gunpowder for the further pros-
ecution of slaving raids, or booze to soothe the vanities of leading
men.

The good Abbé Proyart, who observed all this with an intelligent and sympathetic eye, having an admiration for the people
among whom he lived, records the nature of the goods that Europeans used for buying captives. One day he buys his own domestic slave, a man aged twenty-two. This costs him goods to the
value of thirty "pieces." The "piece" was a notional unit of value,
much like the similarly notional "trade ounce" used by the English on the Guinea coast; it was designed to ease the difficulties
of a trade conducted largely without money. The actual content
of a "piece" varied with supply and demand of the different trading items, most of which were clothing stuffs, metal pots or bars,
firearms, and alcohol. The whole art of trading was to manipu-
late the value of such items, expressed in so-and-so many
"pieces". An enormous amount of negotiation was consequently
inseparable from any deal, with each side striving for its own
advantage.

Seventeen and a half of the thirty pieces paid by the abbot for
his slave are clothing stuffs of seven different sorts, varying in
materials, texture, or color. Besides this he gives two guns, reckoned each at one piece, two small barrels of gunpowder, similarly
agreed, two small sacks of lead bullets, and two swords. As well
as all that, his thirty pieces are completed by two dozen small
knives, two iron bars, five pots of painted earthenware, two
strings of beads, and four measures of brandy.

Rather an odd transaction for a messenger of God? But the
abbot gives more of the same. To clinch the deal, he has to present the king's agent with guns and gunpowder, swords and
brandy, to the value of another six pieces.[4] Evidently the missionary was content; the interesting point lies in the agent's
commission. It comes out at 20 per cent. And it is in this, of
course, as in the customs dues and other tribute exacted by the
king, that one sees the peculiar attraction of the trade for ruling
men. These black rulers might argue that they generally pre-

[4] Ibid., pp. 116–18.

vented their immediate fellow countrymen from becoming victims. But their ruthless eyes were on their profits, and their profits were relatively great.

Multiplied by countless such exchanges, this was the actual nature of the slave trade so far as Africans were concerned. Even where it was carried on peacefully between the agents on either side, it contained and could contain no single developmental feature capable of advancing methods of production as distinct from methods of trade. It could lead in Africa to no improved technologies, no enlarged productive systems, no creative change in productive relationships.

Far from that, the slave trade in Africa induced a steady loss in productive labor. Was this its principal effect? The loss was certainly large. Just how large is hard to measure. Professor Curtin's researches suggest that the total number of slaves imported to Brazil was about 3,600,000 from first to last.[5] Most but not all of these came from South Atlantic seaboard states such as Kongo and Loango; these states, on the other hand, also sent captives to other American countries besides Brazil. If the total number of victims, whether by export or death in the course of capture and transport, was possibly double the number actually landed in the Americas, then the Congo-Angolan countries may have lost at least seven million people over four and a half centuries.

This was much in terms of productive health and strength, for the exported captives were almost invariably men and women in their prime. Yet it was clearly not a crippling loss over so long a period, save in local dimensions. These could be extremely severe. As early as 1592 a Jesuit deplored that whereas formerly Angola, by which he meant the seaboard country north of the Cuanza estuary, "did not have a span of land that was not inhabited," slave traders were now having to travel for three months into the interior before finding markets where captives could be bought.[6] Severe though it sometimes was, however, population

[5] Philip D. Curtin, *The Atlantic Slave Trade: A Census,* Madison, Wis., 1969, p. 89.
[6] Abreu de Brito, quoted by C. R. Boxer, *Race Relations in the Portuguese Colonial Empire 1415–1825,* Clarendon, Oxford, 1963, p. 28.

loss was not the principal long-term damage. Far greater in over-all importance was induced frustration of the developmental process.

All those factors of growth inherent in Iron Age systems of African society—making as they had for better mastery of environment, more diversified forms of production, larger settlements, effective law and order, a superb range of creative art—can only have been watered down and denied by the institutions of the slave trade. And this is what the broad historical picture generally confirms.

During the centuries before 1650–1700, the period that marks the slave trade's major upsurge, these societies had passed through much developmental change, whether economic, political, or cultural. After that, with obvious exceptions which only prove the rule, they passed through little. It was then that the "power gap" between white and black structures of society widened from a narrow step to an abyss. It became easy for Europeans arriving after 1850 to think, as their forebears had not thought, that Africans had merely "stood still" in history.

Many factors may explain this. There are at least strong grounds for thinking that the oversea slave trade, itself the very core of the white-black connection, was among the most influential of them. But nowhere else in Africa was its influence so long-enduring and destructive as here in Angola.

PRIMITIVE EXTRACTION: 1600–1850

Installed at a few decisive points along a narrow band of coastal territory running for some 400 kilometers south of the Congo estuary, the Portuguese system was pushed gradually eastward to the inland country. But many years would pass before its presence had any importance beyond a hundred miles from the sea.

Something needs to be said about this system in its early growth, if only because it was then that its permanent features, whether physical or mental, were established. Little can be understood about Portuguese colonialism, or the Portuguese wars of the 1960s, unless these features are kept in mind. Forms were to alter, often very greatly; the essential content of ideas and interests would remain implacably the same.

Then, as later, the governing framework supposed a *mise en valeur*, a material exploitation for the benefit of the Portuguese, as sufficient justification for whatever might be done or not done. Disorderly piracy passed away; legalized piracy took its place. The characteristic note had been struck at the very start by the Crown's "gift" of São Thomé to a vassal whose hands were free to act as he wished, provided always that he barred the way to rival powers. And when organized conquest of the mainland was in contemplation, a century later, nothing changed.

In 1574 a chunk of coastal territory south of the Cuanza estuary was indicated vaguely on a map and "given" to the would-be conqueror, Paulo Dias de Novais. The charter of dona-

tion, including a certificate by two theologians affirming that conquest by force would be beneficial to the interests of the Faith,[1]
made him governor of the royal colony north of the Cuanza estuary and assured him of the "right" to push the frontiers of
this colony as far to the east as his troops could carry them. Dias
was to bear all the costs. In return for these "gifts," he was to receive for himself all the taxation he could squeeze from the inhabitants of his own colony as well as a third of the royal
colony's taxes and sundry other benefits. The Crown expected
1,600 milreis in duty for every captive exported from these territories, but De Novais could send out forty-eight slaves a year, as
part of his personal kickback, without paying duty.

Others followed him in similar efforts to make these territories
"deliver." All these efforts were substantially the same in kind.
Every governor of Angola after Dias de Novais, and there were
sixty-three of them up to 1830, not counting all the lesser governors and commanders of troops, had about three years in office.
They were judged above all by their capacity to deliver revenue
for the Crown. But most of them, otherwise conscientious
though they might be, were in practice bound to judge themselves
by their capacity to deliver revenue into their own pockets. Even
the best of them could operate only within institutions designed
to extract as much wealth as possible at the lowest possible cost.
The worst of them, surrendering to a reckless greed, provoked
revolts and bitterness not only by blacks but also by the colony's
few hundred whites.

Envy and hatred, or at least a sense of outrageous grievance,
became common elements in the feelings between colonists and
officials. In 1666, for example, Governor Tristão da Cunha
arrived from Brazil to find himself, almost at once, faced with a
revolt of the Loanda colonists, who, "raising a tumult against
him, forced him to embark for Brazil in the same ship that had
brought him."[2] The colonists were not, of course, against the system itself. They were part and parcel of it, and they had no

[1] Details in Birmingham, op. cit., p. 46.
[2] José Joaquim Lopes de Lima, *Ensaio sobre a Statística das Possessões Portugueses*, Lisbon, 4 vols., 1844, 1846, 1859; vol. 3, p. 88.

means of existence outside it. But they wanted to work the system their own way; they resented unduly rapacious or interfering governors.

Much would afterward be claimed for their "civilizing presence." Yet theirs was the civilization of petty traders concerned almost uniquely with the slave trade. Few were literate. Most were imbued with an ingrained "racism" which supposed their own God-given superiority. So far as the records show, they had a total indifference to African culture, even a total ignorance of it. Men who would have lived in Portugal as penniless nobles or small employees lived here as little kings, lording it over their domestic slaves, admitting only their own narrow interests. Toward the blacks they kept or sold, their attitudes were those one might expect. These blacks, declared a memorial from the Loanda colonists of 1694, were "brutes without intelligent understanding . . . almost, if one may say so, irrational beings."[3] Others of their kind would say the same for countless years to come. Some are still saying it today.

Many were *degredados,* convicted criminals. A conservative Portuguese of later years was recording no more than the truth when he remarked, ". . . the colonization of Angola was carried out in early centuries almost exclusively by convicted criminals."[4] The practice continued well into the twentieth century. It is not as bad as it may sound, so far as the nature of the colonists has been concerned. Many democrats have found their way to Angola by political sentence of autocratic Portuguese courts; some of them have proved Angola's most enlightened white inhabitants. But in early years, at least, most of the *degredados* were wretched and demoralized victims of Portuguese society; exile to Angola only deepened their disorder.

Was the Church much better placed to "carry civilization"? This, too, has often been claimed. But the Church was also part of the system and could not exist outside it. Almost from the

[3] Boxer, op. cit., p. 19.

[4] Venancio Guimarães, *Angola: Uma Administração ruinosa: Para a História do Reinado de Norton,* Lisbon, 1923. In the spirit of the Luanda revolt of 1667, this turbulent pamphlet was aimed not at the system, but at one of its governors.

first, bishops and lower clergy alike had their quota of slaves who worked in fields and gardens, performed domestic service, carried the litters in which their reverend masters moved about on such journeys as they cared to undertake. If the clergy felt need to salve its conscience, the gesture of baptism proved generally enough: were they not, with that, offering escape from eternal damnation? "On the wharf at Luanda, as late as 1870, there could still be seen a marble chair in which the bishop had sat and baptized by boatloads the poor wretches as they rowed alongside the ship. The Government collected its tax, the pious ecclesiastic received his fee, and the slaves had their first introduction to the white man's religion."[5]

By the end of the seventeenth century all missionary orders working in Angola were supported to some extent by slavery—by revenue, that is, from dealing in slaves by one means or another. Occasionally the Crown granted them special privileges. Establishing a Junta of Missions at Loanda in 1693, the Crown assigned it the right to seven hundred slaves, at the going rate, for its financial support. Thereafter the missionary traffic assumed wider dimensions, others profiting in the same way.[6] There were criticisms of this Church slavery; they made no difference. In 1800, when missionary effort was universally subsidized by slaving, a governor remarked, "We claim to be bringing all the blacks of Angola to the lap of the Holy Mother, while at the same time we promote and maintain the slave trade, two aims that contradict each other."[7] It was the second aim that carried the day.

And so it came about, in Lopes de Lima's words, "that the Christian religion, which had entered this vast African land with such high hopes, was in progressive and marked decay through the 18th century." For this he blamed three things: First, there was a lack of priests. Yet often those who came left much to be desired, for, secondly, there was "the corruption of the clergy,

[5] J. T. Tucker, *Angola: The Land of the Blacksmith Prince,* World Dominion Press, New York, 1933, p. 16.
[6] Lopes de Lima, op. cit., p. 147.
[7] Ibid. The governor in question was Miguel António de Mello.

especially of the regular clergy, Carmelite and Franciscan, sent out here by their prelates in Portugal as being immoral and incorrigible members of the Church"; as it were, religious *degredados*. Thirdly, there was "the inhuman traffic in slaves."[8] And one may add, lest the author of those words may be thought to have been "immoral and incorrigible" himself, that Lopes de Lima was among the most distinguished Portuguese of his day, an experienced administrator, deputy of the Cortes, member of the King's Council.

As to the Africans themselves, the kings and chiefs of areas lying inland from these coastal "kingdoms of Angola and Benguella" were for a long time little disturbed. Considerable inland changes of power took place on the High Plateau—in Huambo and Bié—with the rise of the Ovimbundu constellation of states. While all this was settling down, contact with the coast was sporadic and indirect. This contact would become, in the future, the basis for extending the whole system inland. At the beginning, it consisted of nothing more than trade, whether in captives or other goods.

The system's trade with the inland country came to be conducted by agents of three principal types: First there were the *aviados*, "mobile agents in the bush to whom the inhabitants of Loanda"—that is, the trading colonists—"were in the habit of entrusting a great wealth in business. [These *aviados*] do not always account for it, though. Sometimes they die out there, with all they have. Sometimes they survive, but do not come back."[9] For the colonists, it could make no difference. Whatever might happen "out there," beyond the blue and sepia skyline of the inland hills, lay perfectly beyond their influence, let alone control. Then there were the *negros calçados,* the "shod blacks," all of whom were in white service. Lastly there were the *pombeiros,* the "barefoot blacks" who "are the agents of the *aviados* for the retail trade; at this they are skillful and always give good account of their loads."

These were the men, but especially the *aviados,* who were the

[8] Ibid., p. 148.
[9] Ibid., p. 63.

real "carriers of Portuguese culture" before about 1850, and it
was upon them, save for brief periods of military incursion, that
relations between whites and blacks chiefly depended. They were
the reality of "Portuguese presence" outside the coastal fringe.

African authorities and *aviados* reached agreements according to the opportunities of time and place. Often there was no
agreement; sometimes there was sharp hostility. As early as
1620 it had come to a point where the governor of the day felt
obliged to ban all *aviados* from entry to the inland country. Having denounced "the violence and folly practiced in the interior by
whites, mulattoes, and shod blacks, *aviados* of the merchants of
Loanda, by which they compromise the business they are entrusted with through the dangerous wars they provoke with
chiefs whom they have abused," this governor "forbade under
pain of heavy penalties the entry into the interior of all whites,
mulattoes, and shod blacks, allowing permission only to the *pombeiros*."

The prohibition led to another aspect of the system's penetration of the inland country. Regular markets or fairs were established for the long-distance trade at two or three points along the
lower Cuanza River inland from the coast. These fairs persisted
for many years; others were afterward added farther east. Later
on, when it came to military invasion of the interior, they formed
the springboards for imperial adventure.

There could be little economic growth within this framework,
but there was some. Slaving grew in its dimensions with the exploitation of Brazil. Writing in 1846, De Lima estimated the
export of slaves to Brazil as "many more than 20,000 a year";
his detailed figures for the years 1823–25 show that slaves ac-
counted for 92 per cent in value of all the exports of "the Kingdoms of Angola and Benguella"—for the coastal fringe, that is,
lying between the Congo estuary and a short way south of Benguella harbor. All these went to Brazil: in 1830–32, for example, Luanda received nine ships from Portugal but ninety
from Brazil, mostly from Bahia and Rio.

Angola, as De Lima said, had become far more a colony of
Brazil than of Portugal. This had its influence with the colonists.

For quite a while after the Brazilian colonists had revolted in 1822 against the authority of Portugal, it looked as though the colonists of "Angola and Benguella" would follow suit. Almost at once there was a mutiny of troops in Loanda. They deposed the governor and placed the bishop at the head of a local administrative junta. This junta rejected an offer of confederation made by the newly independent Brazilian government, but a separatist rising in Benguella attempted, though unsuccessfully, to declare a Confederação Brazilica. It was to be a familiar theme.

Anti-Crown sentiments were reinforced by liberalism in Lisbon. In 1836, pressured by other European governments, the cabinet of Sá da Bandeira confirmed the colonists' worst fears by decreeing an end to the oversea slave trade with Portuguese territories. These were renamed oversea provinces, as on other convenient occasions in the future, though without the slightest real effect on their colonial status.

This decree met "implacable resistance"[10] by the Luanda-Benguella colonists. And no wonder. For it struck at the heart of their whole economy. It was generally ignored, and the incumbent governor himself set the pattern: ". . . he made a fortune in bribes by allowing [the oversea slave trade] to continue and sent a cargo of slaves to Rio de Janeiro on his own account."[11] Not for another ten years would the ban on slave exports begin to take effect, and then only by reason of the anti-slaving patrols of the British navy.

To stop slave exports was one thing. It was quite another to bring internal slaving and slavery to an end. No outside agency could do this. Here, again, the system's principle of growth was at work. Internal slave numbers increased, during the early-nineteenth century, by reason of the colonists' attempt to grow sugar on plantations like their fellow colonists in Brazil. In a more intensive sense than before, the "Kingdoms of Angola and Benguella" became slave states. The population figures show an interesting picture.

[10] Duffy, op. cit., p. 76.
[11] Ibid.

According to De Lima's careful researches in 1846 there were
a total of 1,832 whites in the "Kingdoms of Angola and Benguella," only 156 of these being women; and no fewer than 1,466
of them were concentrated in Loanda. There were 5,759 mulattoes, of whom about half were women; only twenty-eight of
these were slaves. There were some 300,000 free blacks. But
there were also about 40,000 black male slaves and 46,000
black female slaves. Most of these 86,000 black slaves were
owned by a few hundred white heads of households and by a
smaller number of mulatto heads of households. What the Portuguese "civilizing presence" had achieved along the seaboard,
aided by African partners, was to create a slave colony where
none had existed before.

If, then, there was growth within the extractive framework,
it was a classical case of growth without development. Nothing
had developed since the installation of Portuguese control and
slaving institutions: all that had happened, and even this in
small degree, was that the control had grown more effective and
the institutions larger. Fastened into the coastal regions, Portugal's presence and all it meant had moved from being a small
parasite into being a big one.

Such was the European "presence" available to Africans in
these lands. And this "presence" had become by the middle of
the nineteenth century a community whose ideas would throw a
baleful shadow for long years ahead. Racist in all essentials, not
least in their sexual use of black women, the men who composed
it had no notion of moving with the times. Their tone and tem-
per were well expressed by a governor of 1856 when replying
to some liberal sentiments let slip by the Oversea Council in Lisbon. Internal slavery and forced labor, the Council timidly suggested, should now be displaced by institutions of free labor. It
was a point of view that seemed absurd in Loanda. "For what
reason," this governor retorted, "may the African negro, who
exercises no useful profession, not be subjected to forced
labor?"[12]

This was to become the *leitmotiv* of Portuguese colonial la-

12 Quoted in Norton de Matos, *A Província de Angola*, Oporto, 1926, p. 268.

bor law. Nobody denied that Africans worked. But that was not the point. "Exercising a useful profession" meant working for the colonists. If Africans would not volunteer for that, they should be forced. This was by now an idea engrained so deeply in the Portuguese mind that the notion of "useful labor" as being equivalent to "labor for whites" became the cornerstone of every Portuguese "labor code" of the modern colonial period.[13]

So little was there any true development within the Portuguese system that the transfer of technology, in so far as there was any, sometimes went from blacks to whites. In 1818 a Swedish mining engineer who had long worked in the mineral-rich interior of Brazil remarked that "the Captaincy of Minas Geráis seems to have been the last in which the use of iron ore and the extraction of iron was learnt from African negro slaves"; and he then goes on to describe methods and equipment that were clearly African.[14]

Yet a new impulse begins to be felt around 1850. Slowly at first, Portuguese imperialism acquires a fresh lease of life. Pressed on by rival powers, Portugal sets out to conquer the interior. It will take a long time, more than half a century. When it is done, however, the ideas and interests of the old framework will still be there, latent beneath a fresh imperialist surface. Not until the 1960s will they be seriously challenged. But when at last that happens, a new world in Angola will begin to emerge.

[13] Cf. B. Davidson, *The African Awakening*, Cape, London, Macmillan, New York, 1955, chs. 17–21.

[14] W. E. von Eschwege, *Journal von Brasilien*, Weimar, 1818, vol. 1, p. 234.

PART TWO

THE YEARS OF SILENCE: 1850-1960

"Since the beginning of our conquest, military force has been the primary and most essential aspect of our colonization."

Lopes de Lima, 1846

"At present practically the entire economy of Angola, Mozambique, and São Thomé is based on forced labor. These colonies produce nothing and transport nothing that is not directly or indirectly dependent on conditions of forced labor."

Henrique Galvão, 1961

1   CARVING OUT A COLONY

In 1846 there were exactly six white men listed as living in the "backlands," east of the narrow belt along the ocean seaboard that formed the colony still then known as "the kingdoms of Angola and Benguella." Even seventy-five years later, when formal conquest was said to be complete, wide areas remained outside effective Portuguese reach.[1] And when, in the middle 1960s, the people of the east began responding to the national movement, their experience of the colonial system was often less than forty years old. Their elders could still recall "the time of our own government." To them, at least, this new resistance of the 1960s seemed a continuation of the battles of their youth.

Directly or indirectly, however, all Angola's peoples were enclosed within the Portuguese extractive framework by about 1925, although more closely in the west and center than the east or south. This enclosure was realized in two chief phases: The first of these, up to about 1900, or later in remote areas, was the work of military invasion and the establishment of "effective presence" by a handful of forts. Europe's concert of imperial powers traced Angola's colonial frontiers as they are today. The second phase, continuing through the 1920s, was concerned

[1] Writing in 1931 of the far southeast, a veteran administrator could note that "our influence, occupation, and territorial organization are incomparably less intense or complete than after the actions of João de Almeida" twenty years earlier; and Almeida had done little but establish a few forts. H. Galvão, *História do Nosso Tempo: João de Almeida (Sua Obra e Acção)*, Lisbon, 1934, p. 303.

with "pacification"; with repressing African resistance; with the beginnings of civilian administration; and, slowly but stubbornly, with extending the institutions of economic extraction eastward from the coast. The third chief phase, which may be called the phase of mature colonialism, included the long effort of the Salazarist period, beginning with the late 1920s, with the purpose of making the colony "deliver." Little fruitful for the regime and its beneficiaries until the 1950s, this effort brought a gradual if erratic enlargement and modernization of the institutions of extraction. Many of these institutions continued to be primitive, especially those relating to African labor, but others acquired a certain sophistication.

No comprehensive history of this three-phase period can be written until the Portuguese archives are thoroughly examined, and, still more important, until liberation can release the tides of memory and judgment on the African side. Yet enough is known to make the outline clear. This outline is the explanatory back cloth to the drama of the 1960s and today. It sets the scene and tracks the logic of events.

Violence has been the key note of Africa's experience of Portugal. Many Portuguese soldiers and rulers have deplored it, though none of them has ever found a remedy. Lopes de Lima was by no means the first. "In no part of the Portuguese world," Alexandre da Silva Correia, a Brazilian soldier and historian, was writing in 1792, "is militia more necessary than in Angola." And he went on to compare the steady trickle of criminals and conscripts sent to the army in Luanda with "the human sacrifice" of the seven Greek youths delivered to the Minotaur in Crete every year, "if one could in any case compare a real torment with an imaginary one."[2] To which, some eighty years later, a governor general responded with the comment, ". . . the normal condition of the administration of this colony is to make war, and to prepare itself for war."[3] Small wonder that the tale of African

[2] Elias A. da Silva Correia, *História de Angola*, Lisbon, 1937 (though completed in 1792), 2 vols.; vol. 1, pp. 69–70.
[3] S. Calheiros e Menezes, *Relatório do Governador Geral . . . 1861*, Lisbon, 1867, quoted by D. L. Wheeler, "The Portuguese Army in Angola," *J. of Modern African Studies*, 7, 3 (1969), p. 425.

response has been so often written in desperate rejection and the tumult of revolt.

The scale was modest until recent times, but formed the pattern for later enlargement. Through much of the nineteenth century the two chief garrisons at Luanda and Benguella composed with a few smaller ones a "first line" army, mainly white, that was never more than a couple of thousand men, save for rare occasions when expeditions appeared from Portugal. Often its total was far smaller. In 1845, this "first line" army consisted of 708 men under a major, a ragged force in which nobody who could avoid it would take a command. "Until the final colonial campaigns of 1890–1920, many officers were second-raters, and few of them fit for promotion, even in Angola. The lower ranks were filled with *degredados* (transported convicts), army deserters, disappointed fortune-seekers, and untrained Africans, sometimes forcibly recruited for service."[4]

Whenever large raids or looting wars were in hand—and they often were—the governor could also call on a "second line" army, known as the *guerra preta* ("black army"), consisting of a larger number of African warriors. These were raised on a vassal basis by chiefs of the coastal belt whom the Portuguese had terrified, corrupted, or otherwise persuaded into co-operation. In 1819 this *guerra preta* was said to have numbered as many as twenty thousand warriors. Later it was organized on a regular but lesser scale: in 1843 it consisted of 1,558 black troops commanded by a handful of white officers under a colonel.

Two persistent features of the system had thus appeared. White soldiers ran the colony at all decisive points, civil as well as military; and their feeble power was buttressed by black mercenaries or conscripts. These features would remain. Though on a far larger scale, the situation of the 1960s would be no different. Military men again run the colony; the *guerra preta* once more numbers many thousands.

These black warriors in Portuguese service always included a number of volunteers: in 1968, as many as one quarter of black

4 Ibid., p. 427.

troops were claimed by a Portuguese military source as having volunteered for service.[5] Even if this greatly exaggerated the proportion of black volunteers, why had these joined? The answer lies in the confusion of the times, but also in the history of Angola. As in other colonies where Europeans raised black troops to fight other black troops, there was never much difficulty in setting one people or group of peoples against others. Any idea of a national Angolan loyalty and cause was still in the future. Meanwhile men followed their chiefs; when these saw their interest in co-operating with the Portuguese, recruits were easily forthcoming, though seldom with any sense of personal commitment. Or else men joined in refuge from the scourge of slavery or forced labor, or in hope of loot, or for some other mercenary reason. In the 1960s, for example, some of the black volunteers in Portugal's eastern garrisons were ex-gendarmes from the Katanga, where they had fought for secession in Moise Tshombe's service. Thoroughly corrupted, they had nowhere else to go.

Conscript or volunteer, pressed or willing, these black troops were the chief military arm of Portuguese penetration eastward. "Available for every task of administration, policing, or warfare," recalled one of the best leaders of that enterprise, "they were, in the end, the most regular forces that we had."[6] So vital were these "irregulars," and so central a role did they play upon the scene, that they, too, may be regarded as one of the main "structural achievements" of Portuguese rule. Appropriately, they reflected in their attitudes and actions the system of primitive extraction they served. "Exemplary" among them were such men as Orlog, who, "audacious and intelligent, became a chief of irregulars . . . an authentic robber captain who lived from the

[5] Al. J. Venter, *The Terror Fighters*, Cape Town, 1969, p. 16, quoting a garrison commander in the Dembos zone. Opposition Portuguese have told me that the proportion of volunteers is in fact insignificantly small. This is borne out by another of Venter's military informants, who told him (p. 43): "The Africans are conscripted in Angola . . . ; like the local Europeans and those from Portugal, they are required to spend two years' fighting the insurgent threat."

[6] João de Almeida, quoted in Galvão, *História do Nosso Tempo*, p. 272.

assaults and raids he repeatedly made among native peoples. . . ."[7]

Such troops were indispensable, but they were also the despair of idealists like Almeida. For men like him, they expressed
the facts of Portuguese colonialism in terms of an intolerable
contradiction. They were necessary to the "Portuguese civilizing
mission"; yet how could one possibly "civilize" by a process of
assault and battery, robbery and rape? "Our soldiers, if only we
could make them so, should become true missionaries who,
while guaranteeing our defense and occupation, our prestige and
order, could teach the natives our customs and traditions, and
in this way integrate them with our nationality."[8] But, Almeida
added wearily, it was not to be done. Fifty years afterward, in
1962, other Portuguese commanders would approach the same
mission and meet the same contradiction. They would set out
to "teach our customs and traditions" and to counter African
nationalism; once again it would be seen that Almeida had
been right. You cannot win the hearts of men by assault and
battery.

In these circumstances, military penetration of the interior
called for leaders of unusual courage and the skill of leadership.
Some of those who responded had both qualities; several had
them in abundance. In these respects, at least, the record of
Portugal's colonial effort is starred with brave and brilliant
characters. From the European imperialist standpoint, few
commanders anywhere achieved as much on means so slender
as Artur de Paiva, João de Almeida, and two or three others.
Yet, not one of these, caught in that intolerable contradiction
where ideals met reality, failed to send up his *cri de coeur*.

"Of any you could possibly imagine," wrote De Paiva of the
1890s, "our army in Africa is the most incompetent, whether to
govern our dominions or make itself respected. The only thing
to do with it is to disband it straight away," and build a better.
Its defects of indiscipline, faintheartedness, demoralization,
"added to an absolute poverty of military appearance, make it

[7] Ibid.
[8] Almeida, *Sul de Angola*, p. 111.

absurd in the eyes of the many foreigners who travel our lands."[9]

De Paiva knew what he was talking about; he had done a lot to lead the way. In 1839 the coastal colony had managed to establish a small fort, successor to one of the old fairs along the Cuanza, at Duque de Bragança, some 250 miles due east of Luanda. Its function being to supervise long-distance trade, local African authorities tolerated its presence. In 1862 another such fort was built, at Malange, again pushing eastward the probing point of Portuguese influence. Another twenty years passed before this led to any attempt at what, in the wake of the "Scramble for Africa" conference at Berlin of 1884–85, was now being called "effective occupation." By then it was clear that either the Portuguese must make good their claims or risk losing them to stronger European rivals. Besides, another interest had appeared. The Ovimbundu of the central plateau were producing large quantities of rubber. Rubber became for a while Angola's chief export. It seemed desirable to control its sources.

In 1886 an expedition under De Paiva marched eastward from the coast. It had fifty-two white troops and as many black, one field gun of small caliber, and 226 oxen for transport. De Paiva established two new forts on the confines of the central plateau. Three years later he pushed into the Ovimbundu heartland of Bié, unseating an "insubordinate" king there. Next year he marched southeastward on another show of force in a pattern that would many times repeat itself. This was in no sense an occupation of the country. Forts were established, but in isolation; they were difficult to garrison and supply. Yet they traced the lines of future control.

More pioneers followed. As in other colonies, they were drawn by a mixture of personal ambition, patriotism, and duty, and often ended their careers in bitter hostility to hesitant home governments which they believed had let them down. Yet there was always just enough official support to keep the operation in

9 Artur de Paiva, memoirs, ed. G. S. Dias, Lisbon, 1938, 2 vols.; vol. 1, pp. 96–97.

existence. Almeida revived the strongest motive in 1908, on the
eve of his great march to the far southeast: "Either we occupy
and guard what is ours, or we run the grave risk that others
who are more practical and farseeing will do it instead."[10] He
was thinking of the Germans in South-West Africa and the
British in Northern Rhodesia. "An immediate occupation of
the regions in the extreme south and east of our sphere of influence is necessary, so as to avert irreparable losses in a vast territory, or at least future diplomatic complications. . . ."

They gave him a small column and let him go. In two and a
half months Almeida took this column right across Angola to
the eastward, fixed posts along the border with German colonial
power in South-West Africa, and then returned from Mucusso
to Sá da Bandeira, a distance of more than a thousand miles, in
thirty-eight days. For various reasons, diplomatic or political,
this remarkable feat brought him small thanks. "All this effort
at occupation, carried out as it was under exceptional conditions, evoked from superior authority . . . not a word of thanks
or esteem for those who, at the cost of bitter sacrifice, guaranteed to Portugal the possession of a vast territory which others
would have seized."[11]

Yet the effort was somehow made, if with feeble means. Already in 1895, "so as to avert English expansion westward
from Barotseland [Western Province of modern Zambia] into
our eastern territories, it was decided to establish a penal colony
in the region of Moxico."[12] Captain Trigo Texeira had been
duly dispatched with seventy-two *condenados de Depósito de
Luanda* (inmates of Luanda Prison) to carry out this task.
These poor wretches were taken out of jail and marched from
Benguella in August 1895. Those who survived reached their
destination, some 950 miles to the eastward, in the following
March.

Once more the old tradition had held firm: the pioneers of
colonialism were again the parasites or victims of Portuguese

[10] Almeida, op. cit., p. 134.
[11] Ibid., p. 207.
[12] G. S. Dias, *Ocupação de Angola*, Lisbon, 1944, p. 41.

society. Whatever this little convict colony may have achieved in Moxico remains hidden in the archives. But as with other such installations, there followed the familiar insurrection by Africans resenting white interference and taxation. In 1912 "the peoples of Moxico rose against us, and were put down with difficulty by a column under Capt. Pereira Cardosa."[13]

In these ways, with many setbacks and defeats, the system was extended and affirmed. Yet only with the second governorship of Norton de Matos, in 1921–24, did it begin to acquire administrative coherence, regular principles of action, and that kind of "doctrine" which could make it yield at least some of the fruits that were hoped for.

[13] Ibid.

2   EXTENDING THE SYSTEM:
From Slavery to Forced Labor

The soldiers carved out a colony, wielding their swords with a crude energy; it remained for less romantic men to show what profit could be had from it. What kind of colony was this to be? What in particular was it to mean for the Africans?

Three principles had emerged in earlier times; they were retained, the cornerstones of colonial policy. Like other colonies then in the making, Angola was to yield a net annual revenue to the Crown (or the Republic). Secondly, Angola was to be a colony of white settlement, whether as an administrative convenience in the dumping of criminals or political dissenters, or as an outlet for Portugal's "surplus" labor, or even, in moments of imperialist euphoria, as a heroic and therefore glorious enterprise in spreading Lusitanian culture.

Thirdly, these two great objectives, revenue and settlement, were to be realized by enrolling the labor of Africans. As Professor Caetano was to say, "the blacks were to be organized and enclosed . . . as productive elements in an economy directed by whites." There could be, it was assured, no other way. Even if enough settlers could be found—and in this sense there have never been enough at any time—"they could not labor in the tropics." Here, as in the Americas, the myth of white inability to work in tropical latitudes was to be a constant justification for obliging others to work for them.[1]

[1] A constant theme. Cf. Guimarães, op. cit., p. 31, for a characteristic statement.

Within this framework of ideas, nothing essential has changed from first to last. All that has changed, details apart, has been the relative effectiveness of the extractive system. This has continuously worked for a larger transfer of wealth from blacks to whites. In the old days of the slave trade, at least some of the native populations could take a share in productive or trading profit on terms that, if not equal, were not grossly unequal. Kongo and Kimbundu were among these from the earliest days. Much later, during the nineteenth century, Ovimbundu rubber collectors were able to capture quite considerable profits. The devices of the twentieth century put a stop to this kind of sharing. Export crops were then grown by administrative order, being "farmed" to white concession companies, which have paid African growers whatever prices they have thought fit. More and more, the actual growers have been squeezed between the rapacity of the concession companies and the coercion of the colonial administration.

It follows that the history of the Africans under this system can be written, at all decisive points, in the history of labor laws and practice. Many influences have shaped the consciousness of Angolans during this past century: their own temperament and that of their colonial masters, the slow attrition of intercourse between communities enclasped in distant solitudes, the close and tortuous imbrication of interest and motive on either side. But nothing has counted for a tithe as much as labor laws and practice. As nothing else can, they sketch the guiding outline.

Slavery in Angola was to end, according to a decree of 1858, by a process of transformation to free labor. This was to culminate in 1878. The settlers were to have twenty years in which to adjust to the revolutionary moment when Africans would be able to sell their labor on an open market. The settlers found this outrageous. In what the *Grande Enciclopédia Portuguesa e Brasileira* calls *grandes e nefastas resistências,* "great and

tragic resistances,"[2] they set about subverting the decree of
1858, just as, twenty years earlier, they or their forerunners had
refused to stop exporting slaves till deprived of ships by the
British navy.

But ministers in Lisbon were liberal or under liberal pressure from London patrons, and persisted with reforms. The
years 1869–75 of the twenty-year "grace period" were even
marked by a decree that, as Salazar's chief labor doctrinaire
would indignantly deplore long afterward, actually "protected
the sacred right of idleness."[3] It provided, in other words, that
Africans should have the right to work for themselves rather
than being forced to work for Europeans. Another decree of
1875, reflecting the push and pull of Lisbon's rising bourgeoisie
and other expanding oversea interests, obliged freed slaves to
work for two years for their former masters; only after that, at
least in principle, were they to be allowed to sell their labor on
the market. Finally, in 1878, the end of slavery was formally
enshrined in a regulation declaring that no man could be com-
pelled to enter into a labor contract unless he were a recognized
vagrant.

The apologist Da Silva Cunha has described this regulation
of 1878 as introducing "an amply liberal regime." Even for him
this appears somewhat excessive. In practice, as all available
records indicate, only the outward form of labor usage changed:
instead of buying slaves, settlers now obtained them by "contract." Either they "contracted" them—that is, bought them—
from chiefs willing or able to sell prisoners or other victims,
and who often paid a ransom of their own people so as to win
relief from white coercion; or else, this resource failing, settlers
"contracted" labor from administrative officers who seized "recognized vagrants" and delivered these, vagrant or not, according to the terms of the regulation.

Either way, it was a system that opened the gate to administrative corruption; and this gate was regularly widened by the
temptations of administrators whose salaries were minimal and

[2] Ibid., vol. 2, p. 646.
[3] J. M. da Silva Cunha, *O Trabalho Indígena*, Lisbon, 1949.

hopes of official improvement no better. If anything, the plight of the worker was now worse than before. "The employer felt less obligation to the contracted labourer than he had formerly to his slaves. The *serviçais* ['contracted workers'] were maintained at subsistence level. Many died or failed to return to their villages, especially those exported to São Thomé, and some parts of Angola were almost emptied of their inhabitants; from other areas the Africans fled into the deep interior. Some workers, driven to desperation by the distance from their villages and the inhumanity of the treatment given them, revolted and formed fierce little bands of warriors. . . ."[4] It was to be another persistent theme. Ninety years later, this response to forced labor would be precisely what gave an especial bitterness to the Kongo rising of 1961.

Officially, of course, none of this was true: officially, slavery and forced labor were alike at an end, displaced by "an amply liberal regime." But official Lisbon has never possessed what a British diplomat, reacting to comparable claims at the end of the 1880s, once defined as any sense of their own absurdity.[5] This is how another Portuguese empire builder of those days described the "amply liberal regime" in Angola after 1878:

"It was the custom in those days to give them [the *serviçais*, or 'contract' workers] the rudest and most difficult work . . . above all in the matter of porterage, in which they took the role of humble animals. For the slightest fault they were often cruelly punished by being beaten with the hippopotamus-hide whip, which cut their skin horribly. Very frequently one heard in the late hour of a warm mysterious African night piercing shrieks of pain from the poor wretches. . . ."[6]

Other "amply liberal" regulations of this kind were to follow down the years to 1961 and after. But in 1899 there came one of a different kind, one that was frankly realist. History has shown that it defined the extractive system, then and later, at its

[4] Duffy, op. cit., p. 154.
[5] Sir Villiers Lister; cf. A. J. Hanna, *The Beginnings of Nyasaland and NE Rhodesia 1859–85*, 1956, p. 129. Oxford University Press.
[6] António Júlio Belo de Almeida, *Operações militares . . . ,* Lisbon, 1942, pp. 7–9, quoted by Duffy, op. cit.

central point. This decree codified the settlers' assumption, already decades old, that blacks had a "duty" to work for whites, and that only when they did so work could blacks be regarded as better than brutes. It affirmed accordingly that all Africans had the moral and legal obligation to acquire by labor the means of subsisting and of bettering their social condition.

The need for any such decree might be unusually absurd on the mere face of things. Since Stone Age times, after all, Africans had acquired the means of "subsisting and bettering their social condition" by working for themselves in stage after stage of their own development. But the decree was not absurd to those who framed and worked the system. On the one hand, they could not roundly admit that their exploitation of Angola rested on forced labor pure and simple; where, if they did, was the "civilizing mission" they used in argument with rival imperial powers? On the other hand, the futility of earlier decrees proclaiming a free labor market was so manifest as to need some restorative cover. So they raised to the rank of benevolent doctrine the settler notion that Africans were working only when they worked for whites. They justified forced labor under the pretense of rejecting it.

Thus "transformed," slavery continued. It continued under inadmissible conditions, whether on the sugar and cocoa island of São Thomé or on mainland plantations. Officially, as before, all this was denied: were not the laws of Portugal enlightened and benign? Unofficially, this servitude was as necessary to the dynamics of settler and administrative life as fuel to an engine. Travelers did not fail to note the fact.

Late in 1904 a journalist famous in his day, Henry Nevinson, went to Angola on assignment from *Harper's Monthly* to test the truth of travelers' tales. He walked across the inland plateau to that belt of "Hungry Country," remembered even now as such, which forms the most westerly part of Moxico District. This was the route by which captives from the eastern peoples—Ambwela, Chokwe, Mbunda, and others—were marched by black or white agents to the coast. Even today, as I have heard myself, these eastern peoples still talk of the slaving raids from which they suffered as "the wars of *kwata kwata,*" the wars of hunt and kidnap.

Once they were west of the Hungry Country, Nevinson found, their shackles were struck off by their captors. "The Cuanza [river] is just in front, and behind them lies the long stretch of the Hungry Country, which they could never get through alive if they tried to run back to their homes. So it is that the trees of the Hungry Country bear shackles in profusion—shackles for the hands, shackles for the feet, shackles for three or four slaves who are clamped together at night. The drivers hang them up with the idea of using them again when they return for the next consignment of human merchandise. . . ."

Nevinson also found shackles "scattered up and down the path" through that same Hungry Country toward the little post of Moxico, now long since overshadowed by the town of Luso. They were, he thought, the shackles of men who had died on the journey. For "that path is strewn with dead men's bones. You see the white thighbones lying in front of your feet, and at one side, among the undergrowth, you find the skull. These are the skeletons of slaves who have been unable to keep up with the march, and so were murdered or left to die. . . ."[7]

Officially, as usual, Nevinson was denounced as a liar. Lisbon did its best to blacken his name as it would with other Nevinsons in later days. Nobody outside Portugal took that seriously. And among those who were stirred to action by his revelations were the Quaker owners of English chocolate firms who drew their cocoa from São Thomé. Disturbed by the accusation that they were indirectly using forced labor, they made further inquiries; not long afterward they declared a boycott of the island's product. It was the first time that large commercial interests would respond with boycott to the persecution of Africans.[8]

[7] H. W. Nevinson, *A Modern Slavery*, Harper and Brothers, 1906. Repr. Background Books, London, 1965, pp. 64–65.

[8] See a copious literature on the subject, e.g. W. A. Cadbury, the English chocolate maker who led the way, in his *Labour in Portuguese Africa*, Routledge, London, 1910. Prof. James Duffy has reviewed the whole story in *A Question of Slavery*, Clarendon, Oxford, 1967.

For the rest, the records of Angola speak for themselves. The unofficial ones for this period include the vibrant testimony of Angolan journalists and political thinkers who, as will be seen, became the forerunners of the national movement of half a century later. Nevinson was aware of some of these, too, and gave them credit. "A little newspaper appears occasionally in Loanda (*A Defeza de Angola*), in which the whole system is exposed, at all events with courage. . . ."[9]

But it was not only unofficial opinion, whether liberal Portuguese or educated African, that felt the system must defeat all hope of realizing any sort of "civilizing mission." The years of silence under Salazar have sunk the memory of these protesters so deeply under the floods of authoritarian repression as to make it easily seem that official Portugal has never produced a single dissenting voice. In fact, they were many, as they are today; but some of them stood then at the summit of administrative power. When the first republican government took office in Lisbon in 1910, it appointed as its governor general in Angola a man who had long lived there, and from 1891–96 as a political exile. He "tried to end forced labour and in 1911 he deported eleven Portuguese for this offence . . . , fought a losing battle and . . . resigned in disgust in March 1912. At the same time, a settler-trader coalition allied with influential men in Lisbon forced the dismissal of the Governor of Mossâmedes [south Angola], who had acquired a reputation for opposition to forced labour."[10]

These men, like João de Almeida, were caught in the contradiction of the system: its ideal supposed good for the Africans, its reality ensured the reverse. Nowhere else in history, perhaps, may one more starkly see the true relationship that has linked the capitalist development of the Western world with the systematic impoverishment of colonized peoples. For while the Portuguese economy during these years at least began to liberate itself from the stagnation of aristocratic rule,

[9] Nevinson, op. cit., p. 15.
[10] D. L. Wheeler, in *Angola* (with R. Pélissier), Praeger, New York, and Pall Mall, London, 1971, pp. 109–10 of London ed.

latifundia, and a primitive commercialism, its rate of progress was increasingly determined by men and interests dependent on the forced labor of Africans. Other men on the spot might cry out in protest at the consequences; like the Governor of Mossâmedes in 1911, they were invariably removed.

Nothing shows the process better than the career of José Mendes Ribeiro Norton de Matos. Appointed governor general in 1912 in the wake of his disgusted predecessor, Norton was to be the chief architect of the extractive system's extension through Angola, and of its regulating principles and practice. Little that has happened there since, in terms of colonial policy and action, has done more than add to the structures he raised. Like Lugard in Nigeria, Milner in South Africa, Lyautey in the French African empire, Norton had the arrogant intelligence and drive of an imperial proconsul, tough and dictatorial, paternalist toward Africans when not totally contemptuous, impatient of metropolitan politicos, still more impatient of the petty trafficking of smalltime settlers, blithely impervious to arguments of budgetary cost. His long career in Angola encapsulates the system in which he was involved, and which broke him in the end.

He, too, set out to rid the system of its necessary support in forced labor, innocently thinking, at least to begin with, that this was merely an abuse. "When I arrived in Angola in the middle of 1912," he recalled in 1926, by which time he was not only in retirement but also in disgrace, "I found in the Province a system of native labor that, with rare exceptions, could not be called free labor."[11]

He worked to redress this grievance. Writing long afterward, with a characteristic self-deception, he claimed that by 1915 "the remnants of former enslavement, and of the new slaves who were more or less disguised [as *serviçais*], had completely disappeared. To forced labor there had succeeded the contractual regime. . . . Administrative action, by methods ever more gentle and persuasive . . . was thrusting the whole sys-

11 Norton de Matos, *A Província de Angola,* Oporto, 1926, p. 126.

tem by long steps toward entirely free labor." It was a gross exaggeration, but there was something in it at the time.

What was in it did not stay for long. In 1915 Norton was brought back to Lisbon as Minister for the Colonies, and then, almost at once, transferred to the Ministry of War at a time when Portugal had to find troops for the Allied Western Front in France against the Germans. This proved a bitter experience, but it was nothing to what he suffered later.

The First World War over, Norton returned to Angola in 1921, this time as high commissioner, a republican title briefly substituted for that of governor general. Everything, he found, had slipped back to the position of 1912. A series of decrees passed during his absence had reversed his "transformation" of one pattern of forced labor into a less oppressive one. They had produced a lamentable state of affairs. "A veritable leprosy of corruption covered almost everything that touched on native labor, and it cost me much in my first two years [1921–23] to cauterize and suppress it."[12]

Once again, Norton met with frantic opposition from the settlers and their Lisbon partners. This time they ran him into the ground, though not until 1924. In memoirs of 1953 he could still turn a bitter phrase against those who had brought him down.[13]

The sticking point came over Norton's decrees affecting the delivery of "contract workers" to private users of labor. There was no question of denying forced labor to the administration, though the administration was careful not to call it that. The administration could not otherwise have functioned, nor could Norton have built the Angolan roads of which he was afterward so proud. But Norton's decree 40 of 1921, issued only four months after his return, declared, ". . . no law can permit forced labor [*trabalho compelido*] for the benefit of private employers [*particulares*]." This decree put the settlers in an uproar; once again, the flywheel of their economy seemed threatened with destruction. They deployed the same *grandes e*

12 Ibid., p. 127.
13 Norton de Matos, *África Nossa*, Lisbon, 1953, e.g. p. 109.

nefastas resistências as their forerunners had used to sabotage the anti-slavery decrees of half a century earlier.

Norton had "struck a deep wound into the emergent agriculture and industry of the Province," declared a fairly typical pamphlet written in scathing anger by one of his opponents in Lisbon. The writer went on to compare Norton's "ruinous administration" with the beneficent wisdom of his contemporary in Mozambique, High Commissioner Brito Camacho, under whose rule private employers in Mozambique were assured of ample and continuing supplies of native labor, raised by "contract" between the state and the employers in question.[14]

In evidence of this the indignant writer quoted from a contract which has its interest in the story, for it displays once again the blunt reality behind the bland paternalism of legal language. This contract of 1923 committed the High Commissioner for Mozambique, and his subordinates, "to guarantee for a period of twenty years the delivery (*fornecimento*) of three thousand native *serviçais* who shall work permanently in the manufactories" of the Hornung sugar company, adding that these arrangements would meet "the requirement for natives" in such and such a preferential order, all these natives "being delivered in the precise terms of Article 94 of the regulation on native labor of October 14, 1914."

What did this article stipulate? It merely recognized the existing situation, the same for Mozambique as for Angola. It repeated that "the native who does not carry out voluntarily the obligation to work that is the duty of every Portuguese will be caused, as a vagrant, to do it by the authorities, who will adopt the necessary measures, so as to educate and civilize him." Three thousand natives every year, in this case, were to enjoy the supreme advantage of being educated and civilized by toiling for the Hornung sugar company at starvation rates of pay, fixed by agreement between their masters. In practice this was the situation that Norton now denounced as "a veritable leprosy of corruption." The settlers saw Norton's attack as a gross betrayal, and set about getting him sacked.

[14] Guimarães, op. cit.

Norton undoubtedly had some feelings about the welfare of forced workers, and rightly believed that a regime of modified coercion would be more productive than one of outright slavery. But what he really cared for was the weakening of settler pretensions. Imperialist and authoritarian, he was above all concerned to suppress every trend toward settler separatism from Portugal, toward the "Brazilianizing" of the colony. At the same time, he was determined to build a civilian administration, for the whole area now claimed as a colony, that should be centrally and permanently controlled from Lisbon. In these respects he was quite largely successful; it was ironical that he should have suffered eclipse afterward. In all these ways, he prefigured the attitudes of Salazar and Salazar's New State, and laid the groundwork for subsequent policy and action.

He claimed more than was true, being also in this a typical imperialist figure. Writing of the achievements of his two periods of office, he felt able to say in 1926 that they had witnessed "the disappearance from the minds of civilized colonists in Angola of the notion that there could be any gain in dividing Angola into various parts, making each of these an independent colony as a first step toward a federal state."

But the idea of independence from Portugal stayed in the minds of many Angolan Portuguese. It was reinforced by political exiles after the military *coup* of 1926, which opened the way for Salazar's dictatorship. Then "the chief cities of Angola that had political exiles were centers of intrigue and political opposition."[15] Yet Norton's fundamental work was to prove easily able to contain such opposition. When he quit in 1924, his successors had only to build on his foundations.

[15] H. Galvão and C. Selvagem, *Império Ultramarina Português,* 1952, vol. 3, p. 136. A youthful supporter of the military *coup* of 1926, though "never an *ardent* supporter of the regime" (clandestine letter to me from a Lisbon prison, dated Sept. 19, 1956), Galvão became one of Portugal's most distinguished and literate colonial officials, long serving in Angola in senior posts.

Like others before him, his experiences outraged his sense of patriotism and decency, and he turned into one of the regime's most courageous and, in colonial matters, most authoritative liberal critics. In 1952 he was given a life sentence for political opposition, but escaped from prison and reached South America, afterward leading the seizure of the *Santa Maria.* Cf. his *Santa Maria: My Crusade for Portugal,* Weidenfeld & Nicolson, London, 1961.

He extended "colonial service" rule—by district officers and police—at the expense of the direct army rule which prevailed in the interior. He moved against all those inland African authorities who still retained some power, or occasionally, as with *Mwene* Bando of the Mbunda, a great deal of power. These authorities he destroyed or ruined, driving their people into the control of his *chefes de pôsto;* he built dirt roads and spent money to these ends. He tried once again to realize the old dream of widespread settlement by "sturdy colonists" from home; in this, too, he had some success. The thirteen thousand-odd whites of 1911 had become about twenty-five thousand by 1931; much of this growth was attributable to the policies Norton had introduced.

There were other ways in which Norton prefigured the Salazarist colony. He embodied with a new emphasis the ideal of Portuguese beneficence that would make it possible for a Salazarist scribe of 1955, in a book called *Angola: Heart of the Empire,* to say without the slightest hint of self-ridicule, ". . . in truth, Angola must be regarded as a Portuguese nation rather than a colony";[16] and this, moreover, at a time when census figures showed fewer than eighty thousand whites against some 4,140,000 Africans. But the latter, of course, were not regarded as Portuguese, and so, in any properly human sense, were not regarded as being there at all.

Norton had all the Salazar regime's dizzily dithyrambic capacity for self-praise in public contradiction with facts no one privately denied. "Through our long and brilliant colonial history, three factors have always predominated in relations between the State and the populations we have discovered and conquered: the accommodating and mild manner with which we treat the natives; the respect for the natives' habits and customs; the absolute purpose of admitting no other sovereignty near our own."[17]

[16] A. C. V. T. dos Santos, *Angola: Coração do Império,* Lisbon, 1955, p. 126.
[17] Norton de Matos, *A Província de Angola,* p. 263. The third "factor" is an accurate translation but remains obscure. Perhaps he means Portugal's (vain) attempt to prevent the encroachment of imperialist rivals?

The records display exactly the contrary. If Norton put white settlers on a closer rein, he worked to reinforce their numbers and the supremacy of their interests over those of the Africans. If he began by slightly enlarging the powers of the provincial legislative council in Luanda, even allowing representatives of associations of African or mulatto *assimilados* to sit as "civilized persons" along with whites, he very soon reversed himself, destroyed these associations, and abolished a flourishing little free press which had no fewer than three newspapers expressing a non-Portuguese standpoint. He arrested spokesmen for opposition interests and deported them to distant places. He prepared the way, as Professor Wheeler has remarked, for "the colonial mystique" of the years of Salazar.

Norton's "mystique," like that of those who followed him, might make much of missionary education; it remained entirely hostile to any education except in the Portuguese language, and even this was to be primitive in scope. As for "respect for the natives' habits and customs," a chief effect of Norton's rule was the systematic undermining of any African authority that still survived. He it was who introduced the policy of "village regrouping" into supervised communities, into what the Chokwe called the *ndandandas*—a policy the military were to revive in the 1960s. He carefully applied the principle of "divide and rule" that was to emphasize "tribal rivalries" in later times.

His decree 137 of 1921 set about the systematic splitting up of large ethnic collectivities, the wide cultural groupings of precolonial history, into much smaller ones. By this principle of microethnicity, peoples were to be regrouped in *aldeias* (village settlements) "under the direct chiefship of native *regedores*" appointed by the administration. This "concentration of native peoples is to be done by tribes, chiefships and families subordinate to the same *século* (subchief). . . ."

"All the natives of the Province of Angola are to be regrouped in places chosen for the founding of native settlements."

"From the date of promulgation of this decree no native may

build his hut within a perimeter reserved for the founding of urban residential centers for Europeans or civilized natives (*assimilados*), nor may these last build houses in places destined exclusively for native peoples."

Not only tribalism, but also *apartheid*.

"The concentration of native inhabitants in such settlements is to be completed within a maximum period of two years, after which the administrative authorities will destroy all huts found outside the designated localities."

A strange way of showing "respect for the natives' habits and customs"? Norton did not think so. His successors, if that were possible, thought so even less.

3   THE YEARS OF SALAZAR

Was it so very different in other African colonies of white settlement? In all these, to one degree or other, Africans found
themselves pressured by various devices into the white man's
economy; were made to understand that their future must lie
in accommodating themselves to the white man's needs and
attitudes; and were offered, in exchange, an ample diet of high-
flown sentiment. If they protested they were punished, whether
by whipping, imprisonment, or forced labor. If they rebelled
they were hunted down and crushed. If they sought to accommodate too skillfully to the white man's pattern, and turn this
to their own advantage, they were checked and frustrated.

To all this the records of settler opinion, whether in private
conversation or in public debate, bear monotonous witness. So
also does the sequence of African response and initiative,
whether in individual acts of "insubordination," in rebellions, in
dissident Christian church movements, in millenarian hopes and
prophecies, and, finally, in the growth of political movements
of anti-colonial protest. All the colonies of settlement, whether
British, French, Belgian, or Portuguese, reveal the same underlying social morphology during these years.

Yet there were considerable differences of style, intensity,
and potential. In all these colonies the Africans were increasingly enclosed within an economy organized and directed by
Europeans for European benefit. This colonial economy was

not, however, in any sense an isolated or autonomous organization, but the projection of its governing metropolitan economy. And this governing metropolitan economy, in turn, was molded by its own national history and the interplay of its own social forces. Throughout the middle and later years of the colonial period, or from about 1920 onward, there was accordingly a "metropolitan factor," political as well as economic, which worked on colonial policy and action in varying and sometimes very different ways.[1]

In British colonies of white settlement, a part of this "metropolitan factor" worked under liberal influence for the idea of a "supremacy of the interests of the majority over the minority"; to a lesser extent, it did the same in comparable French colonies. It worked, in short, for the principle of possible reform to African advantage; out of this reformism, during the 1950s, came acceptance of the idea of decolonization, of African political independence. In the British African empire it failed only in the case of South Africa, where local whites had acquired a virtually sovereign power in 1910, and of Southern Rhodesia, where they achieved much the same in 1923.

But the "metropolitan factor" in Portugal's colonies contained after 1926 no element of radical pressure or opinion, and consequently no element of reformism. There had been room, before then, for a certain measure of liberal advocacy inside Portuguese legality. Though it may seem strangely surprising now, the Pan-African Congress led by the late William E. Burghardt Du Bois had been able, in 1923, to hold some of its sessions in Lisbon and find sympathy and support there.

All this, after 1926, was submerged in clandestinity or destroyed. Brought in by soldiers whose principal theme was the "anarchy and irresponsibility" of democratic governments—and these, in Portugal, had certainly reflected the corruption and incapacity of an immature bourgeoisie—the new regime drew its doctrine from a combination of the ideas of Italian Fascism

---

[1] A point discussed in many books. My own views are in "Pluralism in Colonial African Societies: Northern Rhodesia/Zambia," in L. Kuper and M. G. Smith (ed.), *Pluralism in Africa*, Univ. of Cal. Press, 1969.

and medieval Catholicism. As in Italy, the men who acted were the agents of an oligarchy of wealth, narrower in Portugal, whose initial power came from military protectors and whose "worthiness and virtue" were preached by an authoritarian Church opposed to any serious social change.

They found an appropriate leader in Oliveira Salazar, a professor of economics and entirely a man of their persuasion. An interesting character who remains to be properly studied, Salazar had great if limited capacities. Taciturn where Mussolini, in Italy, was verbose; puritanical in his personal life where Mussolini was the reverse; fanatically attached to Portuguese Catholicism, Salazar appears as a man of conviction where Mussolini was merely a rascal. Declaring in a well-known interview of 1954, "I do not believe in universal suffrage. . . . I do not believe in equality, but in hierarchy," Salazar spoke what he believed. It seems never to have crossed his mature mind that reality might be other than he had conceived it in his youth.

Irreducibly provincial, never traveling outside his own country, Salazar appears from the first to have seen himself as the strong bastion that would turn back the tides of evil; and he saw the tides of evil as being anything that could undermine the God-ordained hierarchy of his dreams. When he thought of "communism," accordingly, he included everything from Russia to the Liberal or Labour party of Britain, or the Democratic Party and the United Automobile Workers of the United States. Relentlessly diligent, he thrust all the energy and passion of a powerful and powerfully repressed character into the shaping of Portugal and, by extension, of Portugal's colonies, to the mold of his beliefs.

But this, of course, he could not have achieved without the leading men and interests who backed him. These were partly large landowners, military leaders and bishops, and partly financial and commercial interests in Lisbon and Oporto, the last being linked to similar though stronger interests abroad, chiefly in Britain. Within the New State which Salazar soon launched, these privileged groups found a shell to guarantee their interests, keep the peasants in subjection, dragoon urban workers into silence, and castrate all serious opposition. And the shell stayed firm. The story of Salazar's Portugal is full of small revolts, demonstrations, illegal strikes, acts of defiance, occasional voting contests carefully controlled by official coercion or corruption. None came anywhere near to breaking Salazar's rule.

The actual posture of the bulk of Portuguese came to resemble, at least in essence, that of the colonized Africans. There were large differences of degree, increasingly smaller ones of kind. Salazar's first concern was to balance the national budget in the interest of his backers; this he did at the expense of the majority of Portuguese. Taxes went up. Social services and real wages went down. The elitist structure of the economy became, as in Africa, increasingly extractive in its impact on the mass of ordinary people. Certain key sectors of the economy were able to grow, chiefly those fueled by foreign capital, but only at the cost of regression or stagnation for other sectors, notably agriculture. In this growth without development—without, that is, any general progress—Portugal became a "backward country," a country of semicolonial status in relation to most of the rest of Europe. As late as the 1950s some two fifths of the population remained illiterate; as late as 1965 agriculture absorbed more than one third of the whole working force, but provided only one fifth of the gross national product.[2]

This combination of minority growth and majority regression can be shown in many ways. Perhaps the emigration figures do it most succinctly. Escaping rural poverty or urban unemployment, about 270,000 Portuguese emigrated to the rest of Europe in 1960–65, while another sixty thousand went to the oversea territories. Throughout the decade of the 1960s, Portugal may have lost upward of a million emigrants; the whole population growth was in any case exported, since the 1970 census figures showed a total Portuguese population of 8.6 million, almost the same as in 1960. Yet the extractive economy

[2] A. W. Wilson, in D. M. Abshire and M. A. Samuels, *Portuguese Africa: A Handbook,* Praeger, New York, and Pall Mall, London, 1970, p. 345.

of Portugal never ceased to grow in size and value during these years.

These trends were reflected in Africa. Norton was forced to resign in 1924 on the grounds that his policies were too liberal, and, being too liberal, also too expensive. He ran up a budget deficit in Angola that could be filled only by heavier taxation of the extractive economy. That was unacceptable even before the military *coup* of 1926; after that, it was unthinkable until the wars of the 1960s forced some yielding in budgetary attitudes.

Norton's ousting was accordingly followed by a period of "retrenchment." Its "major effect was to bring the economy of Angola into line with the economic belt-tightening the new regime was implementing at home"; at the same time, "the drift to autonomy," which had begun again after Norton's departure, "was brought to a halt."[3] Meanwhile, the brakes on using forced labor that Norton had tried to apply were taken off and thrown away.

Otherwise, Norton's policies were carried further. Administrative control was extended. African authorities were altogether reduced to the posture of servants nominated by district officers; most became browbeaten puppets or corrupted intermediaries. "Regrouping" of rural communities continued wherever the needs of labor recruitment found it convenient. The last openings for protest were stopped and sealed.

The general process was noted by African neighbors in Northern Rhodesia. A former British district officer has recalled of the period around 1930 that people emigrating from eastern Angola "were all classed as Ma-Wiko (of the West)" and were said to have "come out of subordination to the Portuguese which was classed as slavery in dishonouring a man in his pride."[4] Thus the differences in colonial rule between Angola

[3] U.S. Dept. of the Army, *Area Handbook for Angola,* Washington, D.C., 1967, p. 42.
[4] Commander T. Fox-Pitt, R.N., of a period when he was in charge of the Balovale (northwestern) District of Northern Rhodesia, in a letter of 1971.

and Northern Rhodesia were already felt as considerable. Later, with the British "metropolitan factor" at work on the side of reform, they were to become much greater.

The process varied in severity. In all those areas where the extractive system had little or no interest, life settled to a drab monotony disturbed only by the scandalous eruption of some more or less demoralized administrator, such as Castro Soromenho has described so vividly from his own experience;[5] by the sordid traffickings of forced-labor impressment; or by conflicts with Portuguese traders in little towns of the "third class" and "fourth class" that now took shape.

Elsewhere the system became more active. The late 1920s saw a considerable expansion of the coastal and central-plateau plantation economy. White settlers went into the growing of coffee, sisal, sugar, and cotton with expanding success. Now it was that the colony began to "deliver" for the first time on any scale. It delivered in two ways. First, its exports began to play a critical part in saving from deficit the general Portuguese balance of payments with the rest of the world; as with Mozambique, this became Angola's principal "national role." Secondly, these exports fueled the profits of large trading corporations which now, increasingly, acquired political influence in Lisbon. The plantation economy itself took various forms. Parts of it were purely in settler hands; larger parts were governed by monopolist companies in Lisbon; other parts, again, were "induced" by forcing African farmers, through the intermediary of Portuguese concession companies, to cultivate certain export crops at prices fixed by Portuguese authority.

In all these forms, the extractive nature of the system was reinforced. As elsewhere in colonial Africa, emphasis on the growing of export crops brought a corresponding decline in the growing of food crops. The trend was general to colonial Africa; in Angola and Mozambique it was possibly far worse than elsewhere. Its effect, in any case, was African impoverishment. There are many examples: In Mozambique, for instance,

[5] *Camaxilo,* supra.

a phenomenal rise was achieved after 1938 in African-grown cotton, a cultivation imposed on the northern districts which "had the immediate boomerang effect of reducing almost equally phenomenally, the natural native crops. Groundnuts, maize, manioc, kaffir corn, and beans all reached almost famine production figures in the north of the colony. . . ."[6]

But the policy was continued. Such were its ravages that the Bishop of Beira, in his *Ordem Anticomunista* of 1950, felt bound to denounce it as a source of hunger and injustice. "In practice, what difference is there between the activities of these natives [obligatorily growing cotton] and those who work as contracted labourers on the farms? None. Or better, yes, a difference does exist: the contract labourers receive a salary; here they receive the price of the cotton if the seeding is successful, and in case it isn't, as occurs in bad years for this kind of crop, they receive nothing." And the bishop went on to speak of a region he knew "which used to be a granary for lands afflicted with hunger. After the cotton campaign was begun there, the fertile fields ceased to supply food for the neighbouring populations and the people of the region itself also commenced to feel hunger. There belongs to my diocese a region in which for six months the black spectre of hunger reaped the lives of the inhabitants. . . ."[7] And still the policy was continued. Six years after this protest, official figures for Mozambique showed 519,-000 Africans as cotton cultivators on behalf of Portuguese concession companies.

This obligatory cultivation of export crops, whether in Angola, Guinea-Bissau, or Mozambique, represented forced labor at second degree. But for other Africans, and in huge numbers, the system's chief economic effect was forced labor of the first degree. There reappeared in rampant epidemic that "veritable leprosy of corruption in everything that touched on African labor" of which Norton had complained in 1921. Not, of

[6] C. F. Spense, *The Portuguese Colony of Mozambique*, Cape Town, 1951, p. 54.
[7] Lourenço Marques, 1950, pp. 140–42; trans. Marvin Harris, "Portugal's African 'Wards,'" American Cttee. on Africa. New York, 1958, pp. 33–34.

course, officially. The founding constitution of Salazar's "New State," in 1933, incorporated the labor regulations of 1928-29. These roundly stated that "all regulations whereby the State may undertake to furnish Native laborers to any enterprise working for their own economic development" were forbidden. Reality was different.

If private employers could not obtain forced labor under administrative regulations, they could still obtain contract labor, and contract labor continued to be the same as before—coercion under another name. On this there is a copious body of evidence, whether from Portuguese sources, from visiting journalists, from Protestant missionaries, or from African protests. Contract labor was recruited by administrative force, direct or indirect, or by licensed agents relying on the same pattern. Here is a testimony, out of the multitude available, from an itinerant correspondent of the New York *Herald Tribune* in a period before the scandal attracted world-wide attention.

"When an Angolan plantation owner requires labor, he notifies the government of his needs. The demand is passed down to the village chiefs, who are ordered to supply fixed quotas of laborers from their communities. If the required number is not forthcoming, police are sent to round them up."[8]

It was the least that could be said. By now inspector general of colonies, Henrique Galvão was in a good position to say more. The worst aspect of the system in Angola, he told a hushed gathering of Salazar's "parliament" in 1947, lay "in the attitude of the State to the recruitment of labor for private employers. Here the position is worse in Angola than in Mozambique; because in Angola, openly and deliberately, the State acts as recruiting and distributing agent for labor on behalf of settlers who, as though it were quite natural, write to the Department of Native Affairs for 'a supply of workers.' This word 'supply' (*fornecer*) is used indifferently of goods or of men."[9]

Seven years later, in 1954, this aspect of the system was explained to the present writer by two large employers of contract

8 A. T. Steele, issue for Feb. 15, 1948.
9 My trans. Full text in Galvão, *Santa Maria*, appendix.

labor in the Benguela region. "Employers who want labour," one then learned, "indent for it from the Government-General. The Government-General allocates *contradados* [contract workers] according to a theoretical calculation of the number available for conscription at any one time. Approved demands for labour—sometimes amended, sometimes [for bigger and wealthier employers] imposing certain medical and housing amenities—are sent to local administrators up and down the country; and the *chefe de pôsto,* through his local chiefs and headmen, is then obliged to conscript the number of men required by the indent or indents he receives." Most of these contracts, it was further explained, were collective. "They are generally signed by the *chefe de pôsto* and the native chief or headman who brings in the conscripted men." Failure to comply meant punishment for the chief or headman, often by flogging.[10] Otherwise, as Mr. Steele noted, "if the required number is not forthcoming, police are sent to round them up."

In 1954 the relevant records of the Native Affairs Department, made available by its administrative chief, showed a total of 379,000 *contradados.* This met with Lisbon's customary denial, issued this time by hand of an Englishman living in Portugal, a Mr. F. C. C. Egerton, who argued that the true total was only 99,771.[11] One more case of an "amply liberal regime"? Another view came from a former Angolan district governor, Snr. Augusto Casimiro, four years later. Then an opposition candidate for the presidency of Portugal, he observed: "No useful proposal, no advantage, no wealth, no benefit to civilisation will be possible or lasting, if, at their very foundations, there is no free labour."[12] Nor was Casimiro's the only legalized Portuguese voice to say it.[13]

A newspaper advertisement for labor that appeared in the *Diário de Luanda* in April 1955 summarizes the whole dismal

10 B. Davidson, *The African Awakening,* Cape, London, Macmillan, New York, 1955, p. 196.
11 *Angola Without Prejudice,* Agency General for the Oversea Territories, Lisbon, 1955, p. 20.
12 Wheeler, *Angola,* p. 129.
13 Discussed in ibid., pp. 140–41.

system of authorized evasion of laws that nobody applied. "Licensed contractor offers duly legalized personnel at Esc. 1,000 each." Yes, a labor market existed, but it was not one that offered Africans any voice in their own fate.

Men such as Casimiro feared the consequences. But the system had no such hesitations. It forged ahead. And what this growth without development really meant could be seen in the case of Diamang, the Luanda diamond-mining corporation in which Lisbon interests shared with British, Belgian, and American investors. In 1947 the company had 17,500 African workers, of whom 5,500 were provided "by intervention of the authorities"; their average wage, characteristically paid in kind as well as in cash (a total of 10,050,000 angolars in wages and rations, and a further 4,450,000 in "various goods") was 830 angolars a year, or about $25.

Diamang thought this perfectly reasonable, even generous. But in 1954 a government concerned with rumblings of African unrest decreed that diamond wages should be doubled. Diamang resented this. Reporting to its shareholders, the company assured them that "discussions are now proceeding with the Government-General in an effort to reach agreement on an increase in wages which might be thought reasonable. . . ."[14] The company balked at adding $410,000 to the wage bill of African miners whose average earnings were about $2.45 a month. This, its directors affirmed, they certainly could not afford. But what they could afford, in that same year of 1954, was to pay out ten times as much in dividends ($4,100,000) to shareholders who, with few or no exceptions, had never so much as set foot in Angola or even knew where Angola lay upon the map. Whose growth? Whose development?

Yet perhaps the spread of modern education could compensate for lack of general economic progress? The merits of spending money on schooling for Africans were argued as in other colonies of white settlement. There were some, rather few, who

[14] Davidson, *The African Awakening*, pp. 212–13.

said that too little was being spent: if civilization equaled assimilation, there must be more schools. There were others, rather many, who replied that modern education was unsuitable for natives, and probably dangerous.

"The better the schooling we provide," concluded a luminary of Coimbra University in 1954, writing of experience in Angola, "the more demoralized and disintegrated becomes the social grouping that one is claiming to civilize." Either the ex-pupil "regresses to tribal mentality" and the money spent is wasted, or he becomes a rootless nomad or urban worker and then there is "the danger of creating a native proletariat, one of the consequences of this educational effort."[15] It was the great colonial contradiction once again. Leave things as they were and there was no "civilizing mission." Take the latter seriously and you had trouble on your hands.

The years of Salazar brought some expansion in rudimentary schooling. This was almost all of missionary provision. Here the Protestant missions, British and American, set the pace; their records show they would have gone much faster if Portuguese suspicion, whether lay or clerical, had allowed. As it was, they went slowly.

Up to the middle 1960s there was no institution of higher learning in Angola. Much was talked of technical education; little was done. "In a territory where most farmers were black, out of fifty students enrolled in the two agriculture schools in 1954, not one was a black African."[16] The figure for "inhabitants of all races who have completed a secondary education," wrote Galvão of 1958, "does not reach 2,500. The majority of these are whites."

In a total population of 4,362,271, 135,355 were registered as being "civilized"; of these, about two thirds were whites. Of the 56,000 "assimilated" non-whites in 1958, 1,101 had secondary education; forty-seven had achieved entry to the universities of Portugal.[17]

[15] Vicente Ferreira, *Estudos Ultramarinos,* Lisbon, 1954, vol. 3, p. 56.
[16] Wheeler, *Angola,* p. 136.
[17] Galvão, *Santa Maria,* Appendix 2, pp. 204–5.

Even without the disruption of providing Africans with an "unsuitable" education, the general outcome of the Salazarist years was a continued dismantlement of indigenous society. Deprived of their own centers of authority, disrupted by outbursts of administrative energy in the direction of "regrouping" *à la* Norton, or driven to contract labor, Angola's people suffered a continual erosion of control over their daily lives, whether as individuals or communities.

The impact differed in degree. Most of the eastern districts remained a zone of minimal administration, save for the diamond area of northern Lunda. Even in 1960, only sixty-two whites were registered in the Luchazi administrative division, centered on Cangamba, and only sixty-three in the Mbunda division, centered on Gago Coutinho, compared with thirty thousand Africans in the first and fifty thousand in the second.[18] Beyond the range of a skeleton of dirt roads linking administrative posts, much remained an "unknown land" traversed only by traders' routes and woodland paths—trails that became, after 1965, the tactical gridwork of the war for independence.

Westward it was different, and had long been so. Colonization was far more intensive, and deeper in its consequences. Among these was a wide range of African initiative and response which led step by step to modern politics.

[18] *3° Recenseamento Geral da População: Prov. de Angola,* 1960.

Just over a century before the risings of 1961, the remote little harbor of Kissembo, on the Atlantic seaboard north of Luanda toward the Congo estuary, was gripped in sudden uproar. This episode of 1860 is worth remembering because it illustrates, with a singular clarity and concentration, the two great themes of African response to Portuguese intrusion: resistance from outside the system, and resistance from within it.

A Kongo nobleman aged about thirty was trying to board a British vessel bound for Brazil, where he hoped to improve his education. This Prince Nicolas was son to a king of Kongo, Henrique II, who had lately died. His noble birth had enabled him to enter the colonial service, but there he had found himself a second-class Portuguese and resented it. "Ambitious for a higher station in life" than an *assimilado* could expect, Nicolas became "dissatisfied with his position in European society."[1] He had also lost his chance of succession to the Kongo throne, the Portuguese army having awarded this to a more "convenient" candidate.

Nicolas decided to contest this strong-arm coronation. In earlier times he might have raised an army and fought it out as Kongo custom allowed. Now he would have had to fight the Portuguese as well; besides, he had not been "westernized" for nothing. What the sword could not do, the pen might yet

[1] Wheeler, *Angola*, p. 87.

achieve. Nicolas wrote letters to the king in Lisbon, to the Brazilian emperor in Rio de Janeiro, and even to the Portuguese public; some were published in the Lisbon press. Their chief argument was that the Kongo kingdom stood in relation to Portugal as a sovereign ally, not a vassal; therefore the Portuguese had no right to interfere in its affairs. Moreover, wrote Nicolas, the interests of Kongo could best be served by a king with modern education: in other words, himself.

For official Portugal this was impertinence, if not sedition. Nicolas was threatened with service transfer to a remote area south of Mossâmedes. Thereupon he secured Brazilian and British consular help for removal to Brazil, proposing to pay for his passage and further education by sale of family slaves to white traders of Ambriz, where his service posting then was. He reacted, that is, by resistance within a system that presupposed African slavery, hierarchical privilege, and Western education. Professor Wheeler says that he was the first Angolan of any importance "to express nationalistic feelings using Western techniques." Putting it another way, he was the first of a long line of Angolans, right down to the 1960s, who sought to transfer to their own country the elitist assumptions and institutions of European nationalism.

Acting from outside the system, other Africans saw things differently. For them, Nicolas was a traitor to his heritage and a sell-out to the whites. They murdered him on the quayside at Kissembo as he was about to board his British vessel for a "scholarship" in foreign parts.

Sketched prophetically in this individual tragedy, the two great themes of resistance were now to occupy the center of the stage and long remain there. They were never to be entirely separate. Yet only in the 1960s would the vanguard of a national movement begin to weave modernizing ideas and traditional loyalties into a coherent whole.

Resistance from outside the system was often violent. Revolts and "subversions" shook the Portuguese military framework

every few years. In the north the Kongo and their neighbors
were in frequent effervescence from the early years of Portuguese occupation in the 1860s. The Dembos area, north of
Luanda, saw a major uprising in 1890. Another followed in
1907, a third in 1913. In 1902 the Ovimbundu of the central
plateau again took to arms. Far in the south, 1904 brought
disaster to a Portuguese expeditionary force at the hands of the
Cuanhama and their neighbors. Out of an invading force of
five hundred, 305 lost their lives, including 109 Portuguese
soldiers and sixteen officers. Not until 1915 in the wake of another defeat, at German hands, were the Portuguese able to
carry the day in the south. Even then they were able to do it
only with the aid of the largest force from Portugal that ever set
foot in Africa until the 1960s, a total of some seven thousand
men and 108 officers.[2]

In these resistances, too, there came a certain modernization. Increasingly, after 1900, Africans were able to buy guns
and learn their use in warfare as well as hunting. All these big
revolts were fought out with guns on both sides, though the
Portuguese had more. Africans seem gradually to have accepted that no serious revolt could be started without at least
some supply of guns and powder. So it was that the eastern
peoples were to judge the efficacy and seriousness of the nationalists who came among them, after 1964, by the nationalists' capacity to bring in rifles. Traveling among them in 1970,
one was repeatedly struck by the vivid power of this tradition.
What they required, by all the evidence, was no persuasion to
revolt, nor even much explanation of its possibilities and consequences, but only the guarantee of rifles. Once rifles were available men would be there to use them, and, if necessary, women
too.

Other Africans, living nearer to hospitable frontiers, preferred to go abroad. This, too, was an old tradition. As early
as 1667 Manuel Barreto complains to the Portuguese Crown

[2] R. Pélissier, "Campagnes Militaires au Sud-Angola (1885–1915)," *Cahiers
d'Études Africaines*, IX, I, 1969, a valuable chronological survey.

of a "want of population" in the country inland from Mozambique, and blames "the bad conduct of the Portuguese, from whose violence the blacks flee to other lands".[3] Three centuries later, Henrique Galvão is telling Salazarist deputies in Lisbon about the "clandestine emigration that, ever more rapidly, is draining away the peoples of Guiné, Angola, and Mozambique; and that, in Angola, is largely responsible for the extremely grave state of depopulation (*anémia demográfica*) one notes in this colony." Between 1937 and 1946, according to this then inspector-general of colonies, about one million Africans left the three territories.

Most of the Angolan émigrés went across the frontiers of Northern Rhodesia (Zambia) and the Belgian Congo (Zaïre) and settled among kindred. But individuals journeyed far and wide. Their biographies[4] tell much about colonial Africa.

Pampa-Sangue ("Pain Doesn't Matter"), an elderly fighter (over forty) of the national movement in Moxico; Ovimbundu origin:

> I went to South-West Africa and worked there twelve years for a German. He had a small gold mine at Windhoek. Then I went through Bechuanaland [Botswana] to the Transvaal [South Africa], and I stayed there on my savings. I went to see how they worked in the mines; but I didn't work there myself. . . .
>
> I left the Transvaal by train to Francistown [Botswana], and there to Bulawayo [Rhodesia], and there to Lusaka [Zambia]. I got to Zambia in 1966. I asked for the man who worked there for the MPLA [the national movement of Angola]. I knew already about the MPLA. . . .

Others went through the ordeal of the mines.

Sundi, another elderly fighter of the national movement, a gentle, smiling man stricken with tuberculosis; Cuanhama origin:

[3] In G. M. Theal, *Records of South Eastern Africa*, 1898, vol. 3, p. 482.
[4] Interviews with B. D., May–July 1970.

I went to Johannesburg in 1942 and I worked there in
the mines for nine years. I walked in there from Pereira de
Eça, our Cape Town [chief Portuguese center in the far
southwest of Angola] and I was recruited by Wenela
[Witwatersrand Native Labour Association, the mines' recruiting organisation] in South-West.

In Angola, before that, I was a waiter, then a cook, then
a policeman for the Portuguese. They beat me on the
hands for any trouble, like not finding a man you go to
catch. Now I try this job, to fight for our country, for
Angola.

Written thus, the words may ring false. But not as Sundi
said them.

Countless individuals defended themselves in this way, moving from a primitive extractive system to another that was more
advanced. "Most of the Portuguese boys, when asked why they
were so anxious to get 'south' from Angola," the American
writer Negley Farson recalled in his book, *Behind God's Back,*
of a visit to Ovamboland (South-West) in 1940, "said: 'Because I am hungry, Mister.'"

Resistance from within the system and its assumptions, using
these as springboards for new forms of self-defense, followed
more complex paths. In western Angola the tradition of this
kind of resistance was almost as old as the other. Before 1540
King Affonso of Kongo had used his Christian loyalty to argue
with the Portuguese king, to play off the Pope against that king,
to speak through ambassadors in Rome as well as Lisbon. Other
kings followed his lead, or tried to.

Later, when institutional Christianity was so firmly hand in
hand with European domination that men despaired of its
fruits, other Africans turned to framing their own version of
the missionaries' message, so as to regain self-respect or even
sovereignty. Of such was Dona Beatrice, the beloved Saint Anthony of multitudes of Kongo people, who was burned alive in

1706. Like neighboring territories, Angola has a long history of religious syncretism, most of it with strong political implications.

Later again, others looked to secular arguments and used the printing press. Theirs, too, is a far richer story than the silence of the years of Salazar could possibly suggest. Between 1870 and the early 1920s Luanda saw the publication of a host of little newspapers written by local Portuguese or assimilated Angolans, and with a freedom of expression that would not appear again until the guerrilla-protected writings of the national movement of the 1960s. For a while, the silence was abruptly broken.

Eloquent and angry, like its counterpart in Lourenço Marques of Mozambique, this Luanda journalism cast a long light ahead. In this respect it was like the polemical writings of such men as J. Africanus Horton and Mensah Sarbah in British West Africa or Louis Hunkankrin in French West Africa. In its Angolan heyday before 1900, it owed its opportunities to Luanda whites and Afro-Portuguese who hoped for independence from Portugal, whether as an independent republic, in union with Brazil, or even as a colony of the United States.[5] Yet its accent was persistently Angolan.

Portuguese dissidents published Luanda's first private weekly newspaper in 1866. They called it *A Civilisação d'África Portuguesa*, making a distinction between "Portuguese African civilization" and "Portuguese civilization," just as the Brazilians did in their own case. They were much pestered but allowed to continue for a while. Where they led, others followed. In 1873 came another weekly, *O Cruzeiro do Sul*, named after the Southern Cross which guides the nightbound traveler as does the Pole Star in northern latitudes. Again the direction was radical, in the sense of being republican and reformist. But *O Cruzeiro* had African as well as European contributors, and thereby signaled "a new era in the history of Angolan nationalism."[6]

5 Wheeler, *Angola*, p. 101.
6 D. L. Wheeler, "'Angola Is Whose House?': Early Stirrings of Angolan Nationalism and Protest, 1822–1910," *African Historical Studies*, II, i, 1969, p. 9.

A memorable spokesman for non-white feelings and convictions now broke upon the scene. Born in 1823 and trained for the law, José de Fontes Pereira was an Angolan who had lived through the last decades of the slaving period, experienced the misery of the seaboard colony in the 1830s, and watched the long and successful effort of white settlers to transform one form of black servitude into another. He had seen the new military expeditions departing for the High Plateau in the 1860s, the steady eastward thrust of the extractive system, the growth of settlers' numbers from the fewer than two thousand of 1846 (in 1900 there were to be about nine thousand) and, with that, the flowering of more oppressive racist attitudes to non-whites, whether African or mulatto. In the relative press freedom after 1870, Fontes began to say what many thought.

"How has Angola benefited under Portuguese rule?" he demands in the weekly *O Futuro d'Angola* of April 1882, and replies: "The darkest slavery, scorn, and the most complete ignorance." Worst of all were the settlers—indolent, arrogant, caring little, knowing less. Yet "even the Government have done their utmost to the extent of humiliating and vilifying the sons of this land who possess the necessary qualifications for advancement." And he adds: "What a civilizer, and how Portuguese!"

Three weeks later he returns to the charge. "The sons of the colonies are allowed a significant role only when the Portuguese need them to elect to Parliament that gang of rogues that the Government chooses so as to gain a vote of confidence: that mess of pastry cooks that robs the official ministers of the action of justice." Sons of the colonies who "possess the necessary qualifications" are being regularly deprived of jobs for the benefit of "certain rats they send us from Portugal. . . . They do not use their intelligence to civilize a people for whom they have no respect, and this is proved by the common saying that *com preto e mulato, nada de contrato!* [with blacks and mulattoes, anything goes]."[7]

7 Ibid., pp. 1, 15.

It was refreshing stuff, but it went down badly with its targets. The administration persecuted Fontes; the settlers abused him in their *Gazeta de Loanda,* and also threatened to kill him. Yet Fontes spoke for many besides himself. After his death in 1890, others stepped into his shoes. Some of their articles were published in Luanda in 1901 in a volume called *A Voz de Angola Clamando no Deserto* (*The Voice of Angola Crying in the Wilderness: Offered to the Friends of Truth by the Natives*). This was a veritable symphony, in music angrier and more bitter than would be heard elsewhere, of all the themes of reformist protest that were now to be developed through the next half century and more, whether in the colonies of Portugal or those of other powers.

Yet the protest in *A Voz* and its kind, like that of *O Brado Africano* (*The African Cry*) in Mozambique, was firmly within the assumptions of the system. Already the isolation of the "assimilated Portuguese" had begun to take effect. Far more than their contemporaries in West Africa, these writers had assimilated the European conviction that Africans had no worthwhile cultures of their own.[8]

Africa needed civilizing, these writers agreed; the trouble was that Portugal could never do the job. The settlers whom Portugal had unleashed upon Angola were "vicious, criminal, and bloody." The civilization they had brought was no such thing, but unrestrained violence and greed. The Africans remained "brutalised, as in their former primitive state . . . leaving this very rich colony stagnant"; and "only the negligence of the rulers explains this state of affairs."[9]

Thus abandoned, the *preto boçal,* the "bush African," could never come to any good. The Portuguese having failed, other Europeans should take their place. Let Britain come and try

[8] Perhaps an overstatement. Since writing it, I have read Christopher Fyfe's wise biography of *Africanus Horton: West African Scientist and Patriot* (Oxford, 1972). The parallels in thought between Horton and Fontes, each so passionately loyal to his African patriotism, and yet each convinced that Africa could achieve civilization only by learning Europe's lessons, are very interesting.

[9] *A Voz,* trans. Wheeler, op. cit., p. 21. See also Mário de Andrade, *La Poésie africaine d'Expression portugaise,* Oswald, Paris, 1969, introduction.

her hand, wrote Fontes at the end of his life, choosing a moment when there was, in fact, some reason to suspect that Britain had the same idea in mind. There was nothing surprising, Fontes continued in an editorial which marked the high point of Portuguese wrath against him, in the fact that foreigners should consider taking over "Portuguese lands which are still preserved in a state of nature, or that they should take advantage of them as potential wealth in order to exploit them and civilise the natives, making them useful citizens for them and for the rest of humanity."

Let such foreigners stop arguing with each other in Europe and speak directly to "Africa's inhabitants, the natural lords of their own lands," and so conclude the necessary treaties. "If the foreigners do this, they will be received with open arms, for it has been proved that we have nothing to expect from Portugal except swindles and shackles of slavery, the only means it has to brutalise and subjugate the natives!" The sons of the land could place no trust in the good faith of "the Portuguese colonial party, whose members are only crocodiles crying in order to lure their victims. We know them too well. Out with them!"

Out with the Portuguese, but not back to independence. Africa must be civilized, and Europe alone could do this. It was a trend of thought among many such men in the years that followed. So it was that as late as 1955 another group of protesters, this time in the clandestinity imposed by Salazar's regime, were to turn in the same direction, and send across the seas a petition designed to place their country under a United Nations trusteeship exercised by the United States. "It is unnecessary," declared this petition in words that echoed those that Fontes had used of Britain long before, "to stress the preponderant role played by the United States of America on the international scene. If God has given those people power, wealth, and intelligence, it is for the good of humanity, or oppressed peoples."[10]

[10] John Marcum, *The Angolan Revolution;* vol. 1, *The Anatomy of an Explosion (1950–1962)*, M.I.T. Press, Cambridge, Mass., 1969, p. 61.

Other aspects of the old tradition of response "within the system" likewise stayed alive. As with Prince Nicolas in 1860, Fontes and his immediate successors wanted reforms that would place the educated "sons of the land" in command of power to protect and promote the interests of the *preto boçal,* the "brutish black" of the backlands, while themselves entering into a partnership with Europeans for the advancement of civilization. They accepted the assumptions about Africa and its cultures that were now to provide the liberal justification for colonial invasion and enclosure. Fontes "espoused an Angolan brand of republicanism while, at the same time, urging non-political reforms in the economy and the government."[11]

This has also had its reflection in our own times. Thus the leader of part of the uprising of 1961, Roberto Holden, could repeat the same theme in 1970, though this time without an anti-Portuguese bias. Discussing the need for Angolan independence, he remarked: "We do not expect the Portuguese to make a radical decision, but I think that the regime must undergo a process of liberalization and find ways and means to satisfy everyone. We expect the recognition of the principle of independence. After that we might perhaps ask them what their conditions are. . . ." Otherwise independence might come as "a poisoned gift"; to avoid this, there should be active and continuing co-operation with Portugal.[12]

It would surely have surprised Fontes to see Holden turning for beneficent co-operation to Portugal, above all to the Portugal of Salazar in the wake of the 1960s; but the underlying thought was the same. Left to their own devices, the Africans would sink; what was needed was to achieve a republican Angola by an agreed modification of existing institutions, of the socioeconomic structures of colonial rule. The difference, of course, was that Holden, unlike Fontes, was living in a time when any mere modification of existing institutions had come to seem grossly inadequate, even a program for disaster, to those Angolans who now saw Fontes as their forerunner.

11 Wheeler, op. cit., pp. 14–15.
12 Roberto Holden, interview with *Continent 2000,* Paris, Sept. 1970, p. 21.

In 1910 the Portuguese monarchy was displaced by a republican regime; its constitution of 1911 gave fresh impulse to ideas of reform. New European parties appeared in Luanda; so did small trade unions. Their program was cautious but liberal. Thus *A Reforma,* the weekly paper of one of them, the Partido Reformista de Angola, formed in 1910, pressed for an end to slavery. They admitted assimilated mulattoes and even assimilated blacks, though the companionship was not an easy one.

In 1912 a number of Afro-Portuguese formed a reformist party of their own, the Liga Angolana. Norton de Matos, now governor general, backed this at first in his campaign against the settlers. Other such groupings appeared over the next years, mainly in Luanda. All of them accepted the principle of Portuguese trusteeship and were loyal to the new republic, though it is hard to know with what degree of conviction. Norton would certainly have tolerated none that called for independence: a local white trend toward independence, after all, was one of his chief targets for destruction. Parallel associations of *assimilados* living in Lisbon reflected the same ideas, but could speak more boldly. Two of them, the Liga Africana (1919) and the Partido Nacional Africano (1921), were able to go further in their campaign against race discrimination and even, as the second's title implies, to introduce the idea of Angolan nationhood.

Some of these little groups survived the *coup* of 1926, though "brought to heel" by Norton even before that. The Partido Nacional continued its agitations, notably against forced labor, and began to speak a slightly different language. "We are not simply Portuguese. Before being Portuguese, we are Africans. We are Portuguese of the Negro race. We are proud of our double quality. . . ." In the circumstances of the early 1920s it was saying quite a lot. Fontes would scarcely have approved, yet there was here a new note, a note even of *négritude,* of "African-ness," in which one may perhaps hear the influence of Du Bois and the Pan-African Congress.

In essence there was little that divided the ideas of reformist nationalism, now beginning to crystallize in the Portuguese colonies, from those of educated Africans in the British and French territories, at least in West Africa. Had a reformist republic endured in Portugal, and its structures become enlarged along lines familiar elsewhere, the *assimilados* of Angola (as of other Portuguese colonies) might well have developed into a position where they would have spoken for "the evolving nation" as a whole, and so carried the ideas of Fontes and other pioneers to their logical conclusion of independence within elitist frames and forms.

No such development was possible under Salazar. There followed twenty years of growing frustration and repression. An opposition press became legally unthinkable. The parties and groupings were reduced to cultural clubs presided over by the administration and bullied by the police. Meanwhile settler numbers grew apace, expanding in Angola from the twenty thousand of 1920 to about forty-four thousand in 1940.

The Second World War brought no changes comparable with those in British and French territories. Other Africans might go to the wars against Mussolini, Hitler, or imperial Japan, and become imbued with new insights and new confidence in themselves, returning to their countries with a determination to change the unchangeable. Nothing like that occurred in the colonies of neutral Portugal. All that happened here was a reinforcement of administrative control, a tougher rate of forced labor. Salazar's regime survived, and saw after 1945 a new danger that other powers might covet its African possessions. Administrative control became ever more oppressive.

Yet something changed, for ideas will always cross the most closely guarded of frontiers. After 1945 there were Africans in the British and French colonies who spoke and thought about the future in entirely new terms. And there were Africans in Lisbon and Luanda, or still farther afield, who began to do the same. Not many. But enough.

5   FROM REFORMISM TO REVOLT

Presiding in the pillared halls of medieval Coimbra, the Salazarist clerisy could still find it possible as late as 1953 to assure their students, and themselves, that Portugal was not only Europe's veteran "teacher and example" in matters colonial, but would remain so.[1]

A "certain disparity between our principles and practice," the same pundit felt able to admit, might be recognized and ought to be corrected. Otherwise the system would not be changed, because it should not be changed. In a substantial sense it was somehow inwardly perfect.

Other peoples, such as the British and French, might lose their nerve, sapped by godless heresies or communistic plots, and give way in their weakness to the powers of evil. But not the Portuguese: they at least would brave the Devil and outdo him. They would hold firm, even though American democracy might now join the squalid chorus of their critics. As Salazar proclaimed a few years later: "We will not sell, we will not cede, we will not surrender, we will not share . . . the smallest

[1] J. M. da Silva Cunha, *O Sistema Português de Política Indígena*, Coimbra, 1953, p. 238: "Portugal há-de continuar a ser mestre e exemplo dos povos educadores de outros povos." This remarkable claim deserves, perhaps, its original text.

144 THE YEARS OF SILENCE: 1850–1960

item of our sovereignty. Even if our constitution would allow
this, which it does not, our national conscience would refuse
it."[2]

So it was said and believed: there were to be no reforms of
substance, because none was required. Yet the underlying situation had vastly changed. The colonial decades had now
taken their effect in a far-reaching dismantlement of traditional ways of life and livelihood. We have touched on some of
the causes of this dismantlement: the intensive use of African
labor outside the rural African economy; the imposition of
cash-crop cultivation even within that economy, and its effects
in African impoverishment; the suppression of all indigenous
forms of self-rule, however humble; the abusive practices of
poor settlers often little above the hunger line themselves; the
still more abusive practices of rich settlers whose plantations
called for an ever enlarged, because ever more wasteful, use of
contract labor.

This undermining of rural society during and after the 1930s
was not peculiar to Portuguese Africa, but it was more general
and intensive here. The consequences were the same in kind.
For one reason or another, whether to escape rural poverty and
boredom; or to find the cash for taxes that, if left unpaid, would
be taken in forced labor; or to avoid the heavy paw of colonial
administration in the villages, rural folk began crowding to the
towns.

All over Africa the towns became encircled by conglomerates
of huts and hovels where people managed to survive, though
little more, thanks to the post-1945 boom in the colonial economy. In South Africa these slums were called locations or
shantytowns; in French they were *bidonvilles,* after the custom
of using beaten-out *bidons,* or tin cans, for walls or roofing;
the Portuguese knew them as *senzalas,* "native quarters," a
word deriving from the times of outright slavery, while those

[2] In M. de Vasconcelos, *"Não!"* Lisbon, 1961, a useful anthology of Salazarist
dicta.

at Luanda, particularly large, were the *museques,* or "sand slums."[3]

People lived badly in these places. In 1954, the *senzala* of Lobito, chief Angolan railhead on the Atlantic, contained about twenty thousand inhabitants and more were coming every month. They had to be content with the bare ground and little more. "All these people must take their fresh water," it was observed at the time, "from five water-points with three taps each; and a Protestant mission has lately, out of its own funds, added a sixteenth tap. This gives a rough average of 1,200 people for each water tap. . . ." There were two elementary schools in this *senzala* and their total enrollment was about 250. "Thousands of children have no hope of going to school; and bend their daily efforts, once they are over the 'apparent age' of about ten years old, to escaping the watchful arm of the police, who are likely otherwise to arrest them for 'vagrancy' and send them to forced labor."[4] Yet the Lobito *senzala* was not an exception.

Once again the extractive system was reaping its fruits. In the old days it had grown through the slave trade; and the wealth of "kings, rich men, and prime merchants" had produced the "development" of trans-Atlantic slavery. Now the system grew again, but this time its corresponding "development" for Africans was displayed in these *senzalas,* while the African beneficiaries were no longer "kings, rich men, and prime merchants" but petty traders, junior officials, and the

[3] The process was already far advanced even in 1950, as the following population figures indicate (*Anuário Estat. de Ang.,* 1956, p. 38):

	1940	1950	% Increase
Luanda	61,028	141,722	132
Nova Lisboa	16,298	28,272	73
Malange	5,299	9,473	80
Lobito	13,592	23,897	75
Silva Pôrto	4,671	8,840	53
In all leading cities:			
Africans	78,244	182,146	132
Europeans	22,289	45,450	103

[4] B. Davidson, *The African Awakening,* p. 223.

colonial army's rank and file. Whether as forced workers in Angola, as migrant workers elsewhere, as squatters on the seaward-pointing spit of Lobito's stones and dust or in the sand slums of Luanda, it was now the case that upward of a third of the whole African population had quit their traditional homes and ways of life.

This was the accelerating process of dismantlement, of dilapidation of all that Africans had built for themselves through the long unfolding of their social history, which now laid the groundwork for the risings of the 1960s. Essentially, these risings were "the result of the irreversible blow dealt to traditional African structures by the market economy introduced under the Portuguese colonial administration." The judgment is that of an Angolan revolutionary, Viriato da Cruz. From a different standpoint, an American historian has reached the same conclusion: "the disintegration of traditional society and the injustice of colonial society had led to widespread disorientation, despair and repression."[5] Thoroughly undermined though they were, traditional structures were replaced by nothing save the misery of hand-to-mouth existence in a kind of helotry where nothing was to be corrected except "a certain disparity between principles and practice."

But misery in itself is no guarantee of effective protest, or even of any kind of protest. Effective protest depends upon the growth of a moral and political consciousness that change is not only necessary, but also possible; and this in turn calls for effective leadership. For a long time there was none. What marked these slums was not the seething agitations of political discontent, but despair and self-abandonment to the harshness of a fate that seemed beyond repair. Drink and demoralization were the badges of their sorrow.

The necessary leadership began to appear shortly before 1950. A few men and women began to search for a workable strategy of change. Necessarily, in the circumstances, they were *assimilados*. Only those with some education could understand

[5] Marcum, op. cit., p. 120.

foreign radio stations, read between the lines of Portuguese newspapers, break through the "barriers of silence" raised around Portuguese Africa by the years of Salazar, and begin to measure the general plight. They were a handful in Luanda (as in Lourenço Marques and Bissau) and a still smaller handful in Lisbon. But they and their work would prove decisive.

Necessarily, too, they turned away from the gradualist reformism of earlier protest. Nothing could now be hoped from that. Permitted "associations" such as the Liga Nacional Angolana had been long reduced to social clubs licensed by the police. As early as 1926 the last of the "old protesters," António de Assis Júnior, had been battered into submission by two periods of jail and years of administrative yapping at his heels. While the rest of colonial Africa reverberated after 1945 with the assemblies and demonstrations of new nationalist movements, all of them pressing on the "reformist option" opened by Britain and France, Portugal remained the same master and example as before.

Yet there remained a few chinks in the armor of stagnation. In 1948 a small group of *assimilados* of Luanda under the leadership of a twenty-year-old poet, Viriato da Cruz, decided to ask permission for a cultural journal. This was a possible project so long as its language remained uniquely Portuguese. As members of one of the permitted associations, Associação dos Naturais de Angola, they duly got their permit. They published the first issue of a journal which they called *Mensagem* (*Message*), and made something of a stir. In 1950 they published a second issue. The stir was greater, and the governor general canceled their permit.

Mensagem was devoted to poetry in Portuguese, but the alarm it raised among the authorities is not difficult to understand. Its poetry said nothing directly political; not even Salazar's police could suppose that its contributors formed any kind of political party. But what was written, rendered all the more emotive by the power of its verse, was indirectly subversive of the whole established order. In this sense its masthead slogan, *Vamos Descobrir Angola* (Let's Discover Angola), formed a radical program in itself. For it supposed that *assimilados* should begin to "deassimilate" themselves and find their African origins, their native identities. It counterposed the idea of African civilization to that of Portuguese civilization. It implied that the first could only prosper in the absence of the second.

The authorities saw all this, if dimly; and for once they saw what was really there. Da Cruz has subsequently explained what the movement of ideas set going by *Mensagem* was intended to achieve. "We wanted to revive the fighting spirit of the African writers of the end of the nineteenth century"—of Fontes and the men who composed *Angola's Voice Crying in the Wilderness*. "But with quite other methods. Our movement attacked the overblown respect given to the cultural values of the West, outdated for the most part; it urged young people to 'rediscover' Angola in every aspect and by an organized and collective effort. . . . Modern trends of foreign culture should be studied," but "so as to rethink and rationalize their positive and valid creativeness" for African situations. Poets should write about the real interests of the Africans and the real nature of African life, "without conceding anything to the thirst for colonial exoticism," to the intellectual and emotional tourism of European prurience and curiosity.[6]

Hence a "program" that cut away from any earlier confidence in the European civilizing mission. The regeneration of Angola could arise only from a bridging of the gulf that separated the *assimilado* from the *preto boçal*, the bush African whom earlier protesters had despised while wishing to protect. If *assimilados* had a duty, *Mensagem* said implicitly in almost all its poems, it was to "de-Portugalize" and "re-Africanize": to escape from Lusitanian isolation, to find contact with "the natives," whether in Luanda's festering slums or out there in the wild *sertão*, the backlands of the bush; and so, bridging the gulf, build an identity which should not be Portuguese, but Angolan.

Reflecting the times, some of its poems said this in terms of an internationalism that could only be, by Salazarist doctrine,

6 Quoted in M. de Andrade, op. cit., p. 12.

a dangerous subversion. Da Cruz's poem *Black Mother: A Song of Hope* strikes the essential note:

> In your voice—
>> the voice of the sugarfields, the ricefields
>> the coffeefields, the rubberlands
>> the cottonlands . . .
>> the plantations of Virginia
>> the fields of the Carolinas
>> of Alabama
>>> Cuba
>>>> Brazil
>> rising from the mills that grind the sugarcane
>> the voice of Harlem District South . . .
>> wailing the blues, breasting the Mississippi
>> chanting the groan of wagon wheels . . .
>> the voice of all America, of all Africa
>> the voice of every voice united
>> in Langston's splendid voice
>> in Guillén's voice of pride. . . .

These writers were only a handful. But in Lisbon there were a few others. And the men in Lisbon, as it chanced, also numbered several with outstanding capacities of intelligence and courage, and who were to make history. One was Amilcar Cabral, who was to be cofounder of the national movement in Angola and founder of its companion movement in Guinea-Bissau. Another was Agostinho Neto, who was to become the leader of Angola's national movement. A third was Mário de Andrade, the first African from Portugal's territories whose voice would reach a wide international audience. A fourth, who died in 1963, was Francisco Tenreiro.

More joined them then or soon after: Lucio Lara, Eduardo dos Santos, Déolinda Rodrigues de Almeida, and others outside Angola. They, too, numbered outstanding characters and talents such as would have made their mark anywhere in a free world: none more so, perhaps, than Déolinda de Almeida, one of the national movement's women pioneers. She had studied at São Paulo, Brazil and Drew University in the United States on Methodist scholarships, before abandoning her career and throwing herself into political work.[7] Her fate was to be a tragic one. In 1962–63 she organized the movement's women's section at Léopoldville (Kinshasa), and was secretary of its medical wing. With several leaders of the movement she was afterward arrested in the Congo (Zaïre) Republic and perished there, with others, from the prison treatment she was given.

"Toward the 1950s," Andrade has recalled, the "little community of students and intellectuals who were then in Portugal became sharply aware of the need to act against the Lusitanian image of the black man"—the image of a man who remained a savage unless and until he became a Portuguese, even a second-class Portuguese—"and to trace out a path to national self-assertion."[8]

Political conditions apart, they found this difficult. They had access to a wider range of information and ideas than their friends in Luanda, Lourenço Marques, Bissau. But the gulf between themselves and the *preto boçal* was also wider, since they were the products of Portuguese higher education. They were the very pillars of Portuguese Africa's academic elite: Cabral a student of hydraulic engineering, Neto of medicine, Andrade a literary critic. They were a million miles from the backland villages. They had even forgotten their mother tongues.

They began with two ideas in mind, aside from completing their studies. First, along the lines of *Mensagem,* they began to re-Africanize themselves, even in an elementary way. They formed with official permission a Center of African Studies with the undeclared aim, Andrade has said, of "analyzing the elements of Africa's cultures," so as "to evoke the sense of belonging to an oppressed world and awaken a national consciousness."

It was much to say; at least it marked a start. Two years passed before the Lisbon authorities had their own awakening

[7] Cf. Marcum, op. cit., pp. 301, 332.
[8] Andrade, op. cit., p. 10.

in this matter and suppressed the Center; but it had not existed quite in vain. Like *Mensagem* in Luanda, the Center published "African poetry in Portuguese" devoted to the emergent themes of protest and self-recognition, and so provided another stimulus to a nationalism still in the womb. Andrade produced a study of the Kimbundu language, reviving in new circumstances the work of Assis Júnior several decades earlier.

Secondly, they examined the possible alternatives to a reformism now utterly defunct. This, too, was far from easy. French-speaking African nationalists might sit in the National Assembly of Paris and affiliate to parties as wide in range as the conservative right or the socialist and Communist left. English-speaking nationalists might find powerful friends in the British Labour Party, or, if they wished, seek opinions from a British Communist Party which, however small, was perfectly legal. But Cabral, Neto, Andrade, and those around them in Lisbon had in this respect only the deeply clandestine and hunted Portuguese Communist Party and one or two other groupings of an anti-Salazarist nature. Yet it seems to have been far better than nothing. "We learned from the sharp conflicts that existed in Portugal," Neto recalled in 1970. "They provided us with useful lessons."

In this way they approached the ideas of Marxism, and these became a powerful strand in the developing fabric of their post-reformist and therefore revolutionary ideas. Yet it also seems to have been the fact—and later years would confirm this—that even in those early years they were aware that the ideas of Marxism, such as they were found in Europe, also needed "Africanizing," reapplying in an African context, if they were to serve a useful purpose. *Déracinés* as they were, these men appear keenly to have felt the gulf between themselves as an elite, and the "masses" upon whose adherence everything would turn. That was the problem which *Mensagem* had posed; it was very much their own.

This gulf was matched by another: the gulf that divided the *possible* conditions for radical change in Africa from doctrines and policies elaborated elsewhere, and for circumstances very

different. If there was to be a revolution it would have to be
indigenous, rooted in African realities; it could never be imported from outside. This clarity was to remain dominant in
their framing of the strategy and policies of the guerrilla movements they were afterward to form and lead. They were to
look to the Communist countries of Europe and Asia for the
guns that would set them going and open their chance of success. But they were also to look stubbornly to African realities
for the political weapons that could prepare and build on any
such success.

Early in the 1950s the Lisbon group went its various ways.
Now a qualified engineer, Cabral returned to his home town of
Bissau and took service in the administration, preparing an
agricultural census. "It was a lucky chance. For two years,
1952–54, he tramped the length and breadth of his country
acquiring detailed local knowledge, growing into an intimacy
with village life, and, as he soon realized, making himself ready
for what should come later." In 1954 the governor, who chanced
to be a man of some liberalism, told him that either he must
stop "talking against the Portuguese" or go to jail. Choosing
neither, and judging the time still premature for clandestine
action, Cabral returned to Lisbon and took one of several offers
of jobs; good hydraulic engineers were hard to come by. He
went to Angola and worked on sugar irrigation in the Benguela
District. Here he found the political agitation more advanced
than in Guinea-Bissau. He became active in its clandestine
discussions.[9]

Neto's life went differently. In 1951 many of his friends in
Lisbon "had tried to play some supporting role in the presi-
dential campaign of Admiral Quintão Meirales, only to find
themselves deprived of this opportunity when the Admiral an-
grily withdrew his candidature. Dr. Salazar had refused to allow the Admiral to nominate any of his supporters to check

[9] For a biographical sketch, see Davidson, *The Liberation of Guiné: Aspects
of an African Revolution,* Penguin, London and Baltimore, 1969. For Mozambican personalities, see, *inter alia,* Eduardo Mondlane, *The Struggle for
Mozambique,* same publisher and date.

the counting of the votes. Once more, Dr. Salazar's nominee was elected without a contest, and the liberals and democrats were obliged to return to illegal private gatherings. The PIDE (political police) decided that Neto should be taught a lesson not to attend these groups. They locked him up for a few weeks."[10] Neto recalled long afterward, "I was active in Portuguese youth organizations for reasons of principle, but also because I liked to get into the action." Friendship should go both ways: if Portuguese democrats were to help Africans, then Africans should help them in return.

The PIDE quickly let him out again but stayed on his trail, alerted also by the moving protest of his poetry:

> My mother
> (black mothers whose sons depart)
> you taught me to wait and hope
> as you had learnt in bitter days
> But in me
> life killed that mystic hope
>
> I am not the one who waits
> but the one who is awaited
> and we are Hope
> your sons . . .
> searching for life.[11]

Besides, the atmosphere was getting worse. Back in Angola, now once more a "province" of the motherland if only for the purpose of denying United Nations investigation of a "non-self-governing territory," *Mensagem* had begun to yield its early harvest. Repression duly stiffened. In February 1955 Neto was again arrested in Lisbon. This time he stayed in prison till June

[10] Peter Benenson, *Persecution 1961,* Penguin, London and Baltimore, 1961, p. 54.

[11] My trans. from original (*in extenso*) in Mário de Andrade, *Antologia da Poesia Negra de Expressão Portuguesa,* Oswald, Paris, 1958, pp. 41–42. A volume of Neto's poems has been published in various languages under the title of *L'Espérance Sacrée,* which I have not been able to trace. See also a selection in French trans. in M. de Andrade, *La Poésie africaine d'Expression portugaise,* Oswald, Paris, 1969.

1957, only then being able to resume his medical studies. Late in 1959, a qualified physician, he returned to Angola and set up practice in Luanda. It was not to be for long.

Andrade contrived to reach Paris in the middle 1950s. There he scraped a living as a critic and editor for Alioune Diop's distinguished monthly review, *Présence Africaine,* then established in the rue Chaligny, while doing what he could to draw public attention to the cause he had at heart. He was able to meet like-minded men from other Portuguese colonies, the Mozambican Marcelino dos Santos, the Angolan Américo Boavida, and others who now converged from Lisbon and Africa. A grouping emerged, and organized co-operation began. Aimed chiefly at propaganda, this took various forms as they searched for their way ahead.

So it was that the leadership of the mainstream of Angolan nationalism, of the inheritance of the "men of the '90s," took fresh shape in Europe as in Africa. It was still far from clear what this leadership could hope to achieve; nothing more than a start had been made. From ideas of reformism they had moved, decisively, to ideas of revolt; but the manner of revolt, the how and the when of it, let alone the manner of its outcome, still lay hidden in the clouds of the approaching storm.

Back in Luanda, meanwhile, events were moving to a climax. Two pressures proved decisive there. One was the stiffening repression of the Portuguese authorities, now with sections of the political police from Portugal to help them turn the screw. The other was the rising protest that Da Cruz and others had set in motion. Taken together, these guaranteed an explosion. When at last it came, this was to be all but fatal to African hopes.

DOCUMENTARY ONE

Few ordinary Angolans have witnessed to their lives during the years of Salazar. In 1943 the veteran American missionary Dr. Merlin Ennis, who had passed most of his life in Angola, was given a long memoir in Umbundu by its author, a carpenter whom he knew well and who had learned to read and write at a Canadian mission in central Angola. Dr. Ennis put this memoir into English and in 1954 gave me his translation, together with much supporting testimony too long for reproduction here.

"Sandele's" memoir is remarkable both for its detail and for the general light it sheds upon a system within which the law was one thing and everyday life quite another. These extracts tell of mistreatment that was never made good, no matter what the law might say. It goes without saying that not all local administrators were as bad as the ones told of here; yet men like them were by no means rare, as the available evidence is enough to prove. Dr. Ennis also knew well the senior of the two administrators, whom he described as an active, intelligent, competent little man, but of great brutality.

"When an African priest complained of his brutalities to the Bishop of Huambo, the Bishop told him that Lelinho [the man in question] had such powerful backing that he, the Bishop, could not do anything about it." But his excesses proved too scandalous in the end. In August 1951 (Boletim Oficial de Angola, Series II, no. 35, p. 757), *he was sacked for taking a relatively huge sum, over the years 1939–51, from private employers for the "recruitment of native laborers." Castro Soromenho, one may note, describes a similar case in* Camaxilo.

*On the 18th day of September 1940 [wrote "Sandele,"
author of this memoir], with a rope about my loins, I suffered bodily hardship because I trusted in the friendliness
of the Portuguese white man. The* Chefe do Pôsto *Lelinho
put me to work building the roof of the office building at
the Post of Cuma. I worked two weeks at the post. When I
discovered that I was working gratis, and the tools were
mine, furnishing my own clothes and eating my own food,
I was afflicted with anger. I refused to work any more for
nothing. I rolled up my things and went all the way to
Ganda.*

*There I found work with a white man who cared for
his people and paid his workers. He was the proprietor of
a saw mill by the name of Silvino. I had worked there
about two weeks when an African who had been sent by
the* Chefe do Pôsto *[Lelinho, at Cuma] came. He said,
'You, they have sent for you.' I went with the man to the
owner of the mill where I was working. The white man
would not agree to let me go. He wrote a letter and put it
in the hand of the one who was sent for me. And then the
messenger took the letter and carried it to the* Chefe do
Pôsto. . . .

[But the Chefe do Pôsto *insisted on getting him back,
and "Sandele" was brought before his assistant, the administrator of Caala.]*

*Then the administrator ordered my incarceration, say-
ing, "Go lock him up." I went into prison on the 14th day
of December 1940. I was in there for 45 days. Then we
saw a messenger come from the* Chefe *to take me away.
That day they hurried matters, with me away to Cuma with
a rope around my waist. The tools remained with the white
man. Now I came to Cuma again. They put me in prison
and locked me up. The next day the* Chefe *came. . . .
They unlocked me and said to me, "Come out." I came
outside. Then they tied me around the waist with a metal
rope which they called a wire. Then the* cipaio *[sepoy: African militiaman or auxiliary policeman] took me to the
office of the* Chefe, *and when I came into his presence he
said to the* cipaio, *"Why did you tie him? Untie him."
Then he untied me. Then he asked me, "Why did you go*

to Ganda?" I answered, saying, "I was looking for work where I could get a living." He said, "There is work here." I then said, "The catch is, that here the work is unpaid." He said, "Now that is too much." He told a cipaio, "Take him away and lock him up." I went off to prison and they locked me up again. . . .

[After four days he was released and agreed to go on working for this Chefe. It was now complained against him and his fellow carpenter that they had written a letter of complaint against the Chefe to the latter's superior; they denied this.]

We went back to work again, and as we began to work we began to consider matters thus: first, we are earning nothing, second, our tools are worn out, third, we are now involved in a complaint. . . . Let us go to Huambo and ask the Intendente about it. . . .

[They accordingly left the Post again and journeyed to the administrative headquarters. There they obtained an interview with the Intendente, who told them to explain their presence.]

Then I began by saying, "We have come to you, the Master of Justice, so that you may decide our case, for we are skilled workmen of Cuma. We are carpenters, and that which troubles us is this, we use our own carpenter tools, we eat our own food, we pay the taxes on our houses with our own money. We know that the Portuguese law does not compel anyone to work without pay. For that reason we have come to you, who are the Master of Justice."

[The Intendente heard their evidence, and confronted "Sandele" and his fellow carpenter with the Caala administrator, Lelinho's assistant. The latter pretended that the failure to pay the carpenters had been an oversight.]

Then the administrator was silent, meditating. After a time he replied, "I have heard all about it, and if you please, sir, permit me to pay these boys at the administration." Then the Intendente agreed, saying, "When you have taken them and paid them, let them go to their villages." The administrator agreed to this.

[But the administrator took them in his car to his Post and locked them up.]

*We were taken into the lock-up and there we passed
the night. When it was morning we awoke. At about nine
thirty we went to the office with the wire about our loins.
When we came into the office they took us in where we
found the administrator. We stood. He said, "What did
you go to Huambo to do?" I said, "We went to ask about
our pay." He reviled us again and again. He said, "I do
not want speeches in here."* [*After further questions of
the same kind*] *he stood up . . . and said, "Oh*, cipaio,
fetch the palmatória." [*A sort of mallet carved from one
piece of hard wood, its head being a disk some three inches
across and an inch and a half thick, patterned with dots
like the five of dice. Under the force of the blow the flesh
is sucked up into these tapering holes, producing intense
pain. The* palmatória *was a standard form of punishment
throughout the years of Salazar, and indeed since.*]

While [*the* cipaio] *was gone to fetch it, my companion
being next to* [*the administrator*], *blows were heaped upon
his head by the administrator himself. The* cipaio *came
with the* palmatória. . . . *When he was tired with beating
my comrade I came in for it. Seventy blows with the*
palmatória *were given to me. . . . When these had been
given he said, "Take off your trousers." We took off our
trousers, and when we were naked he said, "Lie down on
your faces." When we had lain down then the* palmatória
*was applied to our backsides, blow followed blow, thirty
apiece. He said, "Take off your shoes." We took them off
and then he filled them with filth. We came out and went
to the jail and entered it. . . .*

[*Further beatings followed at the administrator's orders,
and eventually these carpenters were sent away to the far
south, to Pôrto Alexandre, where they worked for two
years for the administrator's brother, who had a fishing
business. Their plight was now the usual one of "contract"
workers, and escape from Pôrto Alexandre was next to
impossible. Conditions here were particularly brutal, and
there is much detailed evidence to that effect in Dr. Ennis'
papers. But the carpenters did not lose heart and continued to write complaints. Not until May 1943 did these have
any effect.*]

Then there came the documents to liberate us from slavery. We climbed into the transport on that morning and went all the way to Mossâmedes. We presented our pass. The Secretary asked, "Were you the ones that wrote that brash letter to the Intendente?" We understood and said, "Yes, it was we."

[But they were allowed to return to their own region.] In the evening about ten we came to the area of Caala. We waited four days and then took the train [to Cuma]. On the 17th of June we presented our pass to the Chefe do Pôsto *[Lelinho, the Caala administrator's boss and the original source of their troubles]. He looked up at us and said, "Ah, Sandele, you are not dead?" I said, "I expect to die here in our country." We handed over the money to pay our taxes for three years [their period of enforced absence]. Then he said, "Go to your village and do not let me see you again in my Post, for you are a rascal." I said, "Yes, sir, and thank you." If it were not for the Lord I do not know that we should now be above ground.*

By 1959 no attentive people in Luanda could have been in any doubt that the storm must soon break upon their heads. The first gusts of its wrath had already caught their victims. Early in the year the political police swept dozens into prison; more arrests followed. Rumor and counterrumor ran upon each other's heels, the one more full of menace than the other. A sense of undeclared war now seemed to divide the sand slums from the European city. Individuals watched with growing apprehension, some escaping while there was yet time, others eluding the police on their trail, most awaiting silently whatever fate might bring.

In April, via the governor general, fate brought the Portuguese air force. Their first units gave the tone: "In the morning, they dropped troops by parachute. The first to land, there above Luanda on the hard brown soil, was a regimental padre, Captain Father Martins. . . . Then came the [demonstration] bombing and the target firing and the fanfares of a grand parade, 'agile and athletic, in the German style,' as the *Comércio de Angola* trilled in a long cascade of reportorial magnificence and joy," and as befitted troops commanded by men who had looked to the military schools of Hitler's Germany for their own formation.

Why bring in the air force? The governor general explained in an after-dinner speech that same night: "The air force," he declared, "is not here to make war. . . . [But] peace in our time is possible only when states can wield enough force to confront the threat of agitators and mischief makers, inspired as they generally are by Communism in its darkest guise. . . . We are living in the time of the leaflet. . . . The leaflet has appeared in Angola. . . ."[1] A few weeks later, though with less palaver, two thousand reinforcements for the army likewise arrived from Portugal.[2]

Paratroops, bombing planes, and more infantry might seem a somewhat overdone reply to leaflets, but Europe's "master and example" of the colonizing process was now sorely alarmed. There were reasons in the background for this; those in the foreground were even more persuasive. A year earlier, in 1958, the official opposition candidate for the presidentship of Portugal, General Humberto Delgado, had received 22.5 per cent of the metropolitan vote even under Salazar's peculiar rules; in the oversea provinces, moreover, Delgado was given eighteen thousand votes against seventy-four thousand (also 22.5 per cent) for Salazar's nominee, Admiral Américo Thomaz. Delgado's program was scarcely one of revolution. But it was resolutely anti-Salazarist. Its support in Angola and Mozambique, old centers of Portuguese dissidence, caused anger and apprehension in official ranks, just as it gave new hope to oversea protesters.

These fears—and hopes—were quickened by events in the neighboring Belgian Congo. "Our native," warned the governor of Angola's Congo frontier district in a confidential report written probably in 1957 or 1958, "has learned many things in the Belgian Congo these past years. Among these is that the Congolese are hoping for independence in a few years' time."

Marking these and other sources of political "infection," the governor recommended precautionary measures. One of them was to establish Portuguese Catholic missionaries in frontier areas where British Baptists had influence: "A priest in Lisbon or

[1] B. Davidson, "The Time of the Leaflet," *New Statesman*, London, 21 Nov. 1959.
[2] *The Times*, 27 May 1959.

any other place in the metropole is always a priest. . . . But in Africa, and above all in the [Angolan] Congo the situation is different, because there we are trying to consolidate a Portuguese feeling among the natives." God, apparently, was also Portuguese. Otherwise the governor had little to offer but the familiar recipe: bring in more settlers, send more troops.[3]

Such warnings were noted in Luanda and Lisbon, and even acted on to some extent. But events outran them. In January 1959 the Belgian colonial capital of Léopoldville erupted. Police broke up an African meeting for which no permit had been obtained. It had happened before, but this time the reaction was violent. Furious crowds rushed into the Belgian quarters, smashing cars and invading schools, churches, even hospitals. The Belgian authorities did what they had always done: they sent in their colonial militia, the *Force Publique,* still completely under European officers, and on this occasion the *Force Publique* shot and killed women and children as well as men. The shock in Europe was profound. Within a few days the Belgian government reversed itself completely and announced, through the Belgian king, a "program of reform." This was to provide for local and provincial elections in 1959, while dates were fixed for still wider elections and the establishment of "a government at the national level."

All this was marked by protesters in neighboring Angola. If there, why not here? But it was also marked by the police; among them it appears to have provoked something near a panic. During March they made widespread arrests in Luanda and other cities; in July, with the governor general assembling troops and planes, they followed these arrests with more. In the following months they carried through their "administrative" preparations in the prisons with a customary use of torture; at the end of 1959 they made ready for a mass trial. It was in fact to be a prelude to the all-out effort to eliminate educated Africans that followed later.

[3] Major Hélio A. Esteves Felgas, *Protecção para a Defesa de Angola?,* undated copy in my possession.—B. D.

Three lists were published, and it was at once clear that the
political police had not missed their aim. The first carried the
names of twelve Afro-Portuguese Angolans, three black Angolans, and three foreigners. Among these were Ilidio Tomé
Alves Machado, a postal employee who was also the president elected in clandestinity by the Movimento Popular de Libertação de Angola (MPLA), the group founded in 1956 that was
afterward to grow into the main challenge to the Portuguese;
Carlos Aniceto Vieira Dias, a bank clerk who was also the crea-
tor of a dance ensemble called "Ngola Ritmo," a focal center of
the cultural nationalism that *Mensagem* had set in motion; and
others of the same loyalties and opinions. The foreigners were a
black American, Lawrence Holder (charged *in absentia*), a
Ghanaian called Karl Dogbe (also *in absentia*), and a Cuban,
Francisco Xavier Hernández; all three were sailors.

The second list had seven names; five were Portuguese, and
included a well-known woman physician, Dr. Julieta Gandra,
who is said to have insisted on riding to prison with arrested
Africans instead of taking the special car ("whites only") provided by the police.

The third list was longer, but only twenty-one were under arrest. The dozen charged *in absentia* included Viriato da Cruz,
lately escaped to Europe and then in Paris; Mário de Andrade,
who was also in Paris; and Déolinda de Almeida, who was in
São Paulo, Brazil. They also included the leaders of another
stream of Angolan protest established in the Belgian Congo:
Roberto Holden (under pseudonyms), Eduardo Pinnock, and
others. Of the two whites on this list, one was the Angolan poet
António Jacinto, then in Brazil, and the other an American
journalist, George Barnett, also *in absentia*.[4]

[4] Details in Marcum, op. cit., pp. 33–34; in *Le Procès des Cinquante*, pamphlet issued in Paris on behalf of the newly formed FRAIN (Frente Revolucionária Africana para a Independência Nacional); and other sources. Long
afterward, in 1970, the official and settler attitudes by which these trials were
prepared were to be described in the legal defense of another distinguished Angolan African, the Reverend Joaquim Pinto de Andrade, chancellor of the
Luanda archbishopric, whose years of persecution by the police then began.
"It was the beginning of a systematic and exhaustive aggression, reaching a

Some had escaped, but others had not; and those who had not, included many in the leadership of the growing protest movement. A want of experience in clandestine politics and poor security had made them easy victims. For this the movement was to pay a hard price: it lost its best heads inside the country at the very moment when they were most needed. In the following August, 1960, heavy sentences were handed down after a secret military trial from which legal observers from abroad were barred.[5]

Other trials followed. In November the execution of eight Africans in Luanda Prison was reported; "a 14-year-old African boy who was climbing the wall of the yard was shot dead. He was playing nearby when he heard the shooting and went to see. An African motorcyclist passing near the dead body of the boy tried to carry it away, but was assaulted and arrested."[6] The whole episode betokened the atmosphere of tragedy and anger that now lay heavy on Luanda's Africans, a mingled fear and fury described so well by the Luanda writer Luandino Vieira in his novel about those months of 1960, *The True Life of Domingos Xavier:*

"Zita came back, running, to the little room they lived in. Crossing the yard he saw his grandfather, who was pissing against the fence. The child stopped, breathless, and called:

" 'Pépé, quickly, there's a prisoner!'

"Old Petelo turned around, blinking in the morning light that filtered through their tree.

" 'A prisoner? You saw him yourself?' . . .

paroxysm in 1961, against every man of color who had distinguished himself *in whatever way.* . . . It was the onset of a persecution, as stupid or impious, of all those who could read, had books, possessed a radio, wore spectacles. . . ." Quoted in Mario Brochado Coelho, *En Defesa de Joaquim Pinto de Andrade,* Vila da Maia, 1971, p. 48.

[5] A few months earlier, in May, a British lawyer, Mr. F. Elwyn Jones, M.P., later to be British Attorney-General, had gone to Luanda to express the fears of the International Commission of Jurists that the accused would not receive a fair trial. He found there was nothing he could do. On the defensive, the authorities assured him "that all was quiet and peaceful. . . ." (Letter to Sec. Gen. of International Commission of Jurists, May 20, 1960)

[6] Statement, Aug. 18, 1960, issued for MPLA by its then London representative, João Cabral.

"Outside there were women with children gathered to their skirts, and a man. He was trying to get down from a police truck under the blows of two black policemen. He was tall and thin, very thin, and though his face was swollen beyond recognition, you could see that he was a young man. Getting down from the back of the truck, he collapsed on the sand. . . ."[7]

Such was the atmosphere that was to yield the explosion of the following February. Yet even this might not have taken its effect quite so soon, or so furiously, without the background build-up of the storm.

The end of the Second World War brought new opportunities for colonial growth. Much reduced till 1945 by the dangers of navigation, Portuguese emigration to Angola rapidly soared in the late 1940s and 1950s. From about forty-four thousand in 1940, the white population had risen to fifty-nine thousand in 1950. By 1960 it was past 179,000.

The social consequences were as rapidly felt. Many of these immigrants were from the lowest rungs of the economic ladder, illiterate peasants or semi-skilled urban workers who were glad of any chance of safe employment, even at jobs of little skill or none at all. Most were intended by the authorities as farming settlers who would found rural colonies on the old Roman model. But reality soon found a large number of these colonists crowding back into the towns, preferring the small amenities of wage labor to the backbreaking toil and solitude of the bush.

So it came about that even such jobs as truck driving in the Lobito docks or chambermaiding in the Luanda hotels now began to be filled by poor white immigrants at the expense of local Africans. And a sharper discrimination also made itself apparent, as in every other African colony of white settlement in this post-

[7] Luandino Vieira (José Vieira Mateus de Graça), *La Vraie Vie de Domingos Xavier* (with *Le Complet de Mateus*), trans. M. de Andrade and C. Tiberghien, Présence Africaine, Paris, 1971, pp. 21–22. Arrested in 1961, Vieira was sentenced by the military tribunal of Angola to fourteen years' imprisonment, and sent to the Tarrafal Prison, in the Cape Verde Islands, where he has shared a cell with the poets António Jacinto and António Cardoso.

1945 period. Differential wage levels, not new but now more widely felt, tell their own story:

WAGES OF SKILLED WORKERS IN ANGOLA: 1958[8]

	European		"Native"	
	Escudos	Dollars	Escudos	Dollars
Compositors, manual	4,500	157.50	1,560	54.60
Compositors, mechanical	5,000	175	1,200	42
Carpenters	3,120	109.20	1,690	59.15
Cooks	3,334	116.69	500	17.50
Servants	1,500	52.50	450	15.75
Electricians	3,080	107.80	1,030	36.05
Plasterers etc. etc.	3,640	127.40	1,560	54.60

Some of the "native" workers in such jobs as these were persons of assimilated status: they suffered with the rest. Once again a "certain disparity between principles and practice," tut-tutted over in Coimbra, became on the spot a flagrant outrage.

There might still be room for a number of *assimilados* within the colonial structure; a few of them, during the 1960s, were to be advanced to posts of responsibility. There continued to be room in Portuguese universities for some dozens of African students. Women of *assimilado* families could assure themselves of a "social success" by becoming the concubines or even wives of white settlers or officials. The system was not entirely rigid; in this respect, too, it was nothing if not Portuguese.

But there seems little doubt that a majority of Angola's fifty thousand-odd "civilized natives" now felt the growing pressure of poor-white rivalry for work, and, on top of that, the sharpened edge of racist attitudes among immigrants who, like many of

[8] Thomas Okuma, *Angola in Ferment*, Beacon Press, Boston, 1962, p. 37, quoting Anuário Estat. de Ang. 1958.

those who went from Britain to Rhodesia at this time, found compensation for their own sense of social inferiority by lording it over people still lower in the scale of colonial life. Older settlers, in Angola as in Rhodesia, might deplore this kind of thing, having less need to bolster their self-respect; there was nothing they could do about it. Salazar's Portugal had begun to export its unemployment on a systematic scale.

But the years after 1945 also brought, if erratically, a "colonial boom." Export crops became more in demand. This produced a corresponding demand for more labor: in Angola, above all, for more "contract labor." Coercion increased. Early in 1953 the old slave island of São Thomé illustrated this whole situation with a drama of its own. By now the island had a population of about fifty-five thousand (with another five thousand on nearby Príncipe); the backbone of its economy was provided by about two hundred plantations, chiefly of cocoa and coffee, worked by a dozen Portuguese companies. Like its sugar in the past, São Thomé's coffee and cocoa had always been grown by slaves from the mainland and afterward by *serviçais*, or "contract workers." The island population itself, officially considered as more or less "civilized," had been exempt from forced labor. But early in the 1950s, partly through competition for forced labor on the mainland, São Thomé began to suffer a labor shortage.

In these circumstances a local inspector of "native affairs" published an attack on the "citizen's privileges" of the islanders. This seems to have been interpreted as a prelude to making the islanders subject to the forced-labor regulations of the mainland. Threats on the governor's life were posted on walls. According to the islanders' side of the story, these were provocations arranged by an administration desirous of finding excuses for punishing the islanders. According to the local Portuguese, the islanders now planned to kill them all and declare for independence. What seems certain is that there was fear and fury on either side.

Explosion resulted. One Portuguese officer was killed for certain, but how many non-whites? "The number of deaths among the Natives," reported an American missionary who visited the island for a few hours some weeks later, "is not known, but some persons placed the figure at 'about 200.' The number of arrests, likewise, is not known. . . . It is evident that practically every Native goes about all the time in fear of being denounced and arrested."[9] The islanders themselves claimed that soldiers and settlers had slain more than one thousand of them.[10]

The whole affair was to prefigure Luanda eight years later. Not only no improvement in the way people lived; on the contrary, a toughening of the administrative hand. Not only no reform; but also regression. It was this that gave their chance to the mainland "militants of the revolutionary tendency," as the followers of *Mensagem* now recognized themselves. They found a wider audience among a "petty-bourgeois" population of *assimilados:* African clerks, mechanics, male nurses, elementary schoolmasters, small traders who might otherwise have been content, no doubt, to exploit their privileged position in relation to the "natives" by accepting a process of reform, just as in other African colonies now advancing toward political independence. As it was, they were pushed toward the activists—at first by increased discrimination against them, then by increased repression.

But the activists, their ranks slowly growing in this way, were not content with a "petty bourgeois" audience and following. *Mensagem* had preached the rediscovery of "native" Angola and fraternity with the people of the bush. The activists went into the *senzalas* from which came the people of the bush who had come crowding to the towns. They started clandestine literacy classes in the sand slums of Luanda. They recruited other activists to go out to the villages and backland towns. They spoke for the ideas of an Angolan national culture, a culture of Angola's people, a culture worthy of respect. They "began to circulate leaflets urging

[9] Letter written from Angola on March 30, 1953; copy in my possession.
[10] *L'Isle de São Thomé*, CONCP (Conferência das Organisações Nacionalistas das Colónias Portuguesas), Algiers, 1958.

people to learn, and to prepare for an open struggle against oppression and for independence."[11]

They won a hearing, gained adherents. In 1953 Luanda saw the founding in secrecy of the first party with nationalist aims, in fact a small grouping: PLUA (Partido da Luta Unida dos Africanos de Angola). Another version says that PLUA was founded early in 1956, being preceded by a short-lived Partido Comunista Angolana. It is hard to be sure of the facts about these short-lived early groupings, or their relative weight. Many who formed and worked in them were killed by the Portuguese in the general massacre of *assimilados* and active "natives" that followed the risings of 1961; others, who survived, have still to tell their story. But it matters little. Marxist ideas were undoubtedly active in the 1950s, but they were only one strand in the fabric of developing protest, just as, later on, they were to be only one strand, though a powerful one, in the guerrilla movements of the 1960s.

Many little groupings, though secretly, saw the light; some were in touch with one another, others not. Even in the "forgotten east" of Angola there were new associations and cultural clubs. Those which stood in the mainstream, centered on Luanda, joined in a common front called the MPLA in December 1956. Yet the MPLA, at this time, was far from being able to exercise any consistent lead in non-white opinion. In 1959, moreover, it lost its Luanda leaders, and much would flow from that.

[11] *História de Angola* (*Apontamentos*), Centro de Estudos Angolanos, Algiers, n.d. but early 1960s, pp. 151–52.

All through this period the rising tensions of Luanda were reflected elsewhere in Angola, especially in the plantation regions of the west, northwest, and center, where a sense of coming climax was also present. In all these ways, conditions here were no different from those of Mozambique, nor, essentially, from those of Guinea-Bissau. The storms broke at different moments in these colonies; each of them took shape in the same climate of increasing discrimination and repression. On all this the official and even the unofficial records are defective, and likely long to be so; yet much can be learned from the memories of those who were to embark upon the counterviolence of the 1960s. The burden of their stories is impressively alike, whether for Mozambique, Guinea-Bissau, or Angola. Thus:

Samora Moises Machel, senior commander after 1967 of the fighting units of the Mozambique national movement (FRELIMO) and the movement's president after 1970:

> I was born in 1933 in southern Mozambique. I managed to get some education, and eventually finished a technical course, and became a male nurse [one of the better jobs open to *assimilados* in Portuguese Africa, especially if they had no white relations able to help them]. We were together with whites during our training, but it was only after graduating that we really discovered the very different treatment, the different attitudes to them and

to us. And then, of course, we discovered the different level of wages.

I got to thinking that I could help myself by more education. I began to go to evening courses. In the end I was able to graduate at secondary-school level. This was another thing that should have given me the same status as whites. It didn't.

Gradually, I saw that nothing would help but collective action. A man on his own couldn't achieve anything. At that stage—it was after 1956—I began to understand what the key problems were, the key economic and political problems, and just why it was that we Africans were disadvantaged. Then 1960 taught me more—the independence of the Congo and its tumults. I began to think seriously about the possibilities of Mozambique becoming independent. . . . Then it was that the consciousness of being oppressed, deprived, exploited, began to have its effect, as well as these ideas about independence.

At that time, the Portuguese authorities were increasing their repression of all educated and literate Africans. That was something else that greatly increased our curiosity: to understand why they didn't want us to read newspapers, listen to foreign broadcasts. Yes, and then came 1961 in Angola. . . .[1]

Sebastião Mabote, born in 1942 in southern Mozambique; in 1968 a guerrilla commander in the Niassa District of northern Mozambique, and in charge of military security for the second congress of the national movement, held there in July of that year:

I finished primary school at a mission in the Gaza District called Sikumbane, and then my father advised me to leave our village and go to Lourenço Marques [the colonial capital] and look for a job there. He recommended me to take up shorthand, typing, and wireless telegraphy.

[1] Interview with B.D. in July 1968.

Not such a strange choice, this last: Mabote had done two and a half years in the army, as a conscript, and completed a six months' course in wireless telegraphy. He was apparently rather good at this, for the army kept him beyond what was then the legal term of conscription. After that he continued studying, at first at home and then in Lourenço Marques, where he worked to support himself:

> I worked as a typist in a lawyer's office. His name was Saraiva. He presided over a juvenile court and had a private practice. I was in charge of the private side of his work and I earned 600 escudos a month. But alongside me there was a white girl working, and she didn't know the job, so that most of the work fell on me. But they paid her 3,200 escudos a month, more than five times what they paid me.

> But the injustice [and this Mabote says with a sarcastic humor] wasn't only in the money. It was also in the way they treated me. All the same, they wanted me to accept *assimilado* status. My father was against that; so was I. Why was I? Because I knew the real situation of the *assimilados*. I saw that the *assimilado* and the *indígena* [native] were really in the same situation.

> Later on, I had to become an *assimilado* so as to get a better job. Still, I couldn't find a better job. You could only do that if you knew someone with influence inside Portuguese society [precisely where the Afro-Portuguese "native" could sometimes gain over the purely African "native"]. I didn't know any such person. So I became a very rootless man. I wanted to study, I wanted to live a normal sort of life. But I didn't have a job.

> Even when I was working for that lawyer I had begun to argue angrily with them. And so they began saying I was a politician, a rebel. And they put the PIDE [political police] on my trail, to follow me about, to search my room, to find what radio stations I listened to. . . . I left Lourenço Marques, and I went back to my village again.

In June 1963 I ran away to Rhodesia from Gaza. There I was arrested by the Rhodesian police, who were working with the PIDE. That was in Bulawayo [in western Rhodesia]. They sent me back to Lourenço Marques. I was in prison there for two months and seven days. I came out and went back to work for that lawyer again. But the PIDE stayed on my heels. I couldn't stand it. I went home again. Then my father said, "All right, run away again if you can." And he gave me money to help.

That was in December 1963. One of my brothers was already in FRELIMO. He was in the first group that FRELIMO sent for military training in Algeria, because he'd joined in 1962. . . . So I ran away to Rhodesia again—the only way I knew of getting to the north if you didn't want to risk crossing South Africa. I took advantage of Christmas Day to get across the frontier. . . . I reached Lusaka, in Northern Rhodesia [independent as Zambia a year later]. I contacted our people there. I went on to Dar es Salaam [Tanzania, where FRELIMO had its office]. . . .[2]

Such was "the time of the leaflet" in Mozambique. It was no different in Guinea-Bissau:

Sala N'tonton, about thirty, soldier of the army of the PAIGC [national movement of Guinea-Bissau]:

I was a farmer, and our village was a poor one. We'd pigs and chickens. The Portuguese bought these, but they gave us bad prices. We had to pay a lot of taxes without ever seeing the benefit of them. Where was the school, the clinic? There wasn't any, no matter what taxes we paid. So I joined the Party. I wanted to have a hand in putting things right. . . .

Yes, before that I'd been in the army, the Portuguese I mean. That was in 1957, maybe I was twenty, in Balamo. Two years and six months I served them. They didn't treat us well. The whites had all the promotion. We had

[2] Interview with B.D. in July 1968.

the dirty jobs. Then I went back to my village and I stayed there. That was the time that a comrade from the Party came to our village. He began talking about how things were and what we had to do to put things right. I listened to him. I knew he wasn't telling lies. I knew that things were like he said. I'd seen it for myself. . . .[3]

What manner of men handed out the leaflets, argued the nationalist case?

Pascoal Alves, aged twenty-nine and a senior political commissar in the forests of southern Guiné when interviewed in 1967:

I'm from Bissau. My father was a commercial clerk. I'd just finished primary school when there was the massacre in Bissau [of dock workers, in August 1959], and Cabral came back [from Angola]. I had some friends. They knew about the Party [the PAIGC]. I didn't wait. I joined the Party. We worked hard to mobilise people. We held little meetings; we gave out leaflets. . . .[4]

Nor was it any different in Angola:

Punza (guerrilla pseudonym), from northern Angola, by training a male nurse like Machel and others who took a lead in these movements; in 1970 one of the organizers of the medical service of the Angolan national movement:

My father was a *contradado* ["contract worker"] in Cabinda; my mother lived there, too. I went to school at a Catholic primary school up to the fourth grade [i.e., four years of schooling]. That was enough to get *assimilado* status. But I could have bought that anyway. I knew men who'd paid as much as 40,000 escudos to get it. There were Angolans who did that for the sake of their children, who could then get the status easily. How did you buy it? There were Portuguese who came and sat at the entry of the village, and they acted as middlemen. They gave you

[3] Interview with B.D., October 1967; cf. *The Liberation of Guiné*, p. 36.
[4] Ibid., p. 35.

the time and date for the necessary interview [with the administration]. I accepted *assimilado* status, because it was the only way not to be taken for "contract labor. . . ."[5]

One could offer other such memoirs; several appear elsewhere in this book. All of them illustrate the same essential process; all describe the fuel piled up by frustration and repression.

Yet the fuel required a flame to set it burning. This, too, was duly provided by a colonial service and mentality incapable of reacting to the development of African political consciousness except with the kind of precautions recommended by Governor Felgas of the (Angolan) Congo District: with a prolongation of existing policies, and more repression.

Once again there is a striking similarity of events in each of the three chief colonies. In every case the risings of the 1960s were preceded, in what seems to have been a decisively formative way, by a particularly outrageous use of repressive force.

Thus, in Guinea-Bissau:

The breaking point was in August 1959 [when a strike of dockworkers was organized for higher wages by the clandestine PAIGC at the Pidgiguiti docks of Bissau, the colony's capital town on the Rio Grande]. As you know, by Portuguese law unions have no right to strike—completely forbidden. So the situation was entirely new for the Portuguese when they were confronted with a strike. Their reaction was panic. They called the troops, which came down to the docks and started shooting without even asking questions. As a result, about fifty people were killed, and over a hundred injured. Those hundred were taken to a nearby hospital, but they disappeared during the night. So we decided that the whole approach was wrong. Starting any kind of a democratic procedure in the towns, like a strike or boycott, was meaningless. . . . The only thing to do was . . . to get yourself a gun. . . .[6]

[5] Interview with B.D., June 1970.
[6] Gil Fernandes, interview with *Ufahamu*, University of California at Los Angeles, I, 1, 1970.

Meeting in secret a month later, the leaders of the PAIGC, with Amilcar Cabral in the chair, decided for struggle against the Portuguese "by all possible means, including war."[7] The war began three years later; but Pidgiguiti brought its first shots, and the shots were Portuguese.

And in Mozambique? The late 1950s there saw the emergence of new forms of co-operative mutual aid and incipient political protest in various districts, notably Cabo Delgado in the northeast. This brought protests from Portuguese concession companies, who saw "their natives" beginning to produce on their own account, and for markets where they might have some say in selling prices. It also brought the familiar obstruction from the local government. How to deal with these "natives"? Teach them a lesson.

Alberto-Joaquim Chipande, then aged twenty-two, afterward a leader of the Mozambican national movement:

> [Some of our leaders in the co-operative movement at that time] had made contact with the authorities and asked for more liberty and more pay. . . . After a while, when people were giving support to these leaders, the Portuguese sent police through the villages inviting people to a meeting at Mueda [an administrative center of Cabo Delgado District]. Several thousand people came to hear what the Portuguese would say. As it turned out, the administrator [of Mueda] had asked the governor of Delgado District to come from Pôrto Amélia [its capital] and to bring a company of troops. But these troops were hidden when they got to Mueda. We didn't see them at first.
>
> Then the governor invited our leaders into the administrator's office. I was waiting outside. They were in there for four hours. When they came out on the verandah, the governor asked the crowd who wanted to speak. Many wanted to speak and the governor told them all to stand on one side.
>
> Then without another word he ordered the police to bind the hands of those that stood on one side, and the po-

[7] *Liberation of Guiné*, p. 32.

lice began beating them. I was close by. I saw it all. When
the people saw what was happening, they began to demonstrate against the Portuguese, and the Portuguese simply ordered the police trucks to come and collect those
arrested persons. So there were more demonstrations
against this. At that moment the troops were still hidden,
and the people went up close to the police to stop the arrested persons from being taken away. So the governor
called the troops, and when they appeared he told them to
open fire. They killed about 600 people. . . . I myself
escaped because I was close to a graveyard where I could
take cover, and then I ran away.[8]

That was in 1960. Four years later Alberto-Joaquim Chipande led one of the first little guerrilla bands across the Tanzanian frontier into northern Mozambique, there to root the
armed struggle into the loyalty of people around Mueda, and
soon much farther afield. For "after this massacre," commented
the national movement's leader, the late Eduardo Mondlane,
some years later, "things in the north could never return to normal. Throughout the region it had aroused the most bitter hatred
against the Portuguese and showed once and for all that peaceful resistance was futile."[9] Again the first shots were Portuguese.

And so, too, in Angola. The circumstances were different
here, and yet the same.

While police arrests in 1959 were sweeping into prison the
local leaders of the MPLA and their Portuguese sympathizers,
another leader came back from Portugal. A doctor's plate appeared on a small house in Luanda, that of Dr. Agostinho Neto.
Nobody was in any doubt of Dr. Neto's political views: in Lisbon, after all, he had already served two prison sentences for
acting on them. The PIDE continued with its work:

> In 1960 I was arrested in my consulting room at Luanda
> —not at Icolo e Bengo [his birthplace, near Luanda]. I
> was arrested by a young man who was a police director.

[8] Interview with B.D., July 1968.
[9] Mondlane, *The Struggle for Mozambique*, Penguin, London and Baltimore,
1969.

He came into my office and asked for Dr. Neto. "That's me." "Ah, that's you, is it?" I was working at my medical work. It was towards evening, there were many people about. When they saw me getting into the police car they crowded round it, but they didn't rush it. It was my wife who argued with the police, not understanding what had happened.

What they did to me in prison then was not to beat me but to stop me from sleeping for four days and nights. I was there for three months. Then they took me to the Cape Verdes. . . .[10]

Again it was the beginning of the story, not the end. Neto was already an admired man among his own people of the Luanda District, an African who had "conquered the knowledge of the white man's world" but returned to use it for the benefit of Africans. There followed another Pidgiguiti, another Mueda. No eyewitness accounts have survived, or been collected yet, but the bare facts as given from the African side have not been substantially disputed:

After the arrest of Dr. Neto . . . on June 8, 1960, people from Bengo, the birthplace of Dr. Neto, and from the neighboring village of Icolo decided to go to their district office of Catete, a small town about 60 miles from Luanda, and demand the release of Dr. Neto. When the district officer came to know about the decision he called for reinforcements from Luanda and about 200 soldiers with sub-machine guns were sent to Catete. About a week after the arrest men, women and children from those villages, about one thousand people, arrived at Catete in a peaceful demonstration, but soldiers fired on the crowd without any warning and killed thirty people and injured over 200. On the following day these soldiers went to Icolo and Bengo and killed or arrested everyone who was found in the two villages, which were then set on fire. . . .[11]

[10] Interview with B.D., June 1970.

[11] Statement issued in London on behalf of MPLA, based on an Angolan report, Oct. 10, 1960. Such reports took time to make their way abroad. See also Peter Benenson, op. cit., p. 59.

Outside Luanda in the plantation zones, meanwhile, a recession in the demand for export crops, notably coffee, with its corresponding effect on Africans there, was adding its edge of bitterness.[12] The first explosions now quickly followed. They occurred in the cotton-growing plantation area of Malange, on the central plateau.

Much remains obscure about these turbulent months. Early in January 1961, it seems, an African called António Mariano, eponymous leader of a dissident Christian sect called Maria, "embarked on a campaign against European authority and the whole system of enforced cotton growing":

> January was planting time. Instead of sowing this year, however, many burned their seed, heaped their farm tools at roadsides, and, while singing their militant hymns to Lumumba, Pinnock, and Maria, launched a religious crusade for "independence." They destroyed barges at . . . river crossings, barricaded roads, slaughtered livestock, broke into stores and Catholic missions, and chased away Europeans. This was characterised by African nationalists as "pacific protest," since African *catanas* (cutting tools) and *canhangulos* (vintage muzzle-loader hunting guns) were not used to attack persons but only to level property and kill cattle.

> As Maria's War gained momentum and spread from remote border areas, which seem to have enjoyed some weeks of "independence," into the heart of Malange District, the administration sounded the alarm. Portuguese planes and troops were rushed in to firebomb and strafe villages and to crush all opposition. . . . Portuguese authority was restored in the area, though at a cost of hundreds, perhaps thousands, of African lives.[13]

That was in February and March. And this too was not the end, but the beginning.

[12] Cf. Marcum, op. cit., pp. 123–24.
[13] Ibid., pp. 124–57, quoting Protestant missionary and African sources.

PART THREE

GUERRILLA WAR

"As for you: when it gets to the point
That man is the helper of men,
Think back on us
Forbearingly."

Bertolt Brecht

"Hope is the supreme motivating force in Africa, and the MPLA offers oodles [large quantities] of it."

A South African observer

Even before "Maria's War" had reached its climax on the central plateau, or other and greater upheavals began to shake colonial "calm and quiet" among the Kongo farther north, the gathering tensions in the city of Luanda were snapped with shattering effect.

This Luanda explosion was by no means the largest of the risings of 1961. But in certain ways concerning the development of a revolutionary nationalism it was undoubtedly the most important. Its bloody consequences marked a turning point for the mainstream of Angolan political thought and action deriving from the "men of the '90s" and *Mensagem,* and opened a future that could only be one of armed resistance or obliteration. It signaled the beginning of that long process through which, by 1970, the vanguards of national liberation were to acquire political influence and military power.

On February 4, gathering before dawn, a crowd of Africans from Luanda's sand slums attacked the capital's chief prison. It appears that their main objective was the release of political prisoners before the Portuguese could ship these prisoners out of the country or execute them. Armed with clubs and knives, the attackers were beaten back by police with guns. Seven Portuguese are said to have died on that first day, and forty Africans. Next morning, writes Professor Marcum, "armed European civilians leaving funeral services for the seven policemen turned on Afri-

can bystanders, . . . chased them into a sawmill, and shot them
down." Africans launched a second attack on the prison, failing
again; five days later they attacked another prison, with the same
result.

Catastrophe ensued. Covered by the police, the Luanda
whites took their revenge. They went into the sand slums and
began killing Africans. How many they murdered in these February days remains unknown. An eyewitness who left Luanda
on February 6, two days after the initial assault on the São Paulo
prison, told of having counted forty-nine African corpses. *Time*
magazine of February 24 wrote that a Luanda cab driver had
"told reporters that he saw five trucks loaded with corpses driven
out to a mass burial in the bush." Nearly three weeks later the
São Paulo prison, according to the same report, "still 'stank like
a charnel house' even after being cleared of dead bodies," the
police having apparently turned their guns on political prisoners
during or after the attacks. "While tanks and armored cars pa-
trolled the streets at night and Portuguese gunboats and planes
combed the coastline, a doctor said wearily, 'I don't know how
much more of this I can stand. Every night we deal with men
dreadfully wounded and cut up.'" An American missionary said
that he personally knew of nearly three hundred murdered
persons.

Such were the scraps that reached the outside world through
a frantic censorship. They were incomplete but damningly con-
cordant, and everything that has since come to light has confirmed the picture they sketched. Already badly hit by previous
arrests, the budding national movement was savagely crushed.
Only a few militants managed to get away to the Dembos forests,
north of the capital.

All too clearly, these Luanda attacks were made without effective preparation or well-concerted plan. Costly blunder or necessary act of desperation? Is it that every revolutionary upheaval
demands its initiatory victims, its heroes who are lost, without
exacting whom the gods of progress will not agree to break the

spell of defeat? There is little to suggest that anyone had such thoughts in mind. Otherwise it is hard to be sure, impossible to pass judgment. Too many questions press in.

Did the attackers believe they could do their work without guns, or without inviting massive reprisals? Were they moved by more than a desperate courage? Did there exist, as some observers have proposed, a connection in the attackers' minds between an act of violent defiance and the rumored destination at Luanda of the steamship *Santa Maria*, hijacked in the west Atlantic some days previously by anti-Salazarist Portuguese? Was there someone among them who had noted the rare presence of foreign journalists, attracted by the same rumor? If so, did this have an influence?[1] Were the upheavals in Léopoldville thirteen months earlier taken as a model, in the hope that Lisbon could be induced to do the same as Brussels and "decolonize"?

So many of the participants died then and in following weeks that a sure answer may never be given. With Neto in prison on the Cape Verdes, with Da Cruz and Andrade in Conakry, capital of the recently independent Republic of Guinea, far away in western Africa, and with other leaders in Angolan prisons, the nationalists left in Luanda acted with little or no political experience to guide them. They were also driven on by bitterness. "For some time now," noted a statement issued from Conakry on February 5 by Da Cruz, Andrade, and others of the MPLA's "steering committee" there, "the population of Luanda, outraged by the repressive methods of the Portuguese Gestapo, the PIDE, had planned to liberate MPLA leaders and other nationalists from the capital's prisons. This police stops short at no means of extermination, from the poisoning of food given to prisoners to the summary execution of twenty-five of them in November 1960," three months earlier.

[1] "Foreign correspondents had gone to Angola when it was tipped that the hijacked liner *Santa Maria* might be making for Luanda. Most were recalled about Feb. 1 or 2, when that story collapsed. But about half-a-dozen remained" —until expelled on Feb. 10—"out of curiosity after a lot of bar-room talk around town that 'something was going to happen' at the week-end."—Private communication from Mr. Daniel McGeachie of the London *Daily Express*, who was among them.

The exiles of the MPLA could do little but stand by helplessly
while the disaster took its course. There is not much doubt that
in previous months they had been urged to embark on violent
action, notably by some of the leaders of the Algerian Front de
Libération Nationale (FLN), who had embraced the Angolan
cause and who, arguing from their own experience in Algeria,
believed that it was necessary for Angolans "only to begin," and
"the rest will follow." But the MPLA exiles had dissented. They
counted much on Algerian support and were certainly in favor
of revolt, but they believed the time was premature. Throughout
1960 they replied: Not now; later; we need more time.

So it came about that crucial Algerian backing, whether
through the influence of Frantz Fanon or others, had swung
away from the MPLA at this time in favor of another and very
different Angolan movement, the UPA (União das Populações
de Angola), led by Roberto Holden from headquarters in the
Congo. As Fanon is said to have explained at this time: "I know
Holden is inferior to the MPLA men. But Holden is ready to begin, and they are not. And I am convinced that what is necessary
is to begin, and that an Angolan revolutionary movement will
be forged in the ensuing struggle." It was the Guevarist line
applied to Africa, and it proved terribly mistaken.

For Holden and the UPA did begin, duly backed by the Algerians. And the consequences were to be many times more disastrous than the rising in Luanda.

2   THE RISING IN THE NORTH

On March 15, five and a half weeks after the first attack on the
São Paulo prison, and with "Maria's War" practically over,
northern Angola became the scene of a major insurrection by
large numbers of Kongo farmers joined by local plantation "contract workers" whose homes were in other districts. These men
were poorly armed, or barely armed at all, yet such was their
sudden fury that they rapidly seized control of large areas around
the coffee-growing center of Carmona. They overwhelmed
European farms, trading settlements, police posts. They blocked
access by felling trees across roads, breaking bridges, sinking ferries. Thousands were engaged. For a while, Portuguese authority
more or less disappeared.

But these rebels, unlike those of "Maria's War" and the Luanda attacks, also attacked civilians, murdering and sometimes
mutilating European men, women, and children to a total never
securely known, but probably around the three hundred mark.
What was more, they embarked with similar barbarity on civil
war. They hit with the same savagery at *assimilados,* whether
black or mulatto, evidently regarding these as mere agents of the
Portuguese. Yet of long-term military and political objectives
they appear to have had none, or none that was of practical
effect.

Here is the testimony of Punza, a black *assimilado* who was
there at the time.

When it all began, in 1961, I was working at São Salvador [the principal Kongo administrative center, not far from the Congo frontier] as a male nurse in a government hospital. After the Luanda rising of February 4, I was watched by the Portuguese. But I was able to contact several survivors of the February 4 affair who were escaping to the Congo by way of São Salvador. What they told me was that things were getting constantly worse for all of us.

So I set about organizing a small group for escape into the Congo. When we were still forty kilometers from the frontier, the UPA were sowing panic, killing *assimilados,* whites, Catholics in the *senzalas* who were their own people. It seemed to me a total confusion. At first I thought that all this was spontaneous. But then I noticed that the UPA leaders came and gave orders to do those very things.

If I saved my own life it was only because I found people who disagreed with those orders, and who hid me. Then we found a way for our group of twenty to continue into the Congo. I joined the MPLA there—I'd already had some contact with the MPLA. This was by way of MPLA men who had come into Angola from the Congo in 1959; I remember that a mulatto also came with leaflets in 1960.[1]

In all this killing and confusion, not all MPLA militants made for the Congo. Others, including some who had got away from Luanda to the Dembos forests, continued to attack the Portuguese administration. They met with reprisals even before the rising generalized in the north.

Luisa Caetano, aged about thirty-five, Kimbundu origin, leader of Angolan Women's Organization of MPLA in eastern liberated districts in 1970, when her husband, whom she had not seen for several years, was commander of MPLA units in Cuanza Norte District (northwest):

I have been in the struggle since the beginning, since 1961. I am from Dembos. My father was killed in 1961 by

[1] Interview with B.D., June 1970.

the Portuguese because he was a Protestant pastor. Before
killing him, they tortured him by cutting off his limbs.
That was started by the traders (*os comerciantes*) on
March 13 [i.e., two days before the Kongo rising in the
north].

After that, they tortured him for two months till he was
dead. All that time the Portuguese gave out that he was all
right, he was working; but the cook of the administration
came and told us about the tortures. In that time, too, they
bombed our village, including our house. I was in the bush
of Dembos, after that, for four years; then I got away and
went to Kinshasa [Congo]. You need courage to win and
take revenge.[2]

In those early months of 1961, north of Luanda, few seemed
to have any clear understanding of the situation now taking
shape. Efforts at making common cause with the UPA failed, but
resistance continued.

Kubindama, another black *assimilado* who was there at the
time, a male nurse like Punza; born in 1932, afterward a guerrilla fighter and medical leader in Cabinda and then in the eastern districts:

On February 4 I was in Nambuangongo [a good way
south of São Salvador]. That was when the comrades in
Luanda attacked the prison. In Nambuangongo it broke
out a little later: in March, but before March 15 [date of
the UPA rising].

We had a few personal weapons, some shotguns, tools
like *ketamas* [hoes], and we took arms from the Portuguese. Our commander was Benedicto. We attacked the
Portuguese who were there on the territory of Nambuangongo. For six months we practically drove them out of
there. We killed no women or children or unarmed civilians. But the UPA had no clear program. They didn't act
as a political party. They killed European civilians at
Holden's orders.

[2] Interview with B.D., May 1970.

The Portuguese came in six months later. Before that,
just before that, the UPA tried to attack us, because we
were against the UPA policy of hunting down Europeans,
and hunting down Africans too. They were in the zone of
São Salvador and we were in the zone of Nambuangongo.
When we tried to get to Congo/Kinshasa to make contact
with our leaders, they began to attack us. . . .

The Portuguese army came from two directions, beginning with bombardment. At first our positions held, while
the Portuguese were only in their barracks and garrisons.
But the UPA attacked us, and our strength fell, and the
Portuguese retook the territory we had liberated.[3]

Systematic military operations against these rebels in the
north, whether UPA or MPLA, did not in fact begin till May.
Though the army's over-all white strength at the time was about
two thousand metropolitan troops and rather more conscripted
settlers, its main body consisted of its African troops; these were
the modern descendants of the traditional *guerra preta*, "the
black army" of the past. It seems that there was hesitation in
relying upon them now. Reinforcements were called from Portugal. These began to land at Luanda, with two initial battalions, on May 1.[4]

Helped by fragmentation and napalm bombing from such
aircraft as the air force had then acquired from its allies in the
North Atlantic Treaty Organization,[5] these battalions set out
for the north on May 13. They were well if ruthlessly commanded, and quickly got the upper hand of guerrilla bands
which lacked arms, experience, and unity. By the middle of July,
according to the well-informed account of Hélio Felgas, "the
decline of the terrorist movement was clear, with an evident dis-

[3] Interview with B.D., June 1970.
[4] The best military account from the Portuguese side is that of the ex-
governor of (Angolan) Congo, Hélio Felgas, in *Guerra em Angola*, Lisbon,
1962.
[5] Cf., e.g., Gavin Young in *The Observer*, London, August 20, 1961, for
photographic and other evidence of bombs of U.S. manufacture; missionary
sources (British Baptist Society, London); and, *in extenso, Portugal and NATO*,
Dutch Angola Committee, Amsterdam, 1969.

organization of their groups of bandits." Yet it was only in September that "we completed the reoccupation of all posts and population centers in northern Angola, except for Caiongo," reoccupied on October 3, more than six months after the northern risings had begun.

With that, the northern revolt had manifestly failed, and losses on the African side were now seen to be appalling. Throwing off all restraint after the UPA massacre of European civilians, the settler militias and their army protectors replied with a counter massacre infinitely larger. In these months they went far to eliminate the whole *assimilado* community, not only in the north but in other regions, too.

Small pockets of guerrilla resistance continued to hold out in the forests of Dembos and other northern areas. But they held out in a wilderness that widened as village people fled in multitudes across the frontier to safety among their fellow Kongo in the Congo/Kinshasa Republic. By the middle of June, more than eighty thousand rural people were reported to have fled in this way, escaping from Portuguese reprisals, against which the guerrillas were quite unable to protect them.[6] The disaster seemed complete.

Yet the ruin in the north was only a small part of the picture. The Portuguese massacre of Angolans, whether black or mulatto, continued well into June, but not only in the north. There came a bloodthirsty hunt for every African with any kind of education, however minimal: a "poor white" onslaught on black competitors that was eagerly seconded by the army and political police. "Three weeks after the revolt [of March 15]," wrote a British missionary, "I was myself the confidant of those who were witnesses to the nightly murder of innocent Africans in the outer suburbs" of Luanda. "At that time there was no fighting

[6] British Baptist missionary sources, *The Guardian*, London, June 22, 1961. Several Portuguese who deserted from the colonial army for patriotic reasons have provided eyewitness testimony. For an example see Mário Moutinho de Pádua, *Guerra em Angola: Diário de um Médico em Campanha*, Editora Brasilense, São Paulo, 1963, an account that describes army atrocities—shooting of women and children, decapitation of prisoners, etc.—in early and middle 1961.

within a hundred miles of Luanda, yet wanton killing went on in this way, and even in broad daylight. The educated were again the chief object of attack. . . ."[7]

The same missionary, a veteran in Angola and afterward secretary of the British Baptist Missionary Society, recalled that he "had opportunities of interviewing high officials of the State and they were fully cognizant of what was taking place. It was clear however that they were not prepared to take the risk of protecting Luanda Africans lest they should provoke the antagonism of the white community. If this were not enough, the white terror spread to the south, to the Benguela plateau," where no risings had occurred or, so far as is known, were even threatened.

Foreign journalists told the same grim tale. One of them was Richard Beeston, a special correspondent of the generally pro-Salazarist London *Daily Telegraph:* "A widespread persecution of educated and semi-educated Africans," he reported on July 25, "has been ruthlessly carried out since the uprising in March. . . ." A little earlier, on the twentieth, a special correspondent of the *Sunday Telegraph* reported from Luanda, ". . . the reign of terror and lynching of Africans has at last been stopped—not by public opinion, but by the fear of the authorities that the white militia was getting out of control. It has been followed instead by a series of savage 'precautions' extending to the hitherto peaceful south. Wave after wave of Africans have been arrested, 1500 of them in the Lobito area alone. The local prison holds only 100 and the total disappearance of the arrested Africans has given rise to the most sinister fears."

By the middle of the year the British Baptist Missionary Society concluded that as many as twenty thousand Africans had been killed. Perhaps the true figure was even larger. Another British correspondent, this time of the *Daily Mirror,* reported an army officer's comments to him on May 2: "I estimate that we've killed 30,000 of these animals. . . . There are probably another 100,000 working with the terrorists. We intend killing

---

[7] Clifford Parsons, "The Makings of a Revolt," in *Angola: A Symposium,* Oxford, 1962, p. 72, and for other missionary evidence to the same effect.

them when the dry season starts, in about six weeks' time."
Unlikely views for an army officer? On May 3 the *Daily Telegraph* reported from Lisbon that the Portuguese Defense Minister had told troops leaving for Angola they were "not going
to fight against human beings but against savages and wild
beasts," while Richard Beeston was likewise told "we shall fire
the grass and hunt them like game." The *Daily Mirror*'s correspondent described the behavior of Luanda whites. He saw an
African thrown from the roof of a six-story building, while
"just around the corner another African was torn to pieces by
a mob—a white mob."

DOCUMENTARY TWO

Refugees from Portuguese repression flooded over the Angolan frontier into the western Congo (Zaïre) Republic. British Baptist missionaries in the western Congo established relief centers so as to help these refugees, and began recording brief biographies of those who came for relief. Their records tell a long-continuing tale of horror in many hundreds of such biographies, as the following handful of examples will show:

[*In September 1962*] *the latest Red Cross figures report 215,000 Angolan refugees in the Congo. Many others crossing from Angola have not registered* [*for relief*] *as there has been no official food distribution since January* [*1962*]. *In June* [*1962*] *alone at least 20,000 refugees came over.*

Statement by British Baptist Missionary Society, London, based on reports from the western Congo, Sept. 15, 1962.

Margaret took these notes from a man who came here when I was in Léopoldville. Manuel Agosto: Songo, Uige [*northern Angola*]: (*over 200 started on July 17th but only 50 got across the frontier. Because of the difficulties in the way some decided to find a hiding place while they debated turning back. This was on August 19th. . . . On the 15th July, one woman went early to the water—with two others—and was shot dead and her body mutilated. Her name was Joana Eduardo. They were attacked on the way;*

sometimes the planes flying as late as ten o'clock. There were mines laid in the paths.

Dr. David Grenfell, British Baptist
Missionary Society, Moerbeke, Congo/
Kinshasa, Sept. 1962.

Two men, António Santos, 21, of Zulo Mongo, Songo, and Miguel José, 23, of the same town, came to the house and told me the following story. They arrived at the frontier on the 25th with a group of 22 people. They had been a month on the way, travelling only at night. They were the only people to arrive out of a group of nearly 3,000 that set out from Songo. In spite of travelling only at night, they had been spotted early on the journey, and attacked many times. The last part of the journey was across the Cuimba-Maquele road. They had hid throughout the day about an hour's walk from the road—for all the bush grass had been burnt for a long distance on each side of the road—and about four in the afternoon they sent scouts ahead to see if the road was clear. . . . As they reached the road, they found they had walked into an ambush, and Portuguese soldiers opened fire with machine guns, and even hand grenades. Everyone scattered, most of the people turning back. Just how many have been killed, or injured, is not known. . . .

I asked them why they had come just now. They replied that it was because of the continual bombing by planes of their hiding places, so that they had to move every day to a new hiding place. They said one day they lost five people killed, another two killed; and as the problem of food was becoming increasingly difficult—the gardens were burnt by "gasoline" bombs—they decided to try to get to Congo.

Ibid.

André Yamba, of Gondi, Lucunga, came out with 20 others. They left behind a man and a woman, to care for those who could not make the journey because of injuries. One woman had a broken arm and leg. A second woman had a broken leg, and has lost an ear. The third was a

*man with a broken leg. He described bombs of three types:
those that made a large hole, those that threw iron balls
about, and those that had petrol in them. . . .*

Ibid.

*Some reports recorded today (about refugees arriving
in the western Congo). Pedro Augusto, 40 yrs. of Pamba,
Bembe, with his wife, Graça Sukama. They had no children, but with them were both their mothers and Graça's
grandmother. All were widows. The husbands of the grandmother and Pedro's mother had both died from illness
while hiding in the forest. Graça's mother, Maria Polina,
became a widow in June 1963 when the hiding place was
attacked by ground forces and her husband was caught
and killed along with three others. They had been killed
with knives. . . .*

Ibid., March 22, 1964.

*Lusadiso Ngomba, 33 yrs. of Buzu, Nkanda Hills. Her
husband and six others were killed during a raid on their
hiding place (amongst them were four young children,
killed). The bodies were thrown into the Lufundi river. It
was seen by Pedro Luvakala, who was hiding up to his
neck in the water. Maria Mimosa, 42 yrs., widow, with
four children, of Baka, Lucunga. Their hiding place was
attacked, and her husband and three others were killed
"by knives." The son, Pedro Fernando, saw the bodies,
but they were afraid to bury them because of booby traps
fixed to the body, which explode when they come to bury
the bodies. Others said the same thing. I asked the
teacher of Mula Matumbi, Manuel Kimbangala, if this was
true, and he said, yes, it was quite true.*

Ibid.

*Dias Henrique, 16 yrs., with two children of Kimaria,
Bembe. His wife, parents, brothers and the rest of his
children were caught in 1962 when a raid was made on their
hiding places. No news of them since.*

Barreiro, 32 yrs., of Kindiati, Bembe. His wife and child were killed in an air raid in December 1963.

Isabel Massamba, 36 yrs. with five children, of Sangui, Bembe. Husband was caught when their hiding place was raided in April, 1963, and his head was cut off. She claims the body was recovered and buried, and that she herself was there.

Doneta, 16 yrs., and Josefina, 5 yrs., of Kumusungu, Songo. Mother died in hiding. Father afraid to come out.

Ibid., Kibentele, Congo/Kinshasa,
April 3, 1964.

A large group of Kizele people decided to leave and began the trip on March 3rd. On the 5th, the hiding place was attacked, so many who had decided to stay now changed their minds. One such was Maria Jovita, 34 yrs., five children, whose husband, João Francisco, 38 yrs., was killed in the raid. He was shot while running away. Another man, Pedro Biambia, 18 yrs., was also killed. I asked if they had buried the body of João and they said they had not done so because upon examination they saw that a wire had been fixed to the corpse.

Luiza Alberto, 33 yrs., two children, of Kimbunba Loa, Songo. Husband caught and killed in August 1963. His head was cut off. Two others killed at the same time. The women saw the bodies. She added that the other two had had their ears cut off.

Ibid., April 10, 1964.

André Pululu, 45 yrs., of Sima Congo (Bula Matumbi) Damba. Their hiding place was attacked by parachutists, dropped from several planes, on January 31st, 1964. His wife and four children were killed in the attack. Seven other people were killed. Several were injured but they managed to get away. There were no prisoners taken.

Garcia Mário, 23 yrs., of Vola, with wife. Had two children. One died in the forest, and the other was caught by the Portuguese in a raid of February 3rd, 1964.

João de Sousa, 32 yrs., of Vola. Wife was shot and killed while running away from an attack on the hiding place on September 2nd, 1963. He found the body three days later.

Ibid., April 24, 1964.

Manuel Figuereida, 36 yrs., of Pamba, Bembe, with wife, four children, and mother and four other children in his care. He was very bitter against the Portuguese. On April 11th, 1963 there was a surprise attack on the hiding place. His father was caught and killed by bayonet wounds. They found the body two days later. Two children were missing, believed taken away, but near to the body of his father they found the body of a two-year-old child hanging in a tree.

Samuel Kinkani, 63 yrs. with wife and five children, of Bula Matumbi, Damba. This man is a deacon of our Quibocolo Church. They left the hiding place on March 17th, with a party of ninety-one. They came along the Lufundi valley. At one place the track passes through a gorge, with high rocks on either side. The Portuguese were on the high rocks, but the people were unaware of this. The soldiers opened fire, most tried to escape by returning the way they had come. Eleven were killed, including four women and two children.

Manuel Francisco, 35 yrs., with four children, of Kinsiku, Nambuangongo. Soon after they crossed the Ambriz river, they encountered a patrol. They escaped into the long grass, but two men and two women were killed. Afterwards they returned to get their possessions which they had dropped in the rush to escape. They did not bury the bodies, because one was seen to be wired, and they suspected a bomb.

Ibid., May 1, 1964.

Maria Lo, 35 yrs., of Mpambu Lando, Bembe. Husband killed by bomb on hiding place. Her two children were injured. One was carried out on someone's back, and the other child had to walk.

*André Matos, 25 yrs., of the same town. He was in the
Kuzi ambush. He lost two children when bomb fell on
hiding place. His uncle was wounded in the leg in the Kuzi
ambush. His father was wounded in both legs.*

Ibid., August 24, 1964.

What had set this northern rebellion, this Kongo rising of the
UPA, on its catastrophic course? Who were the men behind it
and what were their plans? Why had these Kongo insurgents in
Angola killed white civilians and *assimilados* who were "their
own people"? Where lay the origins of their hostility to the
MPLA and its fighters during those desperate weeks when unity
among Angolans was so greatly needed?

Those who wish for the detailed evidence, so far as it was
available in 1969, should turn to Professor Marcum's careful
survey. Here I want to consider the substance of the answers
that emerge. This much is essential to any understanding of what
happened later, as well as of what happened then.

A first point is that it would be misleading to draw any clear
line of initial difference between the participants in MPLA-led
risings in the north—for example, in the Nambuangongo area—
and those who were to be led by the UPA. The vast majority
would not have recognized it before the risings began, or even,
here and there, for a little while afterward. If thousands were
drawn in, behind one leadership or another, this was for reasons
basically the same: they wished to raise a counterviolence against
the violence of the regime. Much in the local history of the 1950s
suggests that a unified leadership could have bridged the cultural
and social conflicts that became open and acute only in 1961.
It was precisely this unified leadership that was lacking.

Why was it lacking? There are various answers. The men of
the mainstream, the Luanda nationalists and their sympathizers
elsewhere, had generally an "urban and *assimilado*" coloring;
those who led the March 15 rising of the Kongo, on the other
hand, were strongly within the emotional and intellectual frame-

work of traditional Kongo society. And there were other developments which had helped to accentuate this difference.

In July 1949 a man called Simão Toco, of Zombo origin, the Zombo being a group in the far north related to the São Salvador Kongo, had declared the arrival of a new divine dispensation. Like others shortly before him, like Dona Beatrice long before, Toco preached the imminent coming of decisive godly aid for the Africans. "All whites would become black and all Tocoistas would become white, foreign rule would end, exploitation of the African would cease, and the African would finally rule his own land."[1]

It was substantially the promise of many prophets of the colonial period. Like Simon Kimbangui, who had founded a "New Jerusalem" in the western Belgian Congo in 1921 with a success that has echoed down the decades,[2] Toco was arrested with little delay by the authorities, who saw his teachings as a certain source of trouble for themselves. The authorities were not against God as such. But they were sure that God was white and that only white men could be His prophets.

These authorities were Belgian, not Portuguese. Toco's Christian education had taken place at a Baptist school in the western Belgian Congo. But Toco himself was from northern Angola. Considering him a "foreign native," in the curious colonial jargon of those times, they handed him over to the Portuguese, together with a number of his disciples. The Portuguese gratefully sent Toco to perpetual confinement far in the south of Angola, but put his disciples to work on the roads of the north, except for the literate few among them; these they dispatched to Luanda, where they were allowed to take jobs but were locked up every night.

Literate or not, Toco's disciples duly contrived to escape confinement and contract labor, and began to spread their hopes and beliefs throughout the Angolan north. This went on during

[1] Marcum, op. cit., p. 81, quoting Alfredo Margarida, "L'Église Toco et le Mouvement de Libération de l'Angola," *Le Mois en Afrique,* May 1966.
[2] Cf. P. Raymaekers, "L'Église de Jésus-Christ sur la terre par le prophète Simon Kimbangui . . . ," in *Zaïre,* xiii, 7, 1959. I have discussed this subject at some length in *The African Genius,* espec. ch. 29.

the 1950s, weaving a new messianic strand into the growing fabric of protest among Kongo and related groups. Meanwhile other Tocoistas in the slums of Léopoldville (Belgian Congo) formed a mutual-aid society for Zombo people in 1956. With this, messianic ideas became more directly political ideas. There emerged a "protoparty" called Aliazo (Alliance of the Zombo People). Later again, with the slogans of nationalism resounding in everybody's ears, Aliazo merged into a political organization called the PDA (Partido Democrático de Angola).

At the same time, a far more important trend of protest had crystallized among the Angolan Kongo of the São Salvador region. This was even more traditional in form. In 1955 the then reigning king, the *ntotela* Dom Pedro VII, joined his ancestors. Like other kings before him, Pedro had disliked the things the Portuguese had obliged him to do, such as helping to collect forced workers and taxes; but he had failed to turn his dislike into effective action. He was, moreover, a Catholic. When he died, there were calls for a less dependent man. Leading Kongo kingmakers, above all Barros Necaca and Eduardo Pinnock, urged the candidature of the nephew of Dom Manuel Kiditu, a former king (reigned 1912–15). This candidate, they argued, would press more boldly for reforms. And their group happened to be Protestant.

The last thing the Portuguese desired was a more troublesome king, and they had no thought of introducing reforms. As Protestants, moreover, the opposition candidate and his supporters were all regarded as anti-Portuguese. An alarmed Catholic hierarchy and administration reacted sharply. They forced through the election of their own candidate, Dom António José da Gama, who was duly enthroned in August 1955.

Helped now by Necaca's nephew, Roberto Holden, Necaca and Pinnock looked around from their base in the Belgian Congo for international help toward the reforms they had in mind. As their ideas unfolded, they began to think in terms of a sovereign restoration of the old Kongo kingdom. In 1956 they wrote to a senior U. S. State Department official, then visiting Léopoldville, and told him, ". . . historically and legally the Portuguese

Kongo constituted a territory separate from Angola, to which it had been unjustly joined in 1884"—at the time of the Berlin "scramble" congress. To them, "Angola was the Portuguese colony to the south" of the old Kongo kingdom—"the conquered realm of the *ngola*," the Ndongo kingdom of the Kimbundu people around Luanda. "In their view the Kongo, unlike Angola, had never really been conquered. . . ."[3]

Washing their hands of the rest of the population under Portuguese rule, they added a separatist aim to their calls for reform. In June 1956 they duly addressed the UN Secretary-General with a plea for change in the name of the people of "the Kongo, . . . an ex-independent territory with no treaty with Portugal," and in the following month they formed a political organization, UPNA (Union of the Peoples of Angola) so as to further their separatist aim. They had put into modern guise the ideas of Prince Nicolas of Kongo nearly a hundred years earlier.

They stayed on this line of thought for a while, but found it increasingly weak as a means of gathering foreign support. In an Africa vowed to the gaining of political independence within colonial frontiers, their Kongo monarchism seemed absurdly provincial. In 1958 an unofficial U.S. adviser argued that it might be "difficult to obtain external support" for a policy whose main plank was the resurrection of a sovereign Kongo kingdom.[4] Necaca now agreed that any such plan had better be postponed until "later on when better circumstances allow it." Meanwhile it would be more useful to talk in terms of an all-Angolan nationalism. UPNA's regionally restrictive name was accordingly changed to UPNA (Union of the Peoples of Angola).

At this point Roberto Holden took the lead. Born in northern Angola in 1923, Holden, at the age of two, had been taken to the Congo, where he had remained save for a single short visit in his boyhood, a year's stay at São Salvador in 1941, a three-week visit in 1951, and another ten-day visit in 1955–56. Literate and ambitious, Holden soon became UPA's effective leader.

3 Marcum, op. cit., p. 62.
4 Ibid., p. 64.

Boldly smuggling himself to Ghana in 1958, he was able to attend an All-African Peoples' Congress designed to help the cause of decolonization. There they told him that any idea of concentrating on a restoration of the Kongo kingdom was a "tribal anachronism." Adjusting rapidly to new ideas, as was noticed by those who were there at the time (including the present writer), Holden responded with a manifesto calling for the liberation of all Angola. Yet the UPA remained in all substance what it had been before, a pressure group designed to induce the Portuguese to admit reforms, and capable of operating only within the range of Kongo cultural loyalties.

Out of this sprang a profound hostility to the MPLA afterward deepened by other factors, some of them being linked to Holden's position in the Congo. Holden and his group were men of less education than the leaders of the MPLA. Aside from this, there is much evidence that Holden's non-Angolan contacts, whether official Congolese or official American (and the two were hard to separate, as indeed they have remained), were able to win him for a Cold War position vis-à-vis the MPLA. It was not long before he was talking of the MPLA as the long arm of Russian communism; and the language grew sharper, with corresponding action, as Holden's own position in Kinshasa became increasingly elitist, prosperous, and right-wing under the reign of his like-minded friend President Mobutu.

Separatist but reformist, loyal to the conservative traditions of the old Kongo hierarchy, standing aside from any radical stream of thought, the leaders of the UPA might well have continued as a mere pressure group like others of their kind with bases in the Congo, had it not been for the drive and impulse of the times. As it was, Holden at least seems to have come quickly to a realization that the UPA must act in new and startling ways or else lose ground to others, and above all to the MPLA. Through 1960, accordingly, he set about preparing the ground for a rising, using for this purpose a number of young Kongo who went into northern Angola from the Congo and built up there a clandestine network of contacts.[5]

[5] Ibid., p. 141.

Traveling meanwhile in foreign lands on a passport of the
Republic of Guinea, Holden received some aid from Ghana and
more from Algerian FLN leaders in Tunis; among these, Fanon
became his mentor. Then in midstream of his own intellectual
development, Fanon was still convinced of the supreme virtue
of violent action for its own sake. The MPLA rejected his advice;
Holden accepted it. Some of his young men were given a short
course of military training by the FLN, and arms of FLN prov-
enance were channeled down to them by way of various contacts, including, it appears, the Moroccan representative on the
UN mission then established at Léopoldville.

Meanwhile, again, the Algerians had pressed for the Angolan
unity that Fanon and his FLN colleagues also thought necessary. But unity was by no means welcome to Holden, though
for reasons he did not explain in Tunis. Even so, Fanon pushed
him to the conference table. On January 31, 1960, Holden
signed a joint "declaration of compromise" with four representatives of FRAIN, a newly formed "revolutionary front." These
four were Amilcar Cabral for the PAIGC (Guinea-Bissau),
signing under his pseudonym of Djassi; and Hugo Menezes,
Lucio Lara, and Viriato da Cruz for the MPLA. The Mozambicans of FRELIMO had yet to emerge on the scene.

In this declaration Roberto Holden (signing as José Guil-
mor), committed himself with the others to an agreement that:

> (a) our organizations have decided on joint action in the
> struggle against Portuguese colonialism, a decision we be-
> lieve must be carried out as a patriotic duty;

> (b) the individuality, doctrine, and independence of each
> of our organizations can be retained within this joint action;

> (c) there must be established as rapidly as possible a con-
> crete program of action for 1960 such as can lead our peo-
> ple to independence within the shortest possible time.[6]

But Holden reneged on this agreement, just as he later eluded
many other attempts at winning common action and substantial

[6] My trans. from photostat in my possession.

unity. He continued with his secret plans for the Kongo areas of the north in total absence of co-ordination with anything that others might attempt elsewhere. When Luanda exploded on February 4, he was already well advanced with these plans. It appears that the Luanda eruption, deeply involved as it was with other nationalists, especially of the MPLA, caused him to hasten matters. The pressure now was for a Kongo rising no matter what might follow.

On about February 28, Holden sent several of his young men across the Congo frontier into Angola to launch a rising on March 15.[7] There seems no doubt about this, and at least one non-UPA Angolan then in North Africa was told on March 14, by an Algerian contact, that the war would begin "tomorrow."

It was not, accordingly, a spontaneous outburst, as many thought at the time, including some, like Punza, who were there on the spot. How far spontaneity played a contributing part is another matter: what appears certain is that the mainspring of the rising was Holden's work.

What other instructions did these young men have? On their own evidence, given later, they were to lead the burning down of bridges, crops, and houses, the breaking of Portuguese lines of communication, attacks on airfields. And then? Thousands answered their call without, it seems, any least idea of what should happen next, or of co-ordination for warlike purposes, or of consistent effort to build guerrilla bases for a war that could not possibly be short. The whole affair was conducted in a nightmare of confusion, messianic dreams, bloodshot revenge.

Even so, who gave the orders to kill European civilians and educated Africans? Were there any such orders? In subsequent apologia, Holden presented these wanton and disastrous killings as a "crime" for which he and the UPA were not to blame: the killings were a regrettable "expression of desperation against Portuguese terrorism." Some other reports also claimed that the killings were begun spontaneously by plantation workers. Others again have affirmed that Holden's men brought and gave the orders to kill civilians, white and black, and those who say this

[7] Marcum, loc. cit.

include eyewitnesses such as Punza who narrowly escaped with their lives from UPA rebels. They may of course be making an ex post facto case against Holden. The fact remains that no other nationalist grouping, whether in Luanda or anywhere else, indulged in any such civilian killings, nor have they done so since.

The very least that can be said is that Holden and his agents embarked upon an enterprise they had no understanding of how to conduct. And this, probably, is a more than generous judgment, especially in the light of what happened next.

What happened next, for those who tried to build toward a national movement, was a period of misery and mayhem that practically destroyed their every hope. Its backcloth and scene of action was the western region of the ex-Belgian Congo during a second year of independence no less rife than its first with the murder of men and political reputations. At the center of the scene was the lugubrious city of Léopoldville, afterward renamed Kinshasa, where a sordid battle for power continued its sinister and disgraceful course. If much of the complex detail has little relevance, something needs to be said about the general picture.

The Congo's sudden independence of 1960 had thrust up mushroom parties and a crop of eager politicians. Among these, only Patrice Lumumba and his Mouvement National Congolais promised at least the basis for a stable national movement in much of the country. Overthrown by rivals with the backing of foreign interests fearful of any "radicalization"—though a radical new beginning could alone have saved the Congo from the wretchedness that followed—Lumumba was seized and delivered to secessionist enemies in Katanga, who murdered him. Out of this, in August 1961, there emerged a "government of national union" under a Léopoldville politico named Cyrille Adoula. Adoula's government was neither national nor a union, but it had the local power in Léopoldville and received decisive foreign backing, notably from the United States and Belgium.

In this atmosphere of international intrigue and local machi-
nation, the survivors of Angola's own disaster gathered in ones
and twos during the late months of 1961. Some came from
Luanda and the Dembos forests, São Salvador and elsewhere,
slipping north across the frontier. Others came from North
Africa and Europe. Andrade and Da Cruz closed their office in
Conakry and moved to Léopoldville. They found a very hostile
atmosphere, and almost from the first were harried and beset
as dangerous radicals and troublemakers. If they had any Congolese sympathizers, these were chiefly among the followers of
the murdered Lumumba and his still active successor, Antoine
Gizenga, who was duly arrested by Adoula in January 1962.

But for Holden and the UPA leaders, by the same token, the
atmosphere was warm and favorable. Holden and his family
and friends had long been viewed as "good Kongo nationalists"
who could fit smoothly into the Léopoldville scene. They were
disliked by local Kongo rivals, but soon found powerful friends
in the Adoula grouping and especially in one of its military
men, General Joseph Mobutu. Gradually, their star prevailed.

At first, however, the two leaderships lived uneasily side by
side. Each had some fighting bands left inside Angola, though at
this stage the UPA's were larger, since they could call on Kongo
loyalties across the frontier. Each tried, if with varying degrees
of determination, to reinforce these embattled little units beyond
the border. Each prepared to send reinforcements.

This apparent tolerance did not last for long. Just as the
Adoula-Mobutu faction moved in to smash its rivals, so now did
Holden do the same. On November 23, 1961, the MPLA leadership revealed a somber tragedy. They described the murder by
UPA fighters in northern Angola of an MPLA detachment of
twenty-one fighters led by Tomás Ferreira, who were marching
to the aid of their comrades farther south. This, they affirmed,
had occurred a month earlier. "Through insidious traps, taking
advantage of the brotherly trust of our guerrilla fighters in the
militants of other Angolan political organizations," armed
groups of the UPA had seized Ferreira and his men, and forthwith murdered them.

Strong words; but not, it soon appeared, beyond the mark. At first the UPA leaders denied all truth in the accusation, notably in a communiqué issued in Léopoldville over the names of Rosário Neto, the UPA vice-president, and Marcos Kassanga, the UPA chief of staff. But the scandal had only just begun. Four months later, on March 3, the same Kassanga called a press conference in Léopoldville and declared that the UPA had been responsible for the massacre of Ferreira's column, as well as for other crimes of the same kind:

> Some days after the beginning of the Angolan people's revolution against Portuguese domination and slave exploitation, it was turned into a carnage fomented by the leadership of that party whose chief is Roberto Holden. . . . In all its aspects the armed struggle unleashed in the north of Angola is a real fratricidal struggle. A figure approaching 8,000 Angolans were savagely massacred by tribalist elements of UPA. . . . This inhuman massacre effected by Angolans against Angolans is born of a blind tribalism which presents itself in four aspects: religious, linguistic, ethnic, and ideological. . . .

> [Among those thus killed] we must distinguish the case of Commander Tomás Ferreira and his squad of 21 men sent into the interior by the MPLA . . . ; [they] were captured by UPA militants and barbarously hanged.

> Now there is the sad death of Commander Baptista, Chief of Military Operations in the interior of Angola, a member of the UPA general staff. His death by treachery was motivated by his disagreement with the extermination of Angolans by Angolans, by his not speaking Kikongo, by his not being a native of São Salvador, and by his not being a Protestant. . . .

Holden's office hotly denied all this. Yet it was noted that Kassanga, Holden's first chief of staff, was a "Ganguela," from the east, and that Baptista, Holden's first commander in the field after the early months were over, was a Cuanhama, from the south. And two years later, by then much deeper into his obsessive separatism, Holden himself confirmed that "he had in fact given orders to intercept and annihilate MPLA columns that were trying to infiltrate into Angola."[1]

In this way there was set a pattern which continued. Tomás Ferreira and his companions were not by any means the last MPLA militants to die in this way; prominent among the others could be Déolinda de Almeida. The disaster of 1961 would be still further deepened.

The MPLA survived, and with it the chance of building toward a national movement. But the survival was certainly a close-run thing; not until 1964 did the clouds begin to lighten. Meanwhile the diversions in the Congo continued, and to the same effect. Increasingly identified with Léopoldville politics, and correspondingly sure of himself as these politics acquired their characteristic shape and meaning, Holden continued to close in on the MPLA.

The details, once again, do not greatly matter but have a certain interest. In May 1961 Holden had met Andrade in Monrovia and accepted "close co-operation" in principle; nothing came of it. In June the MPLA tried again without result. In December a number of young militants of MPLA, Aliazo (the Zombo movement), and UPA formed a "Rassemblement Démocratique de la Jeunesse Angolaise"; the UPA members were ordered by their leaders to withdraw, and the project collapsed.

In March 1962 the weary tale continued, but now the conflict sharpened once again. Holden and the leaders of the PDA (ex-Aliazo) formed a coalition, which they named the National Front of Angolan Liberation (FLNA). Nine days later they proclaimed the formation of a "Revolutionary Government in Exile" (GRAE) with Holden as its presiding figure. This "government" at once proceeded in a "declaration of principles" to announce that it embodied "the two authentic representatives of the legitimate aspirations of the people of Angola," leaving the MPLA, as before, in isolation.

[1] Marcum, op. cit., p. 214, quoting two interviews given by Holden. Later it appeared that not all the Ferreira column were killed. Some escaped, including the MPLA's later commander on the eastern front, Hoji ya Henda. See *Vitória ou Morte*, MPLA, Brazzaville, 14 April 1971.

The first foreign government to recognize Holden's "government" was that of President Ben Bella of Algeria, which proceeded to give it a hundred tons of arms, according to the later testimony of its resigned "foreign minister," Jonas Savimbi.[2] Other recognitions followed. In July 1964 the second meeting of the chiefs of state of the Organization of African Unity recommended recognition, and this was granted, being withdrawn only in July 1971.

Holden's victory seemed complete. Late in the summer of 1962 Agostinho Neto had arrived in Léopoldville, having escaped from detention in Portugal, and tried once more for unity. But Neto's arrival was also signaled by a split in the MPLA leadership. Increasingly cut off from Angola by Holden's units, backed as these were by the Congolese army, the MPLA appeared to have reached the end of the road. "Initially the more influential of the two big nationalist movements, the MPLA had fractured, split, and reduced itself to a nullity. With Roberto Holden's UPA steadily gathering strength and allies, the MPLA has ceased to count." The judgment was my own, writing in *West Africa* for December 14, 1963, and it was singularly wrong. But that is what things looked like at the time.

The years that followed saw sporadic efforts at ending this destructive Congo diversion. As late as October 1966, under pressure from the Organization of African Unity, two representatives of Holden's "government in exile" met with four leaders of the MPLA and signed an agreement aimed at ending "the fratricidal strife between the two movements" and achieving unity of action. Its substantial points were:

(1) Immediate end of all forms of hostile propaganda, and supervision of all publications [of the two movements] by OAU representatives.

(2) Immediate freeing of members of the two movements detained by one side or the other.

[2] The ephemeral "literature" of this period is abundant in declarations and communiqués, and I draw upon it here.

(3)   Setting up of a military commission of inquiry of the
      OAU to re-evaluate the situation in Angola and
      make recommendations to intensify a joint and more
      effective armed struggle.

(4)   Following immediately on the end of the commis-
      sion's work, the setting up of a joint committee of
      MPLA and GRAE [Holden's "government"] under
      OAU auspices to study the possible basis for co-
      operation between the two movements, whether in
      military or political activity.

On the very next day, however, Holden in Kinshasa denounced
this agreement on the grounds that his delegates had not been
empowered to sign it. And so it went on. Many watched with
dismay. Some of Holden's most effective men, such as Anibal de
Melo, had long left him for the MPLA; others, like Antoine
Matumona, withdrew from the battle; others again settled into
the relative comfort of "jobs within the structure" of Kinshasa
politics.

Holden himself became increasingly a Kinshasa businessman.
One of the Congo's politicians, a minister under Adoula in
1962–64 and again under Kimba in 1965, was to describe the
Angolan "revolutionary prime minister" as "completely bour-
geoisified, owning four or five buildings in Kinshasa bought
partly with money that the Angolan liberation committee had
placed at his disposal, and partly thanks to American aid and
Mobutu's aid."[3] Malicious or not, the judgment was confirmed
not only by Holden's professed attitudes and opinions, but by
the condition of the movement he led. What this condition now
became also has its place in the story.

For guerrilla warfare, the country of northern Angola is among
the best of any in that vast country, being far more favorable
than the districts of the east and south. Well wooded and wa-

[3] Cléophas Kamitatu, *La Grande Mystification du Congo-Kinshasa*, Maspero,
Paris, 1971, p. 271.

tered, fruitful for a wide variety of crops, broken by many small hills and other useful features of the terrain, northern Angola before 1961 possessed a numerous population with a strong consciousness of its own powerful independence in the past. If skillfully prepared, and with a ready access to the outside world along a frontier difficult to barricade, a guerrilla insurrection here might have saved the local population from the worst excesses of the Portuguese and rooted itself securely into a wide region on an offensive basis. What the MPLA proved able to do after 1966 in the vastly more difficult regions of the east might have been far better accomplished here. But it was not accomplished.

By October 1961 the Portuguese had reoccupied every center in the north of any strategic importance. Huge numbers of rural people had fled to the Congo. Yet fighting units remained in the forests. How many? Speaking in Léopoldville on October 25 of that year Holden claimed, "Our forces include more than 25,-000 guerrillas, armed with automatics and shotguns, [who] occupy vast forest and mountain regions. . . . All administrative posts in the regions called 'reoccupied' are practically encircled by our forces and the enemy can supply himself only by air."

Nobody with any experience of guerrilla warfare would be likely to believe any such figure as twenty-five thousand fighters. Holden continued to repeat it—though his lieutenants did not—and even to inflate it. In 1968 he was claiming to have "nearly 30,000 soldiers".[4] Even if the true figure was only a quarter as large, it was still considerable. A stagnant guerrilla army being a defeated one, either the claims were false, or else this army of the "government in exile" must achieve big and continuous gains.

These gains altogether failed to appear. But the claims continued. In 1971 a veteran Holden spokesman, Johnny Eduardo Pinnock, in charge of the "exile government's" foreign affairs, told a Belgian audience that the "government in exile's" army numbered "more than 10,000 fighters" operating on three fronts: in the north, northeast, and east of Angola, covering a total area

[4] *Afrique Actuelle*, Paris, quoted in GRAE agency bulletin, Aug. 15, 1968.

of three hundred thousand square kilometers, as well as another one hundred thousand square kilometers where "operations are taking place."[5] He went on to explain that each of these "fronts" had its corresponding rear base in the Congo Republic, that of the main northern "front" being at Kinkuzu, not far from Kinshasa.

By 1971 it was clear that these lesser "fronts"—Kasai and Katanga—were little more than imaginary, though great claims were made for them, Pinnock even stating that UPA actions reached as far into eastern Angola as the Luso region along the Benguela Railway. This was in flat contradiction to all the available evidence from foreign observers, including the Portuguese. The true position was evidently indicated by an "exile government" commander interviewed in northern Angola during 1970. "Recently we have been able to establish two new camps in the Congo: one in the northeast . . . and the other in the east at Dilolo in Katanga. . . . For the time being we're still very close to the border. We don't know the country well. . . ."[6]

This was also how the Portuguese saw it. "To boost waning prestige and compete for outside support with its rivals," a South African reporter was told in May 1971, "UPA also sent men into the eastern sector for the first time in April last year. . . ." But the MPLA were "regarded by the Portuguese as the most effective group."[7]

What of Holden's main "front," the Kongo area of northern Angola? Several observers have told their story.

A Swiss journalist, Pierre-Pascal Rossi, spent forty-six days in northern Angola during July, August, and September 1968 and walked about 640 miles. For the first seventeen days beyond the Congo frontier, according to his vivid and convincing account, he and his escort traversed a country that was empty of people. He then reached a liberated zone he estimated as being about seventy miles long, southward from the region immediately south of Bembe, but much smaller in breadth and tapering

[5] *Rémarques Africaines*, Brussels, May 25, 1971.
[6] *Continent 2000*, Paris, Sept. 1970.
[7] Noel Garford, *The Star*, Johannesburg, May 13, 1971.

to a point not far from Nambuangongo. In this zone he found a commander called Margoso Wafuakula who claimed to have a total of about 1,800 guerrillas. Elsewhere, Margoso told Rossi, there were many other UPA/GRAE fighters, altogether about ten thousand.

While traveling, Rossi met another commander called Norbert, "assistant chief of staff at Kinkuzu," the "exile government's" military camp in the western Congo. Norbert said that this liberated area was in the middle of the "Second Region," and that the whole liberated zone was divided into sixteen such regions. "Every year I come into the bush to look at the situation and bring messages to the people."

"What sort of messages?"

"Political orders, words of encouragement from our government."

"Do you think the people can go on resisting for long in these forests?"

"Oh, yes, as long as they must. They are very brave. They are prepared to live under conditions far more difficult than those they knew under the colonial regime, but they prefer to be here, free, while waiting for Angola to become independent."[8]

Rossi was also told by Margoso that Holden did not come into Angola, "because it would be much too dangerous: the Portuguese would do everything they could to seize him." Otherwise one member of the "revolutionary government," Johnny Eduardo (Pinnock) had made a visit, and the government had a permanent representative in the liberated zone.

Much else of Rossi's detailed report, by intention very favorable to Holden's cause, confirmed a general picture of stagnation and waiting upon events.

But perhaps there were other such zones to be seen?

A year later a Swedish journalist, Olle Waestberg, and his wife, Inger Claeeson, made much the same journey and reported much the same things, though in less detail. Remarkably enough, they said they had walked "almost 930 miles" in thirty-nine days; they must have had rather little time for in-

8 P.-P. Rossi, *Pour une Guerre Oubliée*, Julliard, Paris, 1969, pp. 214–15.

quiries on the way. In any event they, too, reached a small liberated zone beginning just south of Bembe and stretching to the southward; and, like Rossi, they saw several hundred fighters. Rossi's commander, Margoso, does not figure in their account. (Commenting on this in 1970, an MPLA leader, Iko Carreira, affirmed that Margoso had wanted to co-operate with MPLA units in the north, but Holden found this out in 1969 and put him into prison.)

Waestberg repeated Holden's claims to have a vastly larger organization and to have control of "about one-sixth of Angola's territory" inhabited by "over a million people" divided into "twenty-eight zones" of which "fifteen have a fully developed administration." There were, he said, about three hundred hospitals and 593 schools in these zones; he himself saw one of each.[9]

Next year, early in 1970, an Austrian journalist named Fritz Sitte repeated the experience once more, and again with substantially the same results. Like the others, he crossed the Congo frontier and walked for many days—eighteen in his case—before reaching "COA," the liberated zone. His marching claim was less remarkable than the Waestbergs: only five hundred miles in forty-seven days, during some of which he lay sick with fever. But huge progress, apparently, had been made since the Waestbergs' visit. According to Sitte's informants, Holden's movement now controlled "more than 2,100,000 Angolans" in "twenty-five zones and countless sub-zones." Doubled since 1969, the total would be nearly one half of the whole rural population. Moreover, Holden's movement had given "a full military training since 1961 to about 30,000 Angolans." But where these vast populations were, and what this great legion was actually doing, Sitte neglected to explain.[10]

Still more inflated claims were to follow. Two Frenchmen made the same journey a few months later. Grand walkers, too —750 miles in fifty days—they reached a point "only two days' march from Luanda," which lay, their account, only thirty-

[9] Olle Waestberg, 3 articles in English, Swedish Features, Stockholm, 1969.
[10] F. Sitte, *Schweizerische Allgemeine,* June 6, 1970.

one miles to the southwest. There they found a Holden commander, called Major Londes, who stated that the liberated zone he himself controlled was about ninety-four miles long, and lay between Bembe in the north and Caxito, just outside Luanda, in the south. Shifted perhaps a little to the west, it was manifestly the same zone the others had seen. "As far as the MPLA you're talking about is concerned," added Major Londes, "you can go all over Angola without running into it. . . ."[11] On this he was talking nonsense. But further "light" there was none.

Discounting the propaganda, one may conclude that Holden's movement between 1961 and 1971 achieved two military objectives. First, they built a small fighting force in the western Congo, based on the camp at Kinkuzu, and used this to seal off the frontier against any use of it by the MPLA. They also sent members of this force on infrequent short-range raids across the frontier. (Thus in June 1971 they attacked a post some dozen miles from the frontier before returning with some Portuguese prisoners.) Secondly, they retained a small guerrilla presence in northern Angola south of Bembe toward Nambuangongo and Luanda. Given their logistic and other advantages, these objectives can only be described as minimal.

This, too, was the opinion of another sort of foreign observer, the Portuguese and their South African allies. For them, beyond any doubt, it was the MPLA in the north, not the UPA/FLNA, who made the running after 1965. Thus the Luanda news magazine *Notícia* carried late in 1967 an article by one of Lisbon's veteran war correspondents, Fernando Farinha, called "Ninety Minutes Under Fire." He describes a clash in the Cuanza Norte District, a little way eastward from the UPA area visited by Rossi and others. No mention of UPA activity. "As usual," he writes, "the first moments of the guerrilla ambush belong to the MPLA. . . ."[12] On February 21, in the same magazine, he reports another operation in Cuanza Norte, again with units of the MPLA. But this time he does mention

[11] J.-J. Dupont and P. Letellier, *Continent 2000*, Paris, Sept. 1970.
[12] *Notícia*, Luanda, Nov. 18, 1967.

the UPA. He argues that there is no need for the Portuguese army to bother with MPLA in the north: "The UPA has undertaken the job of eliminating them. . . . Effectively, the UPA gives the MPLA here in the north one hell of a life (*a vida negra ao MPLA*)."

Portuguese concentration on the MPLA in the north was confirmed by a detailed South African report of late 1968. Flying north from Luanda in a NorAtlas transport, the journalist Al. J. Venter, very much an orthodox white South African according to his book, was surprised by the crew's almost immediate move for action. "We were still only minutes out of Luanda when the four paratroopers on board started preparations for a supply drop" to the Portuguese fortified post of Quicabo. " 'The area below is thick with terrorists,' Captain Martinho said. 'This is the most notorious sector you have heard so much about, the Dembos. It starts here, seventy kilometres from the capital.' "

"The roads are bad," continues Venter, "and the guerrillas are active. It sometimes takes a convoy as much as twenty-four hours to cover a 100 km. stretch. . . . Often road convoys are attacked four or five times in a single outward journey. The return trip can be worse . . . ; the terrorists see the trucks go north and are ready for them on their return."[13]

Who were these terrorists? Venter does not say. What he does say is, "The Portuguese military authorities admit that the MPLA threat is the most serious they have encountered since the start of the war. . . . 'MPLA men are by far the most resilient fighters,' a captain at Nambuangongo told me," adding that the UPA men were weakened by "a lack of discipline."

" 'Whereas MPLA men will ask villagers for food,' [the same captain] continued, 'UPA fighters will take it. MPLA guerrillas rarely touch the women of their hosts—something apparently drummed into them while they undergo training. UPA men have no qualms whatever about attempting to seduce women of local tribesmen—one of the reasons why they have alienated so many tribal Africans in northern Angola.'

---

13 A. J. Venter, *The Terror Fighters*, Cape Town, 1969, pp. 9–10.

"To these simple people," Venter goes on, "young MPLA guerrilla trainees are more reliable than both the Portuguese officials with whom they have fleeting contact and the grab-all UPA terrorists. Hope is the supreme motivating force in Africa, and the MPLA offers oodles [large quantities] of it."[14]

These scraps from the battlefield were all the more revealing in that they came from officers actively engaged in fighting guerrillas in the north, and whose political preference, if any, would be for the conservative UPA rather than the radical MPLA. They confirm the military failure of the UPA, but they also pay a memorable tribute to the MPLA. For the MPLA's units in these northern areas consisted of men and women who had survived since 1961 in almost total isolation from the outside world. Yet they had done more than survive, though that was already much. They had succeeded in maintaining, if on a small scale, the guerrilla morale and initiative that Holden's movement, in spite of all its manifold advantages, had failed to develop since the UPA's boasted "25,000 fighters occupying vast regions" of October 1961.

Only in July 1966 and in February 1967 could MPLA agents in the western Congo at last arrange for the infiltration of reinforcements to these long-lost northern units. They were then able to circumvent Congo President Mobutu's blockade, as well as Holden's, and send in two groups totaling several hundred men, the "Cienfuegos" and "Camy" columns. These men, mostly veterans of the guerrilla fighting in Cabinda, north of the Congo estuary, got through safely to the Dembos forests along the district borders of Luanda and Cuanza Norte. Their feat went unnoticed in the world at large; yet in terms of guerrilla enterprise it was not a small one. Their route imposed weeks of forced marching through terrain very dangerous to them, and they carried spare weapons and ammunition as well as their own. But they got through, and also got back news of their arrival.

"When they reached our people," a veteran MPLA leader, Iko Carreira, recalled in 1970, "they found small and dispersed

14 Ibid., pp. 31–32.

groups, but with good morale, who'd been there since 1961. These people had a good organization of action committees, each with a literate chairman and secretary, and organizations for women [of the MPLA Angolan Women's Organization], for youth, and for military purposes. They were mobilized on the basis of Protestant Christian loyalty, not otherwise":[15] that is, neither Catholic nor Tocoista. No doubt it was the consequences of these reinforcements' safe arrival early in 1967 that led to the comments let fall by Venter's Portuguese informants in 1968.

This balance sheet in the north, so negative for Holden and his movement, has interesting political implications.

If Holden's movement in the field had run into stagnation and corruption, this was because it mirrored Holden's political position. Beginning as a traditionalist organization devoted to merely local ends, and sometimes merely personal ends, the UPA under Holden's leadership had acquired the trappings of Angolan nationalism without acquiring its dynamic content. It remained what it had been in the beginning, a movement led by traditionalist elites; in so far as it evolved at all, it became a movement led by modernizing elites within the reformist structure of the Congo. Even this is probably saying too much. Holden's personal control of the movement had become effectively complete by 1963; thereafter the movement reflected his own position and assumptions, and was increasingly his own "possession."

These assumptions were elitist and reformist; nothing, perhaps, shows this more clearly than Rossi's description of the actual relations that existed between the Kinshasa leaders and its men in the field. Holden himself could not visit them, because it was "too dangerous"; less prominent leaders would "go down" every now and then to carry orders and "words of encouragement." The policy was sufficiently clear: its main objectives were to husband a small striking force in the safety of

15 Interview with B.D., June 1970.

the Congo, while maintaining at least some guerrilla presence inside Angola, against the day when others should have forced the Portuguese to withdraw or try negotiation. Then Holden would present himself as the convenient *interlocuteur valable:* as the man with whom the Lisbon regime could deal on mutually convenient terms.[16]

Waiting for the Portuguese to collapse, Holden and his colleagues continued to concentrate their attention on the Kongo areas while trying to prevent the MPLA from reasserting itself elsewhere. Meanwhile they were repeatedly trapped in their own contradictions. They had called their government "revolutionary" with the same demagogy that would cause Holden's patron, President Mobutu, to erect in 1966 a statue to Lumumba, whom Mobutu himself had been instrumental in handing over to Lumumba's murderers five years earlier. Yet at the same time, as candidates for the "Western preference" which, as they hoped, would eventually lift them into power, they were forced to attack the MPLA for its revolutionary attachments. Thus the "revolutionary" Holden to a French reporter in 1970: "The propaganda of the MPLA is similar to that of the Communist countries. It is unfortunate that the Western countries, in estimating the MPLA as 'the real driving force in the struggle,' have fallen into the trap."

Alternatively, since the argument was thin, the MPLA was not "Communist," but corrupt. "The MPLA," Holden continued in the same interview, "has never wanted to have anything to do with the population. Its followers are in the majority 'civilized,' privileged elements. All the half-breeds who want to maintain their privileges belong to it. . . ." Once again it was reversion to the traditionalist, separatist civil-war mentality of

[16] In this respect he counted on Mobutu's aid and partnership, and evidently with good reason. Thus on Aug. 7, 1971, a South African newspaper, the *Star Weekly* (Johannesburg), reported from New York that Prime Minister Caetano "has agreed to consider enlisting President Mobutu of the Congo as a mediator in Angola. . . . The Portuguese Premier said this to Vice-President Agnew during their recent talk in Lisbon, reports the New York *Times*. In turn, Mr. Agnew is said to have conveyed to Premier Caetano President Mobutu's confidence that Portugal was 'sincerely interested in establishing racial harmony and reaching some degree of self-determination in her African territories.' "

1961. Holden and his men had reached a point where they could see no further than to judge others by themselves.

And they acted accordingly. Together with Mobutu, Holden continued to bar access to Angola by way of the Congo, while his own units in the field, few though they were by now, declined into an "indiscipline" that turned them increasingly into parasites on the surviving population of the areas where they lived. In all this they revealed a striking parallel with other "Holdenites," of the Second World War, notably the Serbian monarchists of occupied Yugoslavia. Similarly trying to conserve their forces so as to profit from a victory that others would have won, these Yugoslav opportunists also turned their arms against their rivals, the partisans of Tito. Arguing the doctrine of the lesser evil, they went into partnership with the German and Italian occupying armies so as to fight these rivals. With this, their units became increasingly demoralized and parasitic till finally swept away.[17]

There are striking parallels. In the Yugoslav case, there were men among the Serbian monarchists who became disgusted by their leader's temporizing with the occupying powers, and who preferred to join the partisans rather than continue standing idly by. Similar reactions appeared among Holden's rank and file, well placed as they were to know how greatly their people had suffered in northern Angola through UPA/GRAE's failure to defend them against the Portuguese Army. In April 1972, Holden's Kinkuzu camp mutinied against his leadership, demanding arms and action. The fact that they possessed no arms is scarcely less surprising than that they numbered only a thousand men. Holden was once again saved by his confederate, Mobutu, who turned out his own army to overawe the mutineers and seize their leaders, said to be in touch with Brazzaville elements—that is, with the MPLA.

The parallels go wider. They can be found in almost every war of national liberation, perhaps in all of them. It may even

[17] See B. Davidson, "In the Portuguese Context," in C. Allen and R. W. Johnson, *African Perspectives*, Cambridge, 1970, p. 337; also Davidson, *The Liberation of Guiné*, p. 91; and Marcum, op. cit., p. 218.

be that there is a general rule by which all movements of resistance produce and deepen conflicts within themselves as the
reformists draw back from the revolutionaries, and, in drawing
back, fall victim to the game of the enemy regime. This has
certainly occurred in each of the "Portuguese African" territories. As a further elucidation of the Angolan case, these parallels tell a great deal.

In Guinea-Bissau the general rise of nationalism similarly
hived off splinter handfuls which established themselves in Dakar, the capital of neighboring Senegal. Their program and assumptions were correspondingly elitist and reformist, opting in
the end for co-operation with the Portuguese against the mainstream movement, the PAIGC led by Amilcar Cabral. But
these Senegalese diversions never acquired the baleful destruc-
tiveness of their parallel in the Congo. The case of the Mozambique liberation movement, FRELIMO, is more instructive.

FRELIMO was formed in Dar es Salaam in 1962 as a coalition of nationalist groupings in exile, one or two of which had
some real following inside Mozambique. Its leaders then and
for some years after felt no driving need to establish unity on
long-term programs of institutional change. The movement
accordingly developed with different aims in the minds of its
leaders. This unresolved and for the most part unadmitted internal conflict may have done a good deal of damage in the
early years, but entered a crisis only in 1968. Then it became
clear that a UPA-MPLA dichotomy had grown far toward maturity inside the movement's leadership, and some degree of
split proved unavoidable. This reached a head in the summer
of 1968.

In July of that year FRELIMO held a movement congress,
the first since its formation in 1962, in the northern Mozambique district of Niassa. It was a risky move, since the approximate date and even the intention to hold it inside Mozambique
had been announced, such were the public pressures that had
now arisen from this internal crisis. As it turned out (and the
present writer was there at the time), it began and continued
safely, a Portuguese reconnaissance plane locating its assembly

point in the Niassa woodlands only on the last afternoon. When
the bombers came next day, all had dispersed. From another
direction, however, the congress faced a more serious threat.

There came to this congress about 150 delegates and elected
leaders from all nine districts of Mozambique; those from the
far south had traveled for many weeks and pushed their way
through manifold dangers. Each of the three districts where
military operations were in progress—Cabo Delgado, Niassa,
Tete—was to send eight political delegates and nine from the
district's fighting units, or seventeen in all. Niassa and Tete
duly sent their seventeen delegates, but Delgado, where the
political and military struggle was furthest advanced, did not.
Delgado sent its nine delegates from the fighting units, but its
eight political leaders refused to come. The nine young men
from Delgado's fighting units enthusiastically supported the
congress and its resolutions, but the absence of the eight political leaders was a stiff blow to unity. What had happened?

Explanation came in the sequel. Returning to Tanzania after
the congress, the re-elected leader of FRELIMO, the late
Eduardo Mondlane, at once secured the calling of an emer-
gency conference under the aegis of the Tanzanian governing
party, TANU, at the southern Tanzanian town of Mtwara early
in August. This four-day confrontation proved sharp and difficult, but Mondlane and the majority prevailed in the end
against the leader of the dissident Delgado faction, the elderly
Lázaro Nkavandame. During these meetings the real aims behind Nkavandame's dissidence, and that of the seven political
leaders who supported Nkavandame, became clear.

Pushed hard by Mondlane and the military delegates,
Nkavandame and his group declared at this meeting that they
would split away from FRELIMO, on the grounds of dissatisfaction with Mondlane's leadership but in fact, as they soon
explained, in order to revert to their initial position before
1962. This position, that of MANU, the Makonde African National Union which became the Mozambique African National
Union and one of the constituents of FRELIMO, had been
aimed at a separatist goal. In this respect, as in some others,

its initial position had been close to the Necaca-Pinnock-Holden Union of the Peoples of Northern Angola which became the Union of the Peoples of Angola.

Early in 1962 Nkavandame, then under pressure from the Portuguese authorities in Delgado because of his success in organizing African co-operatives and agitating for political reforms, had accepted the need for wider action. He had organized a "meeting of the people's leaders"—himself and others —in order "to discuss what we should do to regain our liberty and to drive the Portuguese oppressors out of our country. After a long and important discussion, we reached the conclusion that the Makonde people of Cabo Delgado District alone could not succeed in driving out the enemy. We then decided to join forces with Mozambicans from the rest of the country."[18]

Unlike Holden and the UPA at the same time—and the differences of circumstance were very great—Nkavandame and the established Makonde leaders decided that they could not go it alone. But it became clear in later years that they had not forgotten their idea of ethnic separatism, and that some other Makonde, across the frontier in Tanzania (like some of the Kongo of the Congo Republic), were ready to support them.

What crystallized the split of 1968, apparently, was the feeling of these established Makonde leaders that the revolutionary development of FRELIMO was fast cutting the ground from under their feet: the "new young men" such as Raimundo and Chipande, now acquiring leadership inside Delgado with the growth of the movement and its action, began to be seen as dangerous rivals instead of convenient instruments. The movement in Delgado, in other words, was "getting out of hand," was developing beyond the orbit of conservative and traditionalist thought.

All this broke into the open at the Mtwara conference of August 1968. There, some days beforehand, Nkavandame had already declared that he and his friends would work independently of FRELIMO. Now, at the conference, Nkavandame went further. He demanded of the Tanzanians that they should allo-

[18] Quoted in Mondlane, *Struggle for Mozambique,* p. 117.

cate half the available support in money and supplies to a
breakaway movement which "would be composed of the
Makonde of Cabo Delgado only, and its task would be to liberate that province and declare another Biafra, with the support of Tanzania."[19] In much the same way, Holden's UPA
was clinging to its notion of Kongo separatism with the support
of the Mobutu government in Congo Kinshasa.

The split failed of its effect, because Mondlane and the young
Delgado leaders held firm against such plans, and the Tanzanian authorities then refused to countenance it.

"To cut a long story short (and an unpleasant one at that),"
Mondlane wrote at the time, "I should say that the presence of
TANU leaders at these meetings [at Mtwara] saved us from a
real tragedy, for, while Mzee Lázaro [Nkavandame] insisted
on breaking away from my leadership, hoping that the Tanzanian government would support him and his followers, TANU
leaders and all the rest of FRELIMO leaders including the
military, disagreed and pressured for continued unity under my
leadership. Finally [the chief Tanzanian delegate] had to
openly tell Mzee Lázaro that the government of Tanzania had
no plans to support his group, and that if he cared for the
liberation of his country he should work within the present
structure of FRELIMO. . . ."[20]

Some of Tanzania's Makonde leaders may have wanted
to play Nkavandame's game, but Nyerere was no Mobutu.
Nkavandame was forced to accept unity, together with his separatist friends. But shortly afterward, as though to ram home
the lesson, he defected to the Portuguese, who, quite mistakenly,
welcomed him as a key figure in Mozambican nationalism,
something he had long ceased to be even inside his own District.
And shortly after that again, in another defection (though this
time not to the Portuguese), a second "key figure," the Rev.
Uria Simango, also split away for reasons basically the same.

[19] Eduardo Mondlane, in a letter to the writer, Aug. 16, 1968. At this time,
it may be remembered, the Tanzanian government had recognized the secession
of Biafra from Nigeria.
[20] Mondlane, in another letter, of Aug. 15, 1968.

He too was loud in his denunciations of Mondlane's leadership, but the evidence suggests that he, too, like Nkavandame, had counted on getting rid of Mondlane's leadership and thereby applying a brake to the movement's policies of radical change.[21]

These moves arose from divergences of a fundamental kind, and they have accordingly a general interest. On one side, there were men like Holden, who saw the liberation struggle in opportunist terms: a means, that is, of "making a noise," of assembling international support, and so of pushing the Portuguese to accept at least a measure of institutional reform. On the other side, by now, there were others who believed that the sufferings and effort of guerrilla warfare could not be justified, could not even be upheld, for the sake of any mere modification of existing institutions, but only by a program that called for the building of new and independent institutions, whether political, social, or cultural. They would carry through this program to the end. They would negotiate with the Portuguese, but only for Portuguese withdrawal.

Inside FRELIMO, as in Angola between UPA and MPLA, the split was thus between programs of reform and revolution; and this was again confirmed by what followed. Early in 1969 FRELIMO's central committee drew its conclusions under the shadow of this crisis and of Mondlane's assassination, in February of that year, by a hand of presumably Portuguese propulsion. Other fainthearts, such as Murupa, defected in the wake of this.

For the central committee now derided people in their leadership at Dar es Salaam, safely in Tanzania, who "by the bureaucratic nature of their functions, coupled with the lack of a solid political base, were overtaken by the Revolution. Living outside, wrapped up in their small world of comfortable routine and papers, they lost contact with the reality of the war and became unable to distinguish the principal from the secondary, the immediate from the long-term tasks. So they opposed

[21] Ibid. In 1972 Simango joined with a handful of Mozambican dissidents, living chiefly in Nairobi, Kenya, in another small splinter "movement."

measures aimed at the intensification of the war, at the subordination of all activities to the armed struggle.

"Almost from the very beginning of FRELIMO [1962],
there had been comrades with those erroneous conceptions.
Some of them deserted in the course of the Revolution: they
formed splinter organisations, through which they hoped to
satisfy their personal interests; or, because they were weak, they
surrendered to the Portuguese; or yet again, because their ambitions or greed for money could not be satisfied in the Revolution, they chose an easier way of life and sought employment
in neighboring countries. . . ."[22] Allowing for differences of
detail, these lapidary words had, and were to go on having, a
direct application to comparable persons and phenomena in the
Angolan situation.

Like Mondlane and the Mozambicans who followed him,
the leaders of the MPLA developed away from reformism toward revolution. But the going was worse than rough. Their
survival is not the least remarkable aspect of the story.

[22] *Mozambique Revolution,* Dar es Salaam, March–April 1969, pp. 2–3.
Some of the defectors withdrew into dissidence or commerce, others into European or American scholarships, or, like Nkavandame and Murupa, into outright betrayal (cf. interview with Murupa in *Notícia,* Luanda, Sept. 18, 1971.)

4   RIDING THE STORM

If Angola's people were ever to develop a movement deserving of the aims of national liberation, there would have to be men and ideas very different from those of the UPA. Could the fragmentary survivals of the MPLA supply the need? Their prospects in 1962 were dim.

With many of their militants dead or imprisoned, in flight or grim survival amid the forests of the north, the men and women who still claimed to lead the mainstream of Angolan nationalism, whether present or potential, faced these prospects with heavy handicaps and heavier hearts. For a while they were little more than a handful of anxious exiles in Léopoldville, harried by the Congolese police, penniless, alone.

The "old MPLA" was practically dead, the victim of Portuguese settler and army massacres in 1961. To build a new MPLA in these somber circumstances and relaunch a national movement, seemed more than difficult. They set about trying. In this they proved to be the gainers from their own misfortune: only men and women of courage and conviction stayed with them now. And then they gained from the arrival of Agostinho Neto late in the summer of 1962.

Neto by this time was very much the product of the struggle he had waged: a strong character built stronger by adversity, little given to words, often finding words a waste of time (even when they might not have been), a privileged *assimilado* who had measured himself against the tests of assimilation and academic acceptance but had risen beyond their limits, a poet and scholar who had made himself into a revolutionary. Uninspiring as a public speaker (or so it seemed to the outside ear) though witty and persuasive in private talk, a man whose mildness of manner concealed a tough, unyielding stubbornness, Neto combined an unshakable devotion to his cause with a corresponding moral power.

From his first arrival in Léopoldville, signaled as it was by schism and harassment, he seems never to have doubted that the MPLA could be made to meet the challenge; this, at least, was my own impression when meeting him there at the time. The MPLA could be made to grow into the spearhead of a genuine movement of national liberation. Meanwhile, in its early stages of growth, it could be made to symbolize the future.

Andrade and others had already begun the work. Neto continued it, stamping what was done with the seal of his own strenuous vision. Not everyone admired his style and temperament or liked his leadership; not everyone was prepared to go along. But the work continued. With doctors who had rallied, Dr. Eduardo dos Santos and others, the exile MPLA formed a little string of clinics for the benefit of refugees who continued to stream across the frontier from the devastated north. They appealed to charitable and other bodies in West and East for medical aid, and they received a little.

They sought again for unity with Holden and the UPA, and were rejected as before. They tried to send in reinforcements to the Dembos forests, only to find themselves violently thwarted. More important for the long run, they set about creating a new political structure. Their acting leader in Kinshasa, the poet and critic Mário de Andrade, had at once stepped down in Neto's favor; together, they began to mend what might still be mended, even though the means at hand were small.

If Andrade welcomed Neto's coming, it appears that Da Cruz did not. The latter seems to have forced a quarrel with more than a touch of that familiar exile's malady, *dementia*

emigrantis, which eats into judgment and character alike. It
was said that Da Cruz had wished to impose his leadership
and had refused to accept the majority's decision; thereafter,
in any case, Da Cruz became increasingly dissident. Eventually
he applied for membership in the UPA.

The quarrel came to a head at a movement conference in
December 1962. This was attended by about seventy of the
MPLA's survivors, some of whom were representative of newly
founded women's, youth, workers' and other movement organizations. A new structure was fashioned and approved; with
this, the new MPLA was launched in a systematic way, even if
as yet it was little more than an empty hull. In July 1963, the
majority expelled the dissident Da Cruz "for acts of indiscipline
tending to undermine the movement's unity, and inspired by
personal ambitions for power."[1] Da Cruz retired to Algiers.
Much foul water flowed from this, including stories that the
MPLA had "formed a front . . . with parties known to have
close contacts with the Salazar regime." These stories were given
currency in the report of a goodwill mission sent to Kinshasa
by the OAU, and for a while increased the MPLA's isolation.[2]

Weathering all this as best they could, Neto and his companions set about providing their empty hull with engines,
equipment, and objectives. But the political climate in Kinshasa
soon proved unbearable. In June 1963 their quarters in the
Binza suburb were raided by Congolese gendarmerie, who
seized arms and explosives destined for Angola. In September
Neto was arrested for possessing "false papers," together with
another veteran of the leadership then and since, Lucio Lara:
the fact was that he and Lara had passports issued by African

[1] MPLA statement, Kinshasa, 1963.
[2] Cf. B. Davidson, *West Africa,* Dec. 14, 1963. Da Cruz afterward went to
Peking, where, according to MPLA experience, he played a part in removing
Chinese support. "It was this man who went to China in order to spread his
poison that MPLA was pro-Russian, anti-Chinese, and so on. This is when our
difficulties with the Chinese comrades began." Daniel Chipenda in interview
with D. Barnett, Lusaka, Aug. 28, 1969, Liberation Support Movement pamphlet.
Andrade meanwhile retired to Algiers, though without any open quarrel with
Neto, where he continued his literary and propagandist work until returning
to the scene of action in 1971.

countries still willing to support them, such as Ghana and Guinea. In the same month, the MPLA was mulcted of a fine for the arms seized in June. In October the Congolese police closed down their principal clinic in Kinshasa, although this was concerned with relief to refugees. In November the gendarmerie suppressed the MPLA's Kinshasa office on the grounds that "parties which form the government-in-exile" did not control it. Arrests and other harassments became a daily menace. Meanwhile, many foreign friends had fallen away. Far from riding the storm, it seemed that the MPLA were again sunk beneath the waves.

In the nick of time there came a lifeline from an unexpected quarter. Across the Congo River from Kinshasa in the republic of Congo/Brazzaville, independent in 1960 like the Belgian Congo, the regime changed. The ranting Abbé Youlou, very much a "conservative" along elitist lines, was displaced by a moderate radical government under Massemba-Débat. When Neto and his companions were formally expelled from the Congo/Kinshasa republic, in November 1963, they were able to slip across the river to sanctuary in Brazzaville. There they found shelter from harassment. At last their prospects could begin to brighten.

The light was small and slow in coming. There might be nowhere else to go but up, yet it was hard to see the way. They began with another conference, in January 1964. Known in their history as the *conferência dos quadros*—of cadres, or active militants—this was to be the relaunched MPLA's "founding congress" in a more meaningful sense than the conference of December 1962. It read itself some stiff lessons. The leadership was trounced, or trounced itself, for having miscalculated the situation in the western Congo; for having failed to define effective political and military modes of action; for having given inadequate attention to questions of training; and for having allowed "a certain complex of superiority and militarist spirit" to emerge among guerrilla commanders who "were led to claim a privileged position in the movement." The leadership was further criticized for having failed to establish a military base inside the Cabinda enclave, north of the Congo River, "such as should have been the logical outcome of our operations there," as well as for "the existence within the movement of factions or pressure groups based on personal ambitions and opportunism".[3]

Much else was laid upon the line with a frankness that would prove healthy. "The armed struggle unleashed in our country in February 1961 continues to be essentially insurrectionary in character, disorganized in practice, leaderless, isolated from the majority of the African population confined to a small part of the territory, and short of arms and ammunition." The medicine was meant to be emetic, and there was more.

"Angolan groups who have kept [the struggle] going have done so without co-ordination, without any centralization of command, using rudimentary techniques, and consequently incapable of winning victories that can deepen the army's difficulties or give heart to our people. . . . The number of losses among the civilian population, whether by death or in flight, shows the lack of a military cover capable of defending people from the criminal assault of the Portuguese colonialists." Having got this off its chest, and other points to the same effect, the conference went on to define new modes of operations, new structures, new objectives. These were to be modified in detail as the years passed, but they have remained the guiding framework.

"The installation of the Movement in the interior calls [now] for the rooting into our national territory of one or several groups of Angolan nationalists linked to common principles, inspired by the same revolutionary ideas, and capable of transmitting and spreading these among the masses of the population. . . ." The weight and leadership of the movement could then be gradually established inside the country.

It was one thing to say all this, another to achieve it. Here in Brazzaville they were even more cut off from northern Angola than before. Their first practical move was to make good their effort of 1963 at working and fighting inside the Cabinda en-

[3] *Conferência dos Quadros: Relatório Geral* . . . , Brazzaville, Jan. 1964.

clave, which abuts on the Congo/Brazzaville Republic. Tolerated by the Massemba-Débat regime, which in any case had its own reasons for disliking the Adoula regime in Léopoldville across the river, the MPLA leaders collected arms and recruited volunteers for Cabinda. Though boycotted by possible Western suppliers, they were able to find a hearing in the Communist countries. A little aid began to arrive from the Soviet Union, Czechoslovakia, and elsewhere; a few young men were sent to these countries for military training.

This action in Cabinda had much success in 1964, but later encountered difficulties with a part of the population. According to one of the volunteers who was longest there, a Cabindan whose *nom de guerre* is Petrov, the main difficulty lay with the Bayumbe, who live along Cabinda's frontier with Congo/Brazzaville. This was necessarily the MPLA route of access, but "the Bayumbe are linked to the Kongo; besides, they have never suffered much from the Portuguese, since labor on local *roças* [plantations] has been contract labor from the south and east, while the Bayumbe themselves did little work, or none at all." Those among them who might have accepted the nationalist case "had preferred to flee Portuguese reprisals and take refuge with their Kongo neighbors in the Congo." The Bayumbe region was therefore hard to cross, whereas beyond it, in Bailongo and Cabinda districts, where the consequences of colonization were more intensive, the people proved far more welcoming and ready to participate.[4]

In 1972 the MPLA still had units active in Cabinda. But its main value had lain in offering a "live" training ground. Most of the early guerrilla leaders who opened a new front in the eastern districts after 1965 had already gone through months of active service in Cabinda.

With the opening of this eastern front, the transfer of the weight of the movement inside the country could be carried forward in decisive fashion. From then onward, the MPLA progressively realized its potential and moved from positions of weakness toward positions of strength.

[4] Interview with B.D., June 1970.

Other factors brought encouragement in 1964. The Congo diversion continued to exact its toll, but there were people now, outside the MPLA, who began to see this diversion for what it was. Thus the year brought a reversal of the OAU's previous withdrawal of recognition for the MPLA. But it also brought the beginning of a long crisis inside Holden's organization in the western Congo (Zaïre) Republic.

This crisis erupted in two phases, and with consequences of some importance.

In July 1964 the "foreign minister" in Holden's Kinshasa cabinet resigned in sensational style, taking with him several others. A product, like Da Cruz, of Luanda secondary-school formation, Jonas Malheiro Savimbi was an *assimilado* from the Bié District of central Angola. Having escaped to Switzerland, where he pursued his studies at the University of Lausanne, he seems for a while to have vacillated between joining the MPLA or the UPA, but eventually accepted the post of Holden's "foreign minister." Yet it rapidly grew clear that Holden had no intention of giving this "young Turk" a free rein. Meanwhile Savimbi saw the inside story, and found it horrifying. About a year after his appointment, while in Cairo for an OAU meeting, he decided to resign, and did so with a declaration that rebel opposition to the Portuguese had virtually collapsed and that the rebels, meaning by this the UPA and its "army in the field," had stopped the war. Then and afterward, he proceeded to explain why.

Holden himself, Savimbi accused,[5] was and had been since 1961 a United States creation "to be held in reserve as a buffer inside a divided Angolan nationalism." A willing tool protected by the pro-American government of Adoula, Holden had accepted a number of American advisers, including a certain "Muller, American subject, in charge of public relations for the Adoula government, as personal counselor"; Bernhard

[5] In a letter to *Rémarques Congolaises et Africaines*, Brussels, 21, Nov. 25, 1964.

Manhertz, "engaged in April 1964 to direct the Angolan Liberation Army [the UPA/GRAE military wing]. This American
officer has served in South Vietnam in the American Army";
and Carlos Kessel, "a militant anti-Castroist" with U.S. affilia-
tions through the U.S. trade union movement.

"Experience within the movement, a profound knowledge
of the activities of individuals, and the materialist analysis of
revolutions, have convinced me that no forward movement
[*progressisme*] is possible with individuals who are subjected
[*inféodés*] to American interests, [individuals] who can have
no logistical base except Léopoldville, itself in the hands of
neocolonialists and notorious agents of imperialism." If all that
was not enough, the UPA and its "government" reflected
Holden, and Holden was "flagrantly tribalist"; on this, too,
Savimbi was careful to give chapter and verse.

As for the "army" based on the Kinkuzu camp in the western
Congo, it received absolutely no political training. Its effectives
were encouraged in "a mercenary spirit by paying them a wage
every time they return to Léopoldville from a raid into Angola." They formed "a frontier army." Poorly disciplined, their
actions could only increase the terrors of the population. "I
quote the case of the officer Abreu, who spent more than
a month on the Congo-Angola frontier, shooting buffaloes
[*pakassas*] with army ammunition so as to sell them afterward
at Matadi, without any disciplinary punishment. This officer is
now [1964] a member of the army's general staff." And much
else to the same tune, or worse.

Coming from one of Holden's right-hand men with access to
inside information, these accusations made a powerful effect
on those who were prepared to listen, including the OAU, but
little or none on Holden, who was content merely to have them
denied.[6] As for Savimbi, he concluded his letter with a call for a
united front of all "valid" nationalist organizations (still, apparently, including Holden's), but failed to act in that direction
himself. For a while, he seems to have dallied with the idea of

[6] See long statement by Johnny Eduardo (Pinnock) circulated by Holden's
office in Algiers, Dec. 15, 1964.

joining the MPLA, who, on their side, say that they pressed him to do so. But early in 1966 he showed that what he really wanted was to follow his own leadership and no one else's. In March 1966 he announced the formation of an entirely new organization, UNITA (União para la Independência Total de Angola), with himself as president.

This group was the first to profit from Zambia's October 1964 independence. Savimbi was able to collect UPA supporters among refugees in western Zambia and send some of them into eastern Angola in 1966–67. These eventually raised a number of actions against the Portuguese, including an attack on the frontier town of Teixeira de Sousa, on the Katanga border; but these actions were backed by what appears to have been a very inadequate political preparation and an even less adequate supply of arms. Sporadic operations seem to have occurred after that, whether in northern Moxico or, as claimed, in eastern Bié, but on a small scale. In October 1969 a UN survey noted ". . . there has been no mention of UNITA in the Portuguese military bulletins since 1968,"[7] while reports by Finnish, Italian, West German, and OAU observers in eastern districts, as well as those of the present writer, were unanimous in concluding that UNITA had become, by 1970, little more than another distracting side show. Its bulletins in Western Europe continued to make large claims which were increasingly hard to believe; often they were impossible to believe. These bulletins also became increasingly "revolutionary" in tone, evidently playing up to a certain propaganda support that UNITA was then receiving in Peking; and those who questioned their veracity were abused as liars, mercenaries, and servants of "modern revisionism." In 1972 it remained to be seen what would be the final outcome of this other, if somewhat different, diversion on the national movement's path.[8]

[7] UN A/8012/Add. 3, Oct. 5, 1969, p. 90.
[8] The whole Savimbi story since 1965 has been wrapped in a certain mystery. Expelled from Zambia in 1968 he found support in Cairo, looking for "its own friends"; later in the same year he was evidently able to return clandestinely to Zambia. There his group appears to have allied itself to the Zambian opposition, especially in the Western (Lozi) Province, where the MPLA and UNIP

Meanwhile, back in Kinshasa (ex-Léopoldville) in June 1965, Roberto Holden received fresh blows. A *coup d'état* was mounted against him by a certain Alexandre Taty, then "armaments minister" in Holden's cabinet. Taty announced the formation of a "military junta" in substitution for Holden's "government." Holden's position in Kinshasa being far too strong for such tactics, this failed and Taty fled; a little later he emerged in Cabinda as an ally of the Portuguese against the MPLA. In July Holden's "minister of information," Rosário Neto, resigned and withdrew.

Yet Mobutu's Congo blockade on the MPLA still stood in their way. They might be somewhat fortified by all this public exposure of Holden's true position. But to grow in any realistic sense they must somehow get themselves deeply inside the country: Cabinda was nothing like enough, and Cabinda, in any case, was proving difficult. Its "growth value," at least for the time being, was practically exhausted.

They continued to try for access by way of the western Congo. In July 1966 and February 1967, as we have seen, they were to have some success, getting two strong columns through to the Dembos forests of the north. But the route proved increasingly hazardous. Quitting Léopoldville for Brazzaville in 1963, they had left behind a clandestine apparatus under the command of that same Benedicto who had led the struggle

---

(the Zambian ruling party) were on intimate terms. They also succeeded in penetrating into Angola on a narrow front south of Luso. Manifestly absurd claims for their success were made by UNITA agents in Western Europe, most of them using a flamboyantly "revolutionary" language (e.g., Jorge Valentim, *Qui Libère l'Angola?*, Brussels, 1969); but all witnesses with the MPLA agreed that UNITA had no more than minimal presence. Several foreigners traveled into Angola with UNITA men without producing any credible evidence to the contrary. After some early adventures in the east, Savimbi's units were reduced by 1970 to a small area of northern Moxico near the borders of Bié. Chinese support for UNITA seems to have faded after 1970; in July 1971 a five-man delegation under Neto's leadership visited China at the invitation of the Chinese African Peoples' Assoc., and Neto was received by Premier Chou En-lai and the Chinese chief of staff. Early in 1972 a correspondent of the *Neue Zürcher Zeitung* (13 Mar. 1972), visiting Angola on the Portuguese side, was given to understand by Portuguese intelligence sources that the Portuguese Army left UNITA "far-reachingly in peace," because, they explained, UNITA was in conflict with MPLA. The parallel between UPA/GRAE and UNITA appeared close.

outside Luanda in 1961. In November 1966 the Congolese authorities arrested Benedicto and handed him over to Holden's "government." An MPLA communiqué, undated but evidently of 1968, had this to say about his fate:

> Benedicto is held in an underground cell in the concentration camp at Kinkuzu, where he suffers the worst kind of treatment and humiliation.
>
> In 1967 a vain attempt at escape was followed with fearful tortures.
>
> Ill and almost blind, Commander Benedicto crouches in the cells of Kinkuzu, paying for the crime of being a patriot. . . .

Worse followed. Another statement, of March 18, 1967, issued from Brazzaville, and whose accuracy there has subsequently appeared no reason to doubt, listed other hostile acts by Holden's organization, including these:

> During the month of January 1967, the same criminal gangs left the territory of Congo/Kinshasa in prosecution of a detachment of the MPLA on its way to the MPLA base in the district of Cuanza Norte. The ambush prepared by Holden's forces failed due to the action of the MPLA militants.
>
> On March 2nd, 1967, twenty MPLA militants returning to the Congo following the accomplishment of their mission in the interior of the country fell into the hands of UPA bands. Among them were five young ladies, leaders of OMA [Angolan Women's Organization of the MPLA], including Déolinda Rodrigues [de Almeida]. . . .

And worse again. Holden's men proving too weak to prevent MPLA columns from marching south, Mobutu's were ordered into action. In June 1967 a column of nearly two hundred MPLA men going to Angola was stopped, disarmed, and arrested by the Congolese army some eight miles north of the frontier. By the end of the year, on MPLA count, there were more than a hundred MPLA personnel in the prison cells of the Kinkuzu camp.[9]

Where else to look for access? Another shift in the African political scene came to their aid. In October 1964 the British Protectorate of Northern Rhodesia, lying along the inland flank of Angola, acceded to independence as Zambia. And Zambia's leaders were militantly nationalist.

Zambia's frontier, true enough, marched with those little-populated "lands at the end of the Earth" of which the MPLA leaders then knew scarcely more than the Portuguese, and possibly less. The people who lived there, sparsely in great woodland solitudes, were far from the central and western heartlands of colonial Angola. No final decision could be hoped for there. Yet these eastern lands could provide an internal base as well as a route to the center and the west. They could give the movement its chance of growth.

The idea had begun to shape itself somewhat earlier. Already the independent government of Tanzania had expressed a willingness to help. So in 1964 the reorganized MPLA asked for permission to open an office in Tanzania's capital, Dar es Salaam, and received it. The next step was to test the ground in still colonial Northern Rhodesia. If that proved favorable, then rear communications from the Indian Ocean to the eastern Angola frontier might be assured.

It would always be a daunting means of communication, fraught with appalling difficulties of transport. Nothing but dirt roads joined the Indian Ocean to western Zambia, some two and a half thousand miles, until part of the Zambian sector was tarred in 1969–70. Anyone who should seek to fuel a guerrilla war with supplies over such a route would need to be cast in a heroic mold—even supposing that supplies could be

---

[9] Agostinho Neto, statement in Brazzaville, Jan. 3, 1968. After 1965 the MPLA appear to have taken reprisals against several UPA personnel whom they were able to seize.

obtained, something by no means certain in 1964. There were those who thought the project practically impossible, but Neto was not one of them. Perhaps it was above all now, from the middle of 1964, that this often quiet and tentative man, so much an intellectual, began to assume the stature that marked him later. Deflected by no disappointment or disaster, Neto worked on his grand design for an eastern front: for the front that would at last give hard and practical reality to the words of national liberation.

There were more setbacks. The MPLA's earliest emissaries to Northern Rhodesia, Daniel Chipenda and Ciel da Conceição, were arrested in Lusaka early in September 1964 and sentenced to four months' hard labor for the illegal possession of arms, while Lusaka news reports described them as "Communist agents." Reacting from Brazzaville, the MPLA protested that "the mission of our fellow freedom fighters, as they told the [Northern] Rhodesian authorities, was to organize a relief center for Angolan refugees arriving [in Northern Rhodesia] in increasing numbers. . . . Two arms for their personal defense cannot mean that they were agitators. Similarly, some revolutionary literature they had can hardly lead to charging them with being Communist agents. . . . Our militants' noble mission had no subversive intention."[10]

The Northern Rhodesian authorities paid no attention to this protest; but fortunately they were changed, or at least began to be changed, with independence a month later. In 1965 Anibal de Melo was able to open an office in Lusaka, Zambia's capital, and to start the sending of political workers into eastern Angola. The Zambian government of President Kaunda appears to have made no objection, provided that the MPLA not try to organize Angolans who were already living in Zambia.

But it was vital to know more about the east before going further. Early reports suggested that the Mbunda and Luvale and their neighbors might need little persuasion to act; five years of upheaval and redoubled repression in the rest of An-

10 MPLA, Brazzaville, Sept. 26, 1964.

gola had made them thoroughly aware of the situation. Yet it
seems to have been similarly clear to the MPLA leaders, with
the disasters of 1961 still large in their minds, that a rising
without due organization of supplies, especially of arms, could
only play into Portuguese hands. It also appears that Savimbi
and his group moved right in with appeals for immediate action, were warmly received by the Mbunda on the promise that
they would bring in guns, failed to bring these in, and left behind a legacy of anger and defeat.[11]

De Melo and his militants moved cautiously. Before passing
to action they wanted to be sure of two gains: first, they needed
at least a minimal network of political co-operation in the vast
Moxico and Cuando Cubango Districts, abutting on Zambia;
secondly, they required a steady if initially small flow of military supplies. While Neto worked away at securing these supplies, mainly from the office in Dar es Salaam, De Melo
burrowed toward the first objective. In Zambia he found volunteers. These volunteers began to have success.

Christopher Kibulala, aged twenty-nine in 1970, was one of
them:

> When I was 20 years old, the Portuguese killed many
> people in my region. I hid in the bush for a year after that,
> because the Portuguese came to get hold of the young men.
> Then I went out of the bush. I worked for the administra-
> tion as a clerk [i.e., in 1962–63]. I also went to secondary
> school.
>
> That was in Malange District [in central Angola]. I went
> as far as the fourth grade. I worked in the mornings so as
> to go to school, and my father helped me with money. I
> started organizing people to resist even before I joined the
> MPLA. I joined the MPLA in 1964, after I had gone to
> Zambia.

Sent into Angola by De Melo in April 1965, Kibulala stayed
there. The going was very rough at first:

[11] This was the situation described to me in 1970 by Mbunda and Luchazi
informants among those who had initially welcomed Savimbi's men in 1966–67.

My first mission was to contact the people, and above all the chiefs, and some supported us.

But others did not.

People at first were afraid. And we found it very difficult, because the Portuguese paid money to chiefs to seize MPLA militants. So chiefs took this money, or else this or that man would go privately to report to the Portuguese on politically suspicious people. At that time Moxico was full of Portuguese soldiers. But we managed to gather some cadres for training outside, and in 1966 we began our struggle.

Two years after fighting began in Moxico District, he was wounded by a bomb splinter; they carried him out across the frontier and sent him to Yugoslavia for treatment. He had just returned to Africa when the present writer met him, in the summer of 1970; though still in a wheelchair, he was working as a stores supervisor in a Zambian transit office, a man of unbroken cheerfulness of spirit. We used to have chats in Serbo-Croat, which he had learned as though it were one more easy obstacle on the road ahead.

Moving thus from political preparation, the MPLA launched its first armed actions against Portuguese posts and transport in the east.

With this, a new phase opened.

DOCUMENTARY THREE

Portuguese killing and burning continued in the north. Records of the British Baptist Missionary Society are filled with its misery. Here is another handful among hundreds of similar witnesses from the north, to which many more could now be added from the east.

> *Luiza Daniel, 22, with one child and young brother from Kingengo Nambuangongo. Husband, António Vicente, killed in an air raid on the hiding place in December 1964.*
>
> *António Dundo, 68, two wives and two children, from Kiumba, Bembe. One of the children was married, António Segunda, and his wife and two children were killed in an air raid in 1963. On same [relief] card—same family—Castelo António, 58. His wife, Isabel Umba, was working in the garden when surprised by a Portuguese patrol and captured.*
>
> *António Gonga, 40, with wife, from Kazi Nambuangongo. All their three children died while in hiding.*

Dr. David Grenfell, Kibentele,
Congo-Kinshasa (Zaïre) Republic, April 16, 1965.

While Dr. Shields was at Songo last week—a town with a state dispensary about seven miles from the frontier—there arrived from Angola a large group of men and boys. There were 120 in the group and they had been two months on the journey. . . . All were in utter rags. There is a church in this town in the charge of a refugee evangelist from São Salvador [northern Angola], and morning

*prayers are held there each day. Most of these chaps went
to the service. . . . During the service, the new refugees
asked if they could sing by themselves, and they sang the
hymn "Jesus knows all about our troubles." Most of them
were Methodists from a place just north of Luanda. . . .*

*Domingos João Machado, 20, with wife and baby, from
Senzala Kikabo, a place fifteen kms. from Caxito [some
50 miles northeast of Luanda]. There were 54 in this group.
They had no contact with the Portuguese on the journey,
which was very hard, because of the floods and swamps.
In the place where they have been hiding, they say there
are about 4,000 folk. . . .*

*Three children, aged 12, 5, and 3 years, on uncle's card.
Their mother, Isabel Margarida, was caught in the garden
in 1963 with her eldest son, 14 years, and twins of eight
months. No details concerning the father.*

*Manuel Mpungu, 59, of above town. Wife killed in air
raid in 1963. . . .*

Ibid., April 23, 1965.

*Gomes Lopes, 33, with wife and six children, from
Kingengo Nambuangongo. There were more than 300
people in this group. The journey out was not too difficult,
but was marred near the start by the loss of this man's
daughter, Manjora, 9, who was drowned when she fell
off the raft while crossing the Loge river in March 1965.*

*Santos Barroso, 33, with wife and three children, from
Senzala Gombe Dange. He lost three children and his
mother in an air raid in August 1964. Six others were also
killed. It was impossible to bury any of them.*

Ibid., May 8, 1965.

*I talked with three men [near Kibentele]. I asked if
they knew of any refugees who had returned to Angola
and they said about ten families had gone. . . . It appears
that they thought I had asked how many refugees they
knew who had gone back to Angola* since 1961. *. . .*

*Last April, some women who live in a border village
called Matadi-Vunda were working in their gardens which*

were on the Portuguese side [of the frontier]. . . . The Portuguese came and five of them were caught. On the way to Maquela they stayed the night at Paza, but during the night three of them got away. The other two agreed to stay at a village called Bangu . . . but after a few days they too got away and back to Congo. These two towns are places where the followers of Simão Toco have settled. . . . Last week, both these places were burnt down. It is believed that it was done by soldiers of GRAE. About two weeks ago the soba [chief] ran away to Congo, and it is thought he may have had something to do with organizing it. There is a Portuguese military camp near. This week Portuguese soldiers have been in the Congo villages looking for GRAE soldiers, but they did not stay. . . .

Isabel Manzambi, 32, with four children, from Makala Songo. During a raid on the hiding place at the end of August 1965, one man was killed on the spot and her husband with three other men were caught, tied up, and taken away. She believes they were killed, but she does not really know. . . .

Ibid., October 1, 1965.

Maria Nkengui, 55, with two children, from Tabi Bembe. These were in the Bembe group from Songololo (mentioned elsewhere in same report). There were 167 in the party. They crossed the Noqui-São Salvador road [in northern Angola] on November 4, 1965, then rested until daylight, for there are mines planted in this area. They had just begun to walk again when the Portuguese soldiers arrived about 7 a.m. on the 5th. The tailend of the party caught the main force of the attack. Maria Nkengui's husband, who was blind, had to be abandoned. Five people were missing. . . .

Ibid., January 18, 1966.

Manuel Zawa, 50, with wife and four children, from Kifwata Songo. In an attack on the hiding place just before they left, their daughter Lindeza, 9, was wounded but got away from the attackers. She was carried as they came

*out. They were caught in the attack on the Fuleze river
[mentioned elsewhere in report], and Lindeza was
drowned. The date, November 22, 1965. Their story confirmed the first report [received of this attack.] The
others said that three were drowned, and Lindeza is the
third name we have.*

*Alberto Laza, 33, with two children, from Kipanda. Was
working in the garden in 1964 with his wife when the
Portuguese arrived. His wife was shot, but he got away
with the children.*

Ibid., February 4, 1966.

*Nzumba Adolfina, 40, one child of twelve, from Kitala
Songo. Husband died in hands of the Portuguese in 1961.
Lost four children in the forest.*

*Feliciana, 59, with six grandchildren, from Kitala Songo.
The mother, Albeka, of these children, was lost on the way
out. The Portuguese attacked early in the morning of November 12. Altogether seven people were missing, all believed captured.*

*Munto Mukazi, 35, with wife and three children, from
Kindembe Ambriz. Group of 130 folk. Had crossed the
Bembe road to the coast and were near the river Ambriz
when they were spotted by a plane. . . . The plane
dropped bombs, and later more planes came with parachutists who had machine guns. One woman, Maria Myaku,
was taken prisoner, but twenty adults and five children
were shot dead or died of wounds. August 1965. . . .*

Ibid., February 11, 1966.

*Jeferina António, 25, with wife and two children, from
Kingengo Nambuangongo. Say they were attacked on the
way out near town of Ambriz after crossing river Loge.
About eleven in the morning. Wife shot in the foot and
now in Kimpese hospital.*

*Domingos Milanda, 20, from Seke, Nova Lisboa. Was
on contract labour. He was tied up with two car loads of
contradados in April 1961, and they were taken to the
river Danzi. There they were all hit with a catana at the*

back of the neck, and thrown into the river. The catana
hit this lad just above the neck, and I have taken a photo-
graph of the large scar. Their hands were tied behind their
backs with wire *and again the marks are still visible. He*
got out of the river himself, but it was several hours before
he met someone to undo the tied hands. . . .

Ibid., August 16, 1966.

Anita Garcia, 20, eldest of four children, from Mwungi,
Nova Caipemba. Mother died just before the war. Father
killed crossing a road as they moved to another hiding
place in 1964. Another man and three children shot and
killed at same time.

Joana Kissende, 25, with two children and pregnant,
from Mwungu. After crossing the Ambriz river and walk-
ing through the long grass, they were attacked by Portu-
guese soldiers. It was early in the morning and they had
only just started. Evidently the Portuguese had also been
camping nearby. June 13th. Killed were four [guerrilla]
soldiers who were guiding them, the husband, another man,
and two women. They got to the frontier five days later.
More than one hundred in this group. . . .

Ibid., September 9, 1966.

A small group of six (five men, one woman), from the
area of Quicabo, near Caxito [near Luanda], arrived at
Nkamuna, in Congo, on September 30, 1968. They had
started out with another group from that area, which we
interviewed and clothed at Kibentele [Congo] in Septem-
ber, but they got separated from the others one night and
lost their way, ran into an ambush and three were killed,
including António Pascal, the husband of Eliza Pedro.

Two groups, the first of thirty-four from Banza Sanga,
near Mucaba, and the other of eighty-two from Lembua,
Quimata, Quinsundi, and Mpete in the Damba region. All
these people seem to have had a safe journey. When asked
why they had decided to come out of Angola now, after
eight years of living in the forest, they replied that now

*the Portuguese soldiers know all their hiding places and
food gardens. They move from place to place but the
soldiers follow and never leave them alone. They stayed
originally so as to be there when Independence was granted,
but now they are weary of the constant harassment. . . .
The adults seem to be quite well, but the children are
anaemic and suffering from protein deficiency. After two
or three weeks of regular feeding, vitamins, and iron pills,
they improve considerably and are able to leave [our]
hospital. . . . There is a measles epidemic just now in this
area . . . and many children die due to complications.
They just do not have the necessary resistance needed. . . .*

Ibid., November 1, 1968.

*What happens to the family of a man after he has been
arrested by PIDE (secret police) in Angola? Today at
Kibentele (Congo) we heard the story of one such family.
Tereza Mateus, a nineteen-year-old girl, has just arrived
from the Bessa Monteiro District of northern Angola. Her
father, Vemba Mateus, was the teacher-evangelist of the
village of Kidilu and was arrested in March 1961 along
with many other church leaders and schoolteachers in the
area between Bessa Monteiro and Ambrizete. Vemba was
taken to Ambrizete, then possibly to Luanda or Novo
Lisboa, but the family were never told and have had no
direct word from him since, though they believe he is still
alive. When there was no news of him, and fear of Portuguese soldiers was growing, the mother, Rosa Miguel, led
her family of ten children into hiding in the forest.*

*In 1964 Rosa Miguel was killed by Portuguese soldiers
who raided their hiding place. They caught and carried off
two of her children, a teen-age girl, Maria, and a four-
year-old boy, Luzolo Mateus. Tereza watched from hiding
while her sister was being tied up. They never saw them
again, but later got word that they had been taken to
Luanda. In the forest José (now 23) and Domingos (21),
two of her brothers, act as evangelist and teacher. They
hold frequent church services and run a school. Last year*

there were thirty-five children in the school. They have only three reading books between them. . . .

Ibid., December 19, 1968.

General Situation: *Very few new refugees arrived in this area of Congo from Angola in 1969 and none have reported [to our mission] at Kibentele [Congo] in 1970. . . . With 400,000 already here, the northern part of Angola must be very depopulated. . . .*

Dr. Jim Grenfell, British Baptist
Missionary Society, Lukala, Congo/
Kinshasa, July 3, 1970.

5   THE EASTERN FRONT:
Toward the Atlantic

After 1965 the new front of resistance is widened and made good.

Supplies flow in from the Indian Ocean. Or, rather, they do not flow in, a word suggesting ease and regularity of motion; they are delivered from across the seas in sudden and erratic spurts, their precise contents seldom known in advance, often unexpected, sometimes practically useless. Boxed or baled, they arrive in such trucks as can be found and kept on the road. These are driven day and night from the Indian Ocean, discreetly, even secretly, by men with the needful papers and few words for the curious. MPLA transport crews perform extraordinary feats of physical and moral endurance. Until late in 1969 the whole two thousand miles and more of road will be entirely bad; then the eastern Zambian sector will be tarred, afterward the Tanzanian sector, afterward again the fearful western Zambian sector, where the road, till then, will often be a trail deep in sand.

Zambia remains a transit country; here the MPLA have no facilities for training or long-term logistics. Supplies have to go through as quickly as they can be taken. The taking is a long affair of jagged nerves and small disasters. Trucks break down far from help; weeks will pass before they can be rescued. Rivers must be crossed on ferries; sometimes these ferries are little more than rafts of timber built for walking folk and rural carts, platforms that lumber from one bank to the other in a slewing motion that gives no guarantee of safe arrival. When the rains are down, these rivers swell into moving lakes that suck at anything they catch.

The visitor crosses in a Land-Rover, and there is no problem in that, for a Land-Rover can move, if required, at what is practically no speed at all. A heavy truck is quite another matter. It comes second, carefully unloaded but still top-heavy on its narrow timber platform. Willing hands haul on ropes until the freighted raft has lodged its sodden foretip on the near-side bank. Sighs of relief all around. Too soon. The driver is a man of untiring energy and strength, and knows his business. It's not enough. He's got his front wheels safely on the bank, a short steep bank climbing from the river; but now he has to accelerate, and a truck is not a Land-Rover. He accelerates to get his back wheels off the raft and take the rise of the bank without being stuck in churning mud. The ropes part with a brisk explosion, the raft backs off into the river like a dumb disgruntled cow, and the truck, its front wheels retreating down the bank, slides away into twelve feet of unrepentant water. Nothing, save its canvas ridge-top, stays in sight.

Only men inured to the steady onward plod of a war with never-ending pains and breakdowns can stay as calm as these. Nobody runs about shouting; nobody looks more than cross. "The MPLA, you'll find," someone has remarked a week or so earlier, "are running this war at their own pace, an African pace, the only pace that anyone could run it at and hope to win. That's one reason why the Portuguese are losing it. Time isn't on the Portuguese side. Not that sort of time." A war of long duration; the MPLA maxim of 1964 has its full meaning at moments such as this. Rui says, smiling at the visitor's dismay: "Now it's in the river. Now we'll have to get it out again."

In this apparently hopeless situation, with an irreplaceable truck lodged in twelve feet of water some fifty yards from the bank and a hundred miles from the nearest town, only a miracle can solve the problem. But miracles occur in Africa; not always by magic, either. An immense bulldozer on caterpillar tracks

heaves across the skyline. Its roadmaking driver, taking the
whole thing as routine, shunts down to the bank while Rui and
others swim out with ropes and dive for the truck's submerged
underframe. Within half an hour the truck is dripping on the
near-side bank. Its drenched engine will not turn? Never mind;
an MPLA mechanic can be here in a week or so, and what
does a week or so matter in a war of long duration?

Somehow or other, across these years, the supplies are carried to the frontier. There they are sorted and sent in, split
into small loads that men will carry on their backs for days, for
weeks, for as much as five weeks if they are going to Bié, for as
much as eight if they are going to Malange. "Soon enough,"
Neto is saying, "we shall be able to motor them on the first part
of their journey. In the end we'll need aircraft." Even in 1970
it is a forecast that sounds no longer quite unreal.

Late in 1970 the supplies improve in quantity and quality.
Before that, they have lacked on both counts. Inspecting some
of the supplies that have come in recent years can be a strange
experience: a large load of embroidered tablecloths when men
are freezing at night for want of blankets; two bales of un-
identifiable pieces of green twill whose use nobody can suggest,
but may be some kind of military ankle bands that nobody
needs; bundles of secondhand clothing of more than doubtful
value—distant well-wishers may be doing themselves some good,
but little enough to the MPLA. Yet the MPLA are carefully
silent on this subject. In charge of logistics, Iko looks at those
strange lengths of green twill, hundreds of them, and comments
with a lifted eyebrow: "You don't know what they're for, either? We'll find a use for them."

The arms that come can also leave a lot to be desired. Even
in 1970, as any visitor could see, automatics reaching the
MPLA include many Schmeissers taken from Hitler's armies
during the Second World War. An excellent weapon then,
though rather heavy, the Schmeisser is long since outranged by
later types, while the Portuguese have the best NATO-issue
automatics. These shoot well over six hundred yards, the

Schmeisser barely over two hundred. It makes a difference in
an ambush—too much of a difference. A few better types come,
a few very good types come; up to 1970, in any case, not many
and not enough.

This paucity of supply may be surprising. If one listens to
the Portuguese and their friends, the MPLA have long been the
happy recipients of large and regular deliveries of first-class
Soviet and Chinese weapons. The truth is otherwise. At least to
the end of 1970 the MPLA receive no Chinese weapons, save
for a few that reach them through the good offices of the "liberation committee" of the Organization of African Unity. The visitor sees a handful of Chinese automatics, one or two Chinese
bazookas; nothing more. And weapon supply from other Communist countries, for whatever reason it may be, is manifestly
meager. At least one unit in a critical area of Moxico District
in 1970 is left with a Browning machine gun of First World
War vintage. This antique is said to be better than nothing:
after all, it makes a noise like a machine gun. The visitor is
left to draw his own conclusions.

All the same, after 1965, Neto succeeds increasingly well in
getting some supply; and the supply is indispensable. No
growth is possible without it, for no guerrilla movement can
ensure significant expansion after its initial onset without this
kind of outside supply: the seizure of sophisticated arms such
as automatics, mortars, and small cannon, and, even more,
the seizure of ammunition for these essential guerrilla tools,
then become too difficult in clashes with an alerted enemy. A
few such weapons can be taken and are taken, but nothing like
enough to keep the pressure on the rise. A guerrilla movement
that cannot keep the pressure on the rise is already halfway to
disbandment. But the MPLA, against whatever difficulties, do
keep the pressure on the rise.

Two other achievements have made and make this possible,
each signaling its own victory over physical or mental obstruction. The first achievement has been the systematic mobilization
of active support among the peoples of the eastern districts,

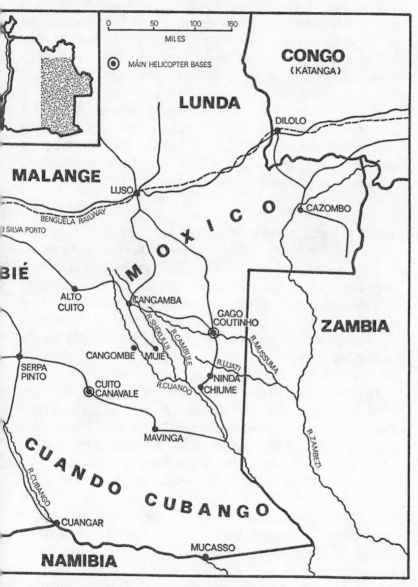

Eastern Angola

256   GUERRILLA WAR

initially among the Luvale, Mbunda, and Luchazi, and then
among their neighbors to the north and west and south. The
second is the intelligent commitment of the veterans of Cabinda,
and their development, together with the rise of local men and
women to positions of leadership, into a vanguard able to lead
a national movement.

Out of this complex process there emerges a movement of a
new type, a mass movement of multiethnic composition which
can embody the aspirations of the early 1960s. With this, the
men and women of the MPLA move from hope to realization.
They begin to reap their harvest from the seed of midwinter.

The first action against the Portuguese army in the east occurred, after due preparation, in Moxico District on March 18,
1966, with others quickly following elsewhere in Moxico and
in eastern Cuando Cubango. These went well. A wide penetration was made good. This enabled a number of rear bases to be
formed in Moxico, duly fed by supplies marched in along what
the Portuguese now began calling the "Agostinho Neto Trail":
in fact, as in Vietnam with the "trail" named after Ho Chi
Minh, a complex network of trails.

To keep the pressure on the rise now meant two things.
First, to extend the war throughout Moxico and Cuando
Cubango; secondly, to push the penetration into Lunda, Malange, and Bié. With military units following after political
units, both were achieved. The first action was fought in Lunda,
north of the Benguela Railway, on May 8, 1968, after which
units continued westward, while the first action was fought in
Bié on June 6, 1969. After that, in 1970 and later, keeping
the pressure on the rise has meant a further enlargement of
actions in the east, and a further progression toward the
Atlantic.

Militarily, this called above all for the continued mobilization
of the eastern peoples and their neighbors to the west. What
really mattered can be told in terms of this mobilization.

Seta, an English-speaking Luvale, aged twenty-eight or twenty-nine in 1970:

> I joined the MPLA in 1965. So did many Luvale of my age. I was trained abroad. I came back to Angola as a unit commander in 1966. Not all of my unit were Luvale.
>
> In the beginning I didn't even know how to use a gun. Then I was trained. But it is difficult to become a unit commander. You have to learn how to plan an attack before you make it. You have to learn the layout of the [Portuguese] post. You have to make a reconnaissance. Then you come back and sit down and work it out in detail. You tell your comrades how you are going to make the operation, how you are going to advance and retreat, and the political reasons why you are going to make it. And after, when it is over, you study together again, and you settle if you did right or if you did wrong. . . .
>
> Starting in 1966, the Portuguese turned all their main posts into fortified barracks. They made many of these, very many. At first the Portuguese had about eighty-five men in each, more or less, Africans as well as Portuguese. . . .

Chapayev, a Luchazi from Ninda, about thirty-five in 1970, militarily trained in the Soviet Union (whence his *nom de guerre*). Speaks no Portuguese but has lately learned in a guerrilla *kimbo* to write ciMbunda; a unit commander and specialist in long-range reconnaissance ("but to walk fast you have to take your boots off"):

> For a long time I tried to find work at home here [apparently between 1951 and 1956] and I could not. Then I went to Rhodesia. But I couldn't support my parents. I came back after six months.
>
> I went a second time. Yes, in 1957. I took a contract with Wenela [Witwatersrand Native Labour Association, the labor-recruiting organization of the Johannesburg

Chamber of Mines, famous throughout southern Africa].
When I came back [from South Africa] I had a radio.
"What do you listen to?" they asked me [at the frontier].
They arrested me, they took away my radio. After I came
out of prison I went back again to South Africa. In 1961. I
returned in two years. I had a bed, a cycle, a radio. But
there was no work for me, so I went to my village. Then,
in 1965, they tried to arrest me again. But I took my things
and went to Zambia.

From Zambia I went to South Africa a third time. But
I came back after only one year. That was in 1966, in
May, and I found the war. I said, "That's it. They've made
us suffer enough. The only way is to fight."

Any previous political activity?

No, but I saw the situation. Zambia was independent.
What else could we do? Why not Angola, too? If I took
up arms, it was because foreign people have our country.
Today the Portuguese have it. They have the power, and
they have the riches. And what do we have—we have no
money, we cannot even earn our living here, we cannot
support our families. . . .

Pupa, courier and fighting man, aged twenty-three in 1970,
a Chokwe from Lumeje, south of Luso, speaks some Portuguese, comes from a village family of eight children:

I have not been to school. In 1961 I began working for
a Portuguese as a boy [domestic servant]. He wasn't bad.
He took me to Uige [northern Angola]. It was all right.
He paid for the breakages. He gave me 150 escudos a
month. He was a trader.

When I got to Uige, at Songo, I heard about the war.
That was in 1962, and the war was hot there. I couldn't
walk about freely. My boss told me that the Kimbundu
ate people. I had no contact with them, with the people
there. I could see the Portuguese columns going on patrol,

leaving with forty men, coming back with thirty, like
that. . . .

The Portuguese said the war was only there, and nowhere else in Angola. My boss said, "If ever the bandits
come here, don't run off into the bush, but into the house;
otherwise the bandits will kill you."

He was fifteen at the time:

But I could see it was a real war. They attacked the
fazendas [Portuguese farmhouses] and I thought, if I stay
here they'll kill me. Better go to Luso [capital of Moxico
District]. I took a train and went [south] to Huambo [a
central district and main area of white settlement]. I
worked there as boy for eight months and got enough for
the ticket to Luso. I went by train to Luso in 1964.

I stayed in Luso till 1966, working as boy for the
whites. I changed bosses. If one didn't pay me, I went to
work for another. At Luso it's the custom that if you don't
work you don't eat, and you're arrested [i.e., as a vagrant,
and thus subject to "contract labor"]. It's better outside
in the country [areas].

I began hearing about the war again. I was told that
the bandits were coming into our part of the country. In
1967 I heard it was a real war again. And I went, too.

Now he was twenty, but he still had to find his way through
the confusion of the times:

I fled from Luso because I didn't want to die there.
Other people might not be hearing about the war, but I did
because I worked for the Portuguese, and the Portuguese
said, "Don't talk about these things to others, that whites
are dying." I was working for a Portuguese policeman. At
that time the Portuguese idea was, "If you see the bandits
give them a demijohn of wine and then come and tell us
and we'll attack them." They also said that the MPLA,
when they came, would take all the people into the bush.

So I fled from Luso to my village. The Portuguese said
then, when I was still in Luso, "If the war comes here
we'll gather the people and kill them all, and the MPLA
will find ruins." And that's what I was afraid of.

All the Portuguese said the same thing. They said, "If
the MPLA come we will kill you all." Then they started
the *ndandandas* [strategic hamlets].

So I fled from Luso and went to Lumeje. That's where
I got information that the war would come there too, that
it was the Angolans who were fighting to liberate our country. I heard this about the MPLA, but the first to arrive
were the people of Savimbi, who came only to mobilize
the people, and had no arms [for them]. Those who
brought the arms were the MPLA. When they arrived in
the Luvale area, Savimbi's people fled to the Congo. . . .

In Lumeje I lived in a *kimbo* [guerrilla-protected settlement in the woods], and it was there that I joined the
MPLA and took part with a grenade in one action. After,
I worked for Iko [Carreira, veteran MPLA militant from
the Luso area, then in charge of that area for the MPLA
and a member of the MPLA's steering committee]. I did
patrols, I made reconnaissances, and when the [political]
activists wanted to go into a village it was me that led them
because I knew the country.

As to the Chokwe, they began like the people here [the
interview took place in Mbunda country]. They began by
fleeing abroad. The Chokwe [who fled] went to the Congo.
But there in the Congo they were often taken and shot.
Those who have stayed behind hold firm and fight. . . .

Selected for training, Pupa turned up one day at the Zambian frontier—"pushing a bicycle," as others recalled, "loaded
with an enormous weight of food," a man with strength well
fitted to the measure of this war. Afterward he was sent into
Mbunda country while awaiting one of the rare opportunities
for training outside Angola.

So it was that a political and military organization grew out of a pioneering effort and persuasion, thrusting up its clarities and individual challenge through a wilderness of muddle and misinformation, pushing aside despair or disbelief, reaching back to old traditions of resistance, transforming these into new disciplines and understanding; and so, little by little, forging a national movement and an army to defend it among communities of scattered people who were also, more and more, angry people ready to fight.

These early units took shape in 1966 and were enlarged in 1967. This was the year in which the cause of the MPLA became rooted into the population of Moxico, a sparse population reckoned in 1960 at some 266,000 people. MPLA communiqués tell the story in detail. For example:

> On June 9, at 07.05, a guerrilla detachment of the MPLA operating in the area of the Mussuma River, near the post of Sessa, shot down a B-27 bomber of the colonialist air force. The aircraft was on a *terra queimada* [destroy-by-fire] mission when it was downed by our forces. . . .

They were to shoot down other aircraft: in 1968, for example, a helicopter whose dead pilot's papers showed him to have been a Rhodesian.

> On June 19, at 16.25, our guerrillas operating on the left bank of the river Cuando [dividing Moxico from Cuando Cubango] ambushed a group of colonialist soldiers on patrol. In a combat lasting about four minutes the enemy lost thirteen men killed and others wounded. . . .

> On March 22, at 16.30, a group of MPLA guerrillas ambushed one truck and three "Jeeps" loaded with Portuguese troops traveling from the post of Ninda to Gago Coutinho. We killed 38 and wounded 17 of them, and suffered no losses. . . .

> On March 25, at 13.30, two trucks loaded with Portuguese soldiers traveling from Cangamba to Muié

were ambushed by MPLA freedom fighters. The enemy
lost 35 killed, and many wounded. . . .

Breaking out from Cabinda and the frontier regions, this
was the "generalization of the armed struggle throughout our
country" for which the leaders of the MPLA had called at the
outset of 1967.

By the end of the year they were ready for another move.
Neto announced it on January 3 at a Brazzaville press conference. The gains of 1967, he said, had allowed a number of
new political and military decisions. "Here is one of them, a
decisive step forward: the seat of our Movement is no longer to
function outside [Angola], and its transfer inside the country
has already begun. . . . This means that the headquarters of
our Movement is no longer Brazzaville, but in one of the regions controlled by our Movement. What this means is that our
Executive thinks the moment right for its members to work
permanently among the people, closer to their problems . . . ,
and it is from the interior that we shall direct all our activities
whether internal or international in scope."

What followed from this was that the MPLA retained its
liaison and communications offices in Brazzaville, Dar es
Salaam, and Lusaka, as well as two or three discreet transit
camps, but that the majority of the steering committee, more
than forty men and women by this time, were to be continuously
inside the country, and visited by touring members of the Executive, including Neto himself. This was the pattern already in
operation by the PAIGC in Guinea-Bissau, and in preparation
by FRELIMO. In Angola it marched in step with modifications
in the structure of the movement and the establishment of interior political training centers. These were the Centros de
Instrucção Revolucionária (CIR), where the shift from revolt
to revolution was now advanced with the movement's growth.

But 1968 brought another development: the first major Portuguese *riposte* in the east. By this time the Portuguese command was sharply aware of a serious threat in regions they

had long regarded as of little or no importance. They had not been quite unmindful of the possible implications of Zambia's independence, and as early as 1962, apparently, had sent across the frontier an agent who inquired of the then *litunga* (traditional ruler) of the Lozi, in western Zambia, whether he would be interested in having Portuguese "protection."[1] But generally they had scoffed at the possibility of serious MPLA action in the east, being still of the view expressed by Roberto Holden in 1970, that the MPLA were "in the majority 'civilized,' privileged elements . . . half-breeds . . . [who have] never wanted anything to do with the population." Now they saw there was something badly astray with this estimate, and mounted a large, multisided operation to regain control. It proved no laughing matter for the MPLA. Iko, speaking of 1968:

> The Portuguese command had the view that Moxico and Cuando Cubango [with only 380,000 people, according to the 1960 census, and fewer in 1968, owing to the flight of refugees into Zambia] were of no great economic importance to them. They would lay waste these regions, scorching the earth along the frontier [with Zambia] as they had already done along the northern frontier. They would hit us as they could, and try to contain us by fixing more and bigger garrisons. Otherwise they would leave these districts to us.

> But west of these districts they would build a tough barrier of defenses designed to keep us out of Bié and Malange—and so out of the coastal regions beyond those central districts. As for Lunda, they thought that the diamond company [Diamang] was quite able to look after itself with its own militia and police.[2]

[1] D. G. Anglin, "Confrontation in Southern Africa: Zambia and Portugal," *International Jnl.* (Canadian Inst. of Int. Affairs) XXV, 3, 1970, who also notes "reports that, immediately after his election in December 1968, the new Litunga received a Portuguese offer of financial assistance." Other sources indicate that Portuguese intrigue among the Lozi has continued, being based, no doubt, on the belief that Lozi traditional leaders might be won for a more overt opposition to the government of UNIP and Pres. Kaunda, of whom the new Litunga has always been a bitter opponent.

[2] This and other quoted interviews were with B.D. in June 1970.

Afterward, when this strategy had failed, the Portuguese would put forth a major effort to corral the whole rural population of the eastern districts within "strategic hamlets" so as to prevent their integration with the MPLA. But this still lay ahead.

The major offensive of 1968 began chronologically in the north, in Cuanza Norte and neighboring areas, where the MPLA had what it now termed its First Region (with Cabinda as the Second, Moxico and Cuando Cubango as the Third, Lunda and Malange as the Fourth, Bié and westward as the Fifth, and a Sixth, toward Mossâmedes, still in preparation). It began in the north, according to the MPLA, in answer to the more aggressive operations of their fighters in the Dembos forests reinforced by the two columns that had got through from the Congo in 1966–67. Iko: "We heard on Luanda radio of an offensive beginning up there. We knew then they'd come our way." He himself was near Luso at the time, and very short of arms. "I was responsible for urban zones around Luso, and I'd only a pistol."

In Moxico this dry-season offensive of 1968 proved a stiff test. Ferried by helicopter, the first time the Portuguese had committed helicopters on any scale in the east, commandos and marines came in to support reinforced patrols from fixed garrisons. There was much bombing, and the bombing hurt. An American sociologist who was there at the time, Don Barnett, has published a graphic account of what it was like: ". . . I began to run again. By this time there were eight planes in the air: three helicopters, three light bombers, and two armed reconnaissance planes. . . ." Recovering from a bout of malaria, Barnett was evidently fortunate to get away as well as he did.[3]

And Barnett, in the wake of these attacks, noted what others would note after him, but what much outside opinion would still disbelieve: the intimate relationship that had come to exist between the movement and the local population. Following the aerial attack in which he and others had to scatter, "it was the

[3] D. Barnett, *With the Guerrillas in Angola*, Liberation Support Committee, 1970.

local peasantry which provided us with the necessary food, shelter and refuge. This support was given freely and in a spirit of full comradeship. It was a reflection of the vital interdependence which now exists between villagers and guerrillas . . . and of the fact that the MPLA's guerrillas are in a very real sense the sons and daughters of the people."

The bombing continued for a while, and did more damage. Late in September a captured villager revealed the site of the MPLA's only staffed hospital then in Moxico, placed in woodlands near the Shekului River. The Portuguese sent in three bombers and three helicopters and harried the place for two hours. Among those killed was the MPLA's only doctor then in Angola, Américo Boavida, one of the founders of the refugee clinics established in the western Congo more than six years earlier. It was a hard loss.

Six months earlier, before the 1968 offensive, the MPLA had suffered an even harder loss: the death in action, while attacking the Portuguese garrison at Caripande, in northern Moxico, of Hoji ya Henda, veteran of Cabinda and commander of all their units in the east. The war was taking its toll of those "privileged elements who have never wanted anything to do with the population." In fact they were giving the population its heroes of today.

Losses in the 1968 offensive were criticized. Iko in 1970: "The truth is that our people had got too confident. We'd had so much success. . . . We allowed the development of large concentrations at fixed points. There were even hours fixed for bathing in the rivers. Not enough attention to security. A serious shortage of arms. And we ran out of food soon after the Portuguese offensive began. . . ." After this, there came a new emphasis on high mobility and on growing more food.

Later offensives in the same area soon went far to erase the memory of the troubles of 1968, and helicopter attacks, though always disturbing, evidently lost much of their demoralizing power. By the end of the year, the situation was more or less restored for the MPLA; penetration westward could begin again. Having reasserted its control of wide rural areas of

Moxico and Cuando Cubango, the movement set about pushing through the "barrier" along the eastern flank of Bié and Malange. The method adopted was the same: first the political units, then the fighting men. Once again the memories tell their tale.

Guahero, aged thirty-one in 1970, one of those who carried out the penetration into eastern Malange:

My father was a European. Our farm was in Cuanza Norte. In the end, after I'd left Portugal to join the struggle, my father agreed with my decision. My mother is an African, and she, oh yes, she certainly agreed!

I got to school all right, and I went to Luanda as well. In Luanda I did all sorts of crazy things, youthful things. I got married. I enjoyed life. Then I went to Portugal and studied at the Fine Arts Academy. But art was only half my life. The other half was driving fast cars. Cars—I was good at that. I drove in competitions. That taught me things too. (He explains that he ran into discrimination, doing well but getting no recognition.) I ran into all that, but I didn't crash with it any more than I crashed my cars. No, I learned about it. And I got to know others who'd learned better. It was in Lisbon that I joined the struggle. That was in 1959, before the wars began.

I got away from Portugal in 1962 [illegally, like other students from Africa who were there at the time], and I went to Algiers. Oh, by one route or another. And from there I went to Brazzaville. The MPLA had already moved there. I became a fighter. I fought in Cabinda. Afterward I was sent down here, to the eastern front. I have been inside the country for a long time. I was sent to help in penetrating Malange. That was in 1969.

He talks about this pioneering expedition:

The eastern border of Malange is formed by a broad river. Our group crossed it with local guides. Our method was to find out the attitude of the local *sobas* [traditional chiefs approved by the Portuguese, as distinct from "chiefs" created by them]. And then to contact them with much discretion. It was easy, because there was no lack of local people who knew about our struggle and were ready to help us. Then we'd go into a selected village and talk to the *soba,* and we'd begin to organize a support group there. I and others of our own group could speak Lunda, the language of the people in that place—they're people who call themselves Bula.

Yes, for example . . . the case of a village about whose *soba* we had good information. We infiltrated one of our comrades into that village. After a while he sent us news. He said, "Follow me in." So we followed him in, and he told us there were good chances of meeting the elders. We stayed . . . and we held meetings in that village, even inside it. The village had five militiamen—Africans armed by the Portuguese with carbines, shotguns. They knew we were there. But they were on our side, too. They gave us information about the Portuguese and their movements. Naturally, it's an anxious business. We keep our arms beside us, though it's not a fighting mission.

We asked about their problems. They said their biggest problem had to do with cultivation. This was because the Portuguese were afraid that as soon as the people went off into the forest, to their clearings, they would make contact with our movement. So the Portuguese had to feed the people, and this they couldn't do, if only because that area had a lot of people. There were four hundred in that village alone. And they had a real food shortage.

Then, too, there's the annual tax (*imposto*). 125 escudos for each male over sixteen. If the husband has gone to the bush, isn't in the village for some reason, then his wife has to pay; the Portuguese tell her she's got to pay because her man's gone to us. To pay this tax they have to sell food. Whether it's dried cassava, rice, maize, groundnuts, they have to sell at the village market to Portuguese traders who come from neighboring towns, sometimes from towns a long way off. Forced labor was still going on in

1969, when I was there, but it wasn't much of a problem for this village I'm telling you about.

We could see that the people wanted contact with us so as to get fresh confidence. And it's a fact that they did all they could to make contact with us. Our job then was to give them courage, to explain how things really were, how things could be. To tell them, for instance, that their children could look forward to a chance of going to school, once the struggle was won. Our job was to counter the everlasting Portuguese propaganda—because the people have lived in ignorance, they've been cut off from information, they haven't been able to understand what's happening, what will happen. . . .

Guahero talks of the sheer physical difficulties, so easy to overlook when glancing at a map:

From the river border, and we were west of that, it took me when I came back fifty-three days of daily marching to reach the Zambian frontier, marching an average six hours a day. It's generally not necessary to march at night, though it may be. A forced march can be eight hours or more, but that's too much when you're carrying a lot of weight, because you're exhausted at the end of the day, and then it's bad if you run into trouble. . . .

What was achieved in eastern Malange was also done in Bié, a central district lying farther south and of crucial importance as being the main gateway to Huambo and its riches, and the road to the Atlantic.

The disadvantages here were great distances and relatively dense road communications capable of being used by the Portuguese army. The advantages were the presence of a big population thoroughly awakened to their grievances. "The oppression was always very great in Benguela, Bié, Huambo, and other Umbundu areas. Hundreds of thousands have been sent to forced labor. Even today there are more Ovimbundu [plural

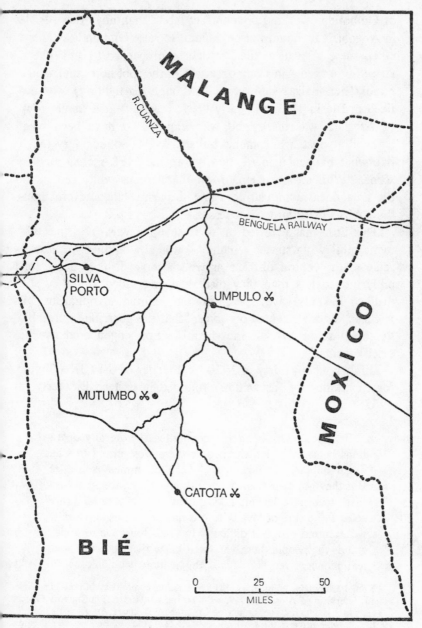

Central Angola: Location of some guerrilla actions in Bié

of Umbundu] working on 'contract labor' than any other people in Angola."[4] It should not be difficult to raise Umbundu country.

To these grievances the Portuguese proceeded to add others. A well-informed American observer on the spot notes that "some minor [nationalist] infiltration (although no fighting) was noticed in Bié in 1967 and early the following year a small group of Africans was discovered who claimed to have been 'vaccinated' against 'white man's bullets.'" This sounds very much like what happened in Moxico before the MPLA came on the scene. "With strong urging from the nervous white settlers in the area, local administrators and the army killed several hundred Africans as an 'object lesson.'"[5]

This little massacre led on to fresh upheavals. The "resettlement" policy of "strategic hamlets" was now applied on a large scale to the central districts as well. People disliked being forcibly moved less than they disliked being killed, but they still disliked it. This gave new ground to militant nationalism. "It is clear," adds this same observer, "that the guerrillas were able to capitalise greatly on the dissatisfaction engendered by the resettlements."

Dilolwa, about thirty in 1970, and leader of the CIR (Center for Revolutionary Instruction) founded in eastern Bié early in 1969:

> In Bié we formed action committees before any operations began. At first, the people there were afraid of what might happen; so far, there'd been no armed resistance. But they got over this. Among groups there, we would ask them to elect a leader, asking them to apply certain rules so as to be sure of loyalty to our national struggle. Usually, we've found no great difficulty in this. You have to understand—the people there very well knew that once the political pioneers reached them, the fighters wouldn't be far

[4] Daniel Chipenda, member of MPLA steering committee, himself an Umbundu; interview of Aug. 28, 1969, with D. Barnett, Liberation Support Cttee.

[5] Gerald J. Bender, "The Limits of Counter-Insurgency: An African Case," 1971, *J. Comparative Politics*, vol. iv, 3 of 1972. Professor Bender, one should add, is careful to make it clear that his paper was in no way committed to the nationalist cause, any more than to the Portuguese. It resulted from months of professional investigation in Angola.

behind. They knew this because they knew it had happened like that elsewhere. First the political pioneers, then the fighting units. . . .

Traitors? No, I can't say we've found any big problem there. Naturally when the Portuguese capture people they can sometimes make them talk. But I don't remember a single case of a man who was in one of our committees and acted as a traitor.

When we first got into Bié the Portuguese put up a big effort at chasing us out again. As they always do when we get active in a new area. They knew we'd arrived—for instance, people fled from the *ndandandas* [strategic hamlets] to our protection. They organized one of their mopping-up operations [*operações de limpeza*]. They brought in helicopters for what they call "vertical attacks." They used commandos from Luanda.

I left Bié to come back here [for treatment of a severe eye ailment; this interview took place outside Angola] at the beginning of January [1970], marching with a column of our people, some of whom were transport men returning from Bié and others men selected for advanced training.

The fighters duly followed. Kubindama, ex-male nurse from the Nambuangongo rebels of 1961:

I came out east in September 1969 after I'd been in Europe on a training course. Before that, I'd been in Cabinda. I was sent to join the units in Bié. It took me a month to walk across Moxico. When I got there I found a guerrilla base with a commander and a commissar; and I worked in the CIR there, which was then commanded by Dilolwa, because we hadn't yet set up a SAM [medical service] there.

We already had several units there, and people were prepared to support us, morally and politically. We began attacking the Portuguese east of the Cuanza. The terrain there is different from Moxico. It's fertile soil, there are hills and forests. And it's the center of Portuguese coloni-

zation, together with Huambo. We attacked their army, beginning in a small way with ambushes and road mining.

I myself was appointed medical chief there, but I did
military service at the same time.

He gives an example:[6]

We attacked the Portuguese post of Umpulo [some
fifty miles on the road east of Silva Pôrto and a few miles
east of the Cuanza]. We were forty divided into groups,
and there were twelve in my group. We laid an ambush
very early in the morning, and waited two days for the
Portuguese. Each group had its own food. Then a truck
convoy, six of them, arrived. We attacked and destroyed
the first three trucks, but the rear three, being a little distant, could turn back and go for help. The first of the
trucks we destroyed went up on a mine, we stopped the
other two with rifle fire. Each had about a dozen soldiers
in it. After the attack we were able to get all the arms
from the first three trucks, because we had covering fire
from our comrades. Then we pulled out.

I myself came back from Bié at the beginning of April
[1970] and marched for twenty-eight days to the Zambian
frontier. My task was to come for medical supplies and
report on the medical work there. Now I shall go back
to Bié.

So it came about that the gateway to the Atlantic was forced
and held open. "Near the end of 1970 the Portuguese began
to move inactive troops from other areas into Bié in an attempt
to stop the guerrillas at the Cuanza River. However, the insur-
gency appears to be rooted among the population and the army
has been unable to dislodge it."[7] By 1970, according to the
MPLA, their units were already fighting west of the Cuanza.

The same progression was reported farther south again,
around Serpa Pinto, in the grasslands there. In July 1970, for
example, the high command in Luanda was claiming a major

6 See map 5.
7 Bender, op. cit.

success "in destroying the structure that the MPLA were trying to implant" in the area of the Cuvelai and Cuito rivers.[8] The MPLA, for their part, said that they had defeated the Portuguese in this operation, destroying two platoons. Common to both accounts was the confirmation of fighting in the southwest. This, too, was a gateway to the Atlantic, and one, moreover, that led to the iron-ore mines of Cassinga, exploited by Krupp of Western Germany for purchasers largely in Japan.

In public the Lisbon authorities and their generals in the field continued to say that they were winning; it is hard to believe they said so in private. Their position had too many obvious weaknesses. They had failed to regain the strategic initiative in the eastern districts. They had failed to prevent their "barrier" to the central districts from being thrust aside. Suffering these defeats, their generals smarted under growing criticism and grew more recklessly destructive. In 1970 they introduced the use of herbicides dropped from the air, another of several "counterinsurgency techniques" they had learned from U.S. examples in Vietnam.

The MPLA also had weaknesses in their position, but did not seek to deny or conceal them. In 1970 they still lacked any sufficient supply of good automatics and mortars, and even of rifles; at least until the closing months of the year, they were quite without the small recoilless cannon used so effectively by the PAIGC against fortified garrisons in Guinea-Bissau since 1967. Of their approximately five thousand fighters in the eastern and central districts, perhaps a half were without modern types of weapons; many had no weapons save grenades.[9] They had still to make contact from the east with their fighters in the far northwest, numbering now between fifteen hundred and two thousand. They had still to battle with the problems of distance and morale inseparable from any guerrilla war.

"It often happens, particularly in rear combat areas, that our fighters are left for months and months without instructions

[8] *O Século,* Luanda, July 22, 1970.
[9] Neto to B.D., June 1970.

or directives from the Steering Committee, even when circumstances are favorable to action. . . . We should organize more actions, more new initiatives." Such was part of Neto's New Year's message of 1970, broadcast from Dar es Salaam on the first day of the year. And there was apparently a good deal to complain about, notably in the crucial zone of central southern Moxico, where men in command were showing a tendency to prefer talk to action. But the record for 1970 was to show this tendency reversed—partly, in the event, by improvements in command.

Reviewing the position early in 1971, a careful US estimate nourished by inside information from Portuguese and other sources could conclude that "1970 marked the greatest increase in the intensity of the war in any single year except 1966 when the eastern front opened. For the first time the insurgents have chosen to stand and fight (300% more often than in previous years) when assaulted by Portuguese units, reflecting better guerrilla organisation, discipline, and arms. In addition, the insurgents initiated over 60% more combat actions than the previous year, resulting in an increase of about 25% in Portuguese casualties. . . . Finally, the number of insurgent attacks against the resettlement militias nearly doubled in 1970. . . ."[10]

The weaknesses were still there, but the military evidence of 1971 suggested that they were being reduced. For 1971 brought the formation of the first of the MPLA's large mobile units of 100–150 men, each unit including an "artillery section" trained in the use of small cannon, large mortars, and portable rocket launchers made available after the fall of 1970. With these, stronger attacks were launched on Portugese garrison posts, and several of these were eliminated. Shortage of food supplies inside the country remained a major problem. Yet the Portuguese were now in greater difficulties than before. In the eleventh year of the war, this was the same as saying that the Portuguese were being defeated.

The political evidence, whether on the Portuguese side or that of the national movement, pointed to the same conclusion.

10 Bender, op. cit.

DOCUMENTARY FOUR

The Government of Portugal is "only keeping up the military police operations necessary for the security of the inhabitants [of the oversea Provinces] who desire to remain Portuguese."

Prime Minister Marcello Caetano in
electoral speech, 1970 (quoted in
United Nations A/8023, Oct. 5
1970, p. 370).

By 1968 Portugal's military effectives totalled 182,000 or 10.1 percent of potential effectives (total of men of military age). This was the highest world percentage, followed by the USA with 8.9 percent under arms, Greece with 8.7 percent under arms, Turkey with 7.7 percent under arms, and USSR with 7.0 percent under arms. But for one understrength division assigned to the North Atlantic Treaty Organisation, as well as base and training troops in Portugal, all of Portugal's effectives were committed to the wars in Africa.

Institute of Strategic Studies,
London, 1968, and comparable sources.

Portuguese National Budget
(millions of escudos)

	Estimated Ordinary Expenditure	Military Defence Actual Expenditure	Security Actual Expenditure
1965	10,712	7,259	446
1966	11,026	7,993	448
1967	12,605	9,785	448
1968	13,663	10,696	466

(United Nations A/8023 Oct. 5, 1970, pp. 54–55. The above figures almost certainly understate the actual amounts spent on warfare and security, some of these expenses being concealed under various "ordinary expenditure" headings.)

Everyone knows that Portugal does not make any aircraft, not even as toys for children.

Amilcar Cabral, in preface to
The Liberation of Guiné, Penguin,
London and Baltimore, 1969.

Since 1961 the Portuguese air force in Africa has used bombers, fighter-bombers, fighters, transports, reconnaissance aircraft and helicopters sold to Portugal, sometimes on highly preferential terms, by Portugal's allies in the North Atlantic Treaty Organization.

Some of these types were specifically designed for NATO purposes: e.g., the Fiat G-91 NATO Type R.4 jet-fighter-bomber. Of these the Portuguese air force secured forty. "These aircraft were supplied to Portugal by West Germany in 1966 for the sum of approximately $10 million. The G-91 is a plane especially designed for NATO. Originally they were built for the U.S.A. in German factories under Italian license. The U.S.A. intended to supply them to Turkey and Greece to be used there for NATO purposes. Later these planes were transferred to the German Luftwaffe. The aircraft consists of an Italian air-

frame, a British engine, French undercarriage, and Dutch electronic equipment. These planes are very suitable for counterinsurgency operations in Africa, as they can take off from a short runway."

> *Frankfurter Rundschau,* Jan. 27, 1966;
> *Daily Express,* London, Jan. 26, 1966;
> *Flying Review International,* March
> 1966, p. 401; *Interavia Air Letter,*
> Jan. 26, 1966. Summarized in S. Bosgra
> and Chr. van Krimpen, *Portugal and
> NATO,* Amsterdam, 1969.

[Portuguese military] bulletins mention the successful use of helicopters to reach nationalist sanctuaries in the east [of Angola that are] inaccessible by land.

> UN summary, 1971.

By 1969 Portugal had been able to buy at least twenty Alouette-2 helicopters and at least sixty-six Alouette-3 helicopters from French manufacturers; a number of (similarly French-made) Puma helicopters; and at least ten Saro-Skeeter West German helicopters. Since then, other and larger types have come into Portuguese service from the same sources.

> *Portugal and NATO* and comparable sources.

Britain and others have supplied small naval vessels, especially for coastal patrols.

In 1968 the West German Blohm und Voss shipyards (Hamburg) undertook a commission to build three 1400-ton frigates for the Portuguese Navy, at an over-all cost of $45 million, an amount, commented the West German Wehrdienst *magazine of December 9, 1968, "that should be compared with the total of $45 million from all West German arms supplies to Portugal up to 1968."*

When West Germany sold the forty Fiat G-91 fighter-bombers mentioned above, the West German Defense Ministry stated: "The sale took place on the basis of the principle of mutual aid between NATO partners. The delivery is subject to a clause agreed on between the Gov-

*ernment of the Federal Republic [of Germany] and the
Portuguese Government which states that the planes are
to be used exclusively in Portugal for defense purposes
within the framework of the North Atlantic Pact."*

*To which a spokesman of the Portuguese Foreign Min-
istry rejoined: "The transaction was agreed on within the
spirit of the North Atlantic Pact. It was agreed that the
planes would be used only for defensive purposes within
Portuguese territory. Portuguese territory extends to
Africa—Angola, Mozambique, and Portuguese Guinea."*

Op. cit., quoting *Flying Review
International,* April 1966, p. 459.

The New York Times *reported on Dec. 9, 1970, that
the State Department had received information from the
U.S. Consulate in Luanda that Portugal had used herbicides to destroy crops grown by nationalists in Angola.
According to this report, U.S. diplomats had been in-
structed to pursue the matter with Portuguese authorities
in Lisbon and Luanda.*

*On Dec. 11, 1970, a spokesman for the State Depart-
ment said that the news reports that it had such information were not true and he added that, "We don't know
what they are doing there." He also said that the U.S.A.
was not investigating the issue. According to the New
York* Times, *however, State Department officials privately
confirmed the accuracy of the article, adding that its publication had "not been helpful."*

*An inquiry of 1970 revealed 303,160 Portuguese living
in France, or 11.4 percent of all foreigners in that country.
Of these, 171,760 were in jobs, of which 58.2 percent
were in the building trade and public works. Nearly half
were in the Paris Region.*

*Portuguese unskilled worker, aged forty, in France five
years:*

*My family's back there in Portugal. I was a farm laborer
at home. I've never worked in the building trade, never;
. . . here I work in the building trade. I earn more here;*

I work more hours. In Portugal I've grandsons and daughters, they're hungry. I came to France and I send money home. . . . Africa doesn't bother me, why should it? We're patriots, we have to go to Angola to defend our country. . . . Angola's a Portuguese colony. . . . I've a son fighting for the country of Salazar, and if the government of Portugal needs me, I'll go to Angola, it's a duty. It's like my own country, it's my blood that's there, it's Portuguese. . . .

Portuguese unskilled worker, aged twenty-eight, in France one year:

Me, I'm talking from experience of the war in Guiné, an experience that cost me my health, I can prove that to you: asthmatic bronchitis. I got so ill I couldn't go on operations in the bush. After eighteen months of Guiné, the medical captain said: "My lad, you'll have to get out." I wanted to all right, and all the more because I'd finished my time three days before, but when the medical captain told the company commander, Lt.-Col. Costa Campes, this one said: "My men go home all dead, or all living." I was really ill, and I had a medical certificate, but they didn't send me home. . . .

[Finally, they did send him home.] I went to Oporto and there they said: "My lad, as you've been in Guiné, which do you choose, Angola or Mozambique?" I said I'd think about it. I went into a café and thought about it, I had half an hour. And you know where I went? I chose France. . . .

Portuguese male, unmarried, no age given, deserter, in France two years:

I got myself smuggled out [o salto]. I came over the mountains. I had to pay eight contos in Portuguese money [about £100: $240] to get here. I'd thought of emigrating when I got back from Angola. That was a moment when emigration was allowed to Germany and France. So I went to the emigration office to put my name down. The woman there said to me: "You'd better get smuggled out [o salto]; otherwise you'll never leave." . . .

What do I think about the war? I think it's a war for the capitalists, because it's only for officers and capitalists. An officer over there gets seven, eight, or even ten contos (£100, £120, or £150: $240, $288, $360) but they don't even give the soldiers enough to eat. . . . I did twenty-one months [of military service] in Portugal, at home, and twenty-seven months in Angola. . . .

I think the Blacks would be right to do thirty thousand times more than they've done. Sooner or later, they'll be independent. . . .

Portuguese male, no details:

As for the slums we live in here [bidonvilles], you've got to see them. You live there because there's nowhere else. Even if you do find something else you haven't got the money to pay for it. They say we're illegal though everyone knows, even Pompidou. But nobody wants to do anything about it. . . . Besides, there's a problem, we've no papers. . . . We get here, and we've no papers. You can't go to a hotel or a hostel. You need papers for that. . . .

Les Travailleurs Immigrés Parlent,
Cahiers du Centre d'Études Socialistes,
Paris, Sept.–Dec. 1970.

Ex-Capt. Jaime Morais, aged thirty-four, deserter interviewed in Stockholm, Sweden, March 25, 1971:

I come from a Portuguese family of liberal views, and was trained as a civil engineer. I have also worked as a public relations officer for the Portuguese government. I did my military service ten years ago. As a student, I was given an officer's training and became a captain in the reserve. . . .

The truth about the present situation in the army is that there are no more officers to be recruited. Nobody who understands anything wants to make a military career. Nobody wants to go to the military academy. . . .

When I was drafted again they started to reach the bottom of the reserve of military officers. I was called up in August 1969. Then I had six months' training in Portugal, including the training of my own men (166 soldiers). In June 1970 we left for Porto Amélia, in northern Mozambique. The ship had a capacity of five hundred men, but it took seventeen hundred. The soldiers had to sleep on the cargo. It was almost impossible to breathe there. The trip lasted twenty-eight days. After six months of service in Mozambique I had made one year of service and was entitled to one month of holiday in Europe. Then I decided to escape. . . .

I never wanted to participate in a war. Not that I did not want to defend my country, but the war in the colonies is not for defense. . . . I had never been to the colonies before. I knew that the official propaganda did not tell the truth about them, but still I was shocked when arriving in Mozambique. It was like when Vasco da Gama went there. Everything I had learned at school about the four hundred years of Portuguese civilising mission was a bluff. . . . The soldiers don't know what they are defending. Before they are sent off to Africa they don't even know where Mozambique is. They are also victims of the war. . . .

Ex-soldier number 04827, Francisco Gomes de Silva, captured and then set free (July 19, 1968) by national liberation army of Guiné:

I was in a Bissau barracks for fifteen days, waiting to be posted. In this barracks there were two militants of the people's army, the PAIGC, who had been captured by the commandos. During interrogation they were beaten day and night with wire whips which cut about half a centimeter into the skin. As the poor devils didn't reply, either because they knew nothing or because they didn't want to betray their cause, the torturers kicked them pitilessly all over the body until the unfortunate prisoners fell exhausted or unconscious to the floor. Many times they were denied water they begged for. When they [the torturers] did give them any they added big quantities of salt, and they laughed in the faces of the poor devils as it was eagerly drunk. Friends, this was the first actual crime I saw in Guiné, but unfortunately it wasn't the last. . . .

Jornal do Emigrante, Paris, 1970.

6 MIDWINTER'S HARVEST:
From Revolt to Revolution

By 1971 the movement could reasonably claim to have achieved much political growth. It had traveled a long way toward that "solid implantation inside the country" called for by the militants' conference of 1964. Even back in 1970, Neto was noting that in the eastern districts alone "we have at present rather more than one hundred and fifty action committees, located according to the dispersal of the populations living there."[1]

These action committees had become the political foundation of the national movement. On them and their extension throughout the country, more than on anything else, there rested the real possibility of achieving major sociopolitical transformations in a liberated future.

But this possibility also rested on the degree in which the MPLA could continue to produce and organize a leadership capable of fending off a number of dangers, whether of elitism, of the "military commandism" from which all guerrilla movements have suffered to some extent, or, from another angle, of the leaders' ideological isolation from the majority of adherents. The possibility of revolutionary change rested, in short, on the degree of working democracy that the leadership could ensure while, at the same time, building a central control sufficient to achieve forward action.

1 Neto to B.D., June 1970.

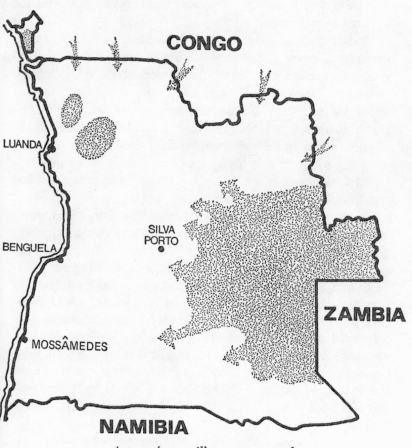

*Areas of guerrilla presence and
penetration, 1971–72, and of national
liberation organization.*

Three main solutions were sought. The first was to improve
the functioning of action committees and to bring new ones
into existence. The second was to promote political education.
The third was to modify command structures in line with the
movement's expansion.

Modification proved difficult. Its difficulties included the vast-
ness of the country, the impossibility of frequent communication with remote areas, and the numerical expansion of the
movement itself. Even if every single one of the forty or fifty
senior leaders of 1970 had been men of political genius and
heroic character, it would still have been difficult to solve the
problem posed by the twin perils of their situation—on one side,
of "going too fast" and losing touch with the bulk of their adherents; on the other, of "going too slowly" and losing political
and therefore military momentum.

This problem had been present from the first. "Portuguese
colonialism will not fall without a fight, and this is why Angola's people can liberate themselves only by revolutionary struggle," the MPLA's founding manifesto had declared in 1956.
"This struggle can be won only by a united front of all Angola's
anti-imperialist forces, irrespective of their color, social situation, religious beliefs, or individual preferences: it can be won
only by a great movement of liberation."[2] The "new MPLA"
remained faithful to the ideas of its origin. It remained "a political organization of the Africans of Angola, irrespective of their
sex, age, ethnic origin, religious beliefs, place of birth, or domi-
cile"—and this meant all the Africans of Angola, no matter what
their color.[3]

This would ensure that everyone might join who wanted national freedom, including any who might shift their ground during the struggle and acquire new courage or understanding from
its success. "We have to distinguish [in this question] between
people who belong to counterrevolutionary groups, and some
who are sincere and courageous, fervently patriotic, but who,

[2] Quoted in M. de Andrade & M. Ollivier, *La Guerre en Angola: Étude
Socio-Économique,* Maspero, Paris, 1971, pp. 69–70.
[3] *Projecto de Estatutos,* Reunião de Dirigentes, Feb. 1966.

for lack of political understanding, have gone off on false trails. We greatly hope that these will recognize the MPLA as the vanguard movement and rally to its position. . . ." All honest Angolans without exception should be free to join this "wide united front of combat against Portuguese colonialism."[4]

But how to ensure, at the same time, that this patriotic "hold-all" should keep and deepen its revolutionary objectives, its conviction that only sociopolitical transformations of a major kind could justify the war?

"We are trying," Neto defined in 1970, "to free and modernize our people by a dual revolution—against their traditional structures, which can no longer serve them, and against colonial rule."

But could this be done with a "wide united front" open to anyone who cared to join, no matter with what level of political understanding? Must there not be a party structure capable of shaping and safeguarding these ideas against the political stagnation or reformism that a "wide united front" could so easily produce? Especially if the time would come when the Portuguese might at last open *political* warfare against the MPLA, and try then to undermine the revolutionary national movement by offering limited reform of the institutions of colonial rule?

The questions were obvious, and were asked. A movement conference of February 1968, held in Congo/Brazzaville for the first and second regions (northwest and Cabinda) "suggested the adoption of a party structure and the expansion of our policy of National Front."[5] Another movement conference, held in Moxico for the Third Region (Moxico and Cuando Cubango) in the following August, "unconditionally supported" this and other ideas of the February conference.

Yet there remained a clear and possibly dangerous contradiction in forming a party linked to specific revolutionary aims— broadly, to the "dual revolution" defined by Neto—while at the same time expanding a national front. A few months earlier, one of the movement's leaders, Spartacus Monimambu, had put

[4] Neto on MPLA broadcasting station, Aug. 24, 1969.
[5] Relatório das Decisãos . . . , Dolisie, Congo/Brazzaville, Feb. 22–26, 1968.

his finger on the problem in an interview with a radical inquirer. "When we become an independent country there is only one way to follow—the socialist way. . . . [But] today we are just a mass movement, a popular movement, and not yet a real party with the structure of a party. Tomorrow there will be a party with its philosophy, its determined ideology, and its structure. And to reach that level we must begin to prepare the way from today. That is why the MPLA is very interested in giving ideological education to our militants. . . ."[6] And that is why, one may add, 1970 saw the functioning of ten CIRs (Centers of Revolutionary Instruction) inside Angola.

One may note in passing that all this was common to the developing experience of the MPLA's companion movements in Guinea-Bissau and Mozambique. Writing after a visit to PAIGC-controlled areas of Guinea-Bissau in 1971, a FRELIMO leader commented:

> In the conditions of our countries and struggle, experience has taught us, it is vital to foresee everything and direct everything from a single center of decision—that is why the role of trained militants [cadres] becomes basic. This means that articulation, a problem always important in every mass party, becomes basic in our countries. . . .[7]

And he went on to discuss the importance given by the PAIGC, as by the other two movements, to the political training of militants.

The transformation of the MPLA into an articulated party was to remain, as with FRELIMO and the PAIGC, a problem for the future. "Only this kind of party can guarantee a democratic future," Neto commented in 1970. "An independent country, in our view, will need a party such as that, and not simply a 'movement.' But its formation would be premature now. So we are trying to train the best and most honest individ-

---

[6] Interview with D. Barnett, Mar. 21, 1968. Liberation Support Movement, 1970.
[7] Oscar Montero, "Un Mozambicain en Guinée," *AfricAsia*, Paris, July 19, 1971.

uals we can find, who will form the backbone of our future party."

The solution for the time being, in other words, would be a compromise: the leaders would promote their ideas and enlarge them by experience, while ensuring as far as they could that the MPLA remained a "wide united front" genuinely open to all who wished for national liberation.

That was one large aspect of the organizational problem. There was another; less difficult, but also not easy. This was to improve the structure of the leadership and its relations with the widening mass of their adherents. The 1964 conference had elected a steering committee, inside which there was to be a political bureau and a military commission. Neto in 1970: "But it didn't work, because it was too diffuse and led to conflicts of decision. Besides, there appeared in the military commission a tendency toward militarism, toward the soldiers' setting themselves aside from the political leaders." It was the common African dilemma: how to get or keep power with soldiers, but how then to prevent the soldiers from taking it for themselves?

The Moxico conference of 1968, now with a strong movement at its back, confirmed the principle of having a steering committee; it was decided that this should have forty-two members and include all the zonal commanders. Political and military functions were united. The military commanders also became the senior political leaders in their respective zones. And these military commanders were to be selected for political merit and understanding as well as for military qualities.

This recognized one of the two great inherent difficulties: that of preventing military issues and persons from taking precedence over sociopolitical issues and persons whose responsibility these issues were—of preventing the guerrilla war from degenerating into a military adventure. It seems unlikely that the 1968 conference fully achieved this purpose. There were local commanders, here and there, who had still to learn the hard but necessary lessons of this always political warfare. Yet the conference at least laid foundations for the future. And when new men of more understanding began to assume positions of local command in the period that followed, they found at least a structure suited to their needs.

The second great inherent difficulty was to ensure a more effective central control over zonal and subzonal commanders dispersed now over many thousands of square miles. Ideally, this supposed sure and frequent communications, including short-wave radio. No such facilities were available in this period. It soon proved too difficult to exercise control through a steering committee whose members were nearly all on active service in widely separated regions. Neto accordingly decided to form a very small executive, called the Committee of Political and Military Co-ordination: in 1970 it had five members, each with a different range of responsibilities, under Neto's chairmanship. Such arrangements left much to be desired, as Neto himself noted in his speech of January 1970. But the results of 1970 soon confirmed that a useful temporary solution had been found.

The resolutions of 1968 still rang, at least to the outside ear, with a certain revolutionary verbalism inherited from earlier years. Yet the conference was manifestly that of a movement which had begun to be in reality what it had long claimed in purpose: an African but non-racist, nationalist yet revolutionary, modernizing though native vehicle of Angolan reassertion and independence. There was far to go, but the political growth was unmistakable, and this political growth continued. The old legacy of Fontes Pereira and the "men of the '90s," of the search for cultural unity and emancipation beyond and outside the caste and color stratifications of colonial rule, was now enlarged to the maturity of a national synthesis, of an Angolan identity matched with the challenge of the times.

Within this identity, the old barriers and divisions increasingly broke down. Men and women came together with a new and creative recognition of their common humanity. That ancient Portuguese category, *mestiço* or mulatto, vanished from the classificatory scheme, and those who were of mixed parentage could step into a national whole and be accepted there.

Racism and tribalism, it was continually asserted, could only play the enemy's game. "If there exists in some of our combatants the idea of a war against the white man, it is necessary that it be immediately substituted by the idea of a war against colonialism and against imperialism; a war against oppression, for the liberty and for the dignity of all men in the world. . . . We must, therefore, look for a political line that will save us from racialism and tribalism, and from the mistakes that were committed in those countries where independence came earlier and by other means."[8]

And such ideas were duly codified in the movement's decisions. Thus the Moxico conference of August 1968 stated its goodwill toward "individuals of white race born or resident in Angola" who showed their sympathy and wish to serve the cause of Angola's people, proposing that they be accepted as *membros simpatizantes* of the MPLA. Authentic because Angolan, modernizing because tilled by the ideas of the twentieth century, the ground upon which the movement now stood was old and yet new, an inalienable development of the history of this country.

In this way, with the struggle for liberation bringing "a forced march along the road of cultural progress,"[9] it proved possible to cope with problems otherwise insoluble. Men who misunderstood their role—and of course there were such—could be checked, corrected, kept within the movement. A good case in point was touched on in an internal bulletin of early 1970. Two leading militants had gone astray. One of them was the deputy commander of the revolutionary instruction center in Bié, the other an ex-member of the command in the southwest.

These men had become "motivated by ambition and a thirst for power" and had tried "to use the people of several zones of

[8] Neto. Broadcast over Radio Tanzania, June 6, 1968, in program "Angola Combatente."

[9] A. Cabral, "National Liberation and Culture," Syracuse University, Feb. 20, 1970.

Moxico in order to realize their objectives." The "whole affair was organized on a tribal basis," although certain complaints against the recognized leadership were accepted as just. These, according to a later bulletin, were concerned with deficiencies of supply and local command. One of the two offenders was demoted, and the other, also after investigation, was criticized but confirmed for the time being in his command.[10]

It would be utopian to suggest that all was done well. The full story, when we have it, will reveal a great many things that were done badly, and continued to be done badly. In these years, however, it appears that sufficient things of basic importance were done sufficiently well; and this, of course, is the point. These men and women were learning, but they were also learning from their mistakes; so long as this was so, the mistakes would not greatly matter.

The Portuguese, on their side, were also learning from their mistakes, but for them it was more difficult. The old contradiction between "doing good" and "colonizing" was now raised to a point of unprecedented sharpness.

Pursuing a psychosocial program of "doing good," launched in the north during 1962 and carried afterward to the center and the east, the Portuguese had it in mind to undermine the nationalists by a new care for the population. Or, rather, some Portuguese had this in mind. But they were obliged to act in the midst of a war, and by means of an armed police and army whose ideas were often quite different. "The soldiers rob and pillage food, animals, clothes, radios, almost any objects of value, indiscriminately and without justification. They have also raped women in the villages, killing anyone who attempts to intercede, then later justifying the killing by accusing the man of having collaborated with the terrorists."[11]

This was not necessarily the general rule. Yet "rural improvement" carried out *manu militari,* and often by reason of local

10 *Informação aos Militantes, 1,* 5/6, 1970.
11 Report by a high government official, quoted in Bender, op. cit.

military needs, could only degenerate into coercion, if not corruption, as in other cases of this kind, not least South Vietnam. The idea was to "regroup" the population so as to provide newly formed villages with schools and other benefits. But this was done in practice under army pressure on one hand and guerrilla pressure on the other; and the results, so far as they could be assessed early in the 1970s, were deplorably negative.

The idea of resettlement was not, of course, a new one. Norton de Matos had applied it early in the 1920s. It was reapplied in the 1940s, though for reasons connected with forced labor and taxation. Writing of conditions in the central area he knew so well, the late Dr. Merlin Ennis was noting of 1943 that the local administrator "made large concentrations. People were not given an opportunity to move with any convenience, nor were they consulted as to the desirability of the sites, but their villages were destroyed ruthlessly. . . . This was done with the usual ferocity. Old and well-established villages with good, well-built houses, schoolhouses, orchards, gardens, irrigation ditches had their houses torn down and the people themselves were herded into inconvenient and unsanitary sites."[12]

It was, after all, the grand tradition: Africans were to be "enclosed in an economy organized and directed by Europeans." There was also the moral and material situation of the men who staffed the administration; rather seldom, so far as the evidence goes, was it an admirable one. This, too, weighed in the balance. Thus "in 1967, when the green light was given to emphasise and expand 'rural resettlement,' many zealous local administrators, often anxious to fulfill what they perceived as a superior's wishes, began to regroup indiscriminately hundreds of thousands of Africans of every type of social and economic system extant in Angola."[13] And then there came, after 1968, increasing army pressure to corral people behind barbed wire so as to deny them access to the national movement; this could only result in the suffering and disarray that foreign observers were noting early in the 1970s.

[12] Journal of Dr. Ennis, pp. 9–10; copy in my possession.
[13] Bender, op. cit.

Even if such "resettlement" could conceivably be to the advantage of the corraled population—and the process was applied to pastoral nomads as well as to settled cultivators—the necessary means of providing "the better life" were largely missing. Food supply within these guarded settlements was soon a sharp and continuing problem. Civil servants and other professionals, such as school teachers, were showing "an understandable reluctance . . . to risk their lives for extremely low salaries and harsh, often dangerous, living conditions. . . . Between 1964 and 1969 an average of only 100 primary school teachers per year were trained in Angola's four teacher-training schools. . . . Moreover, few of the new teachers could have been expected to choose to teach in the rural Eastern areas when severe teacher shortages exist in the safer and more comfortable major cities." And in the east there was still only one secondary school, "attended almost exclusively by Europeans."[14]

On top of all this, in the west and center, there came renewed efforts to enlarge white settlement, with a corresponding eviction of Africans from favorable land. "The government has obviously decided it is of higher strategic importance to have the countryside populated with Europeans," noted the same careful American researcher in 1969, "than it is to develop traditional agrarian sectors."

For these reasons and others like them, the dismantlement of traditional African society, begun by Norton de Matos outside the coastal region forty years earlier, was now carried much further. By 1969 about a million rural Africans, according to the official figures, had been forced from their villages and thrust within "strategic hamlets" of one sort or another, while a large but unknown quantity of others had taken refuge, in towns and cities, from direct army pressure or enclosure behind barbed wire.

In this turmoil and upheaval the old ethnic loyalties had less and less meaning. Resentment against the whole system grew in the same measure, and, as dismantlement continued,

[14] Bender, op. cit.

the need for entirely new structures of society became more apparent. All this, again, could only widen the national movement's opportunity.

With 1971 there came a new Portuguese dalliance with ideas of reform. The uprisings of 1961 had already induced legal and administrative changes, at least on paper. Forced labor was once more declared at an end. So was the division of the population into "civilized" and "native." So, too, was the imposition of company-fixed prices for cash crops grown by Africans. Opinions have differed on how far these reforms became real. Lisbon claimed a great deal for them; African opinion claimed the reverse. In any case, they had in no way lessened the colonial and subject status of Angola as a "province of Portugal."

There were other changes, likewise induced by African resistance. The administration promoted a number of *assimilados* to posts of some authority. Angola's "African-ness" was admitted, at least by the back door, with the regular broadcasting of programs of African music, and the occasional use of African languages. In 1971 the new Prime Minister, Marcello Caetano, began to make gestures in the direction of colonial autonomy.[15] There were even hints of concession to the ideas of African nationalism. Neto in June 1970: "What the Portuguese are trying to find is someone who will pose as a nationalist inside the country."

The search proved difficult. Even if it were successful, it would still remain to be seen whether any concession to African opinion could be carried through against settler and army opposition, each determined, for its own reasons, to stop Lisbon

[15] Cf. an interesting discussion of the regime's options: Eduardo de Sousa Ferreira, "'Evolution und Kontinuitaet' in der Kolonialstrategie Portugals," *Blätter für deutsche und internationale Politik,* Cologne, July 1971. Constitutional amendment in 1971–72 renamed the "oversea provinces" as "oversea states." But the details show that this implies no real transfer of power. Thus the Oversea Minister continues to govern the "oversea states" through officials appointed by himself and subject to his orders and his policies.

from committing any such "betrayal." Meanwhile the MPLA watched the search, and made ready to prevent the confusions that might follow.

In these years, too, there crystallized an African awareness of a threat from another direction.

Angola lay in a position of basic strategical importance not only to the Portuguese colonial system, but also to the Republic of South Africa and its plans for hegemony over the subcontinent. As the national movement gained in Angola, this threat grew more immediate and material. Neto had long foreseen it.

"Yet another danger is appearing and already taking concrete form in certain spheres," he was warning in a broadcast of 1968. "This is the intervention of the racist regime of South Africa. . . . The alliance between these reactionaries and those of Rhodesia with the Portuguese fascist government holds a very great danger for the people of Angola and Mozambique. . . ."

A few months earlier, an MPLA commander had commented:

> We have already found young South African soldiers among the Portuguese troops. At Caripande [northern Moxico], which is open to people coming from Zambia to shop, we have found soldiers who spoke Afrikaans but no Portuguese. Then in Bié they use Afrikaner soldiers to guard the rich foreign-owned Cassinga iron mines.[16] South African helicopters also come to supply their soldiers with ammunition, food, etc., and to do reconnaissance for the Portuguese. . . . And the number of South African troops used in Angola will probably increase in the near future.[17]

Yet the South African regime went cautiously here. Aid was given to the Portuguese, whether financial, diplomatic, or ma-

16 These may, of course, have been local Boer settlers, who number several thousand all together. But 1972 brought fresh accusations by the MPLA of South African military presence inside Angola.

17 Monimambu, in interview with D. Barnett, supra.

terial, but direct military commitment remained small, even very small. This was scathingly noted in the Portuguese army. "You've been sitting on the fence watching us fight this battle, which is as much yours as it is ours, for seven years," a Portuguese officer said to a South African reporter in 1968. Another officer blamed Lisbon for being "not eager to see South Africa increase its influence in this part of Southern Africa." According to this sublieutenant: "It's time we in Southern Africa stood together—but perhaps it's just that, to the exclusion of metropolitan Portugal, that Lisbon is trying to prevent."[18] Born in Angola, this young officer was giving voice to the old settler theme that had won the day in neighboring Rhodesia in November 1965. It was a theme of which more was to be heard in Angola, and from persons of larger authority than a sublieutenant.

A Portuguese defeat in Angola could only be a severe blow to white South Africa's developing plan of political and economic penetration through central Africa. White South Africa could accommodate to any fake autonomy that Lisbon might "concede" to Angola. It could accommodate to a settler regime if that proved possible. It could similarly accommodate, as in Malawi and Malagasy and some other countries, to a black regime that was elitist and "co-operative" in character. But what white South Africa could not accommodate to was an Angola governed by a genuinely independent national movement.

All this became progressively more obvious. Had not Prime Minister Verwoerd, back in 1964, put forward the notion of a Southern African Common Market which South Africa would dominate? Were not certain southern countries, such as Malawi, already "in the net"? Wasn't Prime Minister Vorster ever more active, after 1968, on the same lines? The prospects were sufficiently plain: in Angola, as in Mozambique and Guinea-Bissau, the Portuguese army was fighting in the front line of South Africa's envisaged *apartheid* system for the whole subcontinent.

These prospects were accompanied by others. In 1964 the

18 Al. Venter, *News/Check* (South Africa) July 12, 1968, p. 21.

Lisbon regime was driven to the step of opening Angola to more or less untrammeled foreign investment; and the late 1960s saw a veritable boom in primary exploitation of minerals and other products by companies from the United States, Western Germany, Britain, France, Japan, and elsewhere. But these were the very same companies, or their interlocking partners, that already were major beneficiaries of the *apartheid* system in South Africa. Wasn't the South African danger the harbinger of another and still greater peril: of a general effort to keep Angola (and Mozambique) as part of a wide "neo-colonial" zone of exploitation? Were not South Africa and Rhodesia, as Neto suggested in a broadcast, designated as "the gendarmes of our part of the continent"?[19]

Already Portugal was the recipient of a vast amount of aid from its allies in the North Atlantic Treaty Organization, whether in financial, political, or military terms. With practically the whole of its army in Africa—an army equipped with NATO aid—the Lisbon regime continued to rely for its sophisticated weapons on certain Western countries, mainly France, without whose Alouette and Puma helicopters its troops would lose the only effective arm remaining to them. These suppliers would not welcome a Portuguese defeat; would they tolerate one? And if not, what would they do? Would they encourage South African intervention? Would they perhaps intervene themselves?

The MPLA tried to counter these prospects by multiplying their contacts with Western countries, by appealing for Western aid, by emphasizing their political non-alignment in the world situation. By 1972 they had achieved little success except in neutral Sweden. Meanwhile the Portuguese multiplied their own efforts to present the MPLA (like FRELIMO and the PAIGC) as the "long arm of Communism." They "hammer on the worn-out tune of communism," Neto complained in the same broadcast. "They say the MPLA is Communist. Visits to a socialist country are supposed to be the proof of this. That people fighting for their independence will take aid from wherever they

19 August 24, 1969.

can find it is clear. To win our independence we should even take aid, as they say, from the Devil himself."

As it was, the socialist countries had given indispensable diplomatic, material, and moral aid; moreover, "the MPLA, like other liberation movements, cannot disregard, in their own interest, the enormous potential represented by the socialist countries. But it's one thing to receive aid from the socialist countries and another thing to be a Communist. And I must state that our movement, which has a progressive orientation, embraces all the political and religious trends in our country, all the social strata in our country, all the ethnic groups, all the races. Our movement is an independent organization, building its own political orientation in concord with our people's interests. It doesn't follow with closed eyes the ideas of anybody else. . . ."

This was not only for public consumption. "Our movement," insisted a purely internal bulletin of 1970, "is not subordinate in its general policy to any foreign power or bloc of foreign powers. The *tugas* [colonialist Portuguese] say in their lying propaganda that the MPLA is subordinate to international communism, or that our movement is dominated by the Soviet Union, or that we are directed by China, etc. etc. All this is propagandist fantasy. . . ."[20] It was a theme running through these years, and revealed the dual preoccupation of the movement's leaders: not to be trapped by the "red smear" so lavishly applied by Lisbon and its friends, not to be beaten flat by the hammers of the East-West conflict; but also, at the same time, not to abandon the revolutionary aims and principles of their struggle. Thus an MPLA leader, Chipenda, in 1969:

> Sometimes, I think the imperialists take a very short view, without thinking about the future. All intelligent people know that the Portuguese have no chance of holding onto their colonies in Africa—they have no chance. So if the imperialist corporations keep investing their capital in Angola and Mozambique, they must have some other ob-

[20] *Informação aos Militantes*, 2 of 1970, p. 1.

jective in mind. But if they think that we are prepared to
become neo-colonies of the United States, Western Germany, and so on, they are very mistaken. MPLA and the
people of Angola will continue fighting until we have
achieved complete independence, political *and* economic. . . .[21]

To achieve any such independence must seem a far objective
in the Angola of the early 1970s, and one extremely hard
to achieve. Yet the conviction that Angola's people can in fact
achieve a mastery over their own fate, a mastery at least sufficient to enable their development, and that without such independence there can be no development or none worth striving
for, had become central to these men's inspiration. For them
it was and is the chief justification of their effort and all its
sufferings and sacrifice. Upon this conviction they have taken
their stand as on a rock, waiting for the seas to cease their rag-
ing and the clouds to lift, believing that then they will see everything more clearly, while sure that then, at least, they will be
standing on firm ground.

Why are they thus convinced? What does this conviction
imply for the revolution of which they speak? How does it
match the material needs of development? Is there another
way to ensure development, a better way? With these questions,
too, the long struggle in Angola enters a wider context, whether
in the Africa of the 1970s or perhaps anywhere in the ex-
colonial world.

The nature of the movement's ideas, its chances of realizing
them, the further implications and consequences that may flow
from them—all this concerns directly the universal drama of our
time: the clash between systems of wealth and privilege on one
side, and systems of poverty and deprivation on the other; between the rich with their reasons for being rich, and the
"wretched of the earth" with their hopes of living less badly, or
even of continuing to live at all.

[21] Chipenda interview with D. Barnett, supra.

PART FOUR

THE REVOLUTION OF THE POOR

"What is above all necessary is that the mentality of colonized people be built anew—so that they think freely and feel themselves free, even when their country is not yet free."

Agostinho Neto

"The real locus of revolutionary consciousness is neither in the immediate class, nor in the party, but in the struggle."

Il Manifesto, Rome

"If there is no struggle, there is no progress. Those who profess to favor freedom, and yet deprecate agitation, are men who want crops without ploughing up the ground. They want the ocean without the awful roar of its waters."

Frederick Douglass

1   THE END OF A ROAD

"Farming folk of peaceful temperament," João de Almeida said of the Mbunda and their neighbors more than half a century ago, before the new colonial wars began. They were folk who had traveled the long road of their history slowly but not vainly. They had found their saving balance with nature, here in these harsh northern outliers of the plains of Kalahari sand. They had multiplied and even prospered.

These people of eastern Angola had known no kind of Golden Age. But afterward they would remember their old life without bitterness, and even with a certain proud affection. They had lived in small societies of small political power, but they had seen a virtue in this smallness of scale, clinging to their local loyalties, clasped in social rules and structures framed by "the ancestors who spoke for God."

Their situation had not been bad. If many of the endemic ills from which they suffer now, such as hookworm and malaria, must always have been present, it is much less sure that any serious malnutrition was here as well. Millet and cassava—the second arriving from the West in the seventeenth century—have a low dietary value, but these lands abounded as they do now in small as well as big game, their rivers with good edible fish, their woods with honey-making bees. These people's memory of their precolonial independence is not a sad one.

Their economies were as small as their societies. They had

little interest in long-distance trade, none in any luxury trade, only enough in local trade to furnish metal objects and other artisanship products. This placed narrow limits on any structural growth, narrower still on any productive enlargement, narrowest of all on any personal accumulation. Though not entirely static, these economies had probably realized their developmental potential before the end of the eighteenth century. Even so, their slow-expanding populations might have long continued within traditional frameworks of stability and peace. Here in eastern Angola, at least, the problems of "overpopulation"—of a critically widened gap between numbers of people and means of feeding them—had still to become, in precolonial times, more than faint shadows on the future.

Early Portuguese colonial enterprise had no impact on them till the slave trade reached out and raided their western villages in the eighteenth century. Yet they were too far from the Atlantic for the slave trade to be able to hurt them much, although its raids were painful whenever they occurred. Later Portuguese invasion failed to enclose them till early in the 1920s. But when this happened, there set in a process of structural dismantlement that, carried into our own times at a quickening pace, has now banished all question of "returning to the past." Yet these people would not wish to return to the past even if they could. Their old beliefs may continue to fortify the elders; the young, increasingly, have glimpsed wider horizons, guessed at more worthwhile possibilities than village life could ever offer, become inspired by new challenges, new ambitions.

Today, suspended between the ruins of their past and a future still to be shaped and made, their plight is a painful one, and first of all in a material sense. On the score of health alone they are now a stricken people. At least two medical doctors of their national movement, Américo Boavida and Eduardo dos Santos, have recorded findings in the past few years. Major endemic ills evidently include widespread tuberculosis and syphilis as well as malaria, sleeping sickness, and leprosy, not to mention the all-intrusive hookworm. The malnutrition of mothers and children has been found to be particularly severe. Life expectancy is short, as perhaps it always was; but sterility is now alarmingly high, and hunger has become the common fate.

Their plight is still more serious, in the long run, from another point of view: from that of preparedness to handle the problems of the world they now live in. The colonial system brought them next to no medical care. Still worse, the colonial system brought them no modern education at all; by 1971 the whole of the eastern districts had scarcely sent a single child to a colonial secondary school, let alone university. Even if their hunger could be relieved, their medical condition improved, and their sufferings made less generally severe, they would still be in sore trouble. Nearly 100 per cent illiterate or preliterate, they have been terribly deprived of the means of gaining useful knowledge, and thus of rebuilding their lives on a viable and expanding basis. Faced with this need, they hope that their national movement will win the war and lead them to a better life. But they themselves, apart from the local leaders they give to their national movement, have no idea how this may be done. To be convinced of that, one need only listen to the refugees.

They have come to the end of a road and must find a new one. For them, progress is not only desirable; progress is utterly essential.

Does it greatly matter? It may be said that these people are remote and relatively few. Eastern Angola's population is barely that of a suburb of New York; all Angola's people number little more than half of London's. Yet quantity and geographical position are no guides to the qualitative interest of their problem and its possible solutions.

This interest is a general one. The problem here is inseparable from that of all Angola's people. It is the same problem as that of the peoples of Mozambique and Guinea-Bissau, essentially the same as that of any colonial or ex-colonial people. More distantly and yet still connectedly, it is perhaps the same problem as that of every people anywhere in the world as it is now. The problem for Angola's people is a test case—an extreme one, but also a characteristic one.

For these people have to build a new society. They have to

find a road of advance to political structures such as will enable them to secure a community, a sociopolitical unity, large and strong enough to defend and promote the interests of all its members. They have to move toward social structures capable of yielding a corresponding cultural development, whether in literacy, technical skills, or comprehension of the modern world. They have to build economic structures able to absorb and use the fruits of modern science, technology, organizational progress, but shaped to the scale and service of their own community, their own development, their own history.

It would be a great deal to ask or to expect the full achievement of these aims. Yet reality today is such that nothing short of their substantial achievement can be enough to save these people. By what means can this be done?

2   THE COLONIAL ANSWER

The colonial doctrine says that in one way or another, with changes and reforms, even conceivably with some transfer of political control from Lisbon, the existing system can open a new future for Angola's people. If the system has not done this yet, after decades of "Portuguese presence," still the doctrine insists that it will do so in the future. Lisbon has abounded, now as in the past, with missionary proclamations.

Before considering what reformism might achieve—with or without the support of the national movement, though on that score the outcome had still to be seen in the early 1970s[1]—it will be useful to look briefly at the structure and condition of the system itself.

The system grew much more profitable during the 1960s. In 1970 Dr. da Silva Cunha, Salazar's veteran "African labor expert," who was now Overseas Minister, found Angola "bursting with energy in a spectacular thrust forward in economic development."[2] And he was not overstating the case from the system's point of view. If the general condition of agriculture was far from "bursting with energy," the expansion of industry fully justified Da Silva Cunha's happiness.

---

[1] Meanwhile, the MPLA stood firm against Caetano's tentative reformism, affirming on its tenth anniversary "yet another time that it will not cede to the demagogic tactics of Mr. Caetano. The result of this struggle can only be complete independence. Our struggle will continue, beyond all maneuvers." Statement by Steering Committee, Feb. 4, 1971.

[2] UN A/AC.109/L.699, Apr. 20, 1969, p. 3.

Industrial output had begun to move significantly upward in 1962, and continued rapidly to rise, trebling between 1962 and 1969, an average annual growth rate of 17 per cent.[3] The boom, of course, was an export boom concerned with extraction for export. If "more than 400 authorisations were granted for the installation and alteration of manufacturing activities" in 1968–69 alone, these again were mainly concerned with processing for export. Characteristic of the situation was the rise in cotton exports: these went up in value from the equivalent of £1.5 million in 1967 to more than £6 million in 1970. If there were any local "spread effects" of this "extractive industrialisation," they were minimal, and limited to the privileged white sector of the economy.[4] Yet, within its colonialist limits, the boom was undoubtedly sensational.

The real turning point had come in 1964. In April of that year, giving way to financial pressure caused by its African wars and the urging of foreign partners, the Lisbon regime took an unprecedented step. It opened its colonies to the inflow of foreign capital, and the subsequent outflow of foreign dividends, under terms so generous that "the foreign investor [now] enjoys a higher priority than the Portuguese investor. . . ."[5]

This brought an immediate and growing response. Before 1964, private foreign investment in all Portuguese territories, most of it made long before, was less than 15 per cent of gross fixed capital formation; by 1969 it had risen to 25 per cent and was still rising. Since 1964 "there is only a limited number of activities in which a majority of Portuguese capital is required. More important, any mining activity may be 100 per cent foreign-owned or financed. . . ."[6] Ostensibly fighting to con-

[3] *Financial Times,* London, July 19, 1971. See also Mário de Andrade & Marc Ollivier, op. cit., especially Part 2, ch. 2.

[4] The fairly analogous case of Rhodesia has shown that the local "spread effects" of industrial expansion within this kind of "dual economy" scarcely ever move, in any sense significant for living standards, from the "white sector" to the "black sector." See R. B. Sutcliffe, "Stagnation and Inequality in Rhodesia 1946–68," *Bull.* of Oxford Inst. of Economics and Statistics, vol. 33, 1 of 1971, p. 35.

[5] *Financial Times,* July 23, 1969.

[6] Ibid.

serve a monopoly in its "national possessions" in Africa, the regime was obliged to sell them off, piecemeal, to meet the strain of wars it had failed to win. Unbalanced by any comparable export of Portuguese capital, Lisbon's own neo-colonial plight became clearer than before.

It was to become clearer still. The heart of the boom lay in mineral exports, which doubled between 1965 and 1970, to reach in the latter year a total of $425 million. Almost all were the product of foreign initiative. Angolan minerals had now attracted some of the giants of the Western world such as Krupp of West Germany and Gulf Oil of the U.S.A. South African capital was likewise beginning to find a profitable outlet in Angola, as in Mozambique; and here, too, further expansion seemed assured. In 1971 the Anglo-American copper group, predominantly South African in spite of its name, was "prospecting in eastern Angola where there may be some extension of the Zambian copper-belt and Katanga deposits," while "a company with American links is investigating the phosphate deposits near Benguela."[7] There was more along the same lines. Dr. da Silva Cunha had reason for his words.

The system, in fact, was undergoing another great extension of its scope and intensity. Yet it remained the same system. The blacks stayed exactly in their previous posture of "productive elements organised and to be organised within an economy governed by whites," and for the profit of whites; the only difference now was that profit-taking whites included many more Americans and Germans, Frenchmen, South Africans, and other people in the "rich man's world." Within this system there was absolutely no change in the white-black relationships of power and opportunity. Though accurate figures are hard to come by, there seems to have been a little improvement here and there in non-white wage levels. But the main point was that exported dividends grew, settler incomes grew, and so did settler numbers.

What was being developed, in other words, was not the coun-

[7] *Financial Times,* July 19, 1971.

try as a whole, supposing this to include its five million Africans as well as its three hundred thousand whites, but the extractive system already in place. Rising exports of raw and processed materials only reinforced its implacably colonial nature. Angola might grow more cotton; she still had to buy her cotton textiles from the "motherland." In 1967, for example, Angola bought cotton textiles from abroad to the value of 437 million escudos; of these, textiles worth 386 million came from Portugal. Once again, the "spread effects" of the boom went to oversea benefit.[8]

What was being developed, accordingly, was the machinery of wealth transfer from "underdeveloped" Angola to Portugal and to "developed" countries, now including Japan as a major customer for the Angolan iron ore that Krupp was digging up at Cassinga. To see this kind of process as any form of systematic development of an Angolan national economy, much less the launching of an Angolan capitalist system, was to see what was simply not there. This was just another colonial *mise en valeur,* like so many elsewhere.

It is easy and perhaps useful to demonstrate this a little further. In the matter of infrastructure, for example, the boom went hand in hand with large outlays. But what kind of infrastructure? It was characteristic that the amounts spent on improved transport and communications between 1965 and 1967, when the minerals boom was getting under way, should have been 5.6 times larger than those spent on health and education; and this at a time when very large numbers of Angolans, perhaps more than a million in "resettlement" villages, were in grave need of health and education services. The third "development plan" allocated some two billion escudos to farming and forestry, or about a twelfth of the whole. But the great bulk of it was for the development of white settler communities and export crops; and this, once more, at a time when African farming and food supply were in uncontested crisis.

A survey of July 1971 again showed the way the "develop-

[8] Cf. *Dependency and Underdevelopment: Consequences of Portugal in Africa,* University of California, Riverside, 1971, p. 23.

ment" wind was blowing. There were "high hopes of developing a cattle ranching industry" in the south and east where "there is scope for considerable development by way of settler schemes."[9] These were schemes for white settlers—if any could be found. More land, in short, was to be taken from Africans and handed to Europeans, the latter's installation being subsidized, as usual, by taxes that Africans would also pay. *Robusta* coffee production might have reached its internationally agreed limit, but *arabica* could still be expanded; there were plans for this, too. Once more, it would not be Africans who gained, as the land-holding figures demonstrate.

There are, it is true, about 140,000 hectares under coffee owned by fifty thousand small farmers, many of whom are Africans. But there are 226,000 hectares in big plantations and another 159,000 in small plantations;[10] these are nearly all white, while about 80 per cent of *all* coffee production is controlled by the Companhia Agrícola de Angola: it is easy to see who will get the "development" expenditure.[11]

Meanwhile there were incessant if absurdly optimistic plans for bringing in hundreds of thousands of new white settlers to Angola and Mozambique, and, linked to these plans, large schemes for producing hydroelectric power and irrigation water, mainly with South African capital, from the Cunene River in southern Angola and the Zambezi River at Cabora Bassa in the Tete District of Mozambique. Their declared aim was to enlarge the white sector as well as giving aid to white South Africa.

All this presents a picture already familiar in other colonies of white settlement, most of all in South Africa. As the extractive system grows, so too do the opportunities for profitable foreign investment and white settlement. The contrast between

[9] *Financial Times,* loc. cit.
[10] *Vida Mundial,* Lisbon, Feb. 9, 1967, pp. 31–32.
[11] E. de Sousa Ferreira, "Der Wirtschaftliche Ausbeutungsprozess in den Portugiesischen Kolonien," Univ. of Heidelberg, 1970, p. 16. Angola's most valuable export product (47 per cent of value of all exports in 1965) shows once again the extent to which Portuguese imperialism is merely the fragment of a wider whole. A majority of shares of the Cna. Agrícola de Angola is owned by the French bank of Rallet et Cie.

the mere growth of the system, on one hand, and the failure to induce any all-round development, on the other, becomes ever more sharp.

It may be replied that the economies of the "old British dominions," of Canada, Australia, and New Zealand, were launched on the same extractive pattern, and yet produced an all-round development in the emergence of fully fledged capitalist systems. There is no more than a superficial analogy here. The white settlers of the "old dominions" had historical advantages that the Angolans do not and will not possess: They soon outnumbered and overwhelmed the indigenous peoples; grew from fragments of the British bourgeoisie into new bourgeoisies which could defend themselves; proved able repeatedly to bargain for their autonomous advancement within the world capitalist system. There is nothing in Angola's condition that can promise any such development.

Settler and expatriate employment and profits, whether industrial, commercial, agricultural, or bureaucratic, all expand in the Angolan system. But all remain within the same structures as before; nothing is changed except the quantities, and these do not accumulate into a qualitative change. In many areas of Angola even the quantities do not change by much, no matter what the plans may claim.

In December 1969, for example, the governor general found it wise and well to call for new sacrifices by the rural peoples of the eastern Districts: if they wished to live better they must work harder and yield more taxes. "Yet in April 1970 it was apparent that a great deal of money would be spent in that very area for the construction of asphalt roads whose economic importance is almost negligible, but whose logistic value is of considerable importance to the military. It would appear that the majority of the eastern Angolan population presently living in the strategic resettlements is already making tremendous sacrifices."[12] Those of Muié, to mention only that small place, fully bore out this American observer's conclusion. For the people

[12] Bender, loc. cit.

of Muié and their kind the great boom of the 1960s had as little meaning as the Man in the Moon; rather less, indeed, for they could at least see the latter.

Much the same picture appears from the "scholastic explosion" described by another, though admiring, visitor.[13] Here, too, there was undoubted growth. In the long-neglected field of secondary education, students in academic schools increased from 7,400 in 1960 to 16,000 in 1966, while students in technical schools increased from 4,500 to 15,300. But the statistics carefully omit to say how many were white and how many were black; all available sources agree that the number of blacks remained very small indeed.

There was also a large extension of primary education, at least in the sense of some elementary counting and literacy and acquaintance with the Roman Catholic catechism. But the emphasis remained on assimilation, even if, since 1961, the legal distinction between *assimilado* and *indígena* (native) had been formally abolished. That abolition made no cultural difference of any kind. The object of education remained as before: to "de-Africanise," "de-Angola-ise," and thus promote Portuguese culture and nationalism as the only acceptable standards of loyalty and behavior.

"Schools are necessary, yes," agreed Cardinal Cerejeira, for long Portugal's senior cleric, in a pastoral letter of 1960 on the subject of education for blacks, "but schools where we teach the native the path of human dignity and the grandeur of the nation which protects him."[14]

That the path of human dignity should have to pass through forced labor and political subjugation was perhaps an idea peculiar now to the hierarchs of Portugal, although at one time or other all the colonial powers had thought the same. In Angola, as in Mozambique and Guinea-Bissau, it meant that education for blacks could only be an education for servitude. Even in primitive rural schools the preparation for "de-Africanisation" was already under way: there "the Angolan child learns the

13 R. Pélissier, in Wheeler & Pélissier, op. cit., p. 237.
14 Quoted in Mondlane, *Struggle for Mozambique*, p. 58.

rudiments of Portuguese language, civilisation, history and geography,"[15] but nothing that could teach him the value and potential of his own humanity.

And so we are back once more to the situation against which the "men of the '90s" had raised their outraged voices. The *preto boçal*, the "brutish black," is to learn to read and count a little, and to recite the names of Portuguese heroes; otherwise he is to remain what he was before, the helpless and despised servant of the whites who "organize and control" him. There is still to be no question of developing Angola and its people in their own right, only of increasing those "auxiliaries in the white economy" about whom Prime Minister Caetano was holding forth in 1954, and of making these servants a little more serviceable. The system itself develops; for Angola's people, this remains a growth without development.

Yet perhaps an expansion of the extractive system will eventually serve to raise the economic and political level of the whole population? Perhaps the system's sheer growth will itself burst through the barriers to black enlargement? It is late in the day to nourish any such hope. For this was argued of South Africa's expanding *apartheid* system two or three decades back. And the expansion of South Africa's extractive economy, now far larger than before, has seen no bursting through of barriers; on the contrary, those barriers have never ceased to grow stronger and taller.

Yet South Africa is an extreme case? Even if this were so, there are other and less extreme cases which have shown the same result. Within the colonial framework, for example, there is the striking case of Zambia when it was still the British possession of Northern Rhodesia.

Mining companies began digging for Northern Rhodesia's high-quality copper late in the 1920s. Early in the 1930s there came an industrial "boom" of exactly the same nature as Angola's thirty years later. Northern Rhodesia became one of the world's major sources of copper. What this was worth to

15 Pélissier, loc. cit.

the mining companies may be seen in the value of the dividends they were able to export, before the independent government of Zambia began to put a brake on them:

TOTAL DIVIDENDS EXPORTED BY THE COPPER INDUSTRY[16]
COMPANIES OVER THE PERIOD 1931–1968

	£ million	Period
R.S.T. GROUP LTD. (1)	75.0	Up to June 1939
RHOKANA CORPORATION LTD. (2)	73.0	Up to June 1960
NCHANGA CONSOLIDATED COPPER MINES LTD. (2)	62.0	Up to June 1960
ALL COPPER COMPANIES (3)	202.0	1960–68
TOTAL DIVIDENDS REMITTED	412.0	1931–68

Tremendous growth, clearly; yet, once again, from the standpoint of a break-through to "sustained growth" on any scale meaningful to the population as a whole, it remained growth without development. The mineral boom might expand the "national income" with results that could *seem* expansive for blacks as well as whites. But the "national income" figures said nothing about the nature of the goods produced or about income distribution. The nature of the goods produced was mainly raw or minimally processed copper, which went abroad to foreign factories; it was of no more real value to the bulk of the black population than a flood of cocktail cabinets or suntan oils. They too would have betokened growth, but certainly not development.

If there were some "spread effects" in providing employment for African miners, these were minimal and consciously kept

[16] D. L. Potts, *The Development of the Zambian Copper Economy 1928–1970,* unpublished thesis 1970, quoting:
(1) Sir R. Prain, "Selected Papers, 1958–60," Vol. II, Batsford, London, p. 124.
(2) "Mining Industry Year Book, 1960," Kitwe, Zambia.
(3) "African Development," Sept. 1969, p. 12.

so, just as in Angola. In 1964 the proportion of Africans still living within the "subsistence sector" was still around 80 per cent. Even those in the copper industry, though comprising 88 per cent of all workers in the "capitalist sector," received *less than half* of total labor earnings, the lion's share still going to the 12 per cent of white immigrant workers.[17]

The educational picture shows the same result. Like the Portuguese in Angola, Northern Rhodesia's masters were also inclined to boast of "educational expansion." Given the value of copper profits, there was astonishingly little. With more than half of the total surplus generated in the economy being annually exported even after 1945, there was "no money" for schools. Millions of pounds went annually abroad, but as late as 1958 the country possessed only one secondary school capable of offering African pupils a complete course to the Senior Cambridge Certificate level—to the level, that is, of "middle-term" secondary-school achievement. In 1964 there were scarcely one hundred African graduates in the country, while fewer than thirteen hundred had achieved the Cambridge Certificate. Not a single African worker had completed an industrial apprenticeship.[18]

In this as in other fields, the large expansion of export income following the mineral boom of the early 1930s had "failed to stimulate general and cumulative development."[19] It would be hard to argue that the British system in Northern Rhodesia was less "liberal," less careful of "African interests," than that of the Portuguese in Angola. Yet stimulus to "general and cumulative development" began to appear only with the advent of political independence in 1964, when Zambia's people at last acquired the possibility of developing their country as a whole. But political independence is precisely what the Portuguese have refused to concede to Angola's people.

[17] Potts, op. cit., p. 11.

[18] Potts, op. cit., quoting *Manpower Report,* 1965–66, Govt. Printer, Lusaka, p. 155.

[19] Potts, loc. cit.

If no true development can be achieved within the existing framework, however expanded by foreign capital and ancillary Portuguese investment, what might yet be done within a somewhat reformed framework, a less directly colonial one?

The question was not worth asking so long as Salazar was there: the colonial wars had still to take their full effect. But more than a decade of military frustration, at enormous cost to the people of Portugal as well as to the Africans, had begun to produce a slightly different atmosphere by the outset of the 1970s. A certain element of reform now became thinkable.

There were narrow limits to its practicable scope. Long accustomed to power, Portugal's generals were in no mood to concede defeat. Threatened even by a timid approach to reform, they were more likely to side with the settlers in Angola and Mozambique, and produce something of the situation of "French Algeria" in 1960–61, when French generals and settlers had challenged the reforming intentions of Paris—with the difference that in this situation the Portuguese generals in Africa, counting as they most probably could on the Portuguese generals in Portugal, would be unlikely to fail. Even so, some cautious steps toward a slightly reformed framework were carried into law by Salazar's successor, Caetano, in 1971.

They were minimal. An otherwise serious London newspaper might herald them as "probably the most momentous legislation produced in Portugal for half a century";[20] in fact, they were nothing of the kind. The Portuguese constitution, duly amended, conceded one title of "oversea States" to the African colonies. But its detailed clauses continues to provide that all real administrative, financial, and military authority remained in Lisbon.[21]

These putative provincial states, or autonomous provinces, were to have more authority over their own affairs, at least in principle, and a greater representation in the Lisbon national assembly; but the latter, in turn, was also to have wider powers. The resultant situation remained perfectly colonial. "Assimila-

[20] *Financial Times,* Dec. 4, 1970.
[21] See Note 15 on page 312.

tion" continued as its keynote. And in so far as *any* power was to pass to Angola and Mozambique, it would go to constituted bodies; that is, to councils dominated by local white settlers and officials.

Superconservative politicians in Lisbon deplored even these minimal changes of form.[22] Yet there was little for them to fear. All effective policy, whether financial or political or military, stayed in Lisbon's hands. And since such policy supposed a continued wealth transfer from the colonies to Portugal or to other foreign countries by export of profits, this meant that "development" continued to serve the interests of the "mother country" and its partners. No amount of talk in local legislatures was going to make a pennyworth of difference to that. If the changes of form had any real meaning, they were chiefly to assist the Portuguese regime in smuggling its colonies into the West European Common Market as "integral parts" of itself.

For the argument's sake, however, let us suppose that these reforms were followed by others, going much further, to the point where Angola really became a "country on its own." What could this mean?

Significant power would then pass to an Angolan electorate, as to similar bodies in the other two colonies. In Angola and Mozambique this electorate would be heavily dominated by whites. Voting qualifications (let alone qualifications for standing as electoral candidates) would depend on certain tests; among these would be literacy and the ownership of a certain amount of property, the regular earning of a certain wage or salary. In 1969 some twenty thousand of Portugal's settlers in Angola were illiterate but would presumably be given voting rights along with the rest. On a generous estimate, similar voting rights would be given to a small fraction of the African population, beginning with the one or two per cent who could meet the required qualifications. As in Rhodesia, there might even be provision for some kind of "house of African chiefs,"

---

[22] One of them, the former Minister of Justice Autunes Varela, complained that words such as "autonomy" and "state" had "a bitter taste of renunciation and abdication." *Financial Times,* July 19, 1971.

although these, as in Rhodesia, would all be salaried servants of the regime. Such ornaments would make no difference to the balance of power. This would remain between a government in Lisbon and a settler-dominated legislature in Luanda (or Lourenço Marques).

That is the "best" one could envisage. It is already a good deal more liberal than any reforms seem likely to allow. But let us suppose it were achieved, and even that this settler-dominated legislature were not only fired with patriotic zeal but also filled with a desire for African advancement.

There would be, in that situation, an improvement in the "atmosphere." Censorship might be lifted; local journalism, even African journalism, might be able to take up its work where Norton de Matos had cut it short in 1923. There could be some agitation against abuse, neglect, avoidable poverty, along the lines of the 1880s and 1890s. Parties might be formed; some of these could once more be African. Trade unions might see the light of day; some of these, again, could mobilize Africans.

And then? The resultant situation would be much the same as in Rhodesia since 1923, when the Rhodesian whites acquired self-rule. Political structures ensuring white supremacy would remain untouched, no matter what brave words might be said and written to the contrary. Economic structures ensuring the survival of the extractive system would stay in place, buttressed now by major foreign investment.

All these structures supporting the extractive system have their solid weight and international nature; they are not changeable by mere goodwill. Reform, even at best, means only reform, only the modification of what exists. And the degree of modification could not, in the circumstances, be more than marginal.

It must be merely marginal in Angola or Mozambique because reform in these countries can only be the limited dilution of a rigid autocracy. A little less autocracy rather than a little more: this is the most that reform can yield. The direction of reform can only be toward the displacement of a very narrow elite of rulers by a less narrow one; in any case, the markedly elitist outcome is not in doubt. More local people might take part in deciding and applying policy, but the more would still be a very small minority of the country's population, and this minority would be ever conscious of its privileged position in relation to the non-participant majority. It would be jealously restrictive toward any demand for a broadening of the power base, and, being elitist, increasingly concerned with its own minority advancement. All the experience of history, ancient and modern, African and other, points in that direction.

Africans in government or positions of relative authority could be expected to become less rare. In 1971 they numbered a few dozens; within ten years they might number several hundreds, even perhaps a thousand or two, meanwhile the total African population would have passed the six million mark. The degree of "de-Africanisation" might possibly lessen, so that these privileged Africans might even be able to present themselves as Africans rather than as second-class Portuguese. But what would all this be worth?

Such "promoted Africans"—as, for example, the Angolan African deputy Sincletica Torres of 1970, or the Angolan African Pinheiro da Silva, who was Angolan secretary for education, or others of their kind—might wish for further reforms. Their own privileged positions, as members of the ruling elite, would place a narrow limit on their action. If experience in other countries ruled by elites is any guide, they would take good care to kick away the ladder of privilege up which they had climbed, if only to cut down competition "at the top." Any conceivable reformism, in other words, is bound to create an alliance between whites and privileged blacks, is bound to prolong the structures of authoritarian rule over the bulk of the black population—and thus reinforce the "underdevelopment" of Angola's people as a whole. To say this is to be neither cynical nor malicious, but to see things as they really are.

One need only reflect upon the likely consequences of reformism for populations such as the Mbunda and Luchazi. They might find that a number of "chiefs" would represent them at some annual congress in Luanda. But these representatives would in no sense be an emanation of valid traditional structures, for no such structures any longer exist, nor can they be recalled to life. Or these rural folk might find themselves endowed, in due course, with one or several "elected deputies": in due course, because, as things stand now, there will be no more than the merest handful of these rural populations who could pass the probable income/educational tests for election. But let us suppose they achieved a number of elected deputies. These men, once again, would find themselves elevated to a ranking far above their voters in the villages. If precedents elsewhere are anything to go upon, let alone the sheer force of human frailty, their energies would soon be drawn into the service of their own careers.

Nor could it, in the circumstances, in any case be otherwise. For these "beneficiaries" would find themselves enmeshed in a system that accepted them only as the junior partners of local white beneficiaries who were themselves the junior partners of the Portuguese and other oversea bourgeoisies. These local white beneficiaries might possibly be able to grow into at least the simulacrum of a "national bourgeoisie" in Angola, just as their neighbors in Rhodesia have done; it is quite certain that the black beneficiaries could do no such thing. These would remain, like it or not, the hangers-on of a system they could not conceivably hope to reshape or reorganize.

Not only that: the chances of achieving unity among Angola's populations would be smaller even than before. These black beneficiaries, like others elsewhere, would find that they could "work the system" only by the methods of their white superiors—by competing for their electorate, that is, on "caste and color" grounds. Like others elsewhere in Africa, they would turn themselves into the spokesmen of this or that "tribe"—into "Mbunda spokesmen" or "Luchazi spokesmen" whose language would be "tribalist" in nature.

Politics at the center would become, more and more, a careerist dogfight pitched in terms of micronationalism. By 1970 Africa could point to some terribly destructive examples of this process, whether in Nigeria, Uganda, Kenya, or elsewhere. And the process here could be even more destructive by reason of the smallness of the cake available for cutting, given that the white settlers would undoubtedly insist upon taking the lion's share they have always taken in the past. Here, as elsewhere, elitism and its political reflection, which is "tribalism," would advance together.

Even if the parliamentary deputies of the Mbunda, Luchazi, and other rural "circumscriptions" were to appear as self-sacrificing supermen, resolutely turning their backs on the pork barrels of political and social privilege, how in fact could they become effective modernizing leaders of Angola's people? Like it or not, they would still be clasped within the elitist structures inherent to any reformism. They would still find themselves the helpless instruments of a system, whether local or international, that was far too strong for any control they might hope or wish to exercise. With further development of the extractive system—and it might continue to grow for a while—they would still be faced with a widening gap between the interests of the system and its beneficiaries, and the interests of the majority of Angolans, who would continue to live outside its benefits. As this gap widened, so would there grow a corresponding strain and conflict, a yet greater opposition between the modernizing culture of the towns and the traditional culture of the villages. With that, the very foundations for any over-all development would be removed or increasingly destroyed. Of this, too, Africa in the 1970s could point to plenty of sad examples.

The outcome in a reformist Angola would again be likely to be more destructive than elsewhere by reason of local history. The logical extension of reformist nationalism being micro-nationalism, what justification would remain for a country called Angola? Why, in that case, should not the leaders of the Kongo, or at least those who were their leaders in the 1960s, be given their original demand and allowed to secede as a separate state? What logic should prevent the Mbunda of Angola from joining the Mbunda of Zambia? Why not reunite the Lunda with their brethren in the Congo? The logic, indeed, would be to restore the identity of all the independent states of precolonial Africa. It is thus an argument that ends in the absurd. Yet, much of independent Africa's present framework demonstrates this absurdity, at least when viewed in terms of over-all development. It is an absurdity in which elites flourish while multitudes grow hungrier, and the conspicuous consumption of presidents and parliaments seems often to know no limit. It is an absurdity in which bureaucracies increasingly undermine the validity of institutions intended to be representative. All too clearly, independent Africa needs an entirely new framework in which micronationalism gives way to nationalism, and nationalism to supranational organs of co-operation and continental development.

For Angola, at least, the case is not in doubt. True development must begin with the building of a national unity embracing all its people, and this, to become possible, must mean a national movement of a non-elitist nature. No variant of reformism can do the work. With a grim irony, this is the conclusion that the regime of Salazar/Caetano, in refusing all reforms, has done so much to illuminate and fasten in men's minds, and, as the war for national liberation continues, to make possible and begin to realize.

Yet the likely consequences of a reformism carried to the point of conceding political independence under majority rule, but within elitist institutions, may still be worth looking at in a wider context.

3 THE NEO-COLONIAL VARIANT

The task of true development, as distinct from mere growth without development, is systematic change. This necessity for change of *system* is most obviously and urgently present in the colonial and ex-colonial countries, whether in Africa or anywhere else. These, above all, are the countries that need to reach and pass the watershed between colonial dependence, in whatever form, and the sovereignty that can and does promote systems of sustained and over-all expansion.

In Angola and countries like Angola, the task of development must therefore lie in the making of a great transition from a system of low or primitive production to a quite different system capable of reproducing the fruits of modern science, technology, and organization. But in their circumstances this means that development, in order to succeed, has to ensure the raising of structures that embrace the whole population within social and political institutions capable of promoting an over-all participation.

Participation is absolutely central to their need. If each of the liberation movements of Africa has placed its emphasis on participation, this is for far more than propagandist reasons. Their very survival during the struggle depends on their securing an ever wider participation by the populations concerned. Only this kind of participation can justify their struggle by opening the way to a better life. Without this participation there can be no guerrilla war and no liberation. Short of this conscious effort by the majority of people toward changing their own ideas, beliefs, assumptions, social attitudes, there can be no subsequent transition from one system to another. Orders from above may be well conceived and wise; it is obvious that each of these movements must also stand or fall by the quality of its leadership. Orders from above may be obeyed. But orders from above cannot educate; only the experience of voluntary participation can do that.

"What is above all necessary," Neto has said, "is that the mentality of colonized people be built anew, so that they think freely and feel themselves free. . . ." It is precisely this that a revolutionary experience of participation can achieve. Therein lies the sovereign value of liberation war, which, by its very nature, is revolutionary war as distinct from traditional revolt, outraged upheaval, or violent adventure.[1]

For in this kind of war "the working masses and, in particular, the peasants, who are usually illiterate and have never moved beyond the boundaries of their village or region, lose in their contact with other groups the complexes that constrained them in relation to other ethnic or social groups." They rise above the "tribalism" that is pressed on them by colonial rule.[2] "They realize their crucial role in the struggle. They break the bonds of their village universe, and progressively integrate themselves with their country and with the world. They acquire an infinite amount of new knowledge . . . ; they strengthen their political awareness . . . ; they become more able to play the decisive role of providing the principal force behind the liberation movement."[3]

This is another way of saying that the liberation struggle can solve not only the preliminary problem of regaining inde-

[1] ". . . the phenomenon of national liberation is necessarily one of revolution. . . ." Amilcar Cabral, *Liberation of Guiné*, p. 77.

[2] In 1970, for example, the colonial authorities in Guinea-Bissau, driven hard by military defeat, began to set up "ethnic councils" in which each of the country's ethnicities should have its own and separate "representation," a measure clearly aimed at furthering the ancient policy of "divide and rule."

[3] Amilcar Cabral, *National Liberation and Culture*, Syracuse, New York, Feb. 20, 1969.

pendence from colonial rule, but also the major and far greater problem of ensuring transition from one system to another. It can kick out Portuguese control; it can also build a new Angola. Not inevitably, not automatically; anything but that: the hazards along the way are glaringly obvious, whether in terms of maintaining effective participation or avoiding the perversions of leadership. The argument here is not about utopia; the argument is about the *possible* means of building a new society. And what the evidence of these revolutionary movements goes to show is that they can hope to succeed where reformism is bound to fail.

The positive evidence for this can easily be found in the committees, schools, villages, and fighting units of almost any of the liberated zones of Angola, Mozambique, and Guinea-Bissau; and where it cannot easily be found, this is only because the zone in question is very new or greatly pestered by Portuguese military reaction. But there is also a great deal of negative evidence to the same effect. This negative evidence will be found in countries that have become independent by reformist processes within institutions—within structures—taken over from colonial rule.

The central problem in these newly independent countries is similarly one of participation. Every specialist in development, no matter of what ideological allegiance, has agreed that the progress of the Africans will turn upon the mobilization of the rural multitudes for new and more fruitful methods of production within new and more fruitful relations of production. There is not a single African government without its teams of foreign advisers, experts, analysts, planners; the experience of these specialists is large and various, but all their conclusions point the same way.

Always the argument comes back to the same initial question: how to mobilize the rural multitudes for more work and better work? Only a solution of that problem will make possible any general raising of living standards, any closing of the widening gap between town and village, any advance to appropriate forms of mechanization and industrialization. Only this solution will cut down on costly food imports, supply locally grown food in the sufficiency demanded by burgeoning towns, build the economic basis for a better sociocultural structure of society. Upon this solution, in short, turns the opportunity for transition from one system to another. To another system, one may add, which need in no way aim at "consumption targets" implied by countless motor cars, a continual desertion of the countryside, or bombing planes, but can stubbornly insist on promoting the good of the community *as* a community in line with its own history and development.

Early in the 1970s it was painfully clear that most of the newly independent countries had failed to find any effective answer to this central problem. They were much criticized for this failure, coming as it did when the average annual increase of population in most or all of these countries was touching 3 per cent, a rate of increase capable of doubling Africa's population within less than thirty years. Yet the criticism usually missed the point. For it was usually based on the notion that Africans had inherited perfectly viable institutions for postcolonial development, but had failed to work them. Whereas what they had really inherited were the institutions of colonial extraction. In attempting to develop *these* institutions, they could only deepen their problems.

It is easy to see why. On the political side, these institutions were inherently authoritarian and therefore elitist. In so far as Africans could enter and command them, they could do so only at the price of widening the gap between themselves and the multitudes of their people, even when, as not seldom, individuals tried hard to escape such alienation. Out of this, after independence, came political situations in which elites battled for the spoils of office and were increasingly reduced to silence by the one elite that had effective power, the military.

On the economic side, they were institutions that supposed the continued functioning of the new national economies within the general economic system that had previously dominated them. The new regimes might be able to modify their relationship to this general economic system in which they were clasped, by raising taxation of foreign dividends, increasing mineral royalties, securing foreign loans for this or that individual project, whether of any general use or not. But the modification could only be a small one. Each and all of them remained a fragment of the world capitalist system which had enclosed it while a colony. As time went by, most of the ruling elites became content to accept their position and defend it as best they could against the bulk of their fellow countrymen.

The negative evidence of this kind lies on every side, but one or two examples may be helpful. The oldest of modern Africa's independent countries, save for Ethiopia, offers a good case in point. Like some other countries, Liberia has lately experienced a boom in its economy. "The rate of expansion of the economy of Liberia during the decade preceding 1961 surpassed that of almost any other country in the world. Gross domestic money income more than quadrupled between 1950 and 1959, government receipts increased more than eightfold, tonnage of goods imported nearly quadrupled . . . , the money sector labor force nearly tripled, net money income of tribal households more than quadrupled, and mileage of all-weather roads quadrupled. . . ."[4]

Now, this was a far more sensational growth than that of Angola during the following decade; but it was also, apparently, a growth of the same kind. For these experts, after their researches, wished "to emphasize a central feature of Liberian economy, namely that enormous growth in primary commodities produced by foreign concessions for export has been unaccompanied either by structural changes to induce complementary growth or by institutional changes to diffuse real gains in real income among all sectors of the population." This was exactly Angola's case a decade later.

"Our principal conclusion is that the rapid growth of production between 1950 and 1960 has had little developmental

[4] R. W. Clower, G. Dalton, M. Harwitz, A. A. Walters, *Growth Without Development: An Economic Survey of Liberia,* Northwestern University Press, Evanston, Ill., 1966, p. 24. This survey was undertaken at the behest of the government of Liberia and the U.S. Agency for International Development, the chief official U.S. agency for foreign aid.

impact on Liberia or Liberians. It has increased the wage bill for unskilled labor and has expanded tax revenues received by the government. But the enlarged wage bill has not induced expansion of domestic production of goods bought by wage workers; it has merely raised imports. And increased tax revenues have been spent for the most part in ways that do not apparently increase the productive capacity of the nation."[5]

To shift from mere growth to systematic development, argued these experts at various points in their report, must involve far-reaching structural and institutional changes. But such changes were not being made. "Because the traditional policies and ruling group remain unchanged in the new economic environment of massive iron ore mines and rubber plantations, Liberia is growing but not developing. The overriding goal of Liberian authority remains what it has been for the past 150 years: to retain political control among a small group of families of settler descent and to share any material benefits of economic growth among its own members. . . ."[6]

They said much else to the same effect; it all boiled down to a failure to move out of colonial-elitist structures into structures of over-all participation.

Yet Liberia, it may be objected, had from the first a "settler structure," though black and not white, and is therefore an exception in the Africa of recent independence. Evidently, the argument can only reinforce the hopelessness of any merely reformist solution in a settler-dominated Angola or Mozambique. Even allowing it, though, is the situation any better in countries that do not have a "settler structure"? In a few of them—those which have tried with some success to move out of the elitist institutions inherited from colonial rule—the situation is undoubtedly better than it used to be. Elsewhere the setbacks encountered in the 1960s tell their own distressing tale. Try as they may, these regimes have not been able to reach economic "take-off" or political stability. In this respect, perhaps, the collapse of the first Nigerian Federation (1960–66) has

[5] Ibid., p. vi.
[6] Ibid., p. 5.

provided the most illuminating example. Praised by many foreign admirers as an almost ideal example of economic progress
on "sound" lines, the first Nigerian Federation ended in violence
and disintegration; and there is little doubt that the elitist nature of its regime was a principal reason for this.[7]

The point here is not that the new elites that ruled the first
Nigerian Federation were unable to score any gains for the
country as a whole. On the contrary, they were able to enlarge
and improve several important aspects of the social fabric,
notably the quantity of secondary education. The point is that
they operated (or had to operate) within the assumptions and
restrictions taken over from colonial examples. They wished to
rule the country peacefully and well: in the event, politics became a dogfight between contending groups, formally representative of large multitudes but in fact concerned most nearly
with their own sectional advancement. Putting it another way,
they tried to behave as an emergent national bourgeoisie capable
of imposing on Nigeria a hegemony of ideas and structures
such as could lead to the development of a Nigerian capitalist
system.

Other examples further explain the resultant picture. The
Ivory Coast Republic, in ex-French West Africa, is another
newly independent country where a would-be "bourgeoisie" has
been trying to do the same thing. At first sight, they seem to
have been doing it with success. The last decade has seen a
continued and even notable economic growth, together with the
emergence of a "class" of well-to-do African planters as well
as a relatively comfortable "urban middle class" consisting of
perhaps two thousand heads of families in bureaucratic jobs or
jobs deriving from foreign enterprise.[8]

This, it was argued for the Ivory Coast regime, offered the
evidence of systematic change, and would lead to "take-off" into
an Ivory Coast capitalist system around the year 1970. Here,

[7] Cf. argument *in extenso* in B. Davidson, *Which Way Africa? The Search
for a New Society,* Penguin, London and Baltimore, revised ed., 1971.
[8] Samir Amin, *L'Afrique de L'Ouest Bloquée: L'Économie Politique de la
Colonisation 1880–1970,* Éditions de Minuit, Paris, 1971, pp. 89–90.

if anywhere, was the proof that a native capitalism was not only possible but that it presented, as well, the means of general progress. Yet a more careful look at the facts will suggest the opposite conclusion. This is that the boom in the Ivory Coast is only another example of a colonial-type *mise en valeur*—of growth within a system incapable of achieving the autonomy and inner strength required for any kind of "take-off," whether capitalist or not.

In 1970, far from having reached and passed the watershed between a colonial-type system of extraction and an independent system of sustained and over-all growth, the Ivory Coast appeared to have solved none of its basic problems. The years 1960–67 saw an increase in non-agricultural wage employment of 57 per cent; but the urban population increased far more rapidly, rising by as much as 115 per cent in the capital, Abidjan, where there was said, by 1969, to be massive unemployment. The elites swelled in numbers and individual wealth, but the transfer of wealth to France and other foreign countries swelled at the same time. "There is still no Ivory Coast bourgeoisie, while the 'European' share in non-agricultural revenue—50 per cent in 1965—has certainly increased since that date."[9]

There was no evidence, in short, that these elites had increased the system's independence from France and other foreign investors. "If one may speak of the development of capitalism in the Ivory Coast," Samir Amin has commented, "there is no ground for saying that it is the development of an Ivory Coast capitalism. This society has no autonomy of its own; it has no being without the European society that dominates it. Here the workers are African, but the true bourgeoisie is absent, domiciled in Europe, which provides the capital and the men who use it."

The outcome, accordingly, is a variant of the Liberian situation; and the reader may think it not without interest that four orthodox American experts should arrive at the same general

[9] Ibid., pp. 206–7.

conclusions, almost word for word, as an analysis from a radical standpoint. In the Ivory Coast, as in Liberia, the effective system is one in which a local elite of beneficiaries have gone into partnership with a dominant foreign system. All essential decisions depend directly or indirectly upon this dominant foreign system. But the effect of this dominant foreign system is in no way to develop a systematic change, a native capitalism, an independent entity; on the contrary, its effect is to bolster its continued hegemony by preventing any such development, and, while preventing it, to expand the already existing system of extraction in new ways. With the investible surplus of the Ivory Coast transferred regularly abroad, what is being developed is not the economy which produces the surplus but the economy to which the surplus flows: in this case, largely, the economy of France.

This "neo-colonial" or "late colonial" form of the extractive system differs from the old in many of its appearances but mainly because it affords a place, even if a small one, for local partners. Historically, it has its counterpart in the old days of precolonial independence. In those days the kings, rich men, and prime merchants who ran the slave trade on the African side may be said to have been the beneficiaries of an "early colonial" contract with Europeans for the exploitation of African populations. They, too, in the measure of their time, participated in the "development of underdevelopment,"[10] so that the last state of the slave-trading African countries was almost always worse than the first.

On the European side of the partnership, the slave trade worked as a powerful element in promoting systematic development. It helped to provide the capital, drawn from the sugar trade, which depended on the slave trade, by which England and then France were able to make their industrial revolutions, their major changes of system. But the slave trade brought no

10 The term is that of A. Gunder Frank: cf. *Le Développement du Sous–Développement: l'Amérique latine*, Maspero, Paris 1969; also, idem, *Latin America: Under-Development or Revolution*, Monthly Review Press, New York, 1970.

corresponding stimulus on the African side: if a few slave-trading African societies gained a new means of livelihood, they were only picking up the crumbs, while many other societies, such as those of western Angola, were plunged into ruin. So now today, in different circumstances but with regained political independence, other kings, rich men, and prime merchants once again enter an unequal partnership aimed at the general exploitation of Africans. The "development of underdevelopment" continues.

Thus the Ivory Coast's politico-economic structure is regressive. Its elements prevent it from being otherwise, no matter how much the extractive system may grow. It is regressive "first of all, because the planters are not obliged, by the very functioning of the system, to invest"; they can send their profits abroad, buy real estate in Europe, spend it on as much conspicuous consumption as they wish. Next, because the "rich urban groups do not have the means [to invest], so small is the place left to them by dominant foreign capital." Thirdly, because "the country's native elites are nearly all administrative or para-administrative, and include no more businessmen than elsewhere in black Africa."[11] Two fifths of all the salaries paid by the economy, and above all those paid at high levels, go to Europeans who hold the key jobs.

"There is no exaggeration in saying that the whole capital surplus created in the Ivory Coast—and more than that—is transferred to the centers of the world capitalist system." If bourgeois groups have appeared, "their prosperity is linked to the state and foreign capital, and for their excess revenues they find a remunerative use in real-estate speculation or the promotion of certain services. They play no part in the country's development."

Chiming with conclusions reached elsewhere, Samir Amin thus concludes that the experience of the Ivory Coast over the past twenty years "can be defined as 'growth without development': as growth, that is, engendered and maintained from the

[11] Op. cit., p. 90.

exterior, without the existing socioeconomic structure allowing any automatic passage to a further step, that of self-driven and self-maintained dynamism. This is the 'development of under-development,' described by A. Gunder Frank. For if the Ivory Coast today is no longer in the primitive conditions of 1950, it has since become a true under-developed country, well-integrated into the world capitalist system like its elder brother, Senegal," where the *mise en valeur* began earlier.

Senegal has been somewhat favored over its African fellow republics by a special history of privilege, even if minimal privilege, conceded by its colonizing power. Its period of boom, its *mise en valeur*, was launched at the end of the nineteenth century with the growing of groundnuts for export to France. This in turn produced sectoral economic growth at a relatively early colonial stage, notably in the rise of the Mouride brotherhood and their groundnut enterprises.[12]

Yet these conditions have failed to yield anything remotely resembling an autonomous capitalism capable of carrying Senegal toward a "take-off" stage of all-round socioeconomic development. For the "local beneficiaries" have remained the junior partners of the principal beneficiaries in France. From a detailed review of the various elements in the Senegalese balance of payments, it was possible to conclude in 1971 that "Senegal, it seems, does not *receive* foreign aid; the transfer of wealth goes flatly in the reverse direction: from Senegal to the developed world."[13]

From these and parallel studies it appears undeniable that the post-1945 expansion in colonial economies, whether in Africa or elsewhere, has neither promoted native capitalist systems nor otherwise improved the chances of over-all development. Their general posture, on the contrary, has become ever more subordinate to the development of the capitalist homelands oversea. The distortion of their societies into large sectors of primary poverty and small sectors of conspicuous consumption has re-

[12] See D. B. Cruise O'Brien, *The Mourides of Senegal*, Clarendon, Oxford, 1971; Samir Amin, op. cit., ch. 1.
[13] Samir Amin, op. cit., pp. 194–95.

flected an increasingly monopolistic organization of capital in the major foreign systems which have continued to dominate them. Growing without developing, their economies have fueled the power of giant corporations elsewhere; and "foreign aid" has been little more than a screen to hide the ugly truth.

Comparable studies of another chief area of "under-development," Latin America, indicate the same situation. Here, too, though in otherwise markedly different circumstances, economic expansion has not led to systematic change, but to a deepening frustration expressed most recently in efforts at structural revolution, as in Bolivia and Chile, or, to prevent such efforts, in the rise of governments of a brutally repressive type, as in Brazil. Even the latter, though the largest of all these countries, now ends more than a century of political independence in a condition of more or less total dependence on the policies of the United States, which is playing there, if less directly, the same role as France in Senegal or Ivory Coast.

If a national bourgeoisie has developed in Brazil, it has remained too weak to stand on its own feet. More and more, it has been downgraded to a mere agent of a foreign bourgeoisie which regards Brazil as a part of its own economic hegemony. Once again, as with countries in Africa, the growth of the Brazilian economy appears to have promoted the development of Brazil far less than the further enrichment of its foreign investors.

Between 1947 and 1960, since when the trend has certainly not changed, the volume of private-sector investments from the U.S.A. to Brazil is said to have totaled $1,814 million; meanwhile, the flow of capital from Brazil to the U.S.A., arising from the transfer of dividends, royalties, and other payments, reached $3,481 million, or nearly twice as much.

Figures calculated by the U.S. Department of Commerce for other Latin American countries have revealed the same "reversionary balance."[14] If U.S. aid was given, it was evidently at the price of agreeing to U.S. policies that reinforced this

14 Gunder Frank, *Le Développement* . . . , p. 145.

outward flow of wealth.[15] In view of all this, and much else to
the same tune, it may not be too harsh to say that the attempt
to build independent or national capitalist systems in Latin America has squandered a hundred years of history. Is Africa to
suffer the same?

In August 1971 the Minister of Finance of Ghana, Mr. J. H.
Mensah, made a speech in which he struck a balance of his
country's situation. They had, he said, developed a social and
physical infrastructure without developing the means to pay for
it. "They continued to import more than they exported, and the
expected increase and diversification in exports had not taken
place. Above all, agricultural production had remained stagnant
so that not only did food imports constantly threaten the balance of payments, but the shortage and cost of locally produced
food was largely responsible for inflation. . . ." Industry was
expanding but without being able to absorb all those coming
on the labor market. Unemployment remained a very serious
problem. "The decade 1960–70 represented economically
'wasted years.'"[16]

A little earlier, Samir Amin had also considered Ghana's case
and pointed to an interesting contrast. Ghana's "available physical capital," he concluded, "is relatively large [contrary to a
widespread preconceived idea about under-developed coun-
tries]: per head, it is as large as in Japan. If it has proved
incapable of achieving an independent dynamic growth [*crois-
sance autocentrée et autodynamique*]—that is, a true development—this is because the extractive orientation [*orientation
extravertie*] of production—in other words, foreign domination—
allows the transfer abroad of the potential surplus which this
capital would otherwise constitute. This transfer takes the form
of 'visible' exported profits and of the hidden transfer inherent
in 'unequal exchange,'" in the terms of trade and their conse-

[15] Cf. T. Hayter, *Aid as Imperialism*, Penguin, London and Baltimore, 1971;
e.g., p. 142.
[16] *West Africa*, Aug. 13, 1971.

quences—the adverse movement of import and export prices fixed by foreign firms or by the operations of a "world market," in which Ghana, like any other ex-colonial country, has little or no influence. Essentially, therefore, the "wasted years" were the outcome of economic dependence of a direct and special kind.

It is when one considers the nature of this direct and special dependence that one sees the full futility of any "development plan" conceived according to the theory that a mere adding to what already exists can produce, in these circumstances, more than mere growth of what exists. Most such plans have derived from planners whose basic concepts, with whatever reservations, appear to arise from a crudely lineal notion of development. Of this the best known if also the crudest model has been Professor Rostow's five "stages of growth." Cutting a strange swathe through history, Rostow proposed "to identify all societies, in their economic dimensions, as lying within one of five categories: the traditional society, the pre-conditions for take-off [by which he meant what historians have called 'industrial revolution'], the take-off [i.e., 'industrial revolution'], the drive to maturity, and the age of mass high-consumption."[17] On this view, every country could reach the heavens of the blessed, duly identified by Rostow as the capitalist system of the U.S.A., simply by following capitalist prescriptions; every country could do this, moreover, no matter what its historical posture and present circumstances. Economic plans were duly drawn up or recommended as though this were really possible. Ministers such as Mr. Mensah manfully tried to carry out such plans, and naturally failed.

One may accuse such men of insouciance or naïvety; the fact remains that they have been sold a bill of goods. That their countries remain subordinate fragments of a system they do not control, are unable to develop their own autonomous capitalist systems, but continue to transfer wealth abroad and therefore suffer an ever greater internal dislocation—these are not the fruits of accident or of failure in governmental skill. Aim-

[17] W. W. Rostow, *The Stages of Economic Growth,* Cambridge Univ. Press, 1960, p. 4.

ing at development in these circumstances and within these structures, their leaders have tried to make water run uphill without having the power to pump it there.

All such lineal concepts of development ignore the facts of history.

Much was changed when the African colonies acquired political independence, but not the underlying system which enclosed them. This system took its rise when Britain and France achieved their "industrial revolutions" in the nineteenth century. These revolutions, and others elsewhere, enabled the thus developed countries to put the markets of the undeveloped (= nonindustrialized) world in fee. Out of this there came an international division of labor, with the undeveloped countries supplying raw materials for the industries of the developed countries, and, with this, the gradual creation of a "rich man's world" (if with many poor men) and a "poor man's world" (if with a few rich men).

And "as the world-wide division between developed industrial countries and under-developed primary-producing countries hardened, the dependence of the latter on the former became complete, whether the under-developed countries were direct political colonies or not." There set in, as Barratt-Brown has described with a wealth of detail, the whole long process of colonial growth for the benefit of imperialist development. This colonial growth led to no comparable industrial revolution in the colonies, to no "take-off" there, because it could not do so. The necessary institutions were not created, because they could not be. Thus "the local bourgeoisie [became] but a client or comprador bourgeoisie of the giant corporations of the developed countries which are operating on capital-intensive lines with high profit and high wage rates. There [was], practically speaking, no independent local bourgeoisie," just as we have seen in the case of Ivory Coast.[18]

Since colonial-type systems are regressive, because of their posture in the international division of labor and its conse-

[18] M. Barratt-Brown, *After Imperialism*, Heinemann, London, 1963. The above quotations are from the preface to the Spanish edition, 1971.

quences for wealth transfer, their growth can lead to no general solution of existing problems. This may seem a hard saying. Yet the harder fact is that any such growth, or attempted growth, can only enlarge immediate problems, and so make long-term problems even more difficult to solve. If the economy of Ivory Coast has grown over the past ten years, like that of Liberia a decade earlier, so has the total of urban unemployed (to mention only that aspect of the matter). And the number of people in this category is larger, even much larger, than all the local beneficiaries of growth.

Efforts at colonial-type growth will of course continue. They will not promote development. What they will promote is a still greater distortion of society, and, with the sharpening of conflicts that derive from this distortion, a larger instability and impoverishment. The crucial questions will remain: how to reverse the process of wealth transfer, how to escape from the international division of labor launched in the nineteenth century?

The general solution can lie only in promoting a decisive break from existing structures, a break comparable in degree (though not in kind) with the British and French shift from preindustrial to industrial economies and corresponding sociocultural institutions. This supposes revolution, not reform, just as it did with the "pre-conditions for 'take-off'" in Britain and France. There the advance was not achieved by any process of merely adding to what already existed. Far from that, it was achieved by a profound and all-penetrating sequence of radical breaks with the past, no more identifiable with a reformist gradualism than the English Civil War or the French Revolution. Existing structures and institutions were destroyed or given a new content; different structures and institutions were raised in every field of life.

This is where the "neo-colonialist" answer, the capitalist answer, infallibly breaks down. For everything combines to show, whether in Africa or Asia or Latin America, that the necessary "decisive break" can no longer be made by any attempt to build new capitalist systems, by any effort to promote the hege-

mony of new national bourgeoisies. The time has passed when
that was possible. What must now happen, if you try to do
that, is only another chapter in the "development of underdevelopment": at the best a trial in frustration, at the worst a
signal for the opening of yet another host of secret Swiss bank
accounts.

As matters stand today, any kind of reformism can only
confirm and reinforce the dependence of the weak upon the
strong, the poor upon the rich. Whether positive or negative,
all the African experience demonstrates this; and there is no
evidence that demonstrates the contrary. The case for non-
capitalist policies, eventually for socialist policies, rests not on
any doctrinaire or sentimental preference, but on all the facts
that matter.

It is against this background that the center of the scene in
Africa, during the 1970s, comes to be held by movements,
parties, or governments that have turned toward the finding of
non-capitalist methods of making the major transition their
countries need. Among them alone is anything broadly hopeful
or original to be found; the rest, with whatever good intentions,
and under whatever demagogic labels, are lost in makeshifts
aimed only at raising small islands of survival above the tide
of impoverishment and failure.

And so it is that the liberation movements in the Portuguese
colonies, remote and relatively unimportant as they may appear
at first sight, acquire their full meaning and historical stature.
They have to seek the revolutionary alternative in its most direct
and difficult form. Unlike others more favorably placed by
history, they have to carry their struggle for liberation through
the agonies of war: in their case, only the most heroic effort
can reverse the tide. Yet the scale and nature of their effort has
given them a clarity of understanding from which others may
perhaps have much to learn.

The direction of the road ahead was clear "from the start," at least to those who meant to lead along it. Had not the founding manifesto of the MPLA explained that they would have to tread the road of "a revolutionary struggle" which "will triumph only by the building of a united front of all Angola's anti-imperialist forces, taking no account of color, social situation, religious belief, or individual preference"? This being so, the aim must be to form a vanguard capable of calling a wide national movement into being, and of leading toward a victory in which all could share.

Immediately, the needs were obvious: to drive out Portuguese control; to end a colonial system "which has implanted in Angola's whole body politic the microbes of ruin, hatred, backwardness, poverty, ignorance, and reaction";[1] and, having done that, to construct a new and independent society. What kind of society? The founders of the MPLA had to be content to leave that to the future, being sure only that the process of uncompromising struggle they envisaged would itself carry them and their movement toward original solutions.

This remained the position of the relaunched MPLA of 1963 and after. "Today," observed Neto in 1970, "we are going through the stage of a movement for national liberation, a movement in which all tendencies and persons willing to take part

[1] MPLA founding manifesto, Andrade and Ollivier, pp. 69–70.

in the struggle against Portuguese colonialism are accepted. We are bound together by the common will to fight against Portuguese colonialism . . . [but] while there is one organizational structure there is not one ideological position."[2]

Which ideological position will prevail? Again, the answer lies in the further development of the struggle. The measure in which the position that eventually prevails is non-elitist and non-capitalist and therefore creative and constructive, justifying the sacrifices of the struggle, is the measure in which the national movement and its vanguard can build a unity and consciousness about the needs and possibilities of a new Angola. Putting it another way, the position that eventually prevails will be decided by the ability of the national movement and its vanguard to hold out against military defeat by the Portuguese army and air force, but also against political defeat by surrender to a compromising reformism.

These leaders have undoubtedly thought hard about the future and its needs and possibilities. But little could be gained by trying to codify distant programs. For revolutionary thought, and therefore revolutionary action, are not predetermined quantities or values; they are not the mere outcome of any doctrine however shrewdly framed. As with all original thought and action, they are "a living reality in process of formation,"[3] dialectical and thus dynamic, creating their truth from the interplay between what exists and what can be made to exist.

None of the outstanding leaders of the MPLA, or of its companion movements in Guinea-Bissau and Mozambique, appears to have budged from this standpoint and conviction. If the struggle could be launched and led along the right lines— along lines aimed at revolutionizing the colonial situation, not merely at reforming it—then the struggle would look after the future. This confidence has in no way derived from putting trust in some mysterious working of "the forces of history." On the contrary, these men and women have had to labor

[2] Neto in *Motive*, United Methodist Church, Nashville, Tenn., vol. XXXI, Feb. 4, 1971, p. 60.

[3] Cf. J.-P. Sartre, in *The Socialist Register*, London, 1970, p. 246.

with might and main, and often against terrible discouragement, to bring their movements into being and lead them forward. And this they have had to do in the absence of any
useful blueprint for advance. They have had to manage with
what they have found: peoples extensively demoralized, a "petty
bourgeoisie" of colonial formation, rural multitudes skeptical
of any hopeful change.

Yet at the same time these leaders have also put their faith
in the dynamic quality of national liberation struggles that must
be, by definition of their modes of action and advance, revolutionary struggles—forced marches on the road to any kind of
progress. Once these struggles are well in play, a widening participation, the key to their success, can have its creative effect,
can build the living reality of original thought and action. If
rightly conducted, the testing years of political effort can yield
their reward. They can produce conditions for solving ethnic
and social conflicts otherwise insoluble, for hastening the process of nation forming, for promoting "the emergence of revolutionary drives that will irreversibly mark the conquests of the
nationalist phase"[4]—and so, among other things, give this
nationalism a progressive content.

For if reformist nationalism must lead to tribalism, revolutionary nationalism can do the reverse. And if revolutionary
nationalism can solve intranational conflicts, ethnic conflicts
within a single country, then equally it may also go on to solve
international conflicts, and give the new nations of Africa their
chance of organic unity, whether political or economic. "My own
view is that there are no real conflicts between the peoples of
Africa. There are only conflicts between their élites. . . ."[5]

This reliance on the creative virtues of struggle for national
liberation—a supremely political struggle in which *warfare*, of
course, remains a minor and always regrettable element im-

[4] Mário de Andrade in *La Lutte de Libération Nationale dans les Colonies
portugaises,* Report of a conference at Dar es Salaam, 1965: CONCP, 18 rue
Dirah, Hydra, Algiers, p. 42.
[5] Amilcar Cabral, *Liberation of Guiné*, p. 139.

posed only by the Portuguese or similar obstacles, and otherwise happily absent—may or may not seem optimistic. Either way, it ought not to be confused with any reliance on spontaneity or "voluntarism." These men and women have not placed their trust in spontaneity or "voluntarism" any more than in "the forces of history." Their movements are in no important sense the products of spontaneous response, but of unrelenting toil in political persuasion. Without this toil, "nothing of lasting value" could be done. "This political preparation is the toughest, most daunting, but also most important aspect of the whole campaign for national liberation."[6]

It follows from these considerations that the degree in which the Angolan movement or its vanguard can make good its claim "to guarantee the aspirations of the Angolan people for national independence"[7]—a real and not a fake independence—is the degree in which its leadership becomes rooted in, and continuously nourished by, the living reality of a wide participation. In estimating this degree, the many foreign observers who had traveled in liberated areas by 1971 had reached substantially the same conclusions: here, in a variety of ways according to local circumstance, the concepts of a national movement that was also a revolutionary movement were manifestly taking shape. And they were taking shape because participation was having its effect—the participation of young men and women in fighting units and civilian organizations, the participation of their elders in village committees of self-rule, the participation of all these in working together, learning together, suffering together, solving problems together.[8]

6 Ibid., p. 52.
7 MPLA Steering Cttee., Lusaka, June 25, 1971.
8 E.g., in 1970, a member of the Swedish Parliament in the ruling Social Democratic Party, Mrs. Birghitta Dahl, after a three weeks' tour of liberated areas in Guinea-Bissau: "We found [there] certain things which I believe do not exist elsewhere with the same consequence—clear ideology and a consciousness which reaches into the everyday life of men and women. . . . What I saw has reinforced my conviction and knowledge that our problems are common problems as are our aspirations, and in a certain measure our methods of working. The task of creating a society in which men and women can live in dignity,

Even without the reports of foreign observers of various political beliefs, the presence of a new unity and consciousness about the needs and possibilities of constructive change could still be inferred from the success of the MPLA and its companion movements. These could never have outfaced the military repressions of the 1960s without the convinced participation of increasing numbers of people. They could never otherwise have got the volunteers, food supplies, and local information upon which their survival, let alone their advance, has continually depended. Unless the rural multitudes feel these movements increasingly their own, intimately a part of their own lives and destinies no matter what the cost, these multitudes stand aside from the struggle or stand against it.

Nothing suggests that the winning of participation was an easy or automatic process. In a thousand ways, it could clearly be neither. Nor does this emphasis on participation underplay the "leadership factor"; there is a direct sense in which the varied fortunes of these movements has reflected the nature of their founders and senior leaders, as well as geographical or other peculiarities. Nor does it ignore the obstacles and contradictions that lie along the way.

To achieve in these circumstances an adequate degree of participation—which means a wide but ever-widening one—certainly supposes good leadership. This in turn supposes an interlocking of the leaders and the led to the point where they become inseparable, where the led are constantly providing a harvest of new leaders, whether local or regional or national. And this has to be an on-going process that is felt and seen as one. Otherwise there will be ossification of the structure, and orders "from the center" will increasingly fail through lack of real participation. So the chief problem is a familiar one. It is about the "mediation of power." But here, under guerrilla conditions, the problem is always immediate and acute.

---

peace and equality is a universal problem." Letter to Amilcar Cabral quoted in ibid. "The Eighth Year of our Armed Struggle for National Liberation," Conakry, January 1971.

See also a shrewd report of a visit to Angola by Mme. Cécile Hugel, in *Heures Claires,* Paris, Sept. 1971.

The contradictions have been obvious enough, whether collective or individual. Traveling in liberated areas, one is repeatedly aware of them. There are those, as we have seen, of a largely physical nature. Village committees form a network of self-rule over wide areas, but communications over wide areas are difficult and slow. These committees are formed to act together and so give organizational substance to the living reality of change. But their very effectiveness in acting together brings Portuguese military response and so makes action harder to co-ordinate.

Leadership is exercised, in the nature of things, by a few leaders "at the top." But these depend for their efficacy on the agreement and corresponding effort of a large number of senior leaders scattered around the fighting zones, and these in turn on a still larger number of less senior leaders. Ossification can be prevented only by the persistent presence of leaders among those they lead, and by the mutual correctives they apply to each other. Yet to the extent that this is practiced, communication between the leaders themselves can become, for geographical reasons, more difficult or infrequent. In a country as vast as Angola, where face-to-face discussions between widely separated leaders can be achieved only by weeks of marching, the problem has evidently been among the hardest of all. It goes without saying that its solution has remained critically difficult at certain times and places.

More profound contradictions are implicit in the situation. The MPLA in its large majority is a movement of farmers and rural craftsmen. This is the soil from which an emphatic individualism can and does spring. But the MPLA, so long as it stays true to its objectives, is necessarily pointed in an anti-individualist direction; political preferences quite apart, no other direction could yield any long-term success.

Then, again, the needs of leadership suppose literacy and schooling; and for some, at least, advanced training outside Angola. This means the selection of a small minority of persons; and those with a little education are likely to be preferred if only in the interests of speed. Those with a little education

are also likely to come from "petty bourgeois" backgrounds,
where a personal opportunism, a careerism, will have had its
formative weight. But their training abroad will be useless to
the movement, even damaging, unless it can be made to go
together with a state of mind in which the "personal career"
becomes no longer of personal importance, becomes even con-
temptible. Personal privilege and guerrilla success cannot be
a tolerable contradiction; the hardships of the non-privileged
are too severe. Not a few selected individuals have found this
particular contradiction beyond their strength.

There are other contradictions inherent in the situation. One
of these, already touched upon, is the contradiction between
an all-embracing political front, a united front, and the needs
of revolutionary clarity and purpose. Another, unavoidably
threatening, is the contradiction between "militancy" and "militarism"—between political action, which supposes that you per-
suade, and military action, which supposes that you order. None
of these contradictions can be willed away; their tensions can
only be reduced, their resolution worked toward. Some may
become less dangerous with the onward movement of the struggle; others, and not least the "militarist" tendency, may become
more dangerous.

Yet the quality of these contradictions is also determined,
and in large degree, by the nature of the struggle and its influence on mind and character. The struggles for liberation in
these Portuguese colonies are nothing if not peoples' struggles:
their whole basis of adherence and action rests on the voluntary effort and engagement of people who want, essentially, the
same thing. They want the liberation of their country, and they
find no difficulty in understanding what this means. And the
liberation of their country supposes, in these circumstances, a
continual process of individual emancipation. Intelligent and
critical obedience, not blind acceptance of orders, becomes the
test of their success.

Their leadership is not an elite lifted to the top of the tree
of power by the influence of personal privilege; on the contrary, it is an elite that has had to climb its tree from the bottom,

and constantly to climb down again so as to renew its intimacy with the movement "at the bottom." To this extent, by all
the evidence not a small one, it forms a leadership less open
to the corruptions of power, to the perils of structural ossification.

Now in midstream one thinks in this respect of Neto himself
and his years of political imprisonment. Much older than most
of his companions, having every logistical excuse for "staying
outside," he is nonetheless to be regularly found on tours of
liberated zones. Or of Lara, another veteran of the worst days,
who lately passed the most part of an uninterrupted year in
launching and running the principal center for revolutionary
instruction of Moxico District, camped in woodlands far inside
the country. Or of Iko, another member of the movement's
five-man committee of co-ordination, who spent 1968–69 in
comparable work farther to the north. These, and other men
and women like them, have continued to live in this way.

One thinks as well of the many adults learning to read and
write in the kimbos of the east, of the children gathered in little
woodland schools where no school has ever existed before, of the
all-pervasive education provided by the struggle itself. One
thinks of the hundreds of village militants who pass every year
through centers of revolutionary instruction, inside the country,
so as to provide the leaders of tomorrow. None of this guaran-
tees the absence of ossification, for nothing can guarantee that.
But it does suggest a persistent and dynamic safeguard.

How far can this democratic participation in anti-colonial
struggle be extended into the far more difficult work of postcolonial reconstruction? Only the unfolding of the years can
show; but the argument, once more, is not about utopia: the
argument concerns the better rather than the worse. A revolutionary process is already in play. It is the further unwinding
of this revolutionary process that can carry Angola's people
through new stages of self-development in the time of independence that lies ahead. It is this that can resolve new contradictions inherent in the nature of structural change—can
overcome tensions between a state bureaucracy and the active

initiatives of the mass of citizens; between the state's planned objectives and the hopes of immediate improvement in living standards; between the assumptions of this state and the different assumptions that may exist in other states, whether in Africa or not. It is this that can create the vision and originality required for new solutions which still move stubbornly in line with the self-enlightening processes as of liberation.

For today and the immediate future, the realities are there to be examined. By the early 1970s the Angolans possessed a vehicle for political self-mobilization that enjoyed support, already, in much of the country's rural area and even in towns under strong colonial occupation. Its program spoke of revolution; far more significantly, its structures had acquired a revolutionary nature by the very process of their coming into existence, of their survival, of their political success. They had become "liberationist" in a practical and everyday sense, because they lived and grew by the liberating of minds and modes of behavior from the restrictive fetters of the traditional past and the still colonial present.

The road ahead must be difficult to follow, but they have found its beginning. As in Guinea-Bissau and Mozambique, the achievements of today have acquired their own large significance and value for the future. For it is here that the "wretched of the earth," the most deprived, the least considered, in many ways the least known or ever heard of, have used their reason and their courage to forge conditions for an open-ended liberation: for a process of creative change that need contain no inbuilt termination, that need impose no self-constructed barrier to its broadening scope and purpose.

ACKNOWLEDGEMENTS

Many friends in Africa, Europe, and the U.S.A. have helped to make this book possible. I should like especially to thank Gerald Bender and the Librarian of the University of California at Los Angeles for much bibliographical aid; Michael Barratt-Brown and Robert Sutcliffe for advice and patient criticism; António de Figueiredo for allowing me to draw on his wide knowledge of Portuguese affairs; Hugh MacDiarmid for permitting me to publish part of one of his poems; D. L. Potts for permission to quote from his thesis on the Zambian copper industry; Heinz Kamnitzer for suggesting "forbearance" as the best English equivalent of *Nachsicht* in the lines of Brecht quoted from *An die Nachgeborenen;* my wife for valued textual comments; and Jamie Davidson Licentiate of the Society of Industrial Artists (London) for his careful skill in drawing all the maps. My thanks to Agostinho Neto and his colleagues for documentary material, the opportunity of personal experience, and much hospitality in Angola, are recorded in the book itself. Only I am responsible for what I have written.

B.D.

BIBLIOGRAPHICAL NOTE

The principal works on Angolan history, as distinct from the narrower subject of the history of the Portuguese there, are mentioned in my footnotes. On Angolan-Portuguese relations the reader desiring a more extensive treatment in English should begin by consulting:

D. Birmingham, *Trade and Conflict in Angola: The Mbundu and Their Neighbours under the Influence of the Portuguese 1483–1790,* Clarendon Press, Oxford, 1966;

C. R. Boxer, *Race Relations in the Portuguese Colonial Empire 1415–1825,* Clarendon Press, Oxford, 1963;

J. Duffy, *Portuguese Africa,* Harvard, 1959;
Portugal in Africa, Penguin Books, London and Baltimore, 1962;

J. Vansina, *Kingdoms of the Savanna,* Univ. of Wisconsin Press, 1966;

D. L. Wheeler and R. Pélissier, *Angola,* Praeger, New York, and Pall Mall, London, 1971, chapters 1 to 61; together with their bibliographies, and works on more specialized aspects mentioned in my footnotes. Portuguese studies of African history barely exist. Among studies of Portuguese settlement and expansion, some of which touch briefly though usefully on African history, are:

E. A. da Silva Correa, *História de Angola,* 1792, Lisbon, 1937, 2 vols.

J. J. Lopes de Lima, *Ensaio sobre a Statística das Possessões Portuguêzes,* Lisbon, 4 vols., 1844–59, of which vol. 3 is the most valuable in this context.

R. Delgado, *História de Angola, 1482–1836,* Benguela and Lo-
      bito, onward from 1948, 4 vols. to date.

From the standpoint of Portuguese imperialism, again in order of
date, the following are essential:

G. S. Dias (ed.) *Artur de Paiva,* Lisbon, 1938, 2 vols.

Henrique de Paiva Couceiro, *Dois Anos de Govêrno: História e
      Commentários,* Lisbon, 1910.

João de Almeida, *Sul de Angola: Relatório de um govêrno de dis-
      trito (1908–1910),* repr. Lisbon, 1936.

José de Oliveira Ferreira Diniz, *Populações Indígenas de* Angola,
      Coimbra, 1918.

Norton de Matos, *A Província de Angola,* Pôrto, 1926.

Henrique Galvão, *História de Nosso Tempo: João de Almeida (Sua
      Obra e Acção),* Lisbon, 1934.

Two doctrinal works are similarly essential:

Marcello Caetano, *Os Nativos na Economia Africana,* Coimbra,
      1954.

J. M. da Silva Cunha, *O Sistema Português de Política Indígena,*
      Coimbra, 1953.

There is a large number of lesser works, some of which are mentioned in their context in my footnotes; more light will be shed
when relatively recent Portuguese archives become open to inspection.

INDEX

Adoula, Cyrille, 207, 208, 212, 234, 235
Affonso (Kongo king, 1506–40), 43–44, 71–73, 135
Africa (*see also* specific countries, movements, people, places): history and white man's myths of, 33–46, 119 ff.; independence and development problems in, 322–38 *passim*, 399 ff.; initial cultures of, 47–51, 52–67, 68–76 (*see also* specific aspects, cultures, kingdoms, people, places); initial Portuguese and other European contacts with, 68–76; kingdoms, development of, 52–67, 68–76; national liberation movements in, 160 ff., 170 ff. (*see also* National liberation movements; specific aspects, movements, people); Portuguese colonial exploitation of, 39 ff., 69 ff., 80–84, 85–93, 97 ff., 119 ff. (*see also* Colonialism; Portugal; specific aspects, countries); problems and future of revolutionary struggle and development in, 339–47; reformism, neocolonialism and revolution and, 301–4, 305–21, 322–38, 339 ff. (*see also* Colonialism; Revolution; specific aspects, countries, movements, people); resettlement program, colonialism, and dismantlement of social structures in, 292–93, 302; resistance to colonial exploitation in, 39–46, 79 ff., 119 ff., 160 ff., 170–79, 183 ff., 207 ff. (*see also* Rebellions; Revolution; specific aspects, countries, movements, people, places); significance and ineffectiveness of reformism in, 317–21, 322–38 *passim*; slavery (and slave economy) and colonial exploitation and development of underdevelopment and dependence in, 69 ff., 330–31 (*see also* specific aspects)
Agosto, Manuel, 194–95
Air Force, Portuguese, 160–61, 190–91, 261–62, 340; and bombings (air raids) and guerrilla warfare, 195–99, 245, 247, 261–62, 264–65; NATO aid to, 276–78, 296
Algeria, 18, 173, 186, 204, 211, 315; recognition of GRAE by, 211
Aliazo (Alliance of the Zombo People), 201, 210

All-African Peoples' Congress (1958), 203
Almeida, Déolinda Rodrigues de, 149–50, 163, 210, 239
Almeida, João de, 21, 36, 97 n, 100 n, 101, 103, 111, 301
Alvaro II (Kongo king), 75
Alves, Pascoal, 174
Ambwela, kingdom and people of, 65–66, 109–10
Amin, Samir, 328 n, 329, 331–32, 334
Andrade, Joaquim Pinto de, 163–64, 165 n, 185
Andrade, Mário de, 149, 150, 151, 153 n, 154, 163, 208, 210, 230, 231 n, 284 n, 306 n, 339 n, 341 n
Angola: Central Angola, map of guerrilla activity in, 269; colonial exploitation and frustration of development in, 84, 128, 145, 155 ff. (*see also* Colonialism; Development; Economy; specific aspects); Congo diversions and split in national liberation movement in, 207–28, 229 ff.; Eastern Angola, map of people and guerrilla activity in, 255; emigration from, 133–34 (*see also* Emigration; Refugees); foreign investments and development of underdevelopment in, 306–15, 317 (*see also* Development; Economy); geography and people of, xii–xiv, 3–4, 5, 8–24 *passim*, 27, 35–67 *passim*; guerrilla activity and movement in, 3 ff., 207–22, 229 ff., 252 ff. (*see also* Guerrilla warfare; specific aspects, countries, events, individuals, people, places); history, background, and early development in, 33–46, 47–51; and Hundred Years' War of Ndongo people with Portuguese, 77–80; hunting-and-gathering cultures, 47 ff.; initiative and response to colonial exploitation in, 39–46, 79 ff., 119 ff., 130, 131–42, 143–54, 170–79, 183–86, 187–93, 194 ff., 207 ff. (*see also* specific aspects, movements); initial contact with Portuguese and other Europeans, 68–76, 77–84, 85 ff.; initial cultures and people of, 47–51, 52 ff.; kingdoms, early, 52–67, 68 ff.; liberation struggle, independence, and change, 322–38, 339–47; map of districts, district capi-

Angola (cont'd)
tals, and railways, 32; map of principal ethnic groups, 35; mobilization of
people for resistance to colonial exploitation, 254–61, 264–65 (see also
under National liberation movement,
Angola); national liberation movement
in, 207–28, 229, 252 ff., 275–81, 282–
98 (see also National liberation movement, Angola); political organization
and growth of national liberation
movement in, 282–98 (see also under
National liberation movement, Angola);
Portuguese colonial extractive system
and, 80–84, 85–93, 97–104, 105–18,
119–30, 131–42, 143–54 (see also Colonialism; Development; Economy;
specific aspects); problems and future
of revolutionary struggle in, 339–47;
and reformism (neo-colonialism) and
revolution, 301–4, 305–21, 322–38
(see also Reformism); revolutionary
change in anti-colonial movement in,
282–98 (see also Revolution); rural-
urban population shifts in, 144–46;
significance and ineffectiveness of reformism in, 317–21, 322–38, 339–47;
slavery in (see Slavery); trade, start of,
47 (see also Trade); treatment of
workers by Portuguese in, 155–59 (see
also Labor; specific aspects); white
settlers and, 42–46, 85–93, 97–104,
105–18, 119–30, 131 ff., 137–38, 141–
42, 143–54 passim (see also Settlers;
specific aspects)
Angola: Heart of the Empire (Santos),
116
Angolan Liberation Army (UPA/GRAE
military wing), 236
Arms (weapons), national liberation
movement and, 18, 21–22, 23, 133, 242,
253–54, 272, 273, 274
Army, Portuguese: aid from NATO to,
276–78; black troops in, 99 ff., 190;
and colonial system, 95, 97–104, 105,
120–21, 134; deserters from, 278–81;
and early contact with Angola, 74–75;
GE ("special groups"), 22, 24; and
guerrilla movement, 19, 21, 24 ff.,
212 ff., 221 ff., 244–50, 256–74, 275–81,
282, 290–91, 340 (see also Guerrilla
movement; specific aspects); and Hundred Years' War with Ndongo, 77–
80; manpower and makeup of, 99 ff.,
275–78; militia, 22, 24, 98; and national liberation movement, 290–93;
and reformism (neo-colonialism) policy, 315, 324; and repression of rebellions, 131 ff., 170 ff., 183–86, 187–93,
194–206; and resistance to, 131 ff.,
160–79, 183–86, 187–93, 194 ff., 207 ff.;

revolts in, 91; South African aid to,
294–97
Assimilados, 117, 129, 131, 141, 142,
229–30, 235; Portuguese reformism
and, 293, 311, 315–16; and protest
movement (rebellions), 146–54, 166,
168, 169, 170, 172, 175, 184 ff., 198–
206 passim
Assimilation, Portuguese reformism
(neo-colonialism) and, 293, 311, 315–
16. See also De-Africanization
Assis Júnior, António de, 147
Associacão dos Naturais de Angola, 147
Associations, 147, 169
Atrocities (torture), 119, 127, 158, 162,
183 ff., 189–93, 194–99, 244–50, 290.
See also Repression
Authority (rule, power), political: initial
cultures and development of, 50–51;
kingships and, 52–67; Portuguese and,
68 ff.
Aviados, 89–90

Bailongo District, Angola, 234
Balopwe, and succession to Kongo king-
ships, 60
Bando, Mwene, 20, 21, 50–51, 116
Bantu (culture, languages, and people),
38, 48, 53 n, 60, 66
Baptista, Commander, 209
Baptists (Baptist missionaries), 161, 194–
99, 244–50
Barbot, John, 59
Barnett, Don, 264–65, 286 n, 294 n, 298 n
Barnett, George, 163
Barratt-Brown, M., 336
Barreto, Manuel, 133–34
Bayumbe region and people, 234
Beatrice, Dona, 40–41, 136–37, 200
Behind God's Back (Farson), 135
Beira, Bishop of, 125
Belgian Congo (Zaïre), 134, 161–62, 163,
185, 200, 244–50. See also Congo/
Kinshasa
Belgium, 119, 128, 162, 207
Belo de Almeida, António Júlio, 108 n
Bembe, Angola, 214, 216, 217, 246, 247
Ben Bella, Ahmed, 211
Bender, Gerald J., 270 n, 274 n, 290 n,
291 n
Benedicto, Commander, 238–39
Benguela, city, area, and people of, 62,
74, 90, 91, 97, 99, 103, 127, 152, 268
Benguela Railway, 214, 256
Berlin Conference (1884–85), and "scram-
ble for Africa," 102, 202
Bié District, Angola, 6, 7, 18, 24, 89,
102, 235, 253; and guerrilla activity,
266, 268–72, 289–90, 294
Bisa (people), 62–63
Bissau, Guinea-Bissau, 175–76

Black Mother: A Song of Hope (Cruz), 149

Blacks-whites relationship, 69–76, 77–93 *passim*, 97–118, 119 ff. (*see also* Colonialism; Racism; Settlers; specific aspects, individuals, movements); and African history and myths, 36–46, 59 n, 84, 92, 119 ff.; reformism (neo-colonialism) and, 301–4, 305–21, 322–38 *passim* (*see also* Reformism)

Boavida, Américo, 7, 154, 302; killed in air raid, 265

Bourgeoisie (middle class), reformism (neo-colonialism) and independence movement and, 328–38 *passim*, 341, 345

Brado Africano, O (*The African Cry*), 138

Brazil, 69, 70–71, 72, 83, 90–91, 132, 136, 333–34

Brazzaville, 8, 222, 232–35, 238, 239, 241, 262. *See also* Congo/Brazzaville

British. *See* Great Britain (the British)

British Baptist missionaries, 161, 194–99, 244–50

Brito, Abreu de, 73–74, 83 n

Brito Camacho, Manuel de, 114

Bushmen, 34–35

Cabinda, Angola, 8, 80, 219; guerrilla activity and, 233, 234, 238, 256, 262

Cabo Delgado District, Angola, 176–77, 224, 225–26

Cabra, Dias de, 74

Cabral, Amilcar, and national liberation movement, 9, 149, 150, 151, 152, 176, 204, 223, 276, 289 n, 323 n, 341 n, 343 n

Cadres, national liberation movement and political training of, 232, 286–87

Caetano, Luisa, 188–89

Caetano, Marcello, 69–70, 76, 221 n, 275, 293, 305 n, 312; and Portuguese ideas about Africa and Africans, 69–70, 76, 312

Caiongo, Angola, 191

Calheiros e Menezes, S., 98 n

Cambule River, 4, 10, 15, 20, 30

"Camy" (MPLA guerrilla column), 219

Canavale, Angola, 11, 27

Cangamba, Angola, 24, 130

Cangombe, Angola, 27, 28

Capitalism (capitalist structures): national liberation movements, growth, and development and, 296–98, 305 ff., 322–38 *passim*, 340; problems and future of revolutionary struggle against, 339–47

Caripande, Angola, 265, 294

Carmona, revolt in, 187

Carreira, Iko (MPLA leader), 216, 219–20, 260, 263, 264

Casimiro, Augusto, 127, 128

Cassava, 39, 63, 66, 301

Cassinga iron-ore mines, 273, 294

Castro, Balthazar de, 77–78

Catholics (Catholicism), 40–41, 70, 71, 78, 86, 87–89, 121, 161–62, 188, 220, 311. *See also* Christianity; Church, the; Jesuits; Missionaries

Caxito, 217, 245, 248

Center of African Studies, formation and suppression of, 150–51

Centros de Instrucçao Revolucionária (CIR), 262, 270, 286, 346

Cerejeira, Cardinal, 311

Chapayev (guerrilla pseudonym), 10, 11, 18–19, 28, 257–58

Chiefs (chiefdoms): initial African cultures and, 49, 58–67; neo-colonialism and, 316–17, 318–19; and slave trade, 58 ff., 89

Chile, 333

China (Chinese), 231 n, 237, 254, 297; and aid to national liberation movement in Angola, 297

Chipande, Alberto-Joaquim, 176–77, 225

Chipenda, Daniel, 231 n, 241, 270 n, 297–98

Chokwe (people), 9, 37, 38, 39 n, 109–10, 117, 258, 260

Christianity, 40–41, 71, 78, 86, 87–89, 119, 136–37. *See also* Church, the; Missionaries; specific denominations

Church, the, and slavery and colonial exploitation, 87–89, 121. *See also* Christianity; Missionaries; specific denominations

"Cienfuegos" (MPLA guerrilla column), 219

ciMbunda language, 11, 22, 27, 37

CIR (Centers of Revolutionary Instruction), 262, 270, 286, 346

Civilisaçao d'Africa Portuguesa, A (weekly newspaper), 136

Claeeson, Inger, 215–16

Clinics, MPLA and formation of, 230, 232, 265

Clower, R. W., 326 ff.

Cocoa plantations and production, 109, 110, 167

Coffee plantations and production, 124, 125, 309

Coimbra University, 129, 143, 166

Colonatos (Portuguese farming settlements), 45

Colonialism (colonial system, colonial exploitation): Angolan response to, 39–46, 79 ff., 119 ff., 130, 131–42, 143–54, 282–98, 301–4, 305–21, 322 ff. (*see also* specific aspects, events, movements); and dismantlement of African

Colonialism (cont'd)
  social structures, 292–93, 302; economic aspects of liberation from, 305–
  21, 322–38; guerrilla activity and (see
  Guerrilla warfare); political organization and leadership in movement
  against, 282–98; Portuguese and start
  of extractive system, 68–76, 77–84,
  85–93, 97–104, 105–18, 119–30, 131–
  42, 143–54; Portuguese military expenditures and commitments and, 275–78;
  problems and future of revolutionary
  struggle against, 339–47; rebellions and
  resistance to, 160–69, 170–79, 183–86,
  187–93, 194 (see also Rebellions); reformism (neo-colonialism) and development of underdevelopment and,
  301–4, 305–21, 322–38; revolutionary
  change in movement against, 282–98;
  and revolution of the poor, 301–4,
  305–21, 322 ff.; Salazar regime and,
  119–30 (see also Salazar); significance
  and ineffectiveness of reformism and,
  317–21, 322–38; treatment of workers
  under, 155–59 (see also Labor; specific aspects)
Common Market: South African, 295;
  West European, 316
Communism, 121, 151–52, 160, 221, 234,
  241, 296–97
Communist countries, 234. See also Communism; individual countries by name
Companhia Agrícola de Angola, 309
Conceiçao, Ciel da, 241
CONCP, 168 n
Confederaçao Brazilica, 91
Conferência dos quadros, 232
Congo/Brazzaville, 8, 222, 232–35, 238,
  239, 241, 262; and MPLA and national
  liberation movement in Angola, 232–
  35, 238, 239–40, 241, 262, 285, 287–
  88
Congo/Kinshasa (Belgian Congo, Congo
  Republic, Zaïre Republic), 134, 161–
  62, 163, 185, 189, 190, 191, 192, 194–
  99, 200, 207, 235–40, 244–50; and national liberation movement in Angola,
  207–12, 214, 217, 220–22, 226, 229,
  231–40 passim
Congo River, 52, 59–60, 69, 77; Basin,
  47, 48, 69
Contract laborers (contrados, serviçais),
  108–18, 119–30, 144, 167, 174–75,
  247–48, 267–70 (see also Forced labor); treatment by Portuguese of, 155–
  59
Copper mining industry, neo-colonialism
  and, 307, 308, 312–14
Corporations, investments in Africa and
  neo-colonialism in, 296–98, 305 ff.,
  322–38 passim

Correia de Sousa, João, 79
Cotton plantations and production, 179,
  306, 308
Cruz, Viriato da, 146, 147, 148–49, 154,
  163, 185, 204, 208, 230–31, 235; op-
  position to Neto and reorganized
  MPLA by, 230–31
Cruzeiro do Sul (newspaper), 136
Cuando Cubango District, Angola, 242,
  256, 261, 262, 263, 266, 285
Cuanhama (people), 133
Cuanza Norte District, Angola, 239;
  guerrilla activity and, 217–18, 219, 264
Cuanza River and estuary, 85–86, 90,
  110, 261, 271–72
Cuito River area, 273
Cultural clubs, 169
Cultural nationalism, 141–42, 147–54,
  163, 168–69
Cunha, Tristão da, 86
Cuvelai River area, 273
Czechoslovakia, 234

Dahl, Mrs. Birghitta, 342–43 n
Dakar, 223
Dalton, G., 326 ff.
Damba region, 248–49
Dar es Salaam, 8, 173, 223, 227, 240,
  242, 262, 274
Davidson, B., 59 n, 93 n, 127 n, 128 n,
  145 n, 328 n
De-Africanization, reformism (neo-
  colonialism) and, 311–12, 318–21
Decolonization, 120, 185, 203. See also
  specific aspects, movements
Defeza de Angola, A (newspaper), 111
Degredados (transported convicted crim-
  inals), settlement in Africa by, 87, 89,
  99, 103–4
Delgado, 225. See also Cabo Delgado
Delgado, General Humberto, 161
Dembos forests, region, and people, 184,
  188, 189, 191, 208, 219, 230, 238, 264;
  uprising (1890), 133
Dependence, neo-colonialism and under-
  development and, 301–4, 305–21, 322–
  38 passim, 339 ff.
Development (underdevelopment), re-
  formism (neo-colonialism) and, 298,
  305–21, 322–38, 339–47
Diamang (Luanda diamond-mining cor-
  poration), 128, 263
Diamond mining and miners, 128, 263
Dias de Novais, Paulo, 78–79, 85–86
Dilolo area, 214
Dilolwa (guerrilla pseudonym), 270–71
Diniz, José de Oliveira Ferreira, 20, 36
Diop, Alioune, 154
Diseases (health), 301, 302–3 (see also
  Clinics; specific diseases); life expect-
  ancy and, 302–3

"Disposable persons," 59, 78
Dividends, foreign investments and neo-colonialism and, 306, 313, 326, 333
Division of labor, neo-colonialism and underdevelopment and dependence and, 336–38
Dogbe, Karl, 163
Dos Santos, A. C. V. T., 116 n
Dos Santos, Dr. Eduardo, 149, 230, 302
Dos Santos, Marcelino, 154
Du Bois, William E. B., 120, 141
Dutch, the, 74, 79–80

Economy (economic aspects and structures): and colonialism, 117, 119–30, 292, 303, 311–12 (see also Colonialism; specific aspects); labor and (see Labor); "metropolitan factor" and, 120, 124; reformism (neo-colonialism) and, 301–4, 305–21, 322–38 (see also Colonialism; Development; Reformism; specific aspects, countries); and slavery, 69–76, 80–84, 85–93, 97–118, 119–30 (see also Slave economy; Slavery)
Educated (literate) class, repression by Portuguese of, 171, 191, 200
Education (schools), 117, 128–30, 292; missionaries and, 117, 129, 155; political, national liberation movement and, 284, 286, 328; reformism (neo-colonialism) and, 128–30, 292, 311–12; revolutionary struggle and, 344–45, 346; teachers, 292
Egerton, F. C. C., 127
Elections (voting), reformism and, 316–17, 319
Elitism (elites) and elitist structures, reformism (neo-colonialism) and, 317–21, 326 ff., 340–47
Emigration: Africans abroad, 133–34; African rural/urban population shift, 144–46; Angolans from Angola, 44, 194 ff.; Portuguese from Portugal to overseas territories, 44, 122, 165–66 (see also Settlers)
England. See Great Britain (the British)
Ennis, Dr. Merlin, 155, 158, 291
Ethnic groups, Angola, 35–37 ff.; map of, 35
Europeans (see also Blacks-whites relationship; Settlers; specific aspects, countries): and African history and myths, 36–46, 59 n, 84, 92, 119 ff.; and colonial economy, 119 ff. (see also Colonialism; Economy; specific aspects); reformism (neo-colonialism) and, 301–4, 305–21, 322–38 passim
Export income (export crops): forced labor and, 106–18, 124–30, 167, 179; reformism (neo-colonialism) and, 306–

15, 326–38 passim (see also specific aspects; crops, goods)
Extractive system (see also Colonialism): liberation movement and, 306–21, 322–38 passim; reformism (neo-colonialism) and, 306–21, 322–38 passim

Fairs (markets), 53, 90, 102
Fanon, Frantz, 186, 204
Farinha, Fernando, 217–18
Farson, Negley, 135
February-Four (guerrilla pseudonym), xiii, 4, 10, 12, 18, 28
Felgas, Hélio A. Esteves, 162 n, 190–91
Ferreira, Tomás, 208–9, 210
Figuereida, Manuel, eyewitness account of treatment by Portuguese of, 198
Financial Times (London), 306 n, 307 n, 309 n, 315 n, 316 n
FLN, Algeria, 186, 204
FLNA, 210
Fontes Pereira, José de, 137–38, 139–40, 141, 148, 288
Food production (food cultivation, food supply), 39 (see also Export income; Plantations; specific aspects, crops, kinds); early development of Angola and, 47–49, 66; popular participation in national liberation movement and, 325
Forced labor, 95, 105–18, 119–30, 141, 142, 167 ff., 267–70, 293, 311. See also Contract laborers
Force Publique, Belgium and, 162
Foreign aid, neo-colonialism and, 333–34, 337–38. See also individual countries
Foreign investment, national liberation movement and neo-colonialism in Angola and, 295–98, 306–15, 317, 322–38
Forts, Portuguese "presence" in Africa and construction of, 97–98, 102
FRAIN (Frente Revolucionária Africana para a Independência Nacional), 163 n, 204
France (the French), 42, 112, 119, 142, 143, 147, 296; and aid to Portuguese, 277, 296; and Algeria, 315; and investments in Angola, 296, 307, 309 n; and Ivory Coast Republic, 328, 329, 330; and neo-colonialism, 296, 307, 309, 328, 329, 330, 332, 333, 336, 337; Portuguese Army deserters in, 278–81; and Senegal, 332, 333
Francisco, Manuel, 198
Frank, A. Gunder, 330 n, 332
Free labor, 92–93, 106–18. See also Contract laborers; Labor

FRELIMO (Mozambique national liberation movement), 170–73, 176–77, 204, 223–28, 262, 286, 296; Mtwara conference (1968), 225–28; separatism and splits in, 223–28
Frente Revolucionária Africana para a Independência Nacional (FRAIN), 163 n, 204
Front de Libération Nationale (FLN), Algeria, 186, 204
Futuro d'Angola, O (weekly), 137–38

Gago, Angola, 5, 11
Gago Coutinho, Angola, 130
Galvão, Henrique, 95, 97 n, 100 n, 115 n, 129, 134
Gama, Dom António José da, 201
Gandra, Dr. Julieta, 163
Ganguella (people), 8–9
Garcia II (Kongo king), 74
Gazeta de Loanda, 138
Germany: and aid to Portuguese, 276–78; and investment in Angola, 296, 307; and South-West Africa, 103, 133
Ghana, 204, 232, 334–35
Gizenga, Antoine, 208
Gold, 49–50, 62, 71
Gomes de Silva, Francisco, 281
Gouveia, Father, 70
Graça, J. R. de, 64
GRAE (Revolutionary Government of Angola in Exile), 210–22, 235–40, 246
Great Britain (the British), 91, 103, 110, 112, 119, 120, 123–24, 128, 129, 138–39, 142, 143, 147, 310; and investments in Angola, 296, 307; and neocolonialism, 296, 312–14, 336, 337; slave trade and industrial development in, 330–31
Greece, 275, 276
Grenfell, Dr. David, 195, 244
Grenfell, Dr. Jim, 250
Guahero (guerrilla pseudonym), 266–68
Guerra preta ("black army"), use by Portuguese of, 99 ff., 190
Guerrilla warfare (guerrilla movement), 3–30, 33, 152, 169, 181, 183–86, 187–93, 194–206, 212–22, 229–43, 244–52 (*see also* specific aspects, countries, individuals, organizations); Eastern Angola Front activity and drive toward Atlantic, 252–74, 282 ff.; map of area of guerrilla presence and penetration in Angola (1971–72), 283; MPLA and, 3 ff., 212–22, 229–43, 244 ff., 253–74 ff., 282–98 (*see also* MPLA); MPLA reorganization and, 229–43, 244 ff.; and mobilization of popular participation, 254–61, 264–65, 282–98; political organization and growth in, 260–62, 282–98, 322–38 *passim*; Portuguese

military expenditures and, 275–78; problems and future of revolutionary struggle and, 339–47; revolutionary change and, 282–98, 305–21 *passim*, 322–38 *passim*; split in national liberation movement of Angola and, 207–28; and supplies, 252–54 (*see also* Arms); terrain, strength, and activities of, 212–22, 229–43, 244 ff.
Guimarães (guerrilla pseudonym), 22–23, 105 n
Guinea, Portuguese, 134, 232, 278. *See also* Guinea-Bissau
Guinea-Bissau, 45, 125, 149, 152, 202 (*see also* Guinea, Portuguese); ethnic councils established in, 323 n; national liberation movement in, 170, 173–74, 175, 223, 262, 273, 281, 286, 295, 323 n, 324, 340, 347 (*see also* PAIGC); neocolonialism, 303, 311, 323 n
Guns. *See* Arms (weapons)

Harper's Monthly, 109–10
Harwitz, M., 326 ff.
Health (disease), 301, 302–3, 308 (*see also* specific diseases); life expectancy and, 302–3; MPLA and founding of clinics, 230, 232, 265
Helicopters, use by Portuguese of, 4, 5, 23, 26, 261, 264, 265, 272, 277, 294, 296
Henda, Hoji ya (MPLA commander), 210 n, 265
Henrique II (Kongo king), 131
Herbicides, use by Portuguese of, 273, 278
Hernández, Francisco Xavier, 163
Hoagland, Jim, 26–27
Hoji ya Henda (MPLA commander), 210 n, 265
Holden, Roberto, 140, 163, 186, 189, 201–6, 263; career, elitism, and opportunism of, 202–4, 212, 220–28; and crisis in UPA, 235–40; and GRAE, 210–22; and guerrilla activity, 213–20; and leadership and split in national liberation movement of Angola, 208–28, 230; and MPLA and UPA controversy, 208 ff.
Holder, Lawrence, 163
Hookworm, 301, 302
Hornung sugar company, 114
Horton, J. Africanus, 136, 138 n
Huambo District, Angola, 89, 155–59, 259, 268, 272
Hugel, Mme. Cécile, 343 n
Hundred Years' War, 77–80
Hunkanrin, Louis, 137

Ibn Khaldun, 53

Iko (guerrilla pseudonym), xiii, 44–45, 253

Independence movement(s), 115, 130, 137, 139, 140, 141, 142, 167, 171, 202 (*see also* National liberation movements; specific aspects, countries, events, organizations); liberation struggle and change, 322–38, 339–47; popular participation problem and, 325 ff.; problems and future of revolutionary struggle and, 339–47; reformism (neo-colonialism) and, 305–21, 322–38 (*see also* Colonialism; Reformism)

Industrial development (industrialization) and output, reformism (neo-colonialism) and underdevelopment and, 306–15, 317, 324–38. *See also* Economy; specific aspects, countries

Industrial revolution ("industrial take-off"), neo-colonialism, underdevelopment and dependence and, 335–38

Institute of Strategic Studies (London), 275

Iron Age, 38, 49–51, 57

Iron ore, 307, 308

Italy, 120–21, 276–77

Ivory Coast Republic, growth without development in, 328–30, 331–32, 333, 337

Jacinto, António, 163, 165 n

Japan, 308, 334; and investments in Angola, 296, 308

Jesuits, 70, 78, 83. *See also* missionaries

Joan of Arc, 41

John II, King of Portugal, 68

Kamitatu, Cléophas, 212 n

Kankangala (people), 27

Kasai River, 60, 61

Kasale, Lake, 60

Kasolo ("the Discoverer") bird, 34, 43

Kassanga, Marcos, 209–10

Katanga, 62, 100, 207, 214, 237; copper, 307

Kaunda, Kenneth D., 241, 263 n

Kazembe, kingdom of, 62, 63–64

Kessel, Carlos, 236

Khoi (people), 34–35, 38, 47, 48

Kibentele, Congo, 248, 249, 250

Kibinda Ilunga, 60

Kibulala, Christopher, 242–43

Kiditu, Dom Manuel, 201

Kimbangala, Manuel, 196

Kimbangui, Simon, 200

Kimbos (villages, settlements), guerrilla activity and warfare in Angola and, 11, 12–30, 257, 260, 346

Kimbundu, kingdom and people of, 37, 38, 40, 61, 77 ff., 106, 202

Kingengo Nambuangongo, 244, 245, 271

Kings (kingdoms, kingship): hereditary power and succession and, 57–58, 60–61; initial African cultures and, 49, 50, 52–67; Portuguese and, 68–76, 77–84, 131–32, 136–37, 201–2; and rebellions, 201–2; and slave trade, 89

Kinkani, Samuel, 198

Kinkuzu, 214, 215, 217, 222, 236, 240

Kinshasa (formerly Léopoldville), 162, 185 (*see also* Congo/Kinshasa); and MPLA reorganization, 229, 231–35; and national liberation movement in Angola, 203, 207–10, 211, 212, 213, 214, 220–21, 222, 226, 229, 230, 231–35, 236, 238, 239–44

Kissembo, Angola, 131–32

Kongo (kingdom and people), 37, 38, 40, 41, 106, 226, 320; early kingdoms and kings, 57–58, 59, 61, 201–2; and national liberation movement and risings, 108, 131–33, 160–69, 170–71, 183–86, 187–93, 194–206, 226; Portuguese and early contacts with, 68–76, 77, 78, 79, 80, 83

Kongolo (Luba leader), 60

Krupp (of West Germany), 307

Kuba, kingdom and people of, 61

Kubindama (guerrilla pseudonym), 189–90, 271–72

Labor (workers), 25–26, 92–93, 105–18, 119–30, 171 ff., 278–81 (*see also* Contract workers; Forced labor; Free labor; Slavery); and mobilization for guerrilla activity, 252 ff.; Portuguese emigration to Angola and competition for employment, and 165–68; reformism (neo-colonialism) and, 301–4, 305–21, 322–38; resistance to colonial exploitation and liberation movement and, 170–79, 183–86, 187–93, 194 ff., 252–61, 322–38 *passim*, 343 ff.; treatment by Portuguese of, 155–59; and wages, 166, 171, 293, 307, 327, 329, 331

Labor laws and practices, Portuguese in Angola (and Africa) and, 92–93, 105–18, 119–30

Land distribution (land use), reformism (neo-colonialism) and, 309

Languages, 38, 53 n, 60. *See also* specific languages, people

Lara (guerrilla pseudonym), xiii

Lara, Lucio, 149, 204, 231–32, 346

Latin America, neo-colonialism and underdevelopment in, 333–34

Leadership, national liberation movement and, 146–54, 163, 177–78, 199–206, 208–28 (*see also* Authority; specific aspects, countries, individuals, movements, organizations); elitism

Leadership (cont'd)
    problem and, 282 ff., 341 ff. (see also
    Elitism); failure of Kongo risings and,
    199–206; guerrilla warfare and splits
    and diversions in, 207–28, 229 ff.,
    240 ff.; MPLA reorganization and,
    229–43; political organization and,
    282–98, 339–47; problems and future
    of revolutionary struggle and, 339–47;
    revolutionary change and, 282–98,
    322–38, 339–47
Leaflets (pamphlets), national liberation
    movement and, 87 n, 161 ff., 168–69,
    173–74
Lelinho, Chefe do Pôsto, 155, 156–59
Léopoldville (later renamed Kinshasa),
    162, 185 (see also Congo/Kinshasa;
    Kinshasa); and MPLA reorganization,
    229, 231–35; and national liberation
    movement in Angola, 203, 207–10, 211,
    213, 214, 220–21, 222, 226, 229, 230,
    231–35, 236, 238, 239 ff.
Liberation movement(s). See Independ-
    ence movement(s); National liberation
    movements; specific aspects, countries,
    movements, organizations
Liberia, development and underdevelop-
    ment in, 326–27, 329, 330, 337
Life expectancy, health conditions in An-
    gola and, 302–3
Liga Africana (1919), 141
Liga Angolana, 141
Liga Nacional Angolana, 147
Lima, Mesquelita de, 36
Lisbon, 25, 68–76, 77, 78, 91, 92, 107,
    108, 111, 113, 120, 121, 124, 142, 147,
    149, 152, 185 (see also Portugal; Sal-
    azar); and foreign investments, 296–
    98; and reformism (neo-colonialism),
    307–21 (see also Reformism); South
    African aid to, 294–97
Literacy (illiteracy), 303, 311–12, 316,
    323, 344–45, 346. See also Education
    (schools)
Loanda, Angola, 74, 78–79, 86–92 pas-
    sim, 111 (see also Luanda); revolts in,
    87 n, 91, 131
Loango, kingdom and people of, 76, 80–
    84
Lobito, 145, 146
Londes, Major, 217
Lopes de Lima, José Joaquim, 80, 90–
    92, 95, 97
Lourenço Marques, 172–73
Lozi people, Zambia, 263
Luanda, Angola (district and people), 11,
    74, 88, 91, 98, 99, 103, 117, 128, 202
    (see also Loanda, Angola); and guer-
    rilla warfare, 183–86, 187–90, 193,
    199–200, 204, 205, 217, 219, 245, 248,
    249, 264, 266, 272–73, 278; herbicides

used by Portuguese against, 278; and
    national liberation movement, 137,
    138, 141, 142, 145, 146, 147, 154,
    160 ff., 164–69, 170 ff.; prison in, 103,
    164–65, 183–84, 187; and reformism
    (neo-colonialism), 317, 318–19, 321;
    refugees from, 208; risings in, 178–79,
    183–86, 187–93, 199–200, 204, 205
Luba (people), 60
Lucca, Fr. Lorenzo da, 41
Luchazi (people), 11, 20, 36, 38–39, 65–
    67, 130; and guerrilla activity, 256,
    257; reformism and, 318–20
Luena, 9. See also Luvale, kingdom and
    people of
Lugard, Lord, 112
Lumumba, Patrice, 207, 208, 221
Lunda, kingdom, region, and people of,
    27, 38, 60–62, 63, 64, 66, 73, 130;
    guerrilla warfare and, 256, 263, 264
Lusaka, Zambia, MPLA in, 262
Luseeng (Luba ruler), 60
Luso, Angola, 44–45, 110, 214, 258, 259–
    60, 264
Luta (guerrilla pseudonym), xiii, 10–11
Luvale, kingdom and people of, 9, 38–39,
    64–65; and guerrilla activity, 9, 256,
    257
Lyautey, and French colonialism in
    Africa, 112

Mabote, Sebastião, 171–72
Machado, Ilidio Tomé Alves, 162
Machel, Samora Moises, 170–72
Maize food crop, 39, 66
Makonde people, 225–26
Malagasy, 295
Malange District, Angola, 253, 263, 264,
    266–68; Portuguese fort built at, 102;
    rebellion in, 179
Malaria, 301, 302
Malawi, 295
Malaysia, 69
Malnutrition, 302, 303
Manhertz, Bernhard, 235–36
Manioc, 39, 63, 66, 301
MANU (Makonde African National
    Union, later the Mozambique African
    National Union), 224–25
Marcum, John, 139 n, 146 n, 163 n, 183–
    84, 200 n, 210
Margoso Wafuakula (UPA/GRAE com-
    mander), 215
Mariano, António, 179
Maria sect (Maria's War), 179, 183, 187
Market economy: dismantling of tradi-
    tional African structures after intro-
    duction by Portuguese of, 146; reform-
    ism (neo-colonialism) and, 305–15
Markets (fairs), 53, 90, 102
Martins, Captain Father, 160

Marxism, 151–52, 169. *See also* Communism; Socialism

Massemba-Débat, Alphonse, 232, 234

Matamba, kingdom of, 79–80

Mateus family, eyewitness accounts of Portuguese atrocities by, 249–50

Matos, André, 199

Matumona, Antoine, 212

Mbunda, area and people of, 12, 15, 20–24, 27, 34, 36, 38–39 n, 50, 65–67, 109–10, 116, 130, 241–42, 301; and guerrilla warfare, 12, 15, 20–24, 27, 256, 260; reformism (neo-colonialism) and, 318–20

Mbwila, Portuguese and Kongo battle at, 74–75

Medical care, 301, 302–3. *See also* Health (diseases)

Meirales, Admiral Quintão, 152–53

Melo, Anibal de, 212, 241, 242

Menezes, Hugo, 204

Mensagem (*Message*), cultural journal, 147–48, 151, 153, 163, 168, 183

Mensah, J. H., 334, 335

Mestiços ("mixed blood" people), 43. *See also Assimilados;* Mulattoes

Metal-working, initial African cultures and, 57

"Metropolitan factor," colonial system and, 120, 124

Micronationalism, reformism (neo-colonialism) and, 319–20, 321. *See also* Tribalism

Middle class. *See* Bourgeoisie (middle class)

Millet, 301

Milner, and British colonialism in South Africa, 112

Mineral exports, neo-colonialism and, 307, 308, 312–14

Mining (miners), 49–50, 128, 134–35 (*see also* specific places, products); neo-colonialism and, 306–7, 312–14

Missionaries, 37, 40–41, 80, 82, 83, 88–89 (*see also* Christianity; Church, the; specific denominations); and education of Africans, 117, 129, 155; and rebellions, 161–62, 194–99

Mobutu, Joseph, and Holden (and UPA) and MPLA controversy, 203, 208, 219, 221, 222, 226, 238, 239

Mondlane, Dr. Eduardo, 224, 226, 227, 228, 311 n

Monimambu, Spartacus, 285–86, 294 n

Monteiro, Lt. Filipe, 27

Morais, Jaime, 280

Mossâmedes, Angola, 111, 112, 264

Mouride brotherhood, Senegal, 331

Mouvement National Congolais, Congo/ Kinshasa, 207

Movimento Popular de Libertação de Angola. *See* MPLA (Movimento Popular de Libertação de Angola)

Moxico District, Angola, 17, 24, 44–45, 103–4, 109–10, 237, 242–43, 254–56 ff., 346; MPLA conference (1968), 285, 287–88, 289; national liberation movement and guerrilla activity and movement in, 134, 259–66 *passim*, 270, 294, 346

Mozambiki (guerrilla pseudonym), 4, 11, 28, 35

Mozambique, 43, 45, 95, 114, 125, 126, 134, 138, 161; diversions in national liberation movement in, 223–28; national liberation movement in, 170–73, 176–77, 223–28, 278, 281, 286, 294, 295, 296, 340, 347 (*see also* FRELIMO); reformism (neo-colonialism) and, 303, 307, 309, 311, 315, 316, 317, 324, 327, 340

Mozambique African National Union, 224–25

Mpinda, Congo, 77

MPLA (Movimento Popular de Libertação de Angola), and national liberation movement in Angola, 24–30, 33, 163, 164 n, 169, 174 ff., 177–79, 181, 185–86, 188, 190, 204–6, 208–28, 229–43, 244 ff., 262, 265, 285 (*see also* National liberation movement, Angola; specific aspects, individuals); action committees of, 282, 284; anti-racist position of, 284, 288–89, 339–40; Central Angola activity and, 266–72; Committee of Political and Military Coordination of, 288; conferences, 231–34, 285, 287–88, 289; Eastern Front activity and, 252–74; and foreign aid, 296–98; and foreign investments and intervention, 294–98; founding manifesto (1956) of, 284, 339; and guerrilla activity, 3–30, 208–28, 229–43, 244, 252–74 (*see also* Guerrilla warfare); and leadership and organizational problems, 282–98, 339–47 *passim* (*see also* Leadership); losses in 1968 offensive by, 265; and major offensive of 1968, 264–65; and mobilization of popular participation and support for, 254–61, 264–65, 322–28, 339–47; and opposition to reformism, 305 n; and political organization, 260–61, 262, 282–98; reorganization and effectiveness of, 229 ff., 339; Steering Committee of, 262, 274, 287, 288, 305 n, 342; supplies for, 18–19, 252–54 (*see also* Arms); and tribalism, 289, 290 (*see also* Tribalism); and UPA diversions and splits, 203–6, 208–28, 229 ff., 237, 238–43; Women's Organization of, 149–50, 188, 220, 239

Mtwara, 225–26
Muaant Yaav (Muata Yamvo), 61–62, 63, 64–65
Mueda, Mozambique, 176–77
Muié, Angola, 10, 22, 23–24, 25–26, 27, 28–30, 310–11
Mujimbo ("bush telegraph"), 22, 23
Mulattoes, 90, 92, 117, 137, 141, 191, 288–89. *See also Assimilados; Mestiços*
Murupa, defection from FRELIMO of, 227, 228 n
Mussolini, Benito, 121
Mussuma River, 3–4, 5, 11
Mwungu, 248

Nambuangongo, 189–90, 215, 217, 218, 244, 245, 247, 271
National Front, MPLA and, 285, 287
National Front of Angolan Liberation (FLNA), Holden and PDA coalition and, 210
Nationalism, 101, 115, 132–33 (*see also* Independence movement[s]; National liberation movements; specific aspects, events, individuals, movements, organizations); cultural, 141–42, 147–54, 163; "primitive" (tribalism), 37–38 (*see also* Tribalism); reformist, 319–20, 321 ff., 341 ff.; revolutionary, 282–98, 301–21, 322 ff., 341 ff. (*see also* Revolution)
National liberation movement, Angola, 8, 13–30 *passim*, 33, 43, 44–45, 132–54 *passim*, 183–86, 187 ff. (*see also* Independence movement[s]; MPLA; specific aspects, events, individuals, organizations); colonial exploitation and (*see* Colonialism); foreign aid and, 296–98; guerrilla activity and, 3–30, 33, 43, 44–45, 132–33, 135–54, 207–28, 229–43, 244–50, 252–74 ff. (*see also* Guerrilla warfare); leadership and organizational problems and, 146–54, 235–40, 282–98, 340 ff. (*see also* Leadership); leaflets, use of, 87 n, 161, 168–69; mobilization of popular support for, 11–30 *passim*, 254–61, 264–65, 282–98, 322–38, 339–47; organization and future of, 282–98; political organization and growth in, 229–43, 260–61, 262, 282–98; Portuguese military expenditures and commitments against, 275–78; reformism (neo-colonialism) and, 301–4, 305–21, 322 ff. (*see also* Reformism); resistance to colonial repression and, 160–61, 170–79, 183–86, 187–93, 194 ff. (*see also* Colonialism; Rebellions; Revolution); revolutionary change in anti-colonialism and, 282–98, 301–21, 322 ff., 339 ff.; splits and diversions in, 222–28, 229–35 (*see also*

specific aspects, individuals, organizations); and supplies, 252–54, 273, 274; women and, 149–50, 188, 220, 239; writers and, 137–41, 147–54, 168–69 (*see also* specific individuals, publications, works)
National liberation movement, Guinea-Bissau. *See* PAIGC
National liberation movement, Mozambique, 170–73, 176–77, 204, 223–28, 262, 286, 296. *See also* FRELIMO
National liberation movements, 131–42, 170–79, 187–93, 194–206 (*see also* Independence movement[s]; specific aspects, countries, individuals, movements, organizations); elitism and leadership problems, 199–206, 340 ff. (*see also* Elitism; Leadership); guerrilla movement and, 183–86, 187–93, 196–206 (*see also* Guerrilla warfare); independence and change and, 323–38, 339–43; political organization and growth of, 282–98; popular participation and, 11–30 *passim*, 254–61, 264–65, 282–98, 322–38, 339–47; problems and failures of, 199–206, 282–98, 339–47; reformism (neo-colonialism) and revolution and, 282–98, 301–4, 305–21, 322–38, 339 ff. (*see also* Reformism; Revolution); rebellions and (*see* Rebellions)
NATO, and aid to Portuguese, 190, 253, 275, 276–78, 296
Navy, Portuguese, 277
Naweej (Luba ruler), 60
Naweej II, 64
Ndandandas ("strategic hamlets"), 13–14, 117–18, 260, 264, 270, 271, 290–93, 308, 310–11
Ndongo, kingdom and people of, 70, 74, 76, 202; Hundred Years' War with Portuguese, 77–80
Ndungu, Chief, 65
Necaca, Barros, 201, 202, 225
Negros calçados ("shod blacks"), 89–90
Neo-colonialism (neo-colonial exploitation), 296, 298, 305–21, 322–38 (*see also under* Reformism); problems and future of revolutionary struggle against, 339–47
Neto, Dr. Agostinho, xiii, 6, 13, 18–19, 149, 150, 151, 152–54, 177–78, 185, 211, 229–32, 299, 347; career and background of, 229–32; and foreign aid, 294, 296–97; and guerrilla activity, 6, 13, 18–19, 229–43 *passim*, 253, 262, 273 n; and move of MPLA from Brazzaville to Angola, 262; New Year's message (1970) of, 274, 288; and Portuguese reformism, 293; quoted on popular participation in national liber-

Neto, Dr. Agostinho (cont'd)
ation movement, 323, 339–40; and reorganization of MPLA and national liberation movement in Angola, 229–43 passim, 253, 254, 273 n, 282, 285–87, 288, 347
Neto, Rosário, 209, 238
Nevinson, Henry W., 109–11
Newspapers (journalism, press), and colonialism and national liberation movement, 137–42, 147–54, 317. See also specific aspects, individuals, publications
New York Herald Tribune, 126
New York Times, 278
Niassa, Mozambique, 223–24
Nicolas, Prince, 131–32, 140, 202
Niger-Benue region, early African kingdoms of, 52–53
Nigeria, 112, 319, 327–28
Nigerian Foundation (1960–66), 327–28
Ninda, Angola, 5
"Ninety Minutes Under Fire" (Farinha), 217–18
Nkavandame, Lazaro, 224–26, 228 n
Norbert (UPA/GRAE commander), 215
North Atlantic Treaty Organization. See NATO
Northern Rhodesia (Zambia), 103, 123–24, 134, 240–42, 312–14. See also Zambia
Norton de Matos, José Mendes Ribeiro, 14, 20, 92, 104, 112–18, 125, 130, 141, 317; and decree 40 (1921), 113–14; and decree 137 (1921), 117–18, 130; and Portuguese extractive system and forced labor in Angola and Africa, 112–18, 125, 130, 141, 317; and resettlement programs, 117–18, 291, 292; resignation of, 123
Notícia (Luanda news magazine), 217–18
N'tonton, Sala, 173–74
Nyerere, Julius, 226

OAU. See Organization of African Unity
Ollivier, Marc, 284 n, 306 n, 339 n
OMA (Angolan Women's Organization of the MPLA), 149–50, 188, 220, 239
Oporto, Portugal, 121
Ordem Anticomunista, issuance by Bishop of Beira (1950) of, 125
Organization of African Unity (OAU), 211–12, 231, 235, 236, 254
Orlog, Captain, 100–1
Overseas Council, Lisbon, 92
Ovimbundu, area and people, 37, 38, 65–67, 89, 102, 106, 133, 134; and guerrilla activity, 9, 268–72

"Pacification" program, Portuguese in Angola and Africa and, 98
Paganini (guerrilla pseudonym), xiii, 5, 6–7, 9, 10, 12, 19–23 passim, 25, 27–29, 30
PAIGC (Guinea-Bissau national liberation movement), 173–74, 175–76, 204, 223, 262, 273, 281, 286, 296
Paiva, Artur de, 101–2
Paiva, João de, 70
Pampa-Sangue, and national liberation movement in Angola, 134
Pamphlets, 87 n. See also Leaflets
Pan-African Congress, 120, 141
Partido Comunista Angolana, 169
Partido da Luta Unida dos Africanos de Angola (PLUA), 169
Partido Democrático de Angola, 201, 210
Partido Nacional Africano (1921), 141
PDA (Partido Democrático de Angola), 201, 210
Peasants (peasantry), 301 ff., 322–38 (see also Kimbos; Labor; Poverty; Villagers; specific events, people, places); national liberation movement and, 11, 12–30, 265, 266–68, 322–38 passim, 343 ff.
Pedro VII, Dom, 201
Pélissier, R., 311 n, 312 n
Pereira, Gonsalvo Gaetano, 62–64
Pereira Cardosa, Captain, 104
Petrov (guerrilla pseudonym), xiii, 8–9, 11, 12, 15–17, 24, 25, 27–28, 234
Philip, King of Spain (1605), 75–76
PIDE (Portuguese secret political police), 153, 160, 162–63, 168, 172–79, 183–86, 249, 275
Pidgiguiti, Guinea-Bissau, 175–76
Pinnock, Johnny Eduardo, 163, 201, 213–14, 215, 225, 236 n
Plantations (plantation economy), 124–30, 140, 167 (see also Economy; Food production; Labor; specific crops, goods, products); and rebellions, 170 ff., 178–79, 183–86, 187–93, 194–206 passim; reformism (neo-colonialism) and, 309 ff., 325, 330–31
PLUA, 169
Poets (poetry), revolutionary national liberation movement and, 147–50, 151, 153, 165 n. See also specific aspects, poets, works
Police (PIDE), Portuguese, 153, 160, 162–63, 172–79, 183–86, 249, 275
Political power (authority, rule), initial African cultures and development of, 50–51, 52–67; Portuguese and, 68 ff.
Political protest movement, anti-colonialism and, 119, 131–42, 143–54, 160 ff., 170 ff., 176 ff., 183–86, 187 ff.

Portugal (Portuguese): Angolan (African) response to exploitation by, 39–46, 79 ff., 119 ff., 130, 131–42, 143 ff., 160–69, 170–79, 183–93 *passim*, 194 ff. (*see also* National liberation movements; Revolution); and Angola's history, 33–46, 47 (*see also* Angola); emigration from, 44, 122, 165–66 (*see also* Emigration; Settlers); forced labor of Africans in colonial extractive system of, 80–84, 85–93, 97–118, 119–30, 155–59 (*see also* Colonialism; Economy; Forced labor); and foreign investments (neo-colonialism) in Africa, 295–98, 306–15; and guerrilla movement, 3–30, 207–28, 229 ff., 244–50, 252 ff., 282–98 (*see also* Air Force, Portuguese; Army, Portuguese; Guerrilla warfare); and Hundred Years' War with Ndongo, 77–80; initial contacts in Africa, 62–65, 67, 68–76, 77–80; military expenditures and commitments in Angola and Africa, 275–78; MPLA and, 229 ff., 262 ff., 273 ff., 290–98 (*see also* MPLA); and national liberation movements (*see* National liberation movements; specific countries); "presence" in Africa of, 90, 92, 97, 305; problems and future of revolutionary struggle against, 339–47; reformism (neo-colonialism) and revolution and, 301–4, 305–21, 322 ff. (*see also* Reformism); replacement of monarchy by republican regime (1910), 141; and resettlement programs, 262 ff., 273 ff., 290–93; response to MPLA and national liberation movement in Angola, 262 ff., 273 ff., 290–98; revolutionary change in anticolonial movement against, 282–98, 301–4, 305–21, 322–38, 339–47; Salazar regime, 119–30 (*see also* Salazar); and slavery (slave trade), 39, 40, 58–59, 69–87, 77 ff., 80–84, 85–93, 109 ff. (*see also* Slavery); South African aid to, 294–97; treatment of workers by, 155–59

Potts, D. L., 313 n, 314 n

Poverty (the poor), 301 ff. (*see also* Economy; Labor; Peasants; Villagers; specific aspects); national liberation movement and, 298, 301–4, 305–21, 322–38; neo-colonialism and, 301–4, 305–21, 322–38; reformism and revolution and, 301–4, 305–21, 322–38; significance and ineffectiveness of reformism and, 317–21, 322–38

Présence Africaine, 154

Press. *See* Newspapers (journalism; press); Printing press

Preto boçal ("bush African"), 138–39, 140, 148–54, 312

Priests, 50. *See also* Christianity; Missionaries; specific denominations

Primary school education, 311–12. *See also* Education (schools)

Printing press, national liberation movements and, 137–42, 147–54. *See also* Leaflets; Newspapers; specific publications, works, writers

Private-sector foreign investment, neo-colonialism and, 295–98, 306–15, 322–38 *passim*

Production (*see also* Export income; Food production; Industrial development; Labor): reformism (neo-colonialism) and, 304; underdevelopment and colonial extractive system and, 305–21, 324–38 *passim*

Protestants, 220 (*see also* Christianity); missionaries and missions, 126, 129, 145, 161, 194–99

Proyant, Abbé, 80 n, 81

Punishment, 119, 127, 158. *See also* Atrocities (torture)

Punza (guerrilla pseudonym), 174–75, 187–88, 189, 205, 206

Pupa (guerrilla pseudonym), xiii, 28, 258–60

Quicabo, 218

Racism (race relations), 43, 87, 92, 117–18, 137, 166–68, 294, 311 (*see also* Blacks-whites relationship; Colonialism; Settlers; specific aspects); national liberation movement and problems and solution of, 288–89, 339–40

Raimundo, and FRELIMO, 225

Rallet et Cie, 309 n

"Rassemblement Démocratique de la Jeunesse Angolaise," 210

Rebellions (revolts, risings), 87 n, 91, 104, 108, 119, 131–42, 146, 160–69, 170–79, 183–86, 187–93, 194–206, 207–28, 229 (*see also* Revolution); guerrilla warfare and, 183–86, 187–93, 194–206, 207–28 (*see also* Guerrilla warfare); Kongo uprisings and failure of, 186, 188–90, 191–206; movement from reformism to, 143–54; MPLA and, 229 ff. (*see also* MPLA)

Reforma, A (weekly newspaper), 141

Reformism (reforms), Portuguese colonial system and, 42, 120, 124, 131–42, 162, 168, 201, 305–21 (*see also* specific aspects, movements, people, places); economic aspects and structures, 301–4, 305–21, 322–38; movement to revolt from, 143–54, 220–28, 229 ff., 282–98; and neo-colonialism

Reformism (cont'd)
and national liberation movement, 285,
290, 293–94, 305–21, 322–38, 339–47
(see also Colonialism; National liberation movements); problems and future
of revolutionary struggle and, 339–47;
significance and ineffectiveness of,
317–21; split between leaders and
movements opposed to, 220–28 (see
also under Leadership)
Reformist nationalism, 131–42
Refugees, 194–99, 208, 213, 230, 244–50,
263. See also Emigration
Religion (African religious beliefs), initial African cultures and, 15–18, 48,
50–51
Repression, resistance to Portuguese colonial exploitation and, 160–61, 170–
79, 183–86, 187–93, 194–206. See also
Air Force, Portuguese; Army, Portuguese; Atrocities (torture); Punishment; specific aspects, people, places
Resettlement programs, Portuguese and,
13–14, 260, 264, 270, 271, 290–93,
308, 310–11. See also Ndandandas
("strategic hamlets")
Revolution (revolutionary struggle), 42,
131–42, 183–86, 187 ff. (see also National liberation movements; Rebellions); movement from reformism to,
143–54, 220–28, 229 ff., 282–98, 301–
4, 305–21, 322–38, 339–47; MPLA
and, 229 ff. (see also MPLA); need for
popular participation in, 322–38; problems and future of, 339–47; reformism (neo-colonialism) and, 301–4,
305–21, 322 ff. (see also Reformism)
Revolutionary Government of Angola in
Exile. See GRAE (Revolutionary Government of Angola in Exile)
Rhodesia, 49–50, 167, 173, 294, 295 (see
also Northern Rhodesia; Southern
Rhodesia; Zambia); neo-colonialism
and, 306 n, 316–17
Rifles. See Arms (weapons)
Roman Catholic Church. See Catholics
(Catholicism)
Rossi, Pierre-Pascal, 214–15, 216, 220
Rostow, W. W., 335–36
Rubber cultivation and production, 102,
106
Rui (guerrilla pseudonym), xiii, 30, 252
"Rural resettlement" program, Portuguese
and, 260, 270, 271, 290–93, 308, 310–
11. See also "Strategic hamlets"
Russia. See Soviet Union (USSR)

Sá Benevida, Salvador Correia de, 74
Sa da Bandeira, Marquis, 91, 103
Salazar, António Oliveira, and Portu-
guese colonial system in Angola and

Africa, 98, 107, 111, 115, 116, 117,
119–30, 134, 139, 140, 142, 143–44,
147, 151–69 passim, 170 ff., 221, 231,
315; career and background of, 121–
30; colonial economy and regime of,
119–30; rebellions and, 170 ff., 178–79,
183–86, 187–93, 194 ff.; and reformism
(neo-colonialism), 305–21, 322 ff.
Sand slums (museques), 145–46, 183–84
Santa Maria (ship), seizure of, 115 n,
185
Santos, A. C. V. T. dos, 116 n
Santos, Dr. Eduardo dos, 149, 230
Santos, Marcelino dos, 154
São Paulo de Loanda, 74, 78–79 (see
also Loanda); attack by Africans on
prison in (1961), 183–84, 187
São Salvador, 188, 190, 204, 208, 244–45
São Thomé Island, 59, 69, 70–71, 73, 77–
78, 85, 95, 109, 110; risings in, 167–68
Sarbah, Mensah, 136
Savimbi, Jonas Malheiro, 211, 235–37,
238 n, 242 n, 260
Schmeisser automatic weapons, 253–54
Second World War, 142, 165, 222
Secret police, Portuguese. See PIDE
(Portuguese secret political police)
Self-rule (see also Independence move-
ment[s]): problems and future of rev-
olutionary struggle and, 342–47; re-
formism (neo-colonialism) and, 317–
21
Senegal, 223; neo-colonialism and growth
without development in, 332–33
Senzalas ("native quarters"), 144–46
Senzalas do paz ("peace villages"), 13–
16
Separatism, 202, 203, 210, 221–28, 320.
See also specific aspects, countries, in-
dividuals, movements, organizations
Serbian monarchists, parallel between
Holdenites and, 22
Serpa Pinto, Alexandre, 36
Serpa Pinto, Angola, 33, 272–73
Serviçais. See Contract laborers
Seta (guerrilla pseudonym), 257
Settlements, initial African cultures and,
49
Settlers, white (see also Blacks-whites
relationship; Europeans; Portugal; Racism; specific aspects, countries, people, places): emigration from Portugal
to Africa, 43–46, 165–66; and exploi-
tative system, 85–93, 97–104, 105–18,
119–30, 131 ff., 137–38, 141–42, 143–
54 passim (see also Colonialism; Labor; Plantations); and reformism (neo-
colonialism), 302–21, 322 ff., 327; and
resettlement programs, 291–93 (see
also Resettlement programs); resistance to, 160–69, 170–79, 183–86,

Settlers (cont'd)
187 ff.; treatment of workers by, 155–59
Shekulai River, 4, 17, 18, 19, 21, 27, 34, 265; Forest, 29
Shinde (Luvale chief), 64–65
Silva Correia, Alexandre da, 98
Silva Cunha, Dr. J. M. da, 107, 143 n, 305, 307
Silva Porto, Angola, 24
Silva Porto, António da, 34, 36, 50, 62, 66
Silver, 71
Simango, Rev. Uria, 226–27
Sisal plantations, 124
Sitte, Fritz, 216
Slave economy, Portuguese in Africa and, 69–76, 80–84, 85 ff., 97–118, 119–30 (see also Slavery); forced labor and, 105–18 (see also Forced labor)
Slavery (slave trade), 39, 40, 58–59, 69–76, 77 ff., 80–84, 85–93, 109–18, 302 (see also Slave Economy); end of (1878), 107; European industrial development and, 330–31; purchase price of slaves, 82–83
Sleeping sickness, 302
Slums, colonial system and development in Angola of, 144–46
Socialism, 286, 296–97 (see also Communism; Marxism); neo-colonialism, capitalist structures and case for, 338
Songo, Angola, 195, 197, 244, 246–47
Soromenho, Castro, 46 n, 124, 155
Sousa Ferreira, Eduardo de, 293 n, 309 n
South Africa, 112, 120, 144, 217, 218, 221 n, 257–58; and aid to Portuguese, 294–97; and apartheid system, 295–96; 312; and investments in Angola, 307, 309
Southern African Common Market, 295
Southern Rhodesia, 49–50, 120
South Vietnam, 291
South-West Africa, 103
Soviet Union (USSR), 18, 19, 234, 254, 257, 275, 297; and aid to national liberation movement, 254, 257, 297
Spain, 75–76
Spense, C. F., 125
Stages of Economic Growth, The (Rostow), 335–36
Stanley, Sir Henry Morton, 52
Steele, A., 126 n, 127
Stone Age, 35–36, 47, 48
"Strategic hamlets," Portuguese and resettlement policy and, 13–14, 117–18, 260, 264, 270, 271, 290–93, 308, 310–11
Sugar plantations and production, 59, 69, 70–71, 77, 91, 109, 114, 124
Summers, Roger, 50

Sundi, 134–35
Supplies, Angolan national liberation movement and, 252–54, 273, 274. See also Arms (weapons); specific kinds
Swahili areas and people, 49, 50
Syphilis, 302

TANU, 224, 225–28
Tanzania, 18, 224, 225, 226–28, 240, 252
Taty, Alexandre, 238
Taxes (taxation), 86, 88, 310, 327
Tenreiro, Francisco, 149
Terrorist movement (terrorists), 187–93, 194–206 passim, 218. See also Guerrilla warfare (guerrilla movement); specific aspects, events, organizations
Tete, Mozambique, 62, 224
Texeira, Trigo, 103
Thomaz, Admiral Américo, 161
Tito, Marshal, 222
Toco, Simão, and Tocoistas, 41, 200–1, 246
Torres, Sincletica, 318
Trade, Portuguese in Angola and Africa and, 69–76, 77–84, 85 ff., 89 ff., 97 ff., 302 (see also Economy; specific aspects); forced labor and, 105–18 (see also Forced labor); initial African cultures and, 49, 58–59, 62–66; overseas, 58, 69 ff., 77–84, 85 ff.; slavery and (see Slavery)
Trade unions, 141, 317
Tribalism, national liberation movement and, 37–38, 289, 290, 323, 341; reformism (neo-colonialism) and, 319–20, 323, 341
Tribute, initial African cultures and, 61–62, 64, 82–83
True Life of Domingos Xavier, The (Vieira), 164–65
Tshombe, Moise, 100
Tuberculosis, 302
Tugas terroristas, Os, 13, 14
Turkey, 275, 276

Uganda, 53, 320
Umbundu areas, guerrilla activity in, 268–72. See also Ovimbundu
Underdevelopment, reformism (neo-colonialism), dependence, and, 301–4, 305–21, 322–38, 339 ff.
Unemployment, neo-colonialism, underdevelopment and, 167, 333–34, 337
União das Populacões de Angola (UPA): Holden and crises in, 235–40 (see also Holden, Roberto); and Kongo uprising, 186, 188–90, 191–206; and MPLA and guerrilla warfare, 203–6, 208–28, 229–30, 231, 237–43
UNIP, 263 n

UNITA (União para la Independência Total de Angola), 237–38
United Nations (UN), 24–25, 139, 153, 202, 237, 277
United States, 128, 129, 139, 143, 201–2, 203, 207, 221 n, 235–36, 273, 278, 335; and investments in Angola, 296, 307; and Latin America, 333–34; and Portuguese aircraft, 276
UPNA (Union of the Peoples of Angola), 202–3, 225. See also União das Populacões de Angola (UPA)

Vansina, Jan, 52, 58, 61 n
Venter, A. J., 100 n, 218–19, 220, 295 n
Verwoerd, Henrik, 295
Vieira, Luandino, 164–65
Vieira Dias, Carlos Aniceto, 163
Villagers (villages), 11 ff. (see also Kimbos; Peasants; specific people, places); national liberation movement, guerrilla movement, and mobilization of, 254–61, 265, 266–68, 290 ff., 322–38 passim, 342 ff.; Portuguese Army and, 290 ff.; reformism (neo-colonialism) and, 301–4, 305–21, 322 ff.; regrouping and resettlement programs and, 13–14, 117–18, 130, 260, 264, 270, 271, 290–93, 308, 310–11; relationship with guerrillas, 11–30 passim, 265, 266–68 (see also specific aspects)
Vorster, Balthazar J., 295
Voting. See Elections (voting)
Voz de Angola Clamando no Deserto . . . (The Voice of Angola Crying in the Wilderness . . .), 138, 148

Waestberg, Olle, 215–16
Wages (earnings, wage levels), 166, 171, 293, 307, 327, 329, 331
Wealth (wealth transfer), reformism, neo-colonialism and development of dependence and, 296–98, 301–4, 305–21, 322–38 passim. See also Poverty (the poor)
Weapons. See Arms (weapons)
Wenela (Witwatersrand Native Labour Association), 257–58
West Africa, British and French and, 137, 142
West European Common Market, 316
West Germany (see also Germany): aid to Portuguese and, 276–78; and investments in Angola, 296, 307
Wheeler, D. L., 111 n, 117, 136 n, 140 n
Whites, relationship with blacks. See Blacks-whites relationship; Racism (race relations); Settlers; specific aspects, countries, people, places
Witchcraft (evil), 15–18
World War II, 142, 165, 222
Writers, and national liberation movement, 137–41, 147–54, 163, 164–65. See also Leaflets; Newspapers; Poets (poetry); specific aspects, works, writers

Yaga (people), 73
Yamba, André, 195–96
Yao (people), 63
Youlou, Abbé, 232
Yugoslavia, 222

"Zaga Operation," 24–30
Zaïre. See Belgian Congo (Zaïre)
Zambezi River, 5, 62
Zambia: and early African kingdoms, 61; foreign investments and neo-colonialism in, 307, 312–14; and national liberation movement in Angola, 5, 8, 12, 19, 21, 22, 237–38, 240–43, 252–53, 258, 263
Zhinga, Queen (Dona Ana de Sousa), 74, 79
Zimbabwe culture, 49
Zombo (people), 200, 201, 210